A Celebration of Poets

South Grades 4-6
Spring 2008

A CELEBRATION OF POETS
SOUTH GRADES 4-6
SPRING 2008

AN ANTHOLOGY COMPILED BY CREATIVE COMMUNICATION, INC.

Published by:

1488 NORTH 200 WEST • LOGAN, UTAH 84341
TEL. 435-713-4411 • WWW.POETICPOWER.COM

All rights reserved. No part of this book may be reproduced or transmitted in any form or by any means, electronic or mechanical without written permission of the author and publisher.

Copyright © 2008 by Creative Communication, Inc.
Printed in the United States of America

ISBN: 978-1-60050-189-0

FOREWORD

This edition of our poetry anthology is an important transition for Creative Communication. Since our beginning in 1993, we have called our contest "A Celebration of Young Poets." Having worked with student poets for over 15 years, we realized that the writers who have been accepted to be published are not "young" poets. They are poets. Young or old, they are writers who have proven their worth as poets. These are the poets we celebrate.

We also start this year with a new cover for the anthologies. We are excited about this new look and our new logo of a hand releasing stars. Our logo can represent different things. It could be a teacher or mentor releasing a writer to the world through our publication. It could represent the fact that the stars are limitless and these writers are just starting to shine with their potential. We have become the starting point for thousands of writers and we hope each poet continues to make writing a part of their lives.

What is recorded between these pages is unique. It exists nowhere else in the world and is now recorded forever. Take the time to read what these poets have shared. A part of themselves and their world exists in each poem. Savor it. Enjoy.

Sincerely,
Thomas Kenne Worthen, Ph.D.
Editor
Creative Communication

WRITING CONTESTS!

Enter our next POETRY contest!

Enter our next ESSAY contest!

Why should I enter?
Win prizes and get published! Each year thousands of dollars in prizes are awarded in each region and tens of thousands of dollars in prizes are awarded throughout North America. The top writers in each division receive a monetary award and a free book that includes their published poem or essay. Entries of merit are also selected to be published in our anthology.

Who may enter?
There are four divisions in the poetry and essay contests. The divisions are grades K-3, 4-6, 7-9, and 10-12.

What is needed to enter the contest?
To enter the poetry contest send in one original poem, 21 lines or less. To enter the essay contest send in one original essay, 250 words or less, on any topic. Each entry must include the student's name, grade, address, city, state, and zip code, and the student's school name and school address. Students who include their teacher's name may help the teacher qualify for a free copy of the anthology.

How do I enter?

Enter a poem online at:
www.poeticpower.com
or
Mail your poem to:
   Poetry Contest
   1488 North 200 West
   Logan, UT 84341

Enter an essay online at:
www.studentessaycontest.com
or
Mail your essay to:
   Essay Contest
   1488 North 200 West
   Logan, UT 84341

When is the deadline?
Poetry contest deadlines are December 4th, April 7th, and August 18th. Essay contest deadlines are October 15th, February 17th, and July 15th. You can enter each contest, however, send only one poem or essay for each contest deadline.

Are there benefits for my school?
Yes. We award $15,000 each year in grants to help with Language Arts programs. Schools qualify to apply for a grant by having a large number of entries of which over fifty percent are accepted for publication. This typically tends to be about 15 accepted entries.

Are there benefits for my teacher?
Yes. Teachers with five or more students accepted to be published receive a free anthology that includes their students' writing.

For more information please go to our website at **www.poeticpower.com**, email us at editor@poeticpower.com or call 435-713-4411.

TABLE OF CONTENTS

Poetic Achievement Honor Schools 1

Language Arts Grant Recipients 9

Grades 4-5-6 13
    Top Poems 14
    High Merit Poems 24

Index 259

States included in this edition:

Alabama
Florida
Georgia
Mississippi
North Carolina
South Carolina

Spring 2008 Poetic Achievement Honor Schools

* Teachers who had fifteen or more poets accepted to be published

The following schools are recognized as receiving a "Poetic Achievement Award." This award is given to schools who have a large number of entries of which over fifty percent are accepted for publication. With hundreds of schools entering our contest, only a small percent of these schools are honored with this award. The purpose of this award is to recognize schools with excellent Language Arts programs. This award qualifies these schools to receive a complimentary copy of this anthology. In addition, these schools are eligible to apply for a Creative Communication Language Arts Grant. Grants of two hundred and fifty dollars each are awarded to further develop writing in our schools.

Albemarle School
   Elizabeth City, NC
      Mrs. C. Mann*

Appling County Middle School
   Baxley, GA
      Melanie Clark
      Lynn Hyers
      Melissa Perkins*

Arlington Middle School
   Jacksonville, FL
      Joseph T. Vaine*

Arnold Magnet Academy
   Columbus, GA
      Alicia Yelkovich*

B'nai Shalom Day School
   Greensboro, NC
      Dawn Ross*

Bak Middle School of the Arts
   West Palm Beach, FL
      Jessica Samons Kutz*

Boiling Springs Intermediate School
   Boiling Springs, SC
      Susan Lyda*
      Wanda Sullivan*

Bridgeway Christian Academy
   Alpharetta, GA
      Marcy Clark
      Jan Fowler
      Andrea Harris*
      Allison Johnson

Brogden Middle School
   Durham, NC
      Samantha Magee*

Brooklet Elementary School
   Brooklet, GA
      Ayanna Wright*

The Muslim Academy of Greater Orlando
   Orlando, FL
      Jamila D. Ismail
      Azza Ismail
      Bilquis Sheikh

Buies Creek Elementary School
Buies Creek, NC
    Kerry O'Donnell*

Central Park Elementary School
Plantation, FL
    Ms. Garvin
    Janetta Gonshak*
    Adrianna Leikind
    Mrs. Rivera
    Mark Siegel

Challenger K8 School of Science and Mathematics
Spring Hill, FL
    Mrs. Leon*
    Angela Miller*
    Sarah Pennington*

Challenger Middle School
Cape Coral, FL
    Amy L. Vagi*

Chapin Middle School
Chapin, SC
    Shannon Allonier*

City of Pembroke Pines Charter Central Middle School
Pembroke Pines, FL
    Carline Martin-Hernandez
    Latrice Hubert
    Jennifer Levine

Clearview Avenue Elementary School
Saint Petersburg, FL
    Christine Laurenzi
    Vicki Meredith*

Cool Spring Elementary School
Cleveland, NC
    Aimee Adkins
    Tonya Cassidy
    Jessica Duncan
    Stephanie Flammang
    Kenneth Lindstrom
    Sandra Milholland
    Monica Williams

Corkscrew Middle School
Naples, FL
    Robin Lavin*
    Linda McDonough

Covenant Classical School
Concord, NC
    Lori Balbuena*
    Jane Dearing

East Jones Elementary School
Laurel, MS
    Shirley Sellers*

East Marion Elementary School
Columbia, MS
    C. Ryals*

Elba Elementary School
Elba, AL
    Sherry Butler*

Eugenia B Thomas Elementary School
Miami, FL
    Ms. Brito
    Leslie Deehl*

Freedom Middle School
Orlando, FL
    Mrs. Kirkland*

Freeport Elementary School
Freeport, FL
    Jeanette Skelly*

FSU/City of Pembroke Pines Charter Elementary School
Pembroke Pines, FL
    Laura Coleman
    Mrs. K. De Simone
    Sophia A. Tenn*

Gold Hill Middle School
Fort Mill, SC
    Kathryn Beebe*
    Jenny Burns*

Poetic Achievement Honor Schools

Grace Baptist Christian School
Powder Springs, GA
Misty Brown
Betty Guzman
Windy Hewett
Mrs. Holloman
Mr. Wynn

Grays Chapel Elementary School
Franklinville, NC
Mrs. Henry
Paula Wall*
Annette Walton

Gulf Stream School
Gulf Stream, FL
Mari Bianco*

Heron Creek Middle School
North Port, FL
Mrs. Channing
Mrs. Hager-Knecht*

Holy Name of Jesus School
Indialantic, FL
Kitty Nash*

Indian Harbour Montessori Elementary School
Indian Harbour Beach, FL
Linda Silverthorn*

Irmo Elementary School
Irmo, SC
Emily Barnhill*

J E Holmes Middle School
Eden, NC
Karen Allen
Delores Lawson*
Linda Reynolds*

Lake Park Baptist School
Lake Park, FL
Linda Easley
Mrs. Schumacher*
Patti Woodall

M.A.T.S. Middle/High School
Bradenton, FL
Sharyn Hundley*

McRae Elementary School
Keystone Heights, FL
Alma Lopez-Mitchell*

Morgan Elementary School
Gold Hill, NC
Barbara Hoover*

Mount Zion Christian School
Greenville, SC
Laura Phillips*

North Elementary School
Lancaster, SC
Elizabeth Yarbrough*

North Windy Ridge School
Weaverville, NC
Christopher Schmidt*

Oakland Elementary School
Greenwood, SC
Mrs. Grant
Mrs. Mack
Mrs. Schweikart
Mrs. Wooley

Olde Providence Elementary School
Charlotte, NC
Julianne Bonner
Susie Henry
Mrs. Marcinkiewicz
Mrs. McConnell
Mrs. Mullen
Mrs. Perkins
Mrs. Powers
Beth Smith
Mrs. Willie

Oliver Hoover Elementary School
Miami, FL
Pamela Rodriguez*

Our Lady of Fatima School
Biloxi, MS
Patrice Torricelli*

Palmetto Christian Academy
Mt Pleasant, SC
Gretchen Kroncke
Dianne Williams

Pensacola Beach Elementary School
Pensacola Beach, FL
Susan McLeod*

Pinellas County Jewish Day School
Clearwater, FL
Janice LeVine*
Mrs. Zakrzewski

Pinnacle Elementary School
Rutherfordton, NC
Gail Wilkins*

Pulaski County Middle School
Hawkinsville, GA
Lucy Hanks Gabriel*

PVPV/Rawlings Elementary School
Ponte Vedra Beach, FL
Rita Andreu
Lola Hartford

Queen's Grant Community School
Mint Hill, NC
Tiffany Dunagan*
Mimi Henderson*
Zhanna Shifflet

Ranburne Elementary School
Ranburne, AL
Shana Pollard*

Rock Mills Jr High School
Rock Mills, AL
Brandy Pike*
Mrs. Richardson
Jeffery Thompson

Rosarian Academy
West Palm Beach, FL
Cyndee Hackney*
Sandra L. Richards

Saint Pauls Middle School
Saint Pauls, NC
Donald Weller*

Scotts Creek Elementary School
Sylva, NC
Laura H. Wallace*
Phil Woody

Seven Springs Middle School
New Port Richey, FL
Paula Aycock*

Sharon Elementary School
Statesville, NC
Jessica White*

Shorecrest Preparatory School
Saint Petersburg, FL
Marci Meyer*

Spruce Creek Elementary School
Port Orange, FL
Debra Abadia
Melissa Chadwell
Dottye Citro*
Judith Degler

St Francis Xavier Elementary School
Vicksburg, MS
Liz Fletcher*
Leslie Young

St John's Lutheran School
Winston Salem, NC
Lydia K. Holz*

St Martin Upper Elementary School
Ocean Springs, MS
Mrs. Carraway
Rebecca Cross
Jean Payton
Mrs. Powell
Cindy Robertson

Poetic Achievement Honor Schools

St Mary Magdalen Catholic School
Altamonte Springs, FL
Debbie Kelly*

St Petersburg Christian School
Saint Petersburg, FL
Kristi Henry*

St Thomas More School
Chapel Hill, NC
Hilda Bukowski*
Natalie Dekle
Linda DiGiovanni*
Mrs. Eldred
Jackie Stanley
Jennifer Sullivan*

Stokesdale Elementary School
Stokesdale, NC
Lynn Moses*

Stone Academy
Greenville, SC
Mr. Brown
Ms. Freeman
Sharon Gilstrap
Christen Josey
Mrs. Martini
Candice Moore
Angela Page
Debbie Roper
Ms. Russell
Pat Sandzen

Summit Hill Elementary School
Alpharetta, GA
Danielle Friefeld
Mary Gaut
Bonny Sickinger*

Tabernacle Elementary School
Asheboro, NC
Laura Popp*

Tarpon Springs Middle School
Tarpon Springs, FL
Mrs. Cochran
Patricia Dashiell*
Crisy Mathews*

Tequesta Trace Middle School
Weston, FL
Sherri Ready*

The Sanibel School
Sanibel, FL
Monica DeBarr*
Anna Godsea

Tomlin Middle School
Plant City, FL
Pamela Conte
Virginia M. Wong*

Turkey Creek Middle School
Plant City, FL
Erin Consolver*

Unity School
Delray Beach, FL
Barbara Ferguson*
Jeanette Perrella*

Vienna Elementary School
Pfafftown, NC
Mrs. M. P. Cowan*
Brenda M. White*

Virginia A Boone Highland Oaks
Elementary School
North Miami Beach, FL
Beth Baucom
Phillis Diskin
Mrs. Guerrero
Stephanie Sheir*
Morgan Taylor

Wellington School
Seminole, FL
Mrs. Smith
Mrs. Susens

West Marion Elementary School
Foxworth, MS
Lisa Peavy*

Westlake Christian School
    Palm Harbor, FL
        Mary Barbaccia
        Kimberly Fleming*
        Marla Lee

William S Talbot Elementary School
    Gainesville, FL
        Melissa Ferraro*
        Yvonne Scammacca

Winona Elementary School
    Winona, MS
        Becky Dee
        Leigh DeNoon*

Wrights Mill Road Elementary School
    Auburn, AL
        Shannon Brandt*

Language Arts Grant Recipients 2007-2008

After receiving a "Poetic Achievement Award" schools are encouraged to apply for a Creative Communication Language Arts Grant. The following is a list of schools who received a two hundred and fifty dollar grant for the 2007-2008 school year.

Acadamie DaVinci, Dunedin, FL
Altamont Elementary School, Altamont, KS
Belle Valley South School, Belleville, IL
Bose Elementary School, Kenosha, WI
Brittany Hill Middle School, Blue Springs, MO
Carver Jr High School, Spartanburg, SC
Cave City Elementary School, Cave City, AR
Central Elementary School, Iron Mountain, MI
Challenger K8 School of Science and Mathematics, Spring Hill, FL
Columbus Middle School, Columbus, MT
Cypress Christian School, Houston, TX
Deer River High School, Deer River, MN
Deweyville Middle School, Deweyville, TX
Four Peaks Elementary School, Fountain Hills, AZ
Fox Chase School, Philadelphia, PA
Fox Creek High School, North Augusta, SC
Grandview Alternative School, Grandview, MO
Hillcrest Elementary School, Lawrence, KS
Holbrook School, Holden, ME
Houston Middle School, Germantown, TN
Independence High School, Elko, NV
International College Preparatory Academy, Cincinnati, OH
John Bowne High School, Flushing, NY
Lorain County Joint Vocational School, Oberlin, OH
Merritt Secondary School, Merritt, BC
Midway Covenant Christian School, Powder Springs, GA
Muir Middle School, Milford, MI
Northlake Christian School, Covington, LA
Northwood Elementary School, Hilton, NY
Place Middle School, Denver, CO
Public School 124, South Ozone Park, NY

Language Arts Grant Winners cont.

Public School 219 Kennedy King, Brooklyn, NY
Rolling Hills Elementary School, San Diego, CA
St Anthony's School, Streator, IL
St Joan Of Arc School, Library, PA
St Joseph Catholic School, York, NE
St Joseph School-Fullerton, Baltimore, MD
St Monica Elementary School, Mishawaka, IN
St Peter Celestine Catholic School, Cherry Hill, NJ
Strasburg High School, Strasburg, VA
Stratton Elementary School, Stratton, ME
Tom Thomson Public School, Burlington, ON
Tremont Elementary School, Tremont, IL
Warren Elementary School, Warren, OR
Webster Elementary School, Hazel Park, MI
West Woods Elementary School, Arvada, CO
West Woods Upper Elementary School, Farmington, CT
White Pine Middle School, Richmond, UT
Winona Elementary School, Winona, TX
Wissahickon Charter School, Philadelphia, PA
Wood County Christian School, Williamstown, WV
Wray High School, Wray, CO

Grades 4-5-6

Note: The Top Ten poems were finalized through an online voting system. Creative Communication's judges first picked out the top poems. These poems were then posted online. The final step involved thousands of students and teachers who registered as online judges and voted for the Top Ten poems. We hope you enjoy these selections.

Top Poem Grades 4-5-6

Dreams

Across the floating clouds she drifts,
The wind swirls around her.
She hears the calling owl,
The moon shining in the darkness.
All is peaceful, all is quiet.
Animals are sleeping soundly in their shelters.
She floats on the clouds, soft as cotton,
Drifting slowly through the night
With the moon, a fire in the sky.
Finally her cotton cloud takes her to her window
And sets her down.
She climbs into her bed and drifts asleep.

Katherine Atkinson, Grade 4
The Children's School at Sylvia Circle, SC

Top Poem Grades 4-5-6

The Castle of Spring

Slumbering leaves awake as spring comes near
and buds like babies growing begin to appear.
Spring also brings the song that an elegant bird sings
while beautiful trees rule the forest like kings.
Greening leaves and swaying trees sing their own song
so the forlorn branches of trees will soon belong.
Awaking animals yawn and stretch after a cozy, cold winter
and peer out of their holes for a verdant adventure.
Stately blooms reign like radiant queens,
while blossoming buds await, eager to be seen.
They all abide in nature's castle of royalty
that is buzzing with critters serving with loyalty.
Behold, emerald beds surround gentle streams
while I giggle and twirl under amber sunbeams!
I can hear the rhythm of the enchanting music
as a song bird chirps her whimsical lyric.
Dizzy I fall, then stare at the azure sky,
and enjoy the pictures as the clouds glide by.
Suddenly, they dutifully sprinkle their drizzling
so I pirouette out the gates of the castle of spring.

Cameron Comrie, Grade 4
Bridgeway Christian Academy, GA

Top Poem Grades 4-5-6

Each Little Snowflake

Each little snowflake
Falls to the ground,
Whispering quietly
Not making
A sound.
Taking a ride down
To the dew-covered grass,
Where the wandering people
Will soon come to pass.
Each little snowflake
A small silvery treasure,
Brings each little child
Joy, comfort, and pleasure.
Each little snowflake
Dancing through the wraithy fog,
As if they were going to this winter's ball.
I reach out to touch winter's crystalline jewel
And in a quick flash
It was gone.

Laura Jane Crocker, Grade 5
J Larry Newton School, AL

Top Poem Grades 4-5-6

The Bully

She stands there, towering tall
She stands there, throwing things at me
They are not visible things, but the insults still hurt
I am hiding behind my castle walls
When all of a sudden, a well placed cannonball collapses my forces
Everything is falling down around my ears
She has no idea how much it hurts
I will let her know.
I stand up and throw a cannonball of my own
As soon as she sees it coming, she hides behind her dark red jacket
It is her castle, it defends her
In that split second, I realize that the bully is no more than a coward, towering tall
She hides behind her dark red jacket,
Throwing insult after insult, cannonball after cannonball
I am no longer afraid, for I know the bully, tall and strong,
Is a coward.

Shelby Keating, Grade 6
HE McCracken Middle School, SC

Top Poem Grades 4-5-6

Alone

How can you call for help when your voice cannot be heard?
How can you tell people how you feel when they think it is so absurd?
Most people don't know how it feels,

How it feels to be in a room full of people and still be alone
Or how it feels to be in your house and it still doesn't feel like home.
Or how it feels to go to school like nothing's wrong,
but deep down you feel as though you don't belong.

Constantly I wonder if there is anyone I could pour my problems out to.
With teachers shouting and family feuds what can I do?
What can I say?
But sit in my corner day after day.

If there's anyone out there that can hear my plea
I wish you would come and help me.
Till then I'm all alone waiting, asking, the same question:
How can you call for help when your voice cannot be heard?

Quiesha Lewis, Grade 6
Brogden Middle School, NC

Top Poem Grades 4-5-6

Who?

If I had a wish,
I know just what I'd do.
I would walk and talk with Nature
And spend an hour or two!

Who set the moon in heaven?
Who threw the stars in place?
Who flipped the switch that morning.
That lit the stars in space?

Who used the billows for the wind?
Who poured the river from its glass?
Who sprayed the perfume on each flower?
Who dropped the glitter on the grass?

Who made the snakes to slither?
Who sized the giraffe neck so long?
Who leads the deer to water?
Who made the birds voice a song?

As I think about my wishing.
I can plainly see
To find out all the answers
Will take eternity!

Maleah Mathis, Grade 6
Scotts Creek Elementary School, NC

Top Poem Grades 4-5-6

My Feelings

My feelings can be as…
Sad as a wolf howling to the moon for forgiveness
Bright like the bird talking to the sun about the day
Lonely like the moon and stars trapped out in the middle of nowhere
Dry like a cactus pleading for water
Wet like the Earth drowning in its own tears
all those feelings come down to
one planet…
one day…
one person…
and in one single
Heart.

Kimberly Ponce, Grade 6
Stokes Elementary School, NC

Top Poem Grades 4-5-6

A Visit

As I walked excitedly up to the old brown chair she was sitting in
I could tell she couldn't remember me
Her brain was searching for an answer, but no memory appeared
Even though she couldn't remember my name, or recognize my face
She still gave me a wonderful warm hug
Her thin pale arms wrapped around me tight
Making me feel content
Everyone around us was old and weak
They were trying to remember too
She stared deeply into my hazel eyes
And told me how beautiful I was
Her voice was as quiet as a mouse
We both enjoyed our talk, two peas in a pod
But it was time for me to go
She didn't understand why I had to leave
I told her I loved her and she gave me a hug goodbye
As I sauntered toward the tall glass doors
I felt a warm feeling rush through my body, thinking to myself
I will remember that visit forever
Even though she has passed on
She will always stay in my heart

Caroline Romer, Grade 6
Unity School, FL

Top Poem Grades 4-5-6

Moonlight

A silver beam
goes through my window,
it's as if a waterfall
is filling my room
with a silvery pool.
It's coming in faster and faster.
My bed
lifts off the ground
and bursts out the window.
The beam is like a river,
my bed is like a boat.
I race up to the moon,
the river starts to flow backwards.
I hold on
as I soar back into my room.
The moon floats across the sky.
Falling like a quarter in a fountain,
and then disappears.

Blaise Vance, Grade 5
Rosarian Academy, FL

Top Poem Grades 4-5-6

Struggles

Struggles are stepping stones.
Once you get over one, another comes along.
Struggles can be fun or saddening,
from trying your hardest to solve a puzzle,
to when you find out your grandmother is dead.
Life is made of millions of these small stepping stones.
Life, you could say, is the pond,
and struggles are the way to the other side.

Alison Waldman, Grade 6
CrossRoads Middle School, SC

Adam the Atom
Adam the Atom
Walked down the hill,
His protons were spinning
His neutrons were still.

His electrons were jiggling
All about him,
And he was on his way
To see his friend Tim.

Adam the Atom
Rang Tim's doorbell,
Then charged himself up
To stay atomically well.
Sarah Curtis, Grade 5
Waters Edge Elementary School, FL

Dreams
Dreams take you on a journey
To any place you want to go
You can live in a castle
And be king or queen
Prince or princess
But your dreams can turn to nightmares
Where you can be in the dungeon
And be an enemy
And you will suffer the consequences
Natalie Zeledon, Grade 5
Oliver Hoover Elementary School, FL

Being Invisible
I guess it would be nice
To have someone wave to me
As I walk down the hall,
But they can't
Because I'm invisible.

If someone would ask me
If I thought the test was difficult
I would answer them
But it's hard to
When you're invisible

I would love to have a friend,
Someone to talk to,
Someone to spend time with,
But guess what?
I'm invisible.

Maybe if I talked more
Or moved more
I would end this curse.
Then
I would no longer be invisible.
Taylor Ertel, Grade 5
R.C. Lipscomb Elementary School, FL

I Am
I am nice and smart
I wonder who I really am
I hear the clouds calling my name
I see the flowers blowing in the wind
I want to go back in time
I am nice and smart
I pretend to glide in the sky
I feel like I am a rose
I touch the silkiness of flowers
I worry the world is coming to an end
I cry about my friends
I am smart and nice
I understand who I love
I say you are special
I dream about you
I try to be better at life
I hope to make a lot of money
I am nice and smart
Ashley Miller, Grade 6
Heron Creek Middle School, FL

Tabby
T errific smile
A lways filled with love
B rightens up each day
B rings everyone joy
Y ou're always a friend.
Tabby Herndon, Grade 6
The ELLES School, FL

Tourism
T ourism
O pinion
U nited States
R emove
I gloo
S equoia
M oving
Colton Cook, Grade 4
East Jones Elementary School, MS

Basements
Basements are roomy
and always d
      o
       w
        n
         s
          t
           a
            i
             r
              s
Arielle Diepenbrock, Grade 5
North Windy Ridge School, NC

Courage
What's courage?
   taking the trash out at night
   admitting you don't like something
   saying no to peer pressure
   telling someone your fears
   breaking up a fist fight
   walking by the gang on your street
   going to see the principal
That's courage!
Bradley Ceto, Grade 6
Turkey Creek Middle School, FL

Friends/Enemies
Friends
Nice, kind
loyal, helpful, cheerful,
courteous, obedient, rival, bully
hatred, unfriendly,
mean, cruel
Enemy
Matthew Hood, Grade 5
Queen's Grant Community School, NC

Seasons
Fall and winter are
beautiful seasons, and
so are spring and summer.

Summer has the hot
days and cold nights.
Swimming pools and cool delights.

Spring has a beautiful flower
calling you to pick it.
You know you can grow your own
and maybe see a cricket.

Winter is a time for laughs and fun,
the snow is always a joy.
Fall comes before Winter which is
such a good dinner feast for them all.

Seasons, oh how they are pretty,
with their warm and cold days,
with beautiful fun things for the family.
They are a delight to have in my life.
Gabby Rush, Grade 5
St Martin Upper Elementary School, MS

Prayer
Every night when it's time for bed,
Fold your hands and bow your head.
An angel face, a heart that's true,
You have a friend to pray with you.
Carrie Jamison, Grade 5
Ranburne Elementary School, AL

High Merit Poems – Grades 4, 5, and 6

Rough Play

The willows sway
And the clouds do billow
My battered hair
Is entangled with the wind

Deftly, swiftly
The notorious wind
Leaves an untidy trail

Like a roving soul
It confiscates
Numerous beauties of the Earth
It strips trees of their leaves
While uplifting petals from their spindly stalks

With its ally the cloud
It swirls down to the shore
Picking through
The creatures below

And when its deadly play
Has ceased at last
It proceeds to all those areas
Left untouched by its mighty wrath

Ross Porter, Grade 6
Shorecrest Preparatory School, FL

Green

Green looks like the color of spring trees.
Green smells like Granny Smith apples.
Green tastes like green apple Jolly Ranchers.®
Green sounds like wind rustling in the leaves.
Green feels like the morning dew on the grass.
Green is just alive.
Green is like chocolate mint ice cream.
That is just some of the many great green things green is.

Damian Colley, Grade 4
Tabernacle Elementary School, NC

My Teddy Bear

brown — for your soft fur and ears so fluffy
white — for the fluff that's inside you
blue — for your beady eyes
pink — for the outline of your smile
multicolors — for the clothes that I'll put on you
red — for the heart of love I'll give you

Olyvia Heinz, Grade 6
McRae Elementary School, FL

Prayer

As kids get ready for Valentine's Day
one little girl stops and prays for her daddy in Vietnam
and day by day as she prays
she knows he'll be home soon.

Raegan Levan, Grade 5
Trinity Lutheran School, FL

Seasons

When the water flows through the streams,
When the birds build their nests and sing,
When there are lucky four leaf clovers above the ground.
We can all easily tell that it's spring!

When bathing suits are out in the breeze,
When girls are out for their tanning slumber,
When dads go to Lowes for lumber,
We can all swim into summer!

When the turkey hunters give their call,
When girls plead on their Christmas lists for a new doll,
When we all have to go rake the lawn,
We can all invite our family into fall!

When dads insist that it was Santa they saw,
When your hands are so cold, you always get a splinter,
When kids drop huge Christmas list hinters,
We can all freeze into winter!

Hannah Crow, Grade 6
Providence Classical School, AL

The Thunderstorm

Suddenly, there was a great big boom!
The thunder sent me to my room
The rain started pouring hard
Big puddles and streams formed in my yard

A streak of lightning lit up the sky
Like fireworks on the Fourth of July
Then the lights went out and I couldn't see
Not even my mom right in front of me.

I was a little scared during the storm
But my mom hugged me and kept me warm
Finally, the storm was over
I was as glad as if I'd found a four leaf clover!

Adam Caskey, Grade 4
Edwards Elementary School, SC

Someone Special

Someone special who could it be.
Someone that is caring, understandable,
and there for me when I need help.
When I cry she is there to cheer me up.
She loves me so much that when I come
from school she hugs me so tight that
its like she will never see me again.
She is kind, She buys whatever I want if she could
that is why she is so special.
 I love her and she loves me, We help each other a lot.
If I was separated I don't know what I would do without her.
I don't know what I would do if I need help.
Oh, I almost forgot that someone special is my mom,

Natalia Paredes, Grade 5
Eugenia B Thomas Elementary School, FL

Light
Brightly shining down,
with the energy and pride
of a great lion,
the light of the sun
tried to reach every plant
on the whole planet.

All the marigolds,
tulips, and rhododendrons,
under the pine trees,
had light shed on them.
The green mosses and holly
received nourishment.

Peaches, pears, and plums
all had sun spread on their leaves;
ripening their fruit.
God created light
for his nature and for us;
take care of this gift.
Grace McCartha, Grade 6
Chapin Middle School, SC

Friends
Friends are always there for you,
They'll stick to you like glue.
They will always be there night and day,
Just to make you laugh.
Morgan Katz, Grade 4
St Thomas More School, NC

Cute Little Puppy
I have a cute puppy
He is so little and fluffy
He needs another haircut
Because he is looking kind of scruffy.

He bounces up and down
Like a big bouncy ball,
But you better back up,
Or you will be the one who will fall.
Keara Chapman, Grade 6
Tarpon Springs Middle School, FL

Hot Summer Day
The sun beats down
Like a scorched orange in the sky,
A bad day for football,
The fields are dry to the roots,
A good day for swimming,
And bring out the sun block,
It reached 100 degrees,
It's the Sahara Desert here,
The sun beats down.
Braeden Rozecki, Grade 6
Seven Springs Middle School, FL

The Big Picnic
There once was a huge picnic and Jesus was teaching
People gathered all around to listen to His preaching

Here and there and everywhere
People bowed their heads in prayer

A fellow disciple exclaimed, "Master, Master we have no food,
I could ask them to leave, but that would be rude!"

But Jesus being Master knowing all things
Called upon his Father the King of Kings

According to the Bible from which I have read
Out of the crowd came a little boy with two fish and five loaves of bread

Jesus was praying as He spoke
Each piece of fish and bread He broke

He passed it around to each man, woman and child
Amazingly there was enough to feed them all

So when times are hard and life's not going so good
Just call upon Jesus He fed the multitude.
Suzi Watson, Grade 5
Grace Baptist Christian School, GA

Colors
Purple is as violet as lily flowers dancing in the shimmering midnight moon.
Pink is like popping bubble gum.
Green is shining like emeralds growing on the dirt.
Yellow is the glowing sun in the morning sky.
Red is the setting sun in the evening sky.
Orange is the peach we eat, so sweet.
Blue is the sapphires we wear in our earrings.
White is the silky, smooth, snowy blanket wrapped around my body.
What do you think of the colors around you?
Jamie Libow, Grade 4
Coral Park Elementary School, FL

March Winds
March winds gently blow,
The sun shines bright,
As it rains, the flowers grow,
And get a beam of fresh light.
When you get married you get a ring,
But don't get mad if it's finally spring!
Don't you whine,
Don't you pout,
Wow! Let's go, the sun is out!
I hear the flow,
But how will the sound get low?
Spring is fun and full of surprises,
That's all I really know, but when I go outside and listen to the wind,
And say, "Wow oh how March winds gently blow."
Denecia Cue, Grade 4
Edwards Elementary School, SC

Wookie

There was an enormous ape named Wookie
He loved to eat his cookie
He wouldn't hurt a fly
But he would poke you in they eye
And all his friends would say was "Lookie, Lookie"

Spence Florczak, Grade 5
Ranburne Elementary School, AL

I Am From

I'm from cars and kids and creepy crawlers
and movies and Mondays and mustard's horrible smell.

I'm from love, rubies, and lots of money too
from chess, checkers, and video games.

I'm from rock and roll
from books and bells and really bad smells.

I'm from God and Jesus
from friends and girls and T-shirts too.

I'm from Clemson and South Carolina
and Sunny and Spidey, my dead fish.

I'm from no dogs, no cats, no bunnies
I'm from funny dad and class clown.

I'm from Rambo and rough housing
that's where I'm from.

Scott Wylie, Grade 4
Settles Bridge Elementary School, GA

Talbot

Talbot is great; it's the best place ever
All the fund-raisers help us raise the lever
The teachers are awesome and teach, teach, teach
At all the parties we feel like we're at the beach
We all shout "GO TIGERS" every day we come
Whenever we're here, it's never a bum
We're all proud that we have this school
It's so fun and oh, so cool
Mrs. Ferraro's class is always fun
It always feels like a day in the sun

Geena Schafer, Grade 4
William S Talbot Elementary School, FL

Autumn

Autumn is the time of scaring,
Autumn is the time of fun,
Autumn is the time of turkey,
Autumn is the time of pie,
That is not all autumn is,
Autumn is also when leaves become crunchy,
When they also fall off of the trees.

Zachary Echelson, Grade 6
Challenger Middle School, FL

The War Will End We Pray

I am as mad as a bull seeing red.
I am as sad as a rainy day when I can't go out to play.
I am as lonely as my grandpas when my grandmas went away.
I want to cry every day.
And everyday we pray.
We got a letter from pa in May.
All he had to say was that he was ok.

We are helping the war in every way we can.
With my mother I planted a Victory Garden.
With my brother I collected metal.
With my sister I saved money for a war bond.
We are all doing our part.
The war is hurting our hearts.
We hope the war will soon end.
And father will return to us again!

Rebekah Pinkel, Grade 5
Stone Academy, SC

Spring Is Coming

Spring is coming, don't you see?
I see butterflies and bees flitting around trees.
Spring is coming, just take a look,
Little, tiny fish, swimming in a brook.
Spring is coming, let's give a cheer,
Little green sprouts being sniffed by deer.
Spring is coming, just look outside,
Lovely cherry blossoms growing, I just can't abide.
Spring is coming, I'm jumping with joy,
Month old kittens, playing with a toy.
Spring is coming, I love this season,
Because spring is the sign of life, that is the reason.

Micah Christman, Grade 5
Palmetto Christian Academy, SC

Racing My Cousin

I was racing my cousin.
As I saw the green trees
Passing by me,
I quickly turn around
And saw Brandon catching up with me.
The house was shrinking behind me
As the finish line drew closer.

When I reached the finish line,
I shouted, "I did it!"
Next thing I knew
I was face-to-face
With the hard, gravel road.
I sat up when I saw
Blood dripping down.
The next hour
I looked at the mirror.
My face was as scarred as the gravel road.

Tyler Cavanaugh, Grade 5
East Marion Elementary School, MS

Morning Rush Sky
Rush, rush, rush,
Through the morning sky
We flow,
Rush, blush, through
Rush wind.
Bye, bye butterfly,
In the morning sky
We flow.
Rush, blush butterfly
Through the morning sky
We flow.
Hayli Fisher, Grade 4
Barnardsville Elementary School, NC

Sweet Friendship
Friendship is like candy.
Sweet, enjoyable, and kind,
It sticks together forever.
Just like yours and mine.

Through all of the mishaps.
Through all of the war.
I'm very much for sure.
That it's you I adore.

We talk all the time.
Through every word and rhyme.
It makes the world kind.
It's like we intertwine.
Alexis Nevada Johns, Grade 6
Turkey Creek Middle School, FL

Nature's Song
Spring flowers bloom
Their scent drifts in the air
Petals so lush
Petals so fair
Birds chirp and sing
A beautiful song, heard by all
Fluttering their little wings
The breezy wind, never letting them fall
Tall trees regain their leaves
To animals once more a home
They suit their needs
In the vast fields in which they roam
Brilliant sunlight
It seeps through the forest
Giving the comfort of daylight
To every natural florist
Each and every beautiful thing
Glowing with the start of a new season
Happily and silently nature sings
They all bloom with their own reason
This is the start of spring.
Sydney Blair, Grade 6
Blowing Rock School, NC

Soccer
I am running down the field,
My teammates are calling to me
To pass the ball.
I make my decision to just
Kick the ball.
I was a "bad" kicker,
I made it.
My team won
Because of me.
Tony Lusco, Grade 5
Pensacola Beach Elementary School, FL

Summer
Summer is hot
It's a time of play
All the children are out of school
They shout, "Hip hip hooray!"
They play lots of games,
They swim all the time,
Summer truly is the most fun time!
Peyton Ricketts, Grade 4
Prince Avenue Christian School, GA

Trust
Looks like a butterfly
Tastes like a chocolate chip cookie
Sounds like a music box
Smells like a flower
Feels like heaven
Jana Layton, Grade 5
Ranburne Elementary School, AL

My Brother
He is a Boy.
He is Rough.
He is sometimes Outrageous.
He is most of the time Terrible
When I go into his room,
It is like a Horror movie.
He Eats anything.
His goal is,
To Reach second grade.
Shelby Corbitt, Grade 4
Freeport Elementary School, FL

The Tennis Ball
Smack, there goes the ball,
It's about to fall,
On the baseline it lands,
People clap their hands,
The next match,
I open a batch,
And remember the ball,
That made my opponent crawl.
Jay Karwatsky, Grade 6
Gold Hill Middle School, SC

The Beach
The beach
Calming and soothing
Jump in the waves,
Read a book,
Swim in the water,
Play in the sand
Never get tired.
The beach
Waves
Big and small.
The beach.
Analisa Ruiz, Grade 5
Rosarian Academy, FL

My Sister
I love my sister very much,
She is very sweet and nice,
I think I love her twice,
She's fun and playful as you know,
I really love her so.
Jessica Williams, Grade 6
Gold Hill Middle School, SC

Today Is the Day
Today is the day
I will fly

Today is the day
I will not fail

Today is the day
The sun will shine

Today is the day
The flowers will bloom

Today is the day
I will reach the stars

Today is the day
I will pass the level

Today is the day
I will finish the book

Today is the day
I will smile
Chloé Andrews, Grade 4
Freeport Elementary School, FL

Birds
Birds are beautiful
Fly around with their babies
They build nests a lot
Matthew McClure, Grade 4
Coldwater Elementary School, AL

Snow

The white, frozen flakes that fall to the frigid terrain,
Snow is one of the four forms of precipitation…
Snow, Sleet, Hail, and Rain.
Shoveling snow can be a pain,
Particularly if you live in Maine,
Snow does not melt right away. It will remain.
Snow is a frozen liquid that forms, like rain.

Grant Roger, Grade 5
St Thomas More School, NC

Autumn

The leaves are falling, the trees are almost bare.
It's like they're gloomy drooping to the ground.
It's leading to chills, snow days, and windy days.
School is starting, say goodbye to laughs.
Homework is hard, but it can be easy.
Your teachers are nice, but you want to go play.
Alas, winter break is here, hot chocolate,
Christmas, and cheers.

Robbie Firstman, Grade 4
Queen of Angels Catholic School, GA

My Mom and Dad

My mom and dad love me so
Every day they teach me and watch me grow.

No matter what life puts against me
They'll fight for me.

My mom and dad love me so.

DeTrea Smith, Grade 4
Windsor Elementary School, NC

The Sky

The sky is like an ocean in the air.
I could sleep on its fluffy pillows floating endlessly.
Oh I wish I could fly, so I can reach the sky.
The sky is where I want to be, it's wonderful can't you see.
Whistle — whistle, oh it's the wind flowing past my ear.
Wait! Can it be, I'm flying I'm really flying.
Oh, it's like a dream, but it's real very real.
Believe it or not I'm in the sky.

Seth Cribbs, Grade 6
Gold Hill Middle School, SC

Softball

S trong so you can hit the ball hard.
O utfield is kind of fun.
F ast so you can run the bases.
T hird base is fun to play.
B atting is fun and helps you win.
A ggressive you have to be.
L iable so they can depend on you to be there.
L ine drive would be better than a pop-up.

Perry Gillis, Grade 6
St Francis Xavier Elementary School, MS

Anniversary Dinner

Almost time to dine,
I said, taking out the wine

In they came,
Through the dark glistening rain.

I flipped the steak,
And pies I baked.

My parents anniversary was here,
Celebrated for the 13th year.

Today's the day,
It is no play.

Married 13 years, girl and boy.
A happy day, filled with joy!

Alex Sutterfield, Grade 4
Chancellor Charter School At Lantana, FL

The Mysterious Girl

Masked
Who this girl is, no one will know.
For she is the star,
of her own private show.
Fearless, and ready to fight,
standing alone in the dark of the night.
Her talents lay undiscovered, the beauty is covered,
as she waits for a moment just right.
The knowledge in her mind,
the character in her soul,
is almost to much, for one to know.
She waits and she hides,
the truth and the lies, if only you could see.
Her thoughts are masked,
present and past,
waiting for each to be seen,
She sits and she waits,
she waits to find, someone whom to reveal her mind,
maybe one day,
someone will see,
just how much, this girl could be.

Keith Hearn, Grade 4
Wilkinson Elementary School, FL

Wind

The wind is blowing
I hear birds chirping
In the distance the light blue sky is glowing with blueness
You can smell nothing in the air
The grass is rustling as the wind is blowing
I hear the kids across the street playing basketball
I said I'd love that to be me
But I am sitting here staring at you

Breanna Goins, Grade 5
Southern Pines Elementary School, NC

What Is Courage?
What is courage?
Courage is believing in yourself
when things go wrong.
Courage is being a little elf
and hum a little song.

Courage is being like Louis Pasteur
And making a special cure
Even when times were hard
his friends numbered fewer and fewer.

Courage is going inside a
haunted hall
instead of shopping
at the mall.
Courage is exploring sunken ships
Instead of dressing up
and working on clothes that fit your hips.

Courage is being whoever you want to be
Courage, I think, begins with…ME!!!
Emily Dawn Hansen, Grade 6
Day Spring Academy, AL

Nothing to Do
I'm bored nothing to do
Tuesday night doing some homework
Done with that
To the games
TV, computer, and friends
Make some snacks drink some sodas
Watch TV nothing on
Computer's down
Friends busy
Not fair
Try and go outside rain
Nothing to do
Read a book nah
Study no way
Go to bed definitely not
What's that
Rain stopped
Computers back
Friends free
Favorite show
Something to do
James Hawkins, Grade 6
Gold Hill Middle School, SC

Racing
When I got into a crash
I ended up last
I thought I was the first
But then I was the worst
Nehemiah Blyler, Grade 6
Arnold Magnet Academy, GA

Jake
J ogging
A t the zoo
K nee hurts
E ndless pain
Jake Martensen, Grade 4
East Jones Elementary School, MS

The Miner's Field
There were seven miners
Mining the wall
The first miner broke the wall
And found an ancient mall
The second miner broke his axe
The third found a diamond
The fourth yelled out Max
The fifth came and said "What"
The sixth went very far
The seventh picked up his pickax
And everyone got in the car.
Garet Frank, Grade 6
Tequesta Trace Middle School, FL

I Am
I am a cloud high in the sky,
With no cares, floating along,
When I cry, I pour.
When I fall out of the sky, I become fog.
I greet everybody, including a frog.
I move all around,
With a mean old wind blowing on me.
I am a cloud,
I can be anything.
David Asmar, Grade 5
Cool Spring Elementary School, NC

The Forest
The dark blackness,
The tall, silent trees —
Are in the forest.

Your flashlight casts shadows,
Shadows of the make-believe.
Your eyes dart around,
Trying to make sense of the forest.

Wild animals prowl,
Prowl though the dark.
Their yellow eyes gleam,
Shining in the darkness.

You're running, running,
Trying to escape the silence,
The trees, the animals, the darkness,
In the forest.
Allison Dear, Grade 4
St Thomas More School, NC

God's Creation
God created the plants that yield seeds
And also the animals in need.
He also gave us life.
For that He is nice.
We all need to live
But also forgive.
I see the squirrels in the trees.
I get down on my knees.
I pray.
I feel like I have to stay.
In the pond I see a turtle.
He is really little.
I wonder if he'll get a chance.
I need a good glance
As nature lures.
God created Earth
Which is His greatest birth.
Zac Davis, Grade 6
Mount Zion Christian School, SC

Animals Are Different
Animals are big,
and animals are small.
Elephants are large,
and ants are so tiny
they're smaller than a ball.

Animals have different homes
and different lives.
Whales live in the ocean,
and bees live in beehives.

Animals eat different things too.
Lions eat meat and they aren't tame,
but horses eat grass and they are tame.
But in all animals are animals,
and they are all the same!
Nicole Gouhin, Grade 4
St Thomas More School, NC

The Clouds and the Sun
Happiness is like the sun
Rising over the darkened cloud.
The darkness from that darkened cloud
No longer shrouds the people now.
The people look at it and think,
"This is grand!"
Paul Stegall, Grade 6
Mount Zion Christian School, SC

Fishing
Fishing on a flat
cast after cast, unlucky
finally a bite
Joey Wirtes, Grade 6
J Larry Newton School, AL

High Merit Poems – Grades 4, 5, and 6

The Tiger Who Drank too Much Cider
There once was a tiger
Who had drank too much cider
He always fought with his brother
But never with his mother
The next day he noticed his pants fit on tighter
Because he drank too much of that cider
Trent Williams, Grade 5
Ranburne Elementary School, AL

One In a Million
You…
Yea, you
Do you want to know who the best grandma in the world is?
Here's a hint
She can't walk
but she can roll
She can't take me out to eat
But she can cook like the finest French chef
She can't run around with me outside
But she can entertain me with fun games inside
Her mind is a super computer
She often passes her knowledge on to me
Her wonderful smiles
Make the world stand still
Her love shines down on me like a brilliant star
No matter what I do
She is my number one fan
Do you want to know who it is?
It's my grandma
And I wouldn't want her any other way
James Olson, Grade 6
Unity School, FL

I'm a Boy
I'm a boy who likes to think about something
I'm a boy who can think of anything
One day I had a dream of something bad
It made me feel very sad
I woke up from bed and saw nothing.
Shourik Das, Grade 5
Betton Hills Preparatory School, FL

An Ode to Spring
When spring is near the flowers bloom,
Washing away winters gloom.
Bunnies hopping up and down,
People feeling like a clown.
Petals falling from above,
Flocks and flocks of flying doves.
I see trees all around,
Popping to life without a sound.
Busy birds building a new little nest,
To start the year over like mothers do best.
Everything is done from the new improved sun.
Courtney Herb, Grade 5
Sharon Elementary School, NC

Hunter
Hunter.
Fair, loyal, honest, and hardworking.
Sibling of Holden.
Lover of music, candy, dogs, and my guitar.
Who feels happiness watching UNC play on TV
    playing my guitar and playing with my friends.
Who needs sunshine, rain, love and family time.
Who gives smiles, laughter, and joy in everyone's day.
Who fears mean dogs, rainy days, and bad test grades.
Who would like to see fewer tests, more holidays,
    and more time with my dog to play.
Resident of Bentonville Community, Four Oaks.
Hunter Johnson, Grade 5
Four Oaks Elementary School, NC

I Am
I am a person who likes puppies
I wonder why puppies mark their territory
I hear puppies barking
I see cute little puppies with their owner
I want a German shepherd
I am a person who likes puppies

I pretend I am walking my puppy
I feel that my parents will say yes
I touch their soft fur
I worry sometimes they will say no
I cry because I miss my old puppy Sandy
I am a person who likes puppies

I understand they cost a lot of money
I say that I will take care of it
I dream that my parents will let me get one
I try to convince them on getting one
I hope that I will
I am a person who likes puppies
Sarah St. Jean, Grade 6
Heron Creek Middle School, FL

Weeping Willows
Weeping willows are the saddest of all trees
Looking like they're crying on their knees
Every time you look they're crying
Almost as if someone were dying.
Jack Witner, Grade 6
St John's Lutheran School, NC

Mother
M aking cookies for her kids' scouting meeting.
O ver and over washing dishes.
" **T** ime is up for playing outside!"
H er shift is never-ending.
E verlasting in motherhood.
R etiring? Never!
Kayla Willis, Grade 6
Boiling Springs Intermediate School, SC

Evergreen

I have seen
That evergreen
Standing with the decorations
While we make the preparations
To celebrate the Great One's birth.
The happy ending's all it's worth.
Born in a manger
Died with a stranger
Carried a cross
To save the lost
That's the ending.
There's a new beginning.

Maya Keator, Grade 4
Bridgeway Christian Academy, GA

The Beach

Waves coming and going,
a soft breeze blowing at your face,
sand between your toes
with every step you take.
Seagulls cawing in the distance,
or searching around for food.
Sea life is all around you,
you just have to look closely.

Kristen Cardenas, Grade 5
Rosarian Academy, FL

Friends

F is for family
R is for really great
I is for "I'll help you"
E is for everyone's together
N is for never alone
D is for almost never depart
S is for all the sleepovers
Colby, Lexi, Brooke, Alyssa, B.F.F.L.

Lexi Tate, Grade 5
Ranburne Elementary School, AL

God Is Love

Love is like a sweet smelling flower.
Joy brings you hope in the hour.
God is love and love is He,
All within the sweet trinity.

Christian Chandler, Grade 6
Mount Zion Christian School, SC

Spring

S pecial
P eaceful
R aindrops
I nsects
N ectar
G raceful

Kalei Tischler, Grade 4
Central Park Elementary School, FL

Emily

I am not the kind of person who plays in the marching band,
But sometimes I am the kid who does the best she can!
If you look down past my eyes, not just blue, green, and gold,
You will see a writer, an artist to behold!

Some people see a goofy kid with buck teeth, freckles, and light skin,
But with my pen and pencil, I will do anything to win.
Sometimes I am a coward, a loser, a nerd,
And sometimes a lion — cool and absurd.

So if you think I'm writing this just for it to rhyme,
You should know this fact, forever, and all the time:
I am very funny, sometimes a pleasure to know,
But other times when Aidan makes me mad, it's NOT a wonderful show.

I am a pretty cool person who loves to rhyme and read,
But if you do not know me, please PLEASE take heed —
I can get a little angry if you call me a dork or nerd,
But open upon that insult when it's quite absurd.

So if you're a-wondering about what you see,
The thing you're looking at is…
Me!

Emily Warner, Grade 5
Oakland Elementary School, SC

Birds

Birds are the creators of flight
They spring off a branch and dive below
They never feel lonely when they call to their friends
Birds open their wings and welcome the cool breeze grazing their face
They are never sad but are always chirping a happy tone
They inspire their admirers who wish they could soar through the sky
They fly over treetops keeping a keen watch for food
They look like great spirits when they fly overhead
Birds are the creators of flight

Rohit Reddy, Grade 6
Shorecrest Preparatory School, FL

Sea at Night

Sea at night is a wonderful sight,
The blue and black waves would make you amazed,
When you lie down in the boat and look at the stars.
With the amazement in your mind you don't see it coming from behind;
Suddenly you feel it coming and so does your friend,
Suddenly you look up and see a fin,
And the ripples coming toward your boat,
You start rowing your boat
But your not fast enough
You see it coming out of the water, the teeth biting your boat,
You're almost there
Will you make it?
But suddenly quiet at sea is about,
And anyone who goes to that sea at night never, ever sees the light again.

Chase Moseley, Grade 4
Elba Elementary School, AL

High Merit Poems – Grades 4, 5, and 6

The Beach
B urying each other in the sand
E ating new foods
A great place to relax
C atching lots of fish
H aving a wonderful time

Regan Nesmith, Grade 6
St Francis Xavier Elementary School, MS

Dishes
Doing chores is a waste of time.
I don't really care if they pay me a dime.
The dishes are the worst of all.
Hoping the dishes won't fall.
The meatballs look like basket rolls.
The baked potato looks like chicken mole.
Yesterday's French toast,
Looks like Friday's meat loaf.
Last but not least the dirty jugs,
And the hot cocoa mugs.

Edward Torres, Grade 6
St Mary Magdalen Catholic School, FL

Earth's Giant Herbivores
Slumbering like humans below the surface
Relaxing like vacationers at the Hilton
Gliding gracefully like water ballerinas
Giants narrowly escaping death

Our carelessness has destroyed many
We pollute, we destroy
They do not deserve this senseless slaughtering
People can care and save them
These passive creatures of the sea

Danny Fernandez, Grade 5
Oliver Hoover Elementary School, FL

Pompeii
U **P** , up, and away I blow
Through **O** live orchards, all must go
M t. Vesuvius must be feared
P ompeii will not see another year
E veryone who stays will pay the toll
As **I** sound the death knoll
I will strike again…

Tommy Bilden, Grade 5
St Thomas More School, NC

Sports of Sorts
I like all sports that are played on courts.
I like all sorts of rough house sports.
I give my best behind the bat.
Excitement filled when that ball cracked.
Give me a chance and you shall see
What a champion I can be!

Michael Suarez, Grade 5
Our Lady of Fatima School, MS

Poems
P oems are so lovely, each one telling it's own story
O n come the rhymes, you use them every time
E agles to fish, your poem can be anything you want
M ake your poem a couplet, a triplet, or an initial poem
S o just keep working until your masterpiece is done.

Chad Nussbaum, Grade 4
PVPV/Rawlings Elementary School, FL

My Adventures
What I like is the wondrous adventures.
What I like is the medieval endeavors.
When the horses gallop, and the knights wallop,
It is the best adventure of all.

What I like is the modern adventures.
When I hunt for food, and the cattle moo,
I will share the feast with you.

What I like is the reading adventures.
When I start a new story, I feel all the glory,
And it becomes the most magical story of all.

What I like is the wondrous adventures.
What I like is the medieval endeavors.
When the horses gallop, and the knights wallop,
It is the best adventure of all.

Tyla Gelman, Grade 4
Brevard Jewish Community School, FL

Money
Penny, penny
Worth one cent
Wish you were enough
To pay our rent.

Nickel, nickel
Big and fat
Not worth much
But so is a mat.

Dime, dime
10¢ for me
So shiny I
Think I can't see.

Quarter, quarter
More for me
When I find some
I say wee!

Dollar, dollar
Enough to make me smile
I'm going to be
Happy for a while.

Bryan Lopez, Grade 4
Egret Lake Community Elementary School, FL

Hideaway
I have a secret hideaway
A place I visit every day
A place where serenity lies
And you can lie beneath the sky
Watch as the clouds go by
A patch of grass as soft as a bed
Where you can lie and rest your head
My secret hideaway
A place I visit every day
Marissa Plondke, Grade 5
Queen's Grant Community School, NC

Spring
Spring is near
The sweet smelling flowers are blooming
The birds are cooing
Children come out and play
The snow melts away
The winter is no more
Even though we yearn for more
Spring is here
Alicia Hayworth, Grade 5
Buies Creek Elementary School, NC

Valentine
I need a time to think of others
I need a time to love.

Valentine's Day is here
and lots of love is near.

Spring is here
it's time to cheer.
Let it be loud and clear.
Summer Bowman, Grade 5
Buies Creek Elementary School, NC

Mrs. Richardson
Mrs. Richardson
Smart, beautiful
Happy, proud, friendly
Wealthy, healthy, lovable, caring
Mrs. Richardson
Summer Roberts, Grade 6
Rock Mills Jr High School, AL

Frog
I ribbit to the other frog
I jump to catch my prey
A car stops so he won't run over me
I jump high and fall on a lily pad
I swim fast through the murky pond
I catch a fly and eat it in the road
Then riiiiiiibbit a car runs over me
Megan Cronin, Grade 4
Pensacola Beach Elementary School, FL

Love
you know you're in love
when you can't fall asleep
at night cause your life
is finally better than
you dreams and all you can do
is lie in bed and think about him
and how your life is better
than it will ever be
you close your eyes and
think you can sleep
but all you see
when you close your eyes
is him smiling back
at you
Jenn Rudolph, Grade 6
Shorecrest Preparatory School, FL

Lovely Stars
Lovely stars tonight
Hanging in the sky all night
Moving all the time
Haleigh Riopelle, Grade 6
Seven Springs Middle School, FL

Flight
When we fly,
We go up high,
It is a magnificent sight,
Why are some afraid of flight?
When we go high,
We are actually in the sky,
It is fun,
To almost be as high as the sun!
Katie Rawls, Grade 5
Rosarian Academy, FL

The Cave
In this cave,
There are no grave secrets,
Only answers of melancholy.

No light drags in,
No breaths of life,
Only sorrow.

In this cave,
The past weeps,
For all of humanity,
Is trapped inside.

For future to come,
Secrets are found,
This dark and lonely cave,
Will soon have light.
Campbell Alspaugh, Grade 5
Sardis Elementary School, NC

The Rain
Pitter patter, pitter patter,
The raindrops fall,
I look outside,
I realize,
It is beginning to hail,
Click clack, click clack,
Hail falls,
Click clack, click clack,
Soon I notice sleet,
Pitter patter, click clack,
BOOM! The lightning struck,
Pitter patter, pitter patter,
(the rain it never ends).
Alexis Oeth, Grade 6
Shorecrest Preparatory School, FL

Mom's Flower
My mom is mine. I love her so.
When I'm sick she holds me tight.
When I'm feeling blue, she helps me see.
I'm a very pretty flower blooming.
Diamond Sistrunk, Grade 5
West Marion Elementary School, MS

My Beach
As the ever so bright sun
sinks into the ocean, I
at the glorious shores with
the animals awaiting the
dark.

As the ever so moon rises above
the grassy sands,
I spy upon the sea life made by
the stars of the gleaming
cold night skies.

As I strode past all the
sea life on the desert
shores rather than the ocean,
I am able to see the crabs rise
from the ocean surface, breaking the
water surface. I squint to see minnows
swimming for their lives from the ocean.
Spectators looking for a munch
in the fright of night.
Brett Leaphart, Grade 6
Chapin Middle School, SC

My Friend Crystal
Crystal Nicole Skeen
Likes to eat beans.
She likes to play with her toys
And talk to boys.
Zoë Taylor, Grade 6
Arnold Magnet Academy, GA

High Merit Poems – Grades 4, 5, and 6

He Has Come
Angels sing a holy hymn
God ascends into the heavenly clouds
The holy child descends to Earth like a
Fall leaf gently flowing down from a tree
Another life is in our Father's hands
One more light has brightened
He is born!

Jordan E. Fason, Grade 4
Marietta Center for Advanced Academics, GA

My Memory
I wonder about my memory.
I wonder if it will erase in another century.
Or just run onto my face!!
My memory…
Will go on as far as it can be.
Or just grow old when it does not come back to me?
So see ya…
Come back another day
And remember I love you
My memory…

Courtney Wolfanger, Grade 4
Clearview Avenue Elementary School, FL

The Eyes of a Tiger
There's a big, hungry animal with whiskers so long.
When at the moment, anything can go wrong.
He can pounce and I'll die,
or he'll roar and I'll cry.
I suddenly feel frightened — knowing he will attack.
In the blink of an eye — just like that.
His claws grow longer, out of his skin.
For this fight, surely he'll win.
I quietly take my last few breaths, in and out.
For I'll at least be bitten, there's no doubt.
He circles me hungrily, ready for the kill.
For at least he'll try, he WILL! HE WILL!
A tear passes slowly down my cheek.
My throat feels itchy, I really can't speak.
I fall to my knees, and he snaps back.
His mouth grows wider
and I look into his eyes, the eyes of a tiger.

Alie Presley, Grade 4
Wilkinson Elementary School, FL

Here Comes the Flood
Here comes the flood,
So wild and free!
Here comes the flood,
Find a safe place to be!
Here comes the flood,
Oh, please don't hurt me!
The flood is here,
So wild and free!

Megan Lange, Grade 4
Wrights Mill Road Elementary School, AL

I Am
I am happy and brave
I wonder when I will laugh again
I hear the wind blowing through the trees
I see flowers blooming in the meadow in Spring
I want peace in every country, in the whole world
I am happy and brave

I pretend I'm angry at everyone
I feel like I'm in heaven
I touch heaven's light
I worry when people are mad
I cry when I think of my gram
I am happy and brave

I understand when I am mad
I say to myself just forget about it
I dream of clear blue skies
I try to see all that is good in things
I hope other people do too
I am happy and brave

David Escobar, Grade 6
Heron Creek Middle School, FL

Stars
Stars are like sparkles in the sky,
As some start shooting I wave goodbye.
Twinkling like diamonds way up high
Shining so beautifully. I close my eyes.
And start to dream about stars, in my bed I lie.

Gina Radicchi, Grade 5
The Sanibel School, FL

Winter's Gift
W is for the soft fluffy wool on my blanket.
I is for the ice on the huge frozen pond across the way.
N is for New Year's Eve.
T is for saying thank you to your parents.
E is for enjoying the winter holidays.
R is for the ruby red ribbon on my gift.

Carlos Charre, Grade 4
Julian D Parker School of Science, Math & Technology, FL

Exaggeration
As comfortable as spikes on a pillow
As graceful as dancing hippos
As clean as a mud hole after a heavy rain

As convenient as working hard and not getting paid
As reassuring as jumping off a cliff
As exciting as watching the news when you're tired

As pleasant as a porcupine poking your butt
As welcome as a hungry bear in your house
As easy as tackle football for the first time

Christian Flowers, Grade 5
Covenant Classical School, NC

Spring
The chilly weather,
Flowers blooming every day
It's raining a lot!
Zenaida Ramos, Grade 4
Moyock Elementary School, NC

Haunted House
I went to a haunted house
And saw a ghost in a blouse.
He ate a mouse.
He flew saying Boo! Boo! Boo!
I'll scare you!

David Raba, Grade 5
Buies Creek Elementary School, NC

My Dog Rocky
My dog Rocky is a Boston terrier.
He likes to sit in his carrier.
He likes to go on walks
While I wear my socks.
My dog Rocky smells like feet.
At dinner he sometimes eats my meat.
My dog Rocky really rocks!
Kris Adkison, Grade 5
Elba Elementary School, AL

Winter
I travel the wind
With a sudden chill
The breeze becomes cool
As I loop through the sky
With grace and a feeling
A feeling of purpose
With white flakes I fall
Jacob Scarberry, Grade 4
Pensacola Beach Elementary School, FL

My Cat
I have a cat,
He sleeps all day
And when he wakes up
He loves to play!
He meows at the birds
And he meows at the bees
And he looks for squirrels,
Dancing in the trees!
He jumps at the spiders
Flying down their web
And sometimes he jumps
At baby snake's heads!
I have a cat,
He sleeps all day
And when he wakes up
He loves to play!
Mariah Francis, Grade 6
Seven Springs Middle School, FL

Seasons
Seasons are like leaves, changing color with its different moods.
Spring, summer, winter, fall —
One, two, three, four, count them all.
Spring brings blossoms and beautiful flowers
And wonderful April showers.
The little birds that chirp and sing
Are fun to listen to in the spring.
Summer brings the fun camp outs,
And the lone coyote that mysteriously shouts.
It's time to run and go climb trees,
And sit and lie and go watch the bees.
Fall brings us back to school,
But it's still warm enough to play in the pool.
The leaves start changing into their orange and reds.
And the animals get ready for their hibernation beds.
Winter is the coldest season
That brings its snow and sleet for a reason.
Christmas time will be drawing near,
With its happiest times of the year.

All these seasons make a year, that bring us joy and make us cheer.
And when each season comes around, remember this poem all year round.
Anna Pierce, Grade 6
Scotts Creek Elementary School, NC

Boston Tea Party
In 1775 I'm told our founding fathers wasted tea,
They hated taxes on it and they couldn't be,
They collected 342 crates of that taxation without representations,
They dressed as mohawks, oh how it was some sensation.
People watched in silent approval,
Everyone who watched — watched like a rival,
Bye-bye tea and thank you for this day,
Thanks to the Boston Tea Party that is all I have to say.
Dillon Das, Grade 5
Queen's Grant Community School, NC

The Last Day
I remember strolling through the door,
As I walked in, I looked at her eyes sparkling like diamonds.
She didn't know who I was
But she loved me anyway.
She gave me compliments, knowing we had a connection but not knowing how.
"You're the sharpest knife in the drawer."
I remember hearing the funniest stories about her
And after the stories, we'd all giggle.
My grandma had a heart of gold
I loved her old wrinkly face.
She was sweet with a bright smile
My grandma had snowy white hair and was as tall as a giraffe.
I adored her soft voice
She was as precious as an angel
I admired her loving way.
I keep in mind that she didn't remember me, but still loved me.
Julie Marino, Grade 6
Unity School, FL

The Forked Road

I stand on a road that forks to the left and right.
The right way is where everyone goes
and where everyone wants me to go.
Should I break swift flow
or go my own way?
Even my friends consider going away with the crowd.
Am I on my own cloud
where no one thinks I'm "cool?"
It feels as so.
"Leave without me," I say.
Me, Myself, and I are left.
Then I decide to do the unthinkable
I take the left road
and a blinding light appears.
"Come, my child," says the light.
A smile spreads across my face
as I walk into the light.
When you come across the forked road,
break the flow.
It will all be worthwhile.

Evy Savoie, Grade 5
St Martin Upper Elementary School, MS

The Beach

Early afternoon,
The sun is shining bright,
The seagulls up above,
Squawking in a fight.

Hot and humid,
The day is nice,
The clouds are finally gone except for one,
And this is all at a single place,
With fresh, salty air filling the lung.

As waves crash up against the shore,
With umbrellas propped up close by,
I sink into the sand and listen,
To the noises of the beach from where I lie.

So, as the day comes to an end,
I watch the sun drop down,
With its shadow as dark as the blackest black,
I walk away with a frown.

Lizebeth Longstreet, Grade 6
Heron Creek Middle School, FL

Sweet Home

My sweet home is the place I want to be.
God brought me here to stay and to be free.
My sweet home is the best
and when I'm tired I can have a rest.
I love my sweet home as much as I can because
My sweet home is the best.

Chris Johnson, Grade 5
West Marion Elementary School, MS

My Future

Future, future it is fun.
Future, future it will be done.
Future, future it will be gone.
When I'm twenty,
I'll be in the endzone.
Future, future
When I'm in the NFL
It will be on.

Travon Evans, Grade 4
Clearview Avenue Elementary School, FL

Which Will You Choose

Will you choose drugs or Jesus
Or will you let them both go
Will you stick with the plan God has for you
Or just go with the flow
When you come before God on judgment day
Will your name be in the Lamb's Book of Life
Or will you be with Satan for the rest of your life
Will you spend eternity with the one you hate
Or smile when you walk through Heaven's gate
Which will you choose?

Hannah Wells, Grade 6
Norlina Christian School, NC

Fell Out of My Deer Stand

I got into my deer stand
Climbed 30 feet up a tree.
After I got settled in,
A buck walks out.
I raised my gun and aimed.
I was nervous.
I thought I'd miss, but I didn't.
I squeezed the trigger. Bam!
The buck had dropped in place.
I started to climb down, but I fell.
When I was falling,
I thought about if I was going to live or die.
I tried to catch a limb
Until I had no skin on my hand.
Then I hit the ground.
There was a tear in my eye,
But I managed to get up.
I walked to my four-wheeler.
I was in a whole lot of pain.
I put the deer on back and rode right home.

Randy Wigginton, Grade 5
East Marion Elementary School, MS

Flower Love

The delicate petals of the rose are tender like you,
The morning dew on the violets shine vividly blue,
Lovely flowers are like succulent candy that is sweet,
It is like our hearts when they meet.

Ashley Sanchez, Grade 5
Joella Good Elementary School, FL

Colors of the Wind

Clear blue is the glow of a sparkling stream shimmering in the luminous sunlight.
White is the silky fur of a newborn polar bear wrapped around his mama's coal black paws.
Yellow is the sunlight dancing around the Earth's sapphire green grass.
Green is the jade lilly pads dripping with dawn's dew.
Purple is the violet petals swaying through the cool spring breeze.
Red is the ruby rose reflecting in the moonlight.
Can you see the colors around you?

Juliana Reyes, Grade 5
Coral Park Elementary School, FL

I Love You

I loved you when you were alive and even more when you died.
I love the delicious smell of your Polish pasta as it would draw me into your house.
I loved your gray and white beautiful hair
and the way it would blow around when we were outside.
I loved your crystal clear backyard, and I loved all those beautiful butterflies.
I loved the way you smelled because it was a smell like blooming flowers.
I loved when you would speak English
even though most of the time I did not understand what you were saying.
I loved your home because it felt as cozy as a couch.
I loved you because you shined like the sun.
I loved how you always had sugary chocolate in your house for me to eat.
I loved how when my sister and I would play in your backyard,
you would sit in that chair and you would peal with laughter.
You were an angel.
I loved the way your room looked, so cozy and so safe.
I loved how you would always respect my family in good times and in bad
I loved how you raised and nurtured the best kids, who now help raise and nurture me.
I loved you and I wish you were still here with me.
I love you! I really love you!
I LOVE YOU!

Taylor Micallef, Grade 6
Unity School, FL

The Girl of Wonders*

Calm as the sleeping dog, glowing brightly as the stars shining in the night sky
Persistent as the sun, always burning warmly, loving as the snowy white dove
"Stargirl, Stargirl," they chant, day after day, week after week
They speak the name with much wonder, "Stargirl, Stargirl"
Soft as fresh, white silk, intelligent as scientists
Pleasant as wildflowers, swaying in the breeze, beautiful as diamonds in a diamond shop
"Stargirl, Stargirl," they chant, day after day, week after week
They speak the name with much wonder, "Stargirl, Stargirl"
Fickle as the waves in the turquoise Caribbean Sea, aloof as a sloth to what others think and say
Jaunty and gregarious like a cheerleader would be,
"Stargirl, Stargirl" they chant, day after day, week after week
They speak the name with much wonder, "Stargirl, Stargirl"
Abstruse as algebra or calculus is to a kindergartner
Amazing as the dark night sky, as mysterious as the constellations
Caring as a doctor or nurse, intriguing as the universe
"Stargirl, Stargirl," they chant, day after day, week after week
They speak the name with much wonder, "Stargirl, Stargirl"
No one can bring her down

Sydney Dalton, Grade 6
Trickum Middle School, GA
*In response to "Stargirl" by Jerry Spinelli

Friends

Friends are people who do not lie
they are always by your side.
Friends are people close to you.
They make you smile when you are blue.
They never let you down.
They'll always be there turning your frown upside down.
They lie in bed thinking of you.
Always wondering why or who.
They buy presents for you each holiday,
or even when you're in bed all day.
They sometimes take you out to eat.
They help you even when you get beat.
They are there for you no matter what.
They sometimes take you to pizza hut.
Friends will always be in your heart.

Lauren Carroll, Grade 5
St Martin Upper Elementary School, MS

Valentine's Day

Valentine's Day is about candy and flowers,
sweethearts, and cards
it all drives you bananas.

Everyone loves it
especially the ones who receives balloons,
chocolate, and sweet bubblegum.

The sweetheart you meet
is the one you keep because
he always sweeps you off your feet —

It's best to get one from you-know-who
and run inside to shout Yahoo!

Everyone gives cards and candy too!

Kori Vessell, Grade 6
St Francis Xavier Elementary School, MS

Just Be You

You send me presents and beautiful things.
Five seconds later my phone starts to ring.
You try to impress me but it doesn't work.
For a split second I think you're a jerk.
It's like truth or dare,
There's no easy way out.
You can't walk around with your head in the clouds.
Know where you're going.
Know what to say.
I don't have all the spare time to waste.
You act all macho and act all tough.
I'm here to tell you that I've had enough.
Be a man,
Tell me the truth.
To start it all off…Just be you!

Jordan Mooney, Grade 6
Heritage Middle School, GA

Hurricane Floyd

The flooding rains were rolling in,
The rough seas and high winds struck again.
Another county became a disaster zone,
Millions of families were on the phone.

Another one gone another one dead,
Another day in the shelter being fed.
By now the hurricane was up even further,
It looked like it could be a real thrower.

Tearing the towns up and down,
So many houses lifted off the ground.
Was this disaster ever to be done?
It was like this hurricane was having fun.

Then finally everything was fine,
These days were put down Sept. 14th-18th 1999.
More than seventy-seven deaths were said,
Over 1.6 billion is what the check read.

Now this is old news, stuff has advanced.
The National Hurricane Center got a second chance.
But today people still like to live on the coast,
So don't blame anyone but you if your house becomes toast.

Tabitha Dean, Grade 6
J E Holmes Middle School, NC

Soccer

Running very fast
Down that open field
Running past
To kick the black-checkered ball
Yes, I made a goal
It lifts my soul
I jump in the air
Making sure it's fair and square
I see the referee
He jumps with much glee
Soccer is very tough
But, that is when you get rough
I love soccer as you can see
When I play, I play happily

Emily Atkins, Grade 6
Boiling Springs Intermediate School, SC

Summer

Summer is the time to have
Some fun with your family.
Summer is the smell of the salty water splashing
Up against the rock.
Summer is the time to go on vacation and spend
Time with your friends.
And Summer is a great time for no school,
So be cool!

William Brown, Grade 6
St John's Lutheran School, NC

The Dragon
Once Tripp was bragging
That there was a dragon
It breathed fire
He's not a liar
I went to see
I said, "It can't be"
I ran to town
But I fell down
It took a sheep
It had to eat
The day was hot
And the dragon got shot
Alberto Zavala, Grade 4
Elba Elementary School, AL

Can You Imagine…
A crab with no shell
A school with no bell

An ocean without water
An alligator without a daughter

A villain with no lair
A mammal without hair

No leaves on a tree
A beehive without a bee

A child with no mom or dad
A butterfly acting really bad

A bat with no wings
A rock that sings

The world without grass
A window without any glass?
James Houston, Grade 4
William S Talbot Elementary School, FL

Glory
Fall is arriving
Trees waving back and forth
Beautiful breeze
God has given us glory.
Mariah True, Grade 4
Sangaree Intermediate School, SC

Spring
When the snow is gone
And the cold is away
The flowers start to bloom
Each and every day
I love spring in every single way
To winter's dismay
Daniel Broadnax, Grade 6
Moyock Middle School, NC

Heaven Is Beautiful
Heaven is beautiful
No men without hair
I am so thankful
That God lives there

The streets are gold
The lights flash
I get a souvenir
And see the angels dash

To see him lying in the hay
To see his smile
I'll just stand there and say
I'll be here for a while

When I go to heaven
There will be no confusion
God's bread is leaven
I'll have my last communion
Joanna Gamble, Grade 4
Bayshore Christian School, FL

Fall
Leaves color the ground
Children are jumping
Pumpkins are growing
Temperature is getting cooler
What season is it?
It is fall
Antonio Rodriguez, Grade 5
Rosarian Academy, FL

Best Friends
Best friends
Are people who are.

Best friends
Are people who share.

Best friends
Are people who are fair.

Best friends
Are people who stick together.

Best friends
Are nice to each other.
Anna Sefo, Grade 4
Freeport Elementary School, FL

Night
The stars gleam at night
Night is a beautiful time
It's a time to sleep
Brendan Stewart, Grade 4
St Thomas More School, NC

Spring Things
Spring is here!
Let's say a cheer;
The beauty is everywhere,
Smell the scent in the air!

The flowers and trees will sprout,
The butterflies and bees are out!
Green grass is all around;
Soon April rains pour down!

Cute, fluffy, yellow chicks
Follow in rows of about six;
Piglets snort and squeal,
Looking for the next meal!

Puppies sleep in the sun;
Later they leap and have fun!
The mother cat licks her kittens,
Soon their fur is as soft as mittens!

I watch the sun slowly go down,
As I look all around;
Soon it's a new spring day,
And my memories will not fade away!
Ashley Waldron, Grade 5
Palmetto Christian Academy, SC

Lovely Ponds
Lovely ponds and lakes
shimmer and shine in the light
and drift in the breeze.
Ryan Gleason, Grade 4
PVPV/Rawlings Elementary School, FL

That One
Stars are a small joy to the galaxy
They shine almost as bright as the sun
All but one
It's dim in the back
It's the one who needs that shine it lacks
They drape the sky with a glow
Where is that one
No one will ever know
I know, because it's me
The little cry in the sky
That was me too
No one dares to go far
To find that star that lost its mind
Who cares anyway, right?
Eventually that star will lose its light
That one dim in the back
Still losing light it lacks
Where is that one
It's gone. It's done.
Mariella Rivera, Grade 6
Freedom Middle School, FL

Poetry Is a Passion

Poetry is a passion,
To all who love to write.
You can write a pretty poem,
From whatever is in sight.
You can write a poem of birds and bees,
A poem of leaves and trees.
You can write a poem of the very blue sky,
A very good poem if you just try.
If you follow these instructions,
And do as you are told,
Your poem is going to be as good as gold.

Courtney Marshall, Grade 4
Elizabeth Traditional Elementary School, NC

I Am

I am a skimboarder.
I wonder if I will ever be as good as Michael.
I hear the ripping waves as they splash onto the beach.
I see the birds chirping as they fly overhead.
I want to be a professional skimboarder.
I am a skimboarder.
I pretend to be as good as Michael.
I feel the ocean mist as it gently splashes me.
I touch my skimboard triumphantly as I complete a trick.
I worry that I might fall.
I cry in pain as if I just fell and broke a bone.
I am a skimboarder.
I understand that I am not as good as Michael.
I say I will become a professional skimboarder.
I dream I am a professional skimboarder.
I try to pursue my dream, but others hold me back.
I am a skimboarder.

Jonathan Cain, Grade 6
Heron Creek Middle School, FL

Jack

His name is Jack,
he likes to run track.
He fell in the snow,
and tears started to flow.
He tried to cut a tree,
but he had to pay a fee.
This boy is so poor,
he couldn't afford a s'more.
He met a boy named Max,
who had a big ax.
One day they got in a fight,
when they were out of sight.
Jack started to cry,
and he had to say goodbye.
He entered a contest for a million dollars,
when they finally answered they said they had a million callers.
Now he has a good life,
and a lovely wife.

Charles Thaxton, Grade 6
Brogden Middle School, NC

Life

Life can be deceiving
making you laugh when you're ready to cry.
But life can be cut short
when you're to say goodbye.
Life is special
Don't waste it.
When you see a baby
don't you cry with joy?
Or do you hold your head
because it seems to annoy?
You are no lesser than a human
believe me, it's true.
But why do people hate themselves
for things they didn't do?
Wars go on and on,
Why? Is there a point?
Everything is so sad,
It seems to disappoint.
And so I say it once again…
Life is special
Don't waste it.

Melody Morgan, Grade 6
City of Pembroke Pines Charter Central Middle School, FL

The Firefly

A firefly is like a light
Making noise like a cricket
As gold as a golden egg
Flying like a butterfly
It is like a person running away from you
As beautiful as a flower
Lighting up like a lantern
As scared as a deer

Robert Sevin, Grade 5
Covenant Classical School, NC

Miserable Mistakes

I made a mistake and I can't pretend it's fake
Mistakes affect so much I can't believe it but it is such
I wish I could redo it go back in time a little bit

Bridget Foster, Grade 4
William S Talbot Elementary School, FL

Woodpecker

I saw a woodpecker who could not fly.
I bet he wished he was in the sky.
Oh, woodpecker, woodpecker, why do you cry?
I know you wish to be in the sky.
I pick him up and put him on a branch,
I say, "Fly, woodpecker, fly."
Suddenly, I see him fly.
I see him up, up high in the sky.
I am so happy I almost cry
To see a woodpecker fly in the sky.

Ashley Hinson, Grade 4
Cool Spring Elementary School, NC

Fear

Waiting in line
Butterflies in stomach
I take slow steps
Fear is in the air
It is almost my turn
To ride the roller coaster

Mario Alvarenga, Grade 6
Tequesta Trace Middle School, FL

The Tunnel

This hole dug in the ground
I walk through it
Me being the only sound
I feel like a butterfly
Trapped in my cocoon
I hope to spread my wings quite soon
In the middle of this mess
A mess of love hate and distress
I walk through this dark tunnel
Looking for light
But the tunnel does not end
And I realize it's just life

Emma Ely, Grade 6
Bak Middle School of the Arts, FL

Waiting

I sit here wondering
When you'll show
When it will be
Time to go
You said
Half-past ten
It is now
Eleven
Should I call you
"Baboon"
Or wait
'Till noon
Maybe
I should worry
But I know
You'd hurry
To call
What's that I hear?
It's time to leave?
Oh dear
I'm not ready.

Eliana Meyerowitz, Grade 6
Bak Middle School of the Arts, FL

Spring

Spring is happiness
Spring is time for peace and joy
Spring is colorful

Aidan Bermingham, Grade 4
St Thomas More School, NC

Rapunzel's Desires

The piercing cackles filled my head
As my extravagant yards of gold silk
Ran through the tower high
As I longed for someone to banish my loneliness
Drifting was the hope of mine
The memories of happiness played in my eyes
For none took pity and sought me
My days were filled with sorrow
Oh what 'twas' this cry
The old vile witch calling me again
for I would let down my rows of hair
And she would climb up to meet me
Long the days lurked by all the while I was awaiting my beloved Prince
The one that would save me from this agony
Oh my 'twas not the witch that cried my name but the Prince I had been longing
He freed me from my prison as I stared into his mesmerizing gaze
His eyes pierced through me and I couldn't wait till we become one
Our love is deep right to the core
And now the time had come
That I am free

Anna Foster, Grade 5
Olde Providence Elementary School, NC

The Circus

Grandma watches the whimsical clowns fool around.
Her light and sweet laugh floats through the air
as she watches the clowns tumble to the ground.
Her bright and gleaming smile shines brilliantly across the room.
Her jaw drops in amazement as she watches the flawless magician.
When she sees the adorable animals perform amazing tricks
her eyes sparkle like the luminous stars in space.
Her laughter soothes the ears of everyone around her.
When she sees the dangerous stunts the acrobat's perform,
her eyes widen with fear of them falling.
As she peers at the spontaneous motorcyclist's ride around the small cage,
she looks at them with the fear and excitement of not knowing what will happen next.
As we all left the big top,
She looked at me with her colorful and beautiful eyes and said,
"What a wonderful day."
I will never forget the day that we went to the circus.

Colin Schotter, Grade 6
Unity School, FL

Caleb

Caleb
Athlete
Fast, athletic, kind, and smart
Lover of family, animals, and outdoors
Who believes in God
Who wants peace, to have a good life, and to stop global warming
Who uses Dad's money, God's help, and fishing poles
Who gives presents, help, and money to charity
Who says nothing is impossible if you try your hardest
Fulp

Caleb Fulp, Grade 6
Broad Creek Middle School, NC

Hope

I am a rock, a strong and hard rock.
I am a lion, fighting for my life.
I am 10, glad for double digits.
I am yellow, like the very bright sun.
I am America, a place of liberty.
I am water, I go and go without stopping.
I am hope, for all wars to end.

Jacob Corrigan, Grade 4
Sangaree Intermediate School, SC

Georgia

Georgia is sweet
Georgia is known for its
Sweet peaches
Sweet just like you and me
Its peaches have made
Thousands upon thousands
Of sweet jams and pies.
Yes, Georgia is the peach of my eye.
Georgia is cool as a
Caribbean breeze in the spring,
Hot as molasses in the summer.
But all in all, Georgia is my
Cool breeze with the sweet taste
Of my melody.

Kahlyn Marine, Grade 6
Academy of Lithonia Charter School, GA

What to Be

I sit
I think
What I want to be
A vet, a doctor or even a biologist
But that wouldn't be me
I want to be a
Canine Trainer
I have dreamed my whole life to be the president
But that would not be me
I want to be a Canine Trainer

Lindsey Hall, Grade 6
Gold Hill Middle School, SC

Just Because…

Just because I'm not "popular"
   Don't laugh at what I wear,
   Don't talk trash behind my back.
Just because I'm not "popular"
   It doesn't mean you're better than me,
   It doesn't mean you should pick on me,
   It doesn't mean no one likes me.
Just because I'm not "popular"
   Say what you have to say to my face,
   Can't wait 'till you're in my shoes.
Just because I'm not "popular" — Don't judge me.

Miriam Godinez, Grade 6
Turkey Creek Middle School, FL

Movies

Filming in a dark place.
Eating some buttery, yellow popcorn.
Sitting and waiting for the best part to come.
When it's over you come outside and look at the blue sky.

Ada Folmar, Grade 4
Wrights Mill Road Elementary School, AL

Love

Love is like a silver dove
love is something everyone knows
forever it goes
and always it'll be
maybe someday
when the rain is clear,
the sky is blue,
and the clouds are gone
you'll see
but true love is something to everyone near
no matter how far
how close
or even here.
Love can be helping an old lady across the street
or being nice to someone you meet.
No matter where you are
love is not very far
just look around the corner or wish upon a star.
Love can't be that far.

Megan Merrill, Grade 5
Ranburne Elementary School, AL

A Witch I Know

I know a witch that has a black hat,
I hit it with a new bat.

The witch that has pink hair,
It turns color when she is at the fair.

The witch's skin is green,
She thinks she is a teen.

She likes to wear red,
She knows a boy named Fred.

Her legs are very gray,
She loves to play with clay.

Her shoes are very blue,
She hates going to the zoo.

Her nose is so long,
She likes to play ping pong.

Her arms are so short,
Which makes it harder for her to build a fort.

Christian Rivera, Grade 4
Chancellor Charter School At Lantana, FL

Scarecrow
Gardens are guarded
Saving food for the winter
Crows are kept away
Tyler Parsons, Grade 6
Arlington Middle School, FL

Trapped with the Lord
Trapped with the Lord I will be.
Running from the devil, you will see.
With the Lord you are a winner.
With the devil you are a sinner.

The Lord is strong.
The devil is wrong.
The Lord will lead you in the right way,
The devil will lead you astray.

If you believe, you will receive.
For faith will carry you through.
The Lord is full of greatness,
The devil is full of hateness.
Brandon Hall, Grade 5
Sharon Elementary School, NC

Volleyball
I hit high,
I bump down low,
I set high,
I'm in the zone,
The tension is high,
Nerves are tingling down my spine,
10 seconds to go,
Hit, bump, set, serve
Michelle Harter, Grade 6
Freedom Middle School, FL

Love
Do you love someone?
I'm too young
to know what love means
but this is what I think it means.
When you love someone
you have compassion for them.
You think of them as your best friend,
love is not a game.
You can't cheat in it.
Love is a bond between two people
that care for each other
as they care for their family.
You can't wish for love;
you have to go out there and find it.
I know all of this from watching
my mom and step dad.
That's what true love is.
Rachel Detlefsen, Grade 6
McRae Elementary School, FL

Earth's Gift to Us, Plants
Every branch and every leaf
Each stem and each flower
Has a little something special
It gives us oxygen
Of which we should not devour
So think about what you do
And plants will be a part of you.
Emma Clarke, Grade 4
Barrow Elementary School, GA

Jonathan Tatum
Nice to everyone
Caring for other people
Very handsome
Likes sports
Very cool
Dreams of being a wrestler
Passing 5th grade
And moving on further in life.
Jonathan Tatum, Grade 5
Winona Elementary School, MS

Spring
Spring is
flowers blooming

Spring feels like
the hot sun

Spring walks like
colorful trees moving

Spring tastes like
a fresh hot dog

Spring looks like
a sunny day

Spring things like
the bright blue sky
Brandon Gebris, Grade 4
Tabernacle Elementary School, NC

My Puzzle Puppy
My puzzle dog is very small.
He often comes without a call.
He chews on toys and swings his tail.
When he is locked in his room, he wails.
He runs around and jumps all day.
He also wants everyone else to play.
He steals my toys, intrudes in my room.
To make him leave, you use a broom.
Although he often makes you yell shoo,
He also can be very cute.
Anna Wilson, Grade 6
Gold Hill Middle School, SC

All Because of You
One sad, sad day
I was walking through the rain
I felt like chains
Attached by clangs
Were holding me back
From the things I lack
I darted somewhere near
I felt like I couldn't hear
I couldn't move my back
Everything suddenly went black
I knew I'd never come back
All because of you
Aaron Bradley, Grade 5
Ranburne Elementary School, AL

The Fall
A woosh of air
A hard ground
Mrs. Alice had barely
Gotten out the words
"Watch your step."
When…
　I fell.
　It seemed as if
　The whole world
　Was laughing at me.
　It was the worst
　Day of my life…
　Almost.
Talia Dawkins, Grade 5
East Marion Elementary School, MS

Dentures
Where did they go?
I left them right here.
So I asked my wife.
(oh sweet honey dear).
Where did they run off to?
I'm going psycho.
Please help me find them
they have to run slow.
(You old wise man
look in your mouth.
Last night you didn't
take them out).
Jamie Sawyer, Grade 6
Challenger Middle School, FL

Mike
My brother's name is Mike
He loves to ride his bike
He rides it to school
He thinks it's cool
But he is not supposed to ride it at night
Santremica Howard, Grade 6
Arnold Magnet Academy, GA

High Merit Poems – Grades 4, 5, and 6

Cleaning My Room
My mom always says that I have to clean my room.
I know I have to do it, but I just don't want to.
If I don't, I'll live with these strange creatures.
Cockroaches, spiders, and a lot more.
So, it's best if I just clean it.

It's boring, I know, but I'll do it.
My mom said if I do it now, I can go outside.
Outside is so beautiful.
The birds so cheerful.
Okay, now, I am cleaning my room for good.
I know that when I am done I will feel great.
Wow! I'm done, and now this room looks… clean!
Alan Hernandez, Grade 6
St Mary Magdalen Catholic School, FL

Drawing
Drawing is wonderful; you wonder why,
Because of the peace and quietness.
All the thrill of the sound the pencil makes
When the pencil or pen moves across the paper.

This isn't all, there's more to come.
Just see how fun this can become.
Once you try, then try again.
Because once you start you'll not want to end.
Thomas Henderson, Grade 4
Providence Classical School, AL

Spring
Spring is a magical time of year
Plants and animals are awaking
From the long cold harsh winter
It is a beautiful scene in the making

Small droplets of water fall from the sky
Drip drop drip drop drip drop
The rain is a musical concert on the small leaves and flowers
But the rain will never stop

The birds are singing in many duets
All types of birds are flying around
Making nests in high trees
But never seem to touch the ground

Water flows from the mossy rocks above into a deep silver pool
The waterfalls are an amazing sight
During the day you can see rainbows
On special occasions you can see a moonbow at night

Kids with sticky fingers looking at colorful shops
That are standing tall and proud
Bringing all ages, from children to adults
All coming together in one big crowd
Clara Williams, Grade 6
Holy Trinity Catholic School, MS

I Don't Understand…
I don't understand
   why girls fight over boys
   why boys and girls can't get along
   why we can't get Fridays off from school.

But most of all
   why are they raising the gas prices
   why most people cheer for America instead of Chivas
   why people from different countries can't get along
   why teachers invented homework.

What I understand most is
   why OMAR BRAVO is my favorite soccer player
   why CHRIS BROWN is my favorite hip hop singer
   why I love DJ FLEX
   why I go for CHIVAS!
Yesenia Castizo, Grade 6
Turkey Creek Middle School, FL

Bunorris
Funny
Handsome
Smart
Wishes to be rich
Dreams to be famous
Wants to be a movie star
Wonders how to play football
Fears alligators
Afraid of lions
Who likes to play
Believes in God
Who loves girls, only respectful and pretty ones
Who loves to eat healthy foods
Who loves to learn
Who loves to fight
Who plans to get an education
Who plans to help people
Who plans to be a good citizen
BuNorris Peeples, Grade 5
Winona Elementary School, MS

Good and Bad
Dangerous is bad
Excitement is really good
Sad is terrified
Breana Henley, Grade 6
Coral Springs Middle School, FL

An Ode to Moms
Moms think how, or what, or why to do it.
They help you when you need it.
Moms go to church with you to praise the Lord.
They pray with you at night.
They stick with you, so tight.
Katelyn Summers, Grade 5
Sharon Elementary School, NC

All About France
France is a cool place
The French enjoy wine and cheese
Bon Voyage bye bye

Gray Oates, Grade 6
St Petersburg Christian School, FL

Tubing in the Ocean
The water was clear and cool,
as I jumped into the tube.
I was scared,
nervous and squished.
The tube moved farther and farther away
from the boat, as we started to move.
As we were moving along,
it was a fast and bumpy ride.
I felt the rash I was getting on my leg.
It was burning and itchy.
As we stopped,
they pulled the tube closer to the boat,
and I jumped out.
When I got on the boat,
I was relieved it was over.

Robert Roxas, Grade 6
Lake Park Baptist School, FL

Basketball
B e aggressive
A thletic
S hoot a basket
K eep score
E njoy
T eamwork
B ounce pass
A ces
L earn plays
L earn more about basketball

Austin King, Grade 4
East Jones Elementary School, MS

Twisting Tiger
Lightning and thunder
Crashed and crackled
It's black
Oh now it's turning yellowish red
Hail smashing at house
Weeeeeeeeeeoooooooh
Sirens go off as loud
As little girls screaming
CRACK
Trees just got lifted
Off of the ground
And broken in half
Wooooossssshhhh
The tornado faded away

Rylee Garrett, Grade 4
Sharon Elementary School, GA

Concrete Path
I walk down the concrete path toward my destiny.
On my way I learn many things.
I learn math, English, science, and history.
I learn how to love and show compassion.
I meet friends on the way that come and go but walk similar paths.
While I walk down the path I fall and stumble, but always get up in the end.
I get older, wiser, kinder, smarter, and have made many memories.
I will always be on that concrete path walking toward my destiny.

Summer Warrington, Grade 6
First Flight Middle School, NC

Seasons
Winter. Cold, silent, and still,
Spring. Soothing, bright colorful flowers blooming until,
Summer. The sun; big, bright, hot and spicy
Fall. Graceful colorful leaves float to the ground from tall dark oak trees,
Then it starts all over again.

Caylen Bost, Grade 5
Queen's Grant Community School, NC

My Dog
Buddy big, loving, sweet guy.
He loves to run he loves to play
He loves the water every day.
He has a little sleeping problem but that's ok.
He turns and rolls around throughout the day
He loves me and I love him too and that's perfectly ok.
Me and him, him and me, play all day every day
Forever he will be my sweet loving guy and that's the best and that's ok.

Tyler Drayton, Grade 6
Gold Hill Middle School, SC

What Would It Be Like?
What would it be to have unity in the world
What would it be like to have respect for one another
What would it be like to live in a peaceful world
What would it be like?

What would it be like to be a leader, not a follower
What would it be like to use nonviolence to settle our differences
What would it be like for one person to stand up for change
What would it be like?

Keanu Mobley, Grade 6
Hand Middle School, SC

Spring
When I went outside today
the sun was shining really bright,
I could hear the birds chirping a very beautiful song to each other.
The wind was blowing so gently I barely felt the breeze.
I could hear the rustling of the grass as I walked onto the platform.
I look up at the trees and I can see squirrels jumping from tree to tree.
I could smell the scent of pine just as I stepped outside.
They were all different shapes and sizes, they smelled pretty good.

Armani Easterling, Grade 5
Southern Pines Elementary School, NC

Waves

Up up up
Down down down
That is the way
The waves
Crash down.

Stephanie Schultheiss, Grade 4
Julian D Parker School of Science, Math & Technology, FL

I Love Jellybeans

Almost every morning,
I eat jellybeans while I'm snoring.
And almost every day at two,
I eat them with my foot.

At 2 p.m. I ate 1, at 3 p.m. I ate 2, and at 4 p.m. I ate 3,
All on top of a tree.
Then one morning,
I blended up my jellybeans and made them into stew.

On my 9th birthday,
I cut a piece of cake.
I looked inside,
And it was full of jellybeans.

Then I let out a scream,
"Mom. I don't want any more jellybeans!"

Milagros Pilipiak, Grade 4
Panther Run Elementary School, FL

Puppies

Puppies are cute, puppies are small
Puppies are the greatest pet of all!
Puppies are playful, puppies are furry
Puppies are always running in a hurry!
Most of all, my favorite thing about puppies is that they are
a wonderful pet and companion to have and to play with!

Ashley Williams, Grade 4
FSU/City of Pembroke Pines Charter Elementary School, FL

The White Blanket

The snow falls so peacefully,
Softly drifting to the ground,
A white cotton blanket,
Covering everything around.

Snow is up to my ankle,
Soon it will be up to my knee,
Children are out throwing snowballs,
Shouting and screaming with glee.

Spring is around the corner,
And the fluffy white snow will melt,
Temperatures will rise,
But good-bye goes the happiness you felt.

Alyssa Barre, Grade 6
Gold Hill Middle School, SC

Waves

Whoosh
the wave crashes on
the beach. The never ending sea
whoosh.
The boats rumbling out in the open sea
ready to catch some big fish.
The clouds hang over the sea
like clothes on a clothesline.
The *waves* pounding the sand
like a hammer pounds a nail.
The *swoosh* sound that you hear
when a bird comes in to catch some of the squirmy fishes
trying to hide.
The pristine clean water.
The fresh smell of sea salt carries in the air.
The huge rocks that protect some house
from destruction by storm surges.
Sometimes you can see tiny and other times you see BIG waves.
So peaceful. The never ending sea.

Dalton Davis, Grade 6
Gulf Stream School, FL

Choices

Living is being scorched by imaginary beasts
and cared after by winged celestial beings.

While I breathe there are two paths of decision.
One leading to fire and hatred, and the
other leading to love and joy.

My life is a mystery blended with fairies that guard me
and nymphs who bribe me into their flaring path.

Gabrielle Pura, Grade 6
R D and Euzelle P Smith Middle School, NC

I Am

I am a dream chaser
I wonder what people think about me.
I hear voices in my head cheering me on.
I see kids playing in an empty park.
I want to belong in a group.
I am a dream chaser
I pretend to be an astronaut in space.
I feel like my dreams will come true.
I touch the steering wheel of my life.
I worry that people might laugh.
I cry every time they do laugh.
I am a dream chaser
I understand that I might not succeed in all of my dreams.
I say I can be anything I want to be.
I dream of what might happen when I fulfill my dreams.
I try to succeed in everything.
I hope people will believe in me.
I am a dream chaser

Alyssa Sumaljag, Grade 6
Heron Creek Middle School, FL

A Beautiful Day
I love to lie
in the green grass
in the afternoon
because the clouds fly above me.
Jackson Henderson, Grade 4
Spruce Creek Elementary School, FL

Hairspray!
Hairspray hit my binky,
Hairspray is so stinky.
Hairspray gets so sticky,
Hairspray makes me really icky.
Hairspray please go away,
Hairspray let me play!
Macey Laine Beattie, Grade 5
Morgan Elementary School, NC

Cleaning My Room
My mom is always yelling
"Clean your room"
I tell my mom it's too soon
I look at my room
Wow I say it's a mess
I got to pick up this awful wreck
Heck, now I know why my mom
Is making me pick up this deck
Now I learned my lesson
So I won't keep on messing
Cause I learned my lesson
Alana Garcia, Grade 6
St Mary Magdalen Catholic School, FL

Nights
Cloudy nights
The moon shining bright
High above
The ground all night
Guiding us along the way
Waiting until morning
To hide away
Around the Earth
Until it comes another night
Where it can shine
Until the cycle can start again
And night will finally begin.
Brianna Price, Grade 6
Varsity Lakes Middle School, FL

Cara
Cool
Very funny
Never acts weird
Means face in Spanish
Blonde
Jonathan Earle, Grade 6
St Mark's Lutheran School, FL

I Am
I am a short guy who likes Oreos.
I wonder how they get jelly in donuts.
I hear the jiggly puff song around me.
I see a world filled with Oreos and milk.
I want a golden Lamborghini.
I am a short guy who likes Oreos.

I pretend that I am Super Mario.
I feel the excitement when I run.
I touch the sky and the stars.
I worry about the poor people in Iraq.
I cry when one of my dogs die.
I am a short guy who likes Oreos.

I understand that smoking is horrible.
I say that life isn't always fair.
I dream to see more in the universe.
I try to finish my homework all the time.
I hope that the world will be peaceful.
I am a short guy who likes Oreos.
Gabriel Rodriguez, Grade 5
Oliver Hoover Elementary School, FL

Freedom
Freedom stands tough
and doesn't look back
Freedom feels like
we have just won a war
It smells like fresh roses
Freedom roars like a good victory
Freedom looks like
the flag waving side to side
Freedom moves like a sprinter
Cameron Trotter, Grade 4
Tabernacle Elementary School, NC

Falling in Place
We're falling in place,
Into the empty space of our hearts.
Shooting for the stars.
In a whirlpool of confusion.
We're falling into space that has
Been empty for so many years.
Xavier Gonzalez, Grade 5
Silver Lakes Elementary School, FL

Ocean/Tree
Ocean
Clean, cold
Shining, glimmering, moving
Atlantic, Pacific, redwood, pine
Shading, falling, dying
Brown, huge
Tree
Garry White, Grade 5
Dover Elementary School, FL

I'm So Fresh
I'm so cool
I'm the best

When I go to school
I act so fresh

When I go to lunch the girls say 'hi'
Then I eat some apple pie

I do my homework every day
Recess comes and I can play

My friends and I walk down the hall
Next, we go to the field for football

I like to raise my hand in class
The teacher says that I will pass

I'm so cool
I'm the best

When I go to school
I act so fresh
Aaron Robinson, Grade 4
Park Ridge Elementary School, FL

Prom Night
In my dress
Out the door
To the prom
On my way
With my date.
Ashante Outlaw, Grade 5
Dover Elementary School, FL

Change
The
Young
Girl
Walks
Into
The
Church
With
Her
Father
On
Her
Arm
To
Celebrate
Her
50th
Anniversary.
Kristian Mabe, Grade 6
J E Holmes Middle School, NC

Stars

Stars blazing in the sky
Stars burning in the sky
Stars disappearing in the day and appearing at night
Stars glowing like fire flies frozen in the sky
Stars the sky's night light floating above the clouds

Phillip Ragazzo, Grade 6
Freedom Middle School, FL

Mary Beth Grant

I really love to read,
I'm a little shy so I don't always want to lead!
I love basketball,
But I always seem to fall!
My favorite color would have to be green,
And all the time at school, it's hard to be seen.
I have brown eyes and hair,
I like being me, I'm quite rare.

I like to create,
I'll be really tall at this rate!
I like to write, never liked to fight.
I'm scared of jelly fish, sharks,
Black widows, and dogs that bark!
I hate math and USC,
I love art, music, and PE!

I'm quite good at sports,
I like candy of all sorts!
I want to be a Librarian or an author,
If you're going to ask me to be tidy, don't even bother!
My favorite drink is sweet tea,
I really just love being me!!

Mary Beth Grant, Grade 5
Oakland Elementary School, SC

The Preacher

There once was a man of God
For which he scattered abroad
Though before he was a persecutor
The Christians called him "The Torturer"
But God threw down a blinding light
'Twas then God made him lose his sight
Then at Damascus this man was saved
By the power of God he paved
A road to save the lost Gentiles
His next three journeys lasted a while
To Greece, Rome, and Asia Minor
From church to church this old timer
Made three journeys toward and back
This last journey he wasn't on track
To Rome his captors took him with dread
And he went to heaven when he lost his head
We've now heard of a man of God's call
Why don't we all be just like Paul?

Kyle Brainard, Grade 6
Santa Rosa Christian Academy, FL

Love

Love seeketh not, but anything to please,
And when you have a certain love, it puts everything at ease!
When you have the courage, to let your true love rise,
You won't only get a kiss and a hug,
But also a true love prize!
Love isn't anything, to mock or play with,
To worry or fret over, just understand it, you'll get it.
Just think, it's very important,
After awhile, it's an enjoyment!
When you love someone, let it be true,
Put it deep down in your heart,
You don't know, they might just love you too!
It doesn't have to be Valentine's Day or Christmas,
You can't force ANYONE to love you, not even by wishing.
If you love someone, don't be afraid to tell,
It's not like a nice person would say, "Too bad! Oh Well!"
I've got to go, and put up my pen,
If you want to know more, ask GOD about it.
But never forget love, no matter where you are,
Home, church, or in the mall, remember love!
And goodbye to all!

Martin Murray, Grade 5
Manchester Elementary School, NC

Me in 11 Lines

Joanna
Student
Compassionate, caring, friendly, supportive
Lover of cows, other people, and bookstores
Who believes that "All men are created equal"
Who wants to be an interior designer,
go to college, and be a good friend
Who uses books, tools, and pencils
Who gives money, advice, and care
Who says "Silence is never the answer"
Daniel

Joanna Daniel, Grade 6
Broad Creek Middle School, NC

Dancing

The rhythm flows through my body.
I feel like somebody.
The people watch and gaze.
They are throwing bouquets.
They are in a trance.
Just to see me dance.
I feel beautiful on stage.
Everyone wants to be backstage.
I could dance all day long,
Or just to the end of the song.
To see me dance is a wonder.
The music sounds like thunder.
Pop, lock, swerve, and curve.
I feel like it is in my nerve.

Shelbi Belue, Grade 6
Boiling Springs Intermediate School, SC

Valentine's Day
V alentine's gifts
A lways together
L oving time
E xcellent day
N ever unhappy
T errific day
I ndividual time
N ever apart
E verybody together
Hannah Beech, Grade 4
East Jones Elementary School, MS

My Softball Team
My softball team
We are good so it seems
We hit and we field
We ARE the real deal
When it comes to bases
Those we steal
Grounders and homeruns
They are the most fun
When we face an opponent
They know they are done
We are the best they've ever seen
This is my softball team
Sadie Smith, Grade 5
Ranburne Elementary School, AL

Bluebird
Sitting
on a branch
Waiting
on a worm
Missed it, until next time…
David Mann, Grade 6
Oxford Christian Academy, AL

The Sea
I see a ship
sailing down the sea
he keeps a journal
oh when will it be…
time to come…
time here…
time for him to wipe my tears.

He keeps my tears in a jar
sails away, I say
Goodbye my dear

The tears I made,
The tears he kept,
It probably meant something
True Love I guess?
Leonie Dupuis, Grade 5
Trinity Lutheran School, FL

Reading
Reading
Reading is fun
Reading is cool
I get to do it every day
When I am sad or happy
I read
Kylee Pittman, Grade 5
West Marion Elementary School, MS

Strange to Think
Passing by the park of dreams
Equal poles and opposite
Met and danced to different tunes
Strange now to remember it.

Walking through a field of mines
Souls in harmony at play
Things we never asked to know
Strange to think of it today.

Dreams that pass beyond the fog
Reaching clarity to fly
Look back down with secret smiles
Strange to think it was a lie.
Jasmin Woody, Grade 6
Salem Middle School, GA

Dragon
I like to fly
below dark clouds
in the middle of dawn
because you don't have to look down.
Kenny Acosta, Grade 4
Spruce Creek Elementary School, FL

My Home
My home rocks,
I can take off my socks,

I can jump in my bed,
And rest my head,

They call me a sloth,
And they say they're my boss,

When I sleep, my mind roams,
I'm no longer a kid, I'm grown!
Gavin Bailey, Grade 4
Edwards Elementary School, SC

Glorious Night
Stars in the night sky
Far away in outer space
During the nighttime
Humberto Viana, Grade 6
Tequesta Trace Middle School, FL

Sayde
Sayde
beautiful, sensible
laughs, plays, runs
kind, sweet, lovable, hyper
Sayde
Sierra Williamson, Grade 6
Rock Mills Jr High School, AL

James
J oyfully
A wesome
M y favorite sport is football.
E xcited
S atisfied
James Walters, Grade 4
East Jones Elementary School, MS

Quiet Creeks
Quiet creek flows on
Water reflects off the sun
Trees grow overhead
Creek flows into waterfall
Cranes fly above the cool creek
Bailey Gillespy, Grade 4
St James Episcopal School, FL

Our God
He is the sea.
He saved you and me.
Do not fear He is here.
He died on the cross.
So all is not lost.
He is out of sight.
But we hold Him tight.
Betty Thomas, Grade 6
Challenger Middle School, FL

School
School is cool.
It's like a pool.
You have so much fun.
You play in the sun.
You have a lot of work.
That's no reason to be a jerk.
Always remember school is cool.
Angela Beasley, Grade 5
West Marion Elementary School, MS

Hummingbird
Their colors are like leaves on trees
Or even a red rose
The sound they make is sweet
They move like the wind all day long
When they fly they shine like the sun
Kirsten Blackburn, Grade 5
Covenant Classical School, NC

Taylor

T rack is what I'll take in the tenth grade.
A girl like me likes to swim.
Y elling is what I do almost all the time.
L oving is what I do sometimes to my siblings.
O n TV is where I would like to be now
R esting is what I do at the end of they day.

Taylor Roberts, Grade 5
Winona Elementary School, MS

A Gift for My Soon-to-be Sibling

If I could give a gift to you
I would give you a good, loving, caring, nurturing
mother, sister, and father.

I would also give you a happy easygoing life,
filled with loads, tons, pounds
of love, kindness, and tender, loving attention.
Life with no problems to face or things to worry about.

A gift to develop memories
and grow a strong relationship together.

Melody Quinton, Grade 5
North Elementary School, SC

Have You Ever

Have you ever felt the wind in your hair?
Have you ever grasped for fresh air?
Have you ever felt the sun on your back?
Have you ever felt scared and tried to turn back?
Have you ever felt the warmth of a fire?
Have you ever felt like you have been lifted higher?
Have you ever felt the kindness of a friend?
Have you ever known the sweetness won't end?
Have you ever felt the wings of a dove?
Have you ever felt love?

Chyna Byrd, Grade 6
St Vincent dePaul Catholic School, MS

Last Words*

I wish as I'd grown
there was more to be known
although a lot was shown.
I wish you were here
by me close and near
the world is big and full of people and things
if only you were here
to help with the names
only the pictures, only the frames
I feel the very pains
of not having you here
to make everything clear
for this I dedicate to you
oh the years of life so blue.

Amber Walker, Grade 6
McRae Elementary School, FL
*Dedicated to my great-grandpa.

Other Worlds

On the frozen Arctic realm,
Not many humans strive to live in such climates.
While others study the land
A harsh habitat for survival.

In a tropical aquarium,
Sea creatures sustain life
Only to be blocked by walls of psychic energy
A limited world.

In a dark, murky forest,
Where the sky is like a blindfold.
Shadows creep behind you
A hopeless planet.

Brian Nguyen, Grade 5
Oliver Hoover Elementary School, FL

What's Your Favorite Sport?

S un in your hair
O utfield player
F un
T hrowing the ball
B unting the ball
A ll day tournament
L eague
L ove playing softball

Madison Heggins, Grade 6
St Francis Xavier Elementary School, MS

Crutches

Crutches are something to hold you.
But instead only your past lives in you,
of all the times people doubted
you rewinds back.
Life is short,
live it out people say, to me,
what's the point
it's just going to happen again.
Yelling, put-downs
anything to make me cold from deep inside.
Only, things that don't kill me
can make me stronger.
My crutches broke,
but as strong as I am
I'm still living.

Naquira Walker, Grade 6
Tequesta Trace Middle School, FL

Nature

Giving a relaxed blow is the wind.
Puffing out something black is a volcano.
A still boat in the arctic breeze is an iceberg.
Can you see the colorful waves of an aurora.
Nature is beautiful.

Emil Lopez, Grade 5
Eugenia B Thomas Elementary School, FL

China
China creates hate
Due to its communist state
Let God give them grace
Max Price, Grade 6
St Petersburg Christian School, FL

I Graze in the Grass
I am a horse; I love to run
I am a snake; I can flex my body
I am the wind; I breeze through
I am a bottle; I keep secrets
I am glass; I can break
I am a kickball; I get kicked around
I am a leaf; I go with the flow
I am a camera; I get the picture
Kayla Strickland, Grade 5
Four Oaks Elementary School, NC

The Reef
Under the shallow water where
colorful fish glide.
On the surface
turtles swimming.
Across the ocean floor
vibrant coral spreading.
In the little caves and crevices
creatures hiding.

All around
jellyfish floating.
Through the glassy ocean
the sun shining.
Schools of tiny fish
quickly swim past.
Stingrays soar above
the Great Barrier Reef.

Back and forth
sea anemones sway.
Resting in their homes,
all the creatures
awaiting another busy day.
Oni Jumapao, Grade 5
Rosarian Academy, FL

Love Is in the Air
Love is good and even hard sometimes
Love is all the time coming and going
God made us this way
Everyone should respect love itself
We all have feelings for one another
What could we do without love?
God made us this way for good
God probably even loves someone too
Samantha Ritter, Grade 4
Tabernacle Elementary School, NC

Manly
Darrin
Athlete
Athletic, strong, manly, awesome
Lover of sports, bacon, skateboarding
Who believes in winning
Who wants to be a pro athlete
A winner not a loser and doesn't want to be a hobo
Who uses strength to whoop Nick F. at his house
Who uses a mouth to eat and shoes to keep my feet warm
Who gives people a smack on the butt when they score a touchdown
Who gives thanks
Who gives a sweet touchdown at a football game
Who says, "If you don't make this first down I will smack you"
Delorme
Darrin Delorme, Grade 6
Broad Creek Middle School, NC

Writer
I'm a tree swaying in the breeze
I'm a walking stone
I'm a poisonous flower with a sweet nectar that will make you feel pain
I'm a tall pine tree that the needles never fall from
I'm a fire breathing dragon with a heart of anger
I'm a rose that will bring peace and make you feel the way I do
I am a writer
Gabrielle Brown, Grade 4
Skycrest Elementary School, FL

Hatred
A little bit of hatred, in a person's heart,
Is the only thing needed, to make the world go dark.
Things caused by hatred? Oh, that's lots of stuff,
Here are two of the ones that I know of;
Hatred causes racism, and many, many wars,
But these aren't the only acts, there's many, many more.
Right now these acts are creeping out from behind a slightly open door,
And here's what could keep the door from opening even more:
Love is all it takes,
To fix our hatred mistakes.
Just a little bit of love, in a person's heart,
Is all it takes to get rid of hatred, way before it starts.
Jose Valle, Grade 6
First Flight Middle School, NC

Lifeless Days
As I stand in the cold, I feel as invisible as bacteria on a doorknob.
You know its there, but you don't take the time to notice it.
As I watch everyone around me pass by, I feel lonely and useless.
And days go by lifelessly without any meaning to me.
Humans around me do things, but everything is just a blur.
My eyes strain to see the life and love in the air around me.
Everything and everyone are so absorbed within their own world
That they can't take the time to spot the people who need them.
And then the lifeless days do by without any meaning.
Vanessa Zapata, Grade 6
Freedom Middle School, FL

High Merit Poems – Grades 4, 5, and 6

Lost
Leaves blowing softly,
Heart beating quickly,
Running from troubles unknown.
Helplessly lost
In this dark, cold wood
While my heart continues to roam.
I call for the one
Who can help me get through
This dark and horrible path,
While trying to escape
The evil one
With his dark and terrible wrath.
When suddenly, lo,
An omen, a sign
Sent by the Holy God.
To show the way, To set me free
Just by the wave of his rod.
Now I know I am safe, Know I am free
From all the evil around,
For I have a Savior
I have a friend, And now I am safe and sound.
Sherlee Q. Chandler, Grade 6
St Francis Xavier Elementary School, MS

My Wonderful Teacher
Mrs. Ferraro is my fourth grade teacher.
She is what I call an 'educational preacher.'

She teaches math, writing, science and more,
A bundle of wonderful subjects galore.

Mrs. Ferraro is the absolute best,
I'll leave it to you to find out the rest!
Beverly Ge, Grade 4
William S Talbot Elementary School, FL

White
White is a lightning bolt
Crashing through the night sky.
White is a mine of silver
Waiting to be discovered.
White is a star
Giving light to its worlds.
White is an iceberg
Crashing into the ocean.
White is a blanket of snow
Crunching under your feet.
White is a ray of moon light
Calling to you at midnight.
White is your home
Welcoming you back.
White is a robe,
Worn by Jesus
As he conquers the devil once and for all.
Wesley McGovern, Grade 5
CrossPointe Christian Academy, GA

Friendship
Knotted together
In a friendship forever
Tears in our ears
Screaming together
Happy with each other
Crying with laughter
When we're knotted together
Forever.
Mackenzie Thorburn and Holly Riopelle, Grade 6
Seven Springs Middle School, FL

Florida
Florida is the land of oranges
It is very great
It also is the Sunshine State
It will fascinate

You can go to the beach
Or you can watch the game
(If you go to the beach you will come back peach.)
If you watch the game, it's not lame.

Florida's capital is Tallahassee.
Florida also has the biggest swamp
It's a peninsula
It's the twenty-seventh state

Once Florida was a state, it was a slave state
Florida became a state when Iowa became one
Florida was once a territory
The two Seminole wars were fought in Florida
Jorge Webb, Grade 4
Bayshore Christian School, FL

My Mom
My mom is a mom.
She's like anybody's mom.
But she's too happy all the time.
Every time she walks it's like, happy, happy, happy.
But my head goes boom, boom, boom!
Jamie Green, Grade 4
Camden Elementary School of the Creative Arts, SC

Paradise
Firefighters come to the house burning down.
Only one survivor can be found.
They rush her out of that fiery house.
Her heart beats as faint as a mouse.
The firefighter tells her she's going to be fine.
Then she sees an image so divine.
A familiar man looks down smiling at her.
Suddenly her life becomes a blur.
Hand in hand they soar up to a heavenly gate
Where paradise awaits.
Taylor Pavlica, Grade 5
St Thomas More School, NC

Sean

Sean
Cool, funny, and fun
Son of Susan and Joe
Lover of skateboarding, skimboarding, and surfing
Who feels cool most of the time
Who needs mac and cheese, water and a house
Who wishes he could have more skateboards, give skateboards to the poor, and own a skate park
Who dreams of being a pro-skateboarder, being famous all over the world, and not being poor
Who fears talking dummies who smile, white faced clowns and the boogie-man
Who gives help to the Salvation Army, his mom and Nana
Who wants to visit Hollister, California, Alaska, and Norway
Resident of Largo, Florida
Serra

Sean Serra, Grade 4
Wellington School, FL

I'll Miss You

Why? is all I can ask myself as I glare down at my mother's ghostly figure lying in her death bed. I see her powder-pale face, her blue eyes, that now look gray, and her beautiful corn-silk hair, which now looked as pale as her face. Then I wonder why I must see her like this. And for the millionth time my eyes tear up, my nose gets stuffed, and slowly a knot forms in my throat, because I know that in a matter of minutes she will only exist in my heart.

Theysi Vidal, Grade 6
Freedom Middle School, FL

Green Is…

Green is luck for the scratch off lottery tickets.
It is flavors of kiwi, lime and the outer skin of a slippery watermelon.
Green is the salad you bring on a picnic in the park with your friend.
Throw in lettuce; avocado, cucumbers, broccoli and an Italian dressing dyed a bright, exotic green.
It makes me feel jealous and melancholy. It is pure and fresh with a tad bit of disorganization.
Athletic, active, exciting and funny are words that make me think of green.
Green sounds like nature, with birds tweeping with happiness and the wind crashing against leaves to make a whoosh sound.
Green is getting to go again on the road when the red light changes color. It is the word yes.
Green is how I feel sitting in bed going through uncountable amounts of tissues
Barely being able to breathe with a stuffed nose missing school.
The final loop upside down on a roller coaster makes my stomach turn green with nausea.
Green looks like a pasture roaming with cows waiting to be milked and galloping horses running during the sunset.
Green tastes like gum, specifically spearmint.
Green feels like the algae at the bottom of an unaccompanied pond
Where tadpoles have recently transformed into frogs and hopped off into the open world.
It is the circle of life. Green is our future if we choose to protect the Earth or not.
Green is recycling and caring for the environment.
Billionaires feel green when they lose a close poker game with lots of money at stake.
Being rich is green, being able to buy whatever you want with the snap of a finger.
Green feels relaxing, soothing and enjoyable.
More importantly, St. Patrick's Day, is green!

Will Holland, Grade 5
Summit Hill Elementary School, GA

Brown

Brown is a piece of chocolate cake with powdered sugar sprinkled on top. Brown is chocolate ice cream with chocolate fudge on top cold and delicious. Brown is soft and tender. Wood is brown. Brown is a winter day. Brown is the wind blowing. Brown is a dessert baking in the oven. Peaceful is brown. Brown is a sweet smell. Brown is keeping me warm and cozy. Brown is a poem. Brown is the fall. Brown is packages.

Shaindyl Klein, Grade 6
Pinellas County Jewish Day School, FL

Fly through the air like a bird,
while spinning out of control
rolls quickly over the grass,
only to be gripped firmly
by the palm of a hand

a round white baseball
Austin B. Gammons, Grade 4
Sangaree Intermediate School, SC

Seems to Be Only You and Me
Our hearts beat together
I wish it to last forever
With you I feel not tame
In the wind a flaming mane
Your hooves on ground
The only sound
They seem to echo so
The life of running free is the one I wish to know
Friendship, life and love
Like a broken winged dove
Might seem to shatter maybe even fall apart
But soon will fly and seize thy broken heart
The mountains seem to buzz as we glide on through
And the river seems to flow not noticing me nor you
Taylor Hanson, Grade 6
Kernan Middle School, FL

Wind
I move swiftly across the world.
Blowing leaves down to the forest floors.
I can blow down houses with all my might.
You can hear me blowing "swooohhh,"
But you cannot see me.
I make waves topple into each other.
I bring cold air wherever I go.
If you see things blowing be sure to think of me.
Will Green, Grade 5
Pensacola Beach Elementary School, FL

The Very Shabby Dog
There was once a very shabby dog.
His name was Henry.

He did not have a home
but on the streets.

Harry had to always eat
out of the nasty garbage that people left out
for the garbage men to pick up every Monday.

Harry really never had a family
until one camping trip a family picked him up
and took him home with them.
Ashton Stennett, Grade 6
St Francis Xavier Elementary School, MS

I Feel
I feel as though my gladness is withering away in the wind.
I feel as though my happiness is coming to an end.
I feel as though it's hard to go on.
Because my best friend will soon be gone.
She was just like a sister, I could tell her most anything.
But, like a tired butterfly, I will lower my wing.
She was in all of my dreams, made my wishes come true.
But now my heart has turned to deep blue.
I did not wish for her to leave.
Because that's what makes my heart grieve.
So with this farewell, allow me to say:
I will love you always, and it will be okay.
Lauren Mahoney, Grade 6
Rosman Middle School, NC

Georgia on My Mind
Although Georgia is a great place
We are all a different race
We always have the sun
And we like to have fun.

Georgia is the peach state
And we like to eat lots of cake
I like the way Georgia is made
And all the people that have stayed.

Although Georgia has great sites
Right now I'm not that height
When Georgia is hot
I like to beat on my pot.

When Georgia has games
I like to think of the hall of fames
In Georgia I will be a famous ACTOR
Like Will Smith and the Rafter.
Dakota Dawson, Grade 6
Academy of Lithonia Charter School, GA

The Calmest Dog in the World
I told you about my dog,
That poem is done.
I actually have two dogs,
So now it's time for this one.

I have a very calm dog,
She's calm all the time.
And if you were to pick her up,
You would say, "She's as light as a dime."

She's a blonde cocker spaniel,
She sometimes jumps around
like she's on a million springs.
And whenever she's around me,
Happiness and love is what she brings.
Casey Cummings, Grade 6
Gold Hill Middle School, SC

The Piano
Sitting at the bench to play
"In the Still of the Night."
Start out smooth
Oh, no!
I play F sharp
Not f flat.
OK.
Doing well
Press down the pedal, lift
Shift hands up one octave
Get louder like a truck
Dramatic, faster
Slow down,
Quiet as a mouse.
Wrap it up.
Bow. Bravisimo. Bravo!
I'll do better next time I hope!
Shom Tiwari, Grade 5
Olde Providence Elementary School, NC

Eyes
Blue eyes
Looking seeing
Wondering gazing out
Free curious
Humongous gazing eyes
Big eyes
Jacob McFadden, Grade 6
Tarpon Springs Middle School, FL

Band Fun
What is band?
  playing fun songs,
  learning about instruments,
  showing off your work in parades,
  a joyous place,
  knowing when to play,
  sharing in lots of excitement,
  being the best you can be,
  living a happy life,
  finding people you can relate to,
  an astounding wonder,
  having somewhere you belong,
That is band!
Caleb Nathaniel Green, Grade 6
Turkey Creek Middle School, FL

Spring
S urprises
P eter Cottontail
R ain
I magination
N o work
G reen grass
Tamar Edwards, Grade 4
Central Park Elementary School, FL

What's War?
guns going off
mortar's flying through the air
helicopters flying by
men dying in your platoon
car bombings going off
THAT'S WAR!
Dakota Register, Grade 6
Turkey Creek Middle School, FL

My Dog
Do you think my dog is a good pet?
Why do you have to bring him to the vet?

Why does he step on my sister's hair?
Do you think she even cares?

Do you think he eats the right food?
Isn't he quite rude?

Why does he eat rocks?
Why does he try to break locks?
Ryan Strandberg, Grade 4
William S Talbot Elementary School, FL

Spatula
Flipping frying
Cut onions crying.
Mixing batter
Pancakes splatter.
Slicing dicing
Cover cake with icing.
Making brownies
No more frownies.
Having fun
When it's all done.
Family saying
Yum-yum!
Shelby Robertson, Grade 6
J E Holmes Middle School, NC

The Big Georgia Peach
The peach is big,
The peach is round,
Its color is bright
Like the night light.

It grows in Georgia,
People really love it,
Take a bite,
It's pure delight!

And when you're through,
Do tell me,
That you like it too!
Samoriah Smith, Grade 5
Frank L Stanton Elementary School, GA

TV Remote
Oh my TV remote
Oh my TV remote
I honor you because
You make it easy
To change the channel
So I can stay comfortable.

Oh my TV remote
Oh my TV remote
You make it easy
To change the volume
Cause when my mom
Says it's too loud, I don't
Have to get up.

Oh my TV remote
Oh my TV remote
It is when my mom says
"Shut off the TV"
All I have to push is one
Button.
Brandon Luper, Grade 6
Pinellas County Jewish Day School, FL

Failure Is…
Not being good enough
The opposite of success.
Losing confidence.
Uneased with yourself.
Feeling like your life is over.
When you stop trying to succeed.
Fabrice Telfort, Grade 6
Arlington Middle School, FL

Biblical Times
In the Garden of Eden
lived Adam and Eve.
When they disobeyed God
they had to leave.

When there was a flood
the ark was Noah's.
There were spiders, elephants,
horses, and even boas.

There were three people called
Shadrack, Meshack, and Abendigo.
When the king said bow down
they said, "No, No, No."

Jesus died for
you and me,
up on the cross
at calvary.
Dustin Farrow, Grade 5
Rock Mills Jr High School, AL

High Merit Poems – Grades 4, 5, and 6

Mowing the Lawn
I wake up at dawn, to mow the lawn.
It is not fun but it has to be done,
It can be hot in the Florida sun.
I get covered in grime, as it takes a long time.
The grass grows fast; I hope I don't run out of gas.
The lawn has trees and mounds and many sounds.
I have dirt all over my new shirt.
The grass is very green, the best I've ever seen.

Bevan Rogers, Grade 6
St Mary Magdalen Catholic School, FL

Baseball
Baseball is a great sport to play,
you can play it from spring through fall.

You play the game with a bat, ball, and a glove,
and there are nine positions on the field.

There are fans cheering, coaches yelling,
teammates playing and umpires calling calls.

Pitchers are pitching to hitters,
and fielders are fielding the ball.

One of the teams will win,
but who will be the champion?

Justin Garber, Grade 6
Brogden Middle School, NC

Valentine's Day
Valentine's Day is here yippee
One thing to ask what does it mean?
You bring chocolate and flowers too.
All the colors are pink and red, red and pink
Please tell me what does it mean what do you think
You act sweet and loving and caring
The next day you're not even sharing
I get flowers and paper hearts with candy
This not the start of the answer
There's slow songs sad songs and slow dancing
Sure you're not Cupid but what does it all mean
Everyone is sweet and all gushy
There's only one thing that makes me happy
It makes me happy in that way
The school dance is on Friday!

Amanda Wing, Grade 6
Challenger Middle School, FL

A Rhino Beetle
A Rhino Beetle on a log looks as hard as stone.
It's width thick like butter,
Slowly crawling as the years go by.
As I hear a voice calling me inside,
I hope I see this creature again while I'm outside.

Nathaniel Holmes, Grade 5
Covenant Classical School, NC

The Wonderful World
I am the wonderful world
I am the whistling wind
I am the wise old mountain who consoles the Earth
I am the stars that guide you through the night
I am the wonderful world

I am the water, flowing ever so gracefully in the stream
I am the birds singing outside your window
I am the thunder who speaks to the gods of the sky
I am the wonderful world

I am the fierce tiger who hunts the creatures of the jungle
I am the courageous lion who is so brave
I am the gracious butterfly who flutters about
as if she is a ballerina and the world is her stage
I am the wonderful world

…I am me

Kaitlyn Sanchez, Grade 6
City of Pembroke Pines Charter Central Middle School, FL

About the Witch from Head to Toe
My witch has lot's of thin yellow hair,
and her hair is always messy but she does not care.

My witch is weird because she has a small nose,
and she has really smelly toes.

She has huge red lips,
and she takes gulps instead of sips.

Her eyes are as blue as the sky,
and she could never tell a lie.

Her eyebrows need to be waxed,
and she doesn't like it when she gets taxed.

She has legs that are very strong,
and she won't listen to any old song.

Her fingers are thick,
and she has a pet that is a tick.

That's the witch,
that loves to play pitch!

Kristen Hepner, Grade 4
Chancellor Charter School At Lantana, FL

Sunset
Watching the sunset, is my favorite thing to do
Watching the sunset, you should try it too
orange, purple, and even blue
the sunset is the prettiest thing you will ever see
Watching the sunset, come and watch with me

Brenna Mercado, Grade 6
Challenger Middle School, FL

The River

The river
Lindy laughing
beams of light from the stars
shining brightly at night
happy
exciting
what are they doing?
doing?
doing?

Aurora Martin, Grade 4
Pinnacle Elementary School, NC

Colors

Apples are red;
Along with green.
The sky is blue;
Hanging above the green grass.
I look out the window;
What do I see?
Flowers, plants, and trees;
Just blowing in the breeze.
Being as colorful as can be!

Olivia Brown, Grade 4
West Bertie Elementary School, NC

Sunny Day

Shining yellow sun
In the golden afternoon
On the sandy beach

Prima Lockhart, Grade 6
Tequesta Trace Middle School, FL

Clocks

Tick-tock, tick-tock,
Tick-tock, tick-tock
This is the sound
Of a clock.
Dong, Bong, Clong!
It plays this all day long.
Dong, Bong, Clong!
It plays this little song.
Every 15 minutes,
Every 30 minutes,
Each and every hour
Each dong is like a choir.
Ding, dong, ding
Ting, tong, ting
Ring, rong, ring
Ping, pong, ping
The bells ring and chime.
And they alert us of the time.
Tick-tock, tick-tock
Dong, dong, dong
It plays this all day long.

Fiona McGuire, Grade 4
St Thomas More School, NC

Rain

Clear and crisp shapes are made uniquely different in every way. Sometimes falling on parched earth or going into the colossal rain barrel our ocean. Soft and silent sounds are seldom. Generally pacing with booming immense sounds. Water flowing quickly through dams and rivers. I can hear pit-pat-pit-pat against my saturated windowpane.

Anna Setzer, Grade 5
St Thomas More School, NC

Tommy

Tommy
Nice, good sharer, and caring
Son of Tom and Jerlene Green
Who feels jealous most of the time, sleepy, and sometimes sad
Who needs mac and cheese, clothes and shelter
Who fears bugs, spiders, and heights
Who wishes for a Wii, a PlayStation 2, and that he was a ninja
Who dreams about himself driving a monster truck
Who wishes to visit Ho Chi Nim, Vietnam, New York City, New York and South Africa
Green

Tommy Green, Grade 4
Wellington School, FL

The Beautiful Witch

Once upon a time, there was a beautiful witch,
she didn't look poor because she was very, very rich.
Do you know what her name is, her name is Claire,
and even though she is grown, she still sleeps with her teddy bear.
She has fake nails that are the color of pink,
and her pretty blue eye's sparkle every time she gives you a wink.
Her garden is so beautiful thanks to her magical hose,
sometimes she even takes a flower and wears it on her clothes.
Her skin is very pale, but her clothes make her look bright,
and without ever touching a switch, she can turn on a light!

Jordan Remson, Grade 4
Chancellor Charter School At Lantana, FL

I Learned That…

I learned that people will not always be here.
I learned that you should not yell at your parents.
I learned that if you treat other people right they will treat you the same way.
I learned that you should not talk about people
I learned that when your parents say no they mean that.
I learned that you need teachers to help you when you are stuck on something.
I learned that not everybody is perfect.
I learned that everybody is different from each other.
I learned that making mistakes is ok.
I learned that you shouldn't hit other people
I learned that your life is not always fair.
I learned that my parents care about me.
I learned that friendship can only go so far, but love will last forever.
I learned that to accept people for who they are and not how the person looks.
I learned that you should not touch a lion if somebody is not around you.
I learned that you should always trust your heart.

Crystasia Robinson, Grade 5
Northside Elementary School, SC

I Miss You

I know why you have to go away.
But it's not fair I wish you could stay.
When I moved in I felt so lonely.
You reached out your hand to me only.
You know why I cry, by the look in my eye.
I miss you, I really do.
We've been best friends forever more,
Ever since we met at the local pool's front door.
I miss you!

Gabbie Martin, Grade 4
Holly Ridge Elementary School, NC

Georgia

State of the peach
Home of the brave
Life of the party
Might not never live again

Sound of the people
Voice of our society
Help for our knowledge
Lost and found again

The praise of our people
Mind of our geniuses
Love for our soldiers
Lost and found again, maybe

Ayanna Kelly, Grade 6
Academy of Lithonia Charter School, GA

The Best Bed

Usually, when we're on a long drive
we gently fall asleep one by one
as if we were dominoes falling.
The dreams we have are about our destination
whether it be a house, or a lake,
I personally think its the solitude of the car
that makes these dreams great.

Greyson Piesco, Grade 6
J Larry Newton School, AL

Pretty

Roses are red
Violets are blue.
You're very pretty and you smell nice too.
Your hair is shining like the morning sun.

Your eyes shine like the beautiful moon and the stars.
Your dimples are red like cherries.
Your body is perfect in every way.
Words cannot describe my feelings for you.

And that's why I love you.

Isaiah Cox, Grade 5
Buies Creek Elementary School, NC

Life

Life is wonderful music,
It opens your soul.

Life is a choice,
A choice between slavery or death.

Life is the great blue ocean,
Moving smoothly in the open world.

Life is the bright sunny light,
Shining brightly inside of your soul.

Life is a hug,
Keeping you warm and comfortable.

Life is happiness,
Wearing a great smile of joy.

Life is hope,
Keeping you happy, healthy, and away from danger.

Eber-Andres Espinal, Grade 4
Dante B Fascell Elementary School, FL

Lemonade

L aughing a little
E njoying a drink of cold lemonade
M aking some money
O n a nice spring day
N ow only 75 cents now hurry up
A fresh pitcher of sweet Lemonade is a
D elicious treat so come on
E verybody come buy your lemonade today!

Ariana Jones, Grade 4
St Thomas More School, NC

Friends

Friends, friends, friends,
they're always kind nice and giving
they are pretty sweet and fun
showing kindness every day and
they always give you an extra hand for everything
even if they don't know how to do it

Amanda Shoffner, Grade 4
Spruce Creek Elementary School, FL

Fly Away

I wish I could fly
Like Pegasus
And I imagine sleeping on clouds
I am dreaming under the stars
I once felt my feet off the ground
But now I can't envision that anymore
I seem to want to fly away in more ways than one
But I'm really a dove with a rock tied to its ankle

Alice Leavengood, Grade 6
Shorecrest Preparatory School, FL

The Jaguar

I see a jaguar,
A golden coat of orange,
With lots of black spots.

I see a jaguar,
Hiding in the tall grasses,
Jaguars are fearless.

Jemini Radwan, Grade 5
The Sanibel School, FL

Beautiful Flower

Beautiful flower
Swaying in the summer breeze
Beauty far untold.

Henry Woodyard, Grade 6
Immaculate Conception School, MS

My First Birthday Party

I was turning six.
A lot of people came.
I knew it was going to be fun.
People sang "Happy Birthday."
I was really happy.
They gave me presents and money.
It was so fun.
Children played and played.
Then everybody said bye
And gave me hugs and kisses.
We thanked everybody
For coming to my birthday.

Arlena Tatum, Grade 5
East Marion Elementary School, MS

I Am

I am a kid who loves baseball
I wonder if I will go to the pros
I hear my bat with a raging fury
I see the ball going
I want to beat the homerun record
I am a kid who loves baseball

I pretend I am a pro.
I feel recharged.
I touch my bat with all my power
I worry we might lose
I cry with pride
I am a kid who loves baseball

I understand the game of baseball
I say we are all winners
I dream to beat the all time record
I try my soul in every game
I hope I go to the pros
I am a kid who loves baseball

Jacob Sheldon, Grade 6
Heron Creek Middle School, FL

What Happened to Big Bird?

On my first birthday
I got a Big Bird cake.
At first I was sneaky
About getting into it.
Everybody started asking
If they could have some.
I squeezed it tight!
I ate it quicker too!
After a couple minutes,
I had it all over my clothes.
They laughed at how I
Dropped it and ate it.
If they tried to get any,
I would squeeze it tighter!
I couple of minutes later,
I was full.
I had it on me!
Then I really played in it.
So what happened to Big Bird?
I ate him!

Tamrah Davis, Grade 5
East Marion Elementary School, MS

A Perfect Star

A star in the sky
With a very yellow light
Twinkling in the night

Jessica Christian, Grade 6
Tequesta Trace Middle School, FL

Hamsters

We got hamsters
We thought they were normal
But one said, "Boo!"
Instead of it having a heart attack
I did!

Trenton Davis, Grade 4
Barnardsville Elementary School, NC

What I See

Red is a spicy Spanish chili.
Yellow is a springtime lily.

Pink is a sweet peach.
Brown is a dirty leach.

Blue is a pair of jeans.
Green is a can of beans.

Purple is a vine of grapes.
Tan is a set of linen drapes.

Orange are some seashells.
Black is the bottom of wells.

Elizabeth Louden, Grade 6
Tequesta Trace Middle School, FL

Nature

Nature smells so good
Pine trees swaying in the breeze
Really love those sounds

Maribel Pavarini, Grade 6
Seven Springs Middle School, FL

Darkness

My eyes are not open
I cannot see a thing
My life is a puddle
Of blue darkened seas
My eyes are not open

Dreams are calling
Calling my name
No words I can see
No words I can name

For my eyes are not open
I can't see cloudy skies
The darkness of grass
The darkness of my eyes

It feels like a puddle
Puddle of darkened seas
For my eyes are not open
For I cannot see

Terriyana Goosby, Grade 6
Elba Elementary School, AL

Nature

The sky is blue
The grass is green
Flowers are red, purple, and green

Birds fly
Puppies cry
I always wonder why

The wind blows
The garden grows
In the winter it snows

Caitlin Smith, Grade 5
Brooklet Elementary School, GA

The Marching Band

Symbols thunder, horns blow,
Feet stomp, I go "whoa."

Sun shines, whistle sounds,
Drums bang, hearts pound.

Music stops, crowd cheers,
Now I wait, until next year.

Rachel Lanier, Grade 6
Gold Hill Middle School, SC

High Merit Poems – Grades 4, 5, and 6

What About My Vertebrae
I went to the doctor to see my DNA,
And I found out I didn't have a vertebrae,
I was so surprised I thought I might choke,
But the doctor just laughed, for it had all been a joke.

Kara Kimple, Grade 4
St Thomas More School, NC

Don't Do Drugs
Don't be stupid
do your part.
Don't do drugs
be real smart.
They may try to provoke you,
say it's good —
but you just say no
I'm too good for this 'hood.
They can call you names
but you just take it and say
that's right,
I don't want to get high and go to jail tonight.
They may call you names for the rest of the school year
but again take it and say
I don't give into the influence.
So there.

Mia Nelson-Gauthier, Grade 6
McRae Elementary School, FL

Sorrow
Today is a day that I feel sorrow for the world.
Pain, suffering, death. I feel much sorrow.
War, battle conflict…stop these fools.
Why must this world revolve around madness?
But this is what it's come to be.
And all of this follows sorrow.

J. B. Veliz, Grade 5
Poinciana Elementary School, FL

The U.S. Army
The men and women leave their families.
Don't know if they'll ever see them again.
The roar of planes thunder away.
The soldiers can hear the shooting far away.
The soldiers are flying to Iraq,
To fight the War on Terror.
To get off the plane to be surprised,
In hope that they know no one who dies.
They go to fight for freedom and peace,
To protect the U.S.
They patrol the streets of Iraq.
I hope they do not crack.
That is why the soldiers are my heroes.
They keep us safe in the U.S.
I thank the men and women in Iraq.
They don't really know if they'll come back.

Andy Nelson, Grade 6
Camperdown Academy, SC

The Bright Sun
The sunflower sun is so bright.
Its brightness lights the earth.
So good, so bright, so yellow —
And how it brightens the day!
While the moon brightens the night.
I can't live without the sun.

Flavia Villamonte, Grade 4
Julian D Parker School of Science, Math & Technology, FL

Space Is a Huge Place
There's a place
Where it's the opposite of day
All kinds of bright stars
I wonder where they come from
They only shine through the night.

Oh how I would love to visit this place
And enjoy the looks of its wonderful sights
And see all of its wonderful planets
This wonderful place is called Outer Space.

There's no gravity in this bright galaxy
I would race every day in this huge place
A space race is the best thing to do before leaving this place
And going back home where there isn't much space.

Frank Cherry, Grade 5
West Bertie Elementary School, NC

Beach
I am finally home,
where waves slap the shores,
and the sand is like silk,
as it hides the life below.

I am finally home,
where every night is full of adventure,
and the constant sounds of fireworks,
as their light fills the night sky.

I am finally home,
where the marsh's crabs scurry
across the wet ground
and cranes stand silently waiting.

I am finally home,
where the pier stretches to the sea
and the wind kisses our face
while the ocean sings his sweet lullaby.

Although I may leave
its sandy shores and salty seas
I know I will be coming back to this beach,
my home.

April Epting, Grade 6
Chapin Middle School, SC

The Tree
The tree gave protection
to the birds,
and danced in the wind
to their songs.
While I picked the apples
off its branches,
"Ouch" it yelled
"Be careful."
Gavin Hodge, Grade 5
Summit Hill Elementary School, GA

Love
Candy hearts and flowers
are not what matters
but the love of your heart
will matter.
Julia Allen, Grade 6
Challenger Middle School, FL

Around Me*
Trees on stumps around
And sand all over the ground
With a sidewalk in between
And a big car sound.

People's voices
And grass making noises
With roots that look like snakes
Popping up with so many choices.

There are trees with arms
And buildings like farms
Trees with faces
And stars like charms.
Alessandro Diaz, Grade 5
Pinewood Acres School, FL
*Inspired by Robert Frost

Bee's Buzz
Buzz, buzz goes the bee.
Please don't sting me!
Buzz goes the bee by me.
Fly back to your honey tree!
Buzz, buzz goes the bee.
Why are you after me?
Oh my! I know why!
I'm in the flower garden where you fly.
You need the pollen I see
To return to your tree.
Honey is what you make
So I will move so you can take.
Buzz, buzz goes the bee.
He is happy now I see.
Buzz, buzz goes the bee!
Brittney Jozefyk, Grade 4
Lake Park Baptist School, FL

Drip
drip
drip
slip
slip. slip
running down
the window dink
dink I think it
is coming bink ew now
it is in my drink
Keelee Ladnier, Grade 5
St Martin Upper Elementary School, MS

Family
Family
Lovable and caring
We like to play, jump, and kick
We are funny
Togetherness
Maya Caradine, Grade 5
Winona Elementary School, MS

Fakes
The fiction we live in
Denies the real facts.
The lies are grasping
And they're not holding back.

All the fakes in this world
Have begun to colonize.
Oh the lies!
We're all mesmerized.

Gossip full of rumors.
They live off of, those fakes.
You pour your miserable heart out,
We all make mistakes.

So yet again,
The lies divide us all.
There's nothing to gain,
They all want to see you fall.
Wendy Miramontes, Grade 6
Freedom Middle School, FL

Global Warming
Ice caps are melting,
The ozone layer is breaking.
Carelessness of pollution is spreading,
And nobody does anything.
Even with a warning,
We haven't stopped.
It will be our fault,
If we destroy our beautiful home.
Planet, Earth.
Simone Lim-Hing, Grade 6
Tequesta Trace Middle School, FL

Outdoors
The outdoors is beautiful.
Especially in spring.
The bees swarm.
Before there is a storm.
So go outdoors.
Go outdoors.
As the beautiful sun brights the light.
So go outdoors because outdoors rules.
Oh, yeah!
Fear Churchwell, Grade 4
Barrow Elementary School, GA

Old Man's Beard
I saw an old man with a beard
who was scary and just plain weird
so when he looked down
I had to frown
The old man who I feared
Daniel Burchette, Grade 5
North Windy Ridge School, NC

Snowy Day
Unpleasant snowfall.
The whole ground covered in snow.
Where did the ground go?
Dominique Johnson, Grade 6
Arnold Magnet Academy, GA

Friendship
Friendship is something that you have.
Something that is close to you.
You might fight.
You might not get along.
But when you need that one person.
They are there.
They cheer you up.
Coronda Glover, Grade 6
Saint Pauls Middle School, NC

Storms
I hear my parents
downstairs, yelling
there are gray clouds
in the sky
I hear them say
"divorce" and my dad
stomps down the landing
the palm trees sway
but doesn't break
in the hurricane of
this nightmare
forgiveness is
the eye of the storm,
so I will forgive
Adrianna Wenz, Grade 6
Shorecrest Preparatory School, FL

High Merit Poems – Grades 4, 5, and 6

Toast

Toast, I want toast.
England, Italy, maybe Spain,
I want French toast.

Toast, I want toast.
Cheese toast is what I like the most.

Toast, I want toast.
Colorado, Tennessee, I want Texas toast.

Toast, I want toast.
Salt, pepper, cinnamon, I want garlic toast.

Toast, I want toast.

Reagan Chewning, Grade 4
Edwards Elementary School, SC

Weather

Weather, Weather,
How mighty you are,
With your wind and rain,
Snow and sleet,
Thunderstorms, tornadoes,
But worse, hurricanes.

Weather, Weather,
You can be gentle,
You can be fierce.

Weather, Weather,
You turn water into waves,
Sun to rain.

Weather, Weather,
Knowing what you do
Is a might strong task
In the summer, in the spring.

Do you know what this season will bring?
Weather, Weather,
You will see!

Wesley Sheffield, Grade 4
Irmo Elementary School, SC

911

On this tragic day
These foreign men came
To take away
Something we thought could stay
We never knew that this would happen
For this is something that never happens
But on this day lots lost their lives
All because these men shouldn't have taken a ride

Bridge Harrison, Grade 4
Elba Elementary School, AL

Concerts

Concerts
Exciting, fun
A lifetime memory
Always rushing to buy tickets
Awesome

Michelle Serrano, Grade 6
St Mark's Lutheran School, FL

Dogs

I love my dog very much.
He sleeps with me, every night.
He makes me warm, like the shining sun.
He barks very loud, to wake me up.
I give him treats, to fill his heart with joy.
His hair is white, like the icy cold snow.
He makes me happy, like a newborn chick,
Cuddling with its happy family.
When I play with my dog,
He brings tears of joy to my eyes.
My dog that I love, is named Shilo,
I love my dog so much, I can't live without him.

Rosalinda Andres, Grade 4
Julian D Parker School of Science, Math & Technology, FL

Dirt Bike Racing

Pushing the clutch and shifting the gear
Giving it gas I have no fear.
Going faster and faster on my Honda dirt bike
The wind whipping in my face,
Here is where I want to be in first place.

Colton Trexler, Grade 5
Morgan Elementary School, NC

Pain

Tears falling. I am nothing without you.
I'm a wreck without you.
Look…
Look at me a monster in the darkness.
Without a care about anyone.
If I hurt myself I won't feel the pain.
Come back…
Come back into my arms.
I need you to be by my side or I will die.
Please…
Don't let me die alone.
Don't leave!
Please don't leave!
Please don't leave me with the pain!
When you're by my side you make the pain go away.
Don't go away…
No!
I will be all alone!
No!
Please don't leave me with a broken heart!

Milan Lance, Grade 6
Bak Middle School of the Arts, FL

Cars

Cars are fast
and they last
they take you to places
and they can fit in spaces.
Cars have headlights
and they sure can be bright
they have wheels
and that helps them go up hills.
Cars have windows
and you can play Nintendos
they have heat
and sometimes it can be neat.
Some cars have sun roofs
and you can see the stars.

Brady Lee, Grade 5
West Marion Elementary School, MS

Soccer

S coring Goals
g **O** od sportsmanship
C reating new tricks
pra **C** ticing very hard
athl **E** tic playing
R otating spots

August Parker, Grade 4
East Jones Elementary School, MS

Two Hamsters in One

Peanut
fluffy, cute
scurrying, cuddling, sleeping
companion, pet, enemy, mean
escaping, gnawing, biting
vicious, deadly
Fang

Connor Murphy, Grade 5
St Thomas More School, NC

Big City

The city is big.
Very tall buildings.
All the cars zooming by.
Going up stairs and down elevators.

Willie Stevenson, Grade 4
Spruce Creek Elementary School, FL

Stars

Twinkling stars
sing songs
to me
making pictures
in the night sky
they lull themselves
to sleep with their songs

Daniel O'Hare, Grade 5
Summit Hill Elementary School, GA

Summer Days Are So Fun

Summer days are so fun.
You can roast hot dogs in a bun.
Best of all you don't have to go to school.
My mom says don't play video games all day, don't be a fool.
Playing with friends, it is the best.
My brother likes me going in the store in the summer wearing a vest.

Travis Fortenberry, Grade 5
West Marion Elementary School, MS

Happiness

Happiness is the sound of kids laughing in the pool,
The bright green of new cut grass is happiness,
Happiness is the smell of a picnic full of food,
Tasting the candy you've always wanted to eat, is the taste of happiness,
The touch of happiness is children gently putting their heads on their pillows,
Seeing the happiness of kids smiling.

Soo Baek, Grade 4
Wrights Mill Road Elementary School, AL

All About Andrew

Andrew
Athletic, caring, strong, kind.
Son of John.
Lover of skateboarding, football, and video games.
Who feels excited when he wins, upset when he loses,
Proud when he gets a good grade.
Who needs a kind sister, laughing and playful sister.
Who gives cooperation, help, love.
Who fears bad people, dangerous weapons, riding horses.
Who would like to see the Philadelphia Eagles win, Bruce Springsteen,
And Ryan Sheckler.
Resident of Pfafftown, North Carolina.
Ciaccia

Andrew Ciaccia, Grade 5
Vienna Elementary School, NC

School's Out!

The bell rings!
The students are skipping, yelling, running,
Talking, and stomping their feet down the hallways!

Some students are boarding the bus circle.
Some students are heading for the car line.
Other students are riding their bikes.
A few students find their way home by walking.
I, Shacoria, happily board bus #852 — the yellow bus.

In the meantime, teachers are busily preparing for the next school day.
They are making new worksheets, picking up miscellaneous messes on the floor,
And planning exciting lessons for the upcoming weeks.

Next week, however, all will be quiet here at Clearview.
YAHOO! Spring break is just around the corner…
School's out!

Shacoria Hall, Grade 4
Clearview Avenue Elementary School, FL

Rain
When the sky is grey it's coming soon
Tiny droplets falling from the clouds
The wind is blowing all around
I feel the pressure of the water splashing on my head
Soaking me from head to toe
I run inside near the warm fire
The droplets are still falling
It's raining outside

Abby McCarthy, Grade 4
Queen of Angels Catholic School, GA

Love
Everyone searches for that thing called love
Whether it's in the trees or in the wind
You turn around and it's the bird chirping
It's the water flowing in the ocean
Love is the thing that everyone searches for
No matter what age
It's something you desire

Elizabeth LaChance, Grade 6
Tarpon Springs Middle School, FL

Alice and I
Alice and I are running.
Run, Run, Run.
Our bare feet are touching the ground.
Run, Run, Run.
The wind is running through our hair.
Run, Run, Run.
We are smiling.
Run, Run, Run, Smile, Smile, Smile.
Then suddenly Alice stops.
She screams.
Everything stops.
I see blood running down her leg!
She is crying terribly.
I'm scared, I don't know what to do.
Then…everything turns black.
I wake up in bed,
I just sit there looking confused, thinking.
Then I realized that it was all a
Terrible, terrible dream,
And finally I went back to sleep again,
Feeling relieved, I sleep, sleep, sleep.

Deionna Benard, Grade 6
St Francis Xavier Elementary School, MS

Happiness
Happiness is orange like a pumpkin,
And also like the rim of the basketball hoop.
It bounces through my head.
It reminds me of the time I got a lay-up.
It makes me feel good when playing b-ball.
It makes me want to shout, "Y.M.C.A.!"

Colton Girard, Grade 4
Indian Harbour Montessori Elementary School, FL

My Mom
My mom loves me no matter what I do,
When times get tough,
She helps me through,
She never lets me down,
When I feel discouraged;
She encourages me to do the right things,
When I fall down she helps me up,
The main thing is that,
She loves me so much!

Demeric Washington, Grade 5
Minor Elementary School, AL

Love
Love is something you like with passion
and yet you wondered how that happened.
You came here to find happiness
but instead you found sadness.
You thought he was the one
until he made you cry just enough to make it a ton.
He said it was forever
but for sure he was thinking clever.
Now you know he's just a fake
and you'll never ever make that same mistake.

Joserlys Adriana de la Torre, Grade 6
Freedom Middle School, FL

Hope, Love, and Friendship
It's the most powerful thing
It's the only tune, that alone you cannot sing

We're together forever
When will we leave each other, the answer's never

I've got your back and you've got mine
I hope it'll stay this way 'till the end of time

I hope that this will never end,
But if it did there would be no more time to spend

Always, remember these and do not skip
Hope, Love, and most of all Friendship

Because if you have a friend
The friendship will never ever end!

Jenah McCall, Grade 6
Rosman Middle School, NC

The Old Woman
One day there was an old woman.
She went to town.
She was upside down.
She went around and around to town.
She played all day and went to sleep.

Alisha English, Grade 4
Camden Elementary School of the Creative Arts, SC

North Carolina
I have a cabin there
It is a beautiful place
It has flowers grazing
Upon the mountains
North Carolina
Kaitlin Alexander, Grade 4
Spruce Creek Elementary School, FL

We Are All Different
We laugh differently
We talk differently
We dress differently
We think differently
We look different
But we are all equal.
Alexandria Kaloplastos, Grade 6
Hand Middle School, SC

Game, Set, Match
Feel the grip slipping
As you hit the ball
The rush of adrenaline
Is overwhelming
The ball is returned
You hear it whiz off
His racquet for the last time
As it goes right in to the net
Game, set, match
The point is won
Alexandra Murray, Grade 5
Rosarian Academy, FL

A Beautiful Night
The day is gone
I say farewell
One last time
The silky blackness
Of the night sets in
But then I think
What a beautiful night
I go outside
Quiet as a mouse
Then
What a beautiful sight
Wherever I went
I could always see
The beautiful stars
That light the sky
I took time away
From the night
Not worrying about tomorrow
Overwhelmed by the sight
I lie down and say
Good night.
Mackenzie White, Grade 5
Rosarian Academy, FL

Love
Love is deep
Love is sweet
Love is the one
Who gets you on your feet
Love is right
Love is left
Love can be found everywhere
Love is someone you can meet
Love is the way she looks at me

Love is not helping me
Love has many rhymes and rhythms
Twists and turns
But which one leads to me
Love has many ways
And I went the wrong way
Garrett Rone, Grade 4
Pine Tree Hill Elementary School, SC

Two Run Shot
I saw it
The perfect pitch
I had to swing the bat
That amazing noise
The crack of the bat
The ball went sailing
It kept going,
Kept sailing
It cleared the fence
And the next backstop
It landed at second
It's a two run shot
Zane Gill, Grade 5
Pensacola Beach Elementary School, FL

Soccer
I think soccer's neat,
Because you use your feet.
And I think that goalie stinks,
When I play soccer I'm a hero,
Not a zero.
Grant Hoffner, Grade 5
Morgan Elementary School, NC

Country People
Country people are cool
country people are nice
they are smart too,
and country people
ride in rodeos and
some raise chickens.
Most country people
raise dogs and puppies.
Country people are awesome.
Jazmine Watson, Grade 5
West Marion Elementary School, MS

My Dog
Gracie is cool
She barks like a fool
If you give her a bone
She's one big drool.
Tiffani Wilson, Grade 5
Our Lady of Fatima School, MS

Unique
Snow is unique
each shiny piece
with its own
fingerprint
I feel each
snow crystal
falling on
my dark black
eyelashes
each unique flake
falling
as each child
laughing, playing
happily throwing
each frosty clump up
and watching
the clumps
frolic
down
down
down
Emily Schwenk, Grade 4
Sharon Elementary School, GA

Haunted House
The door creaks open,
I gait inside,
There goes a shiver,
Rushing down my spine,
I'm in a frightening place,
There's a terrified look,
Upon my face.
Its dark as midnight,
Without the moon,
I might want to get out very soon.
Cobwebs droop down,
Touching my head,
I hope there are no spiders,
Way up ahead.
What's that I hear?
An ear bursting stomp, I fear!
I feel it creeping up behind my back,
Getting ready to attack,
No way! It won't get me,
I'm scampering out,
Like a buzzing bee.
Jasmine Voit, Grade 5
Sharon Elementary School, NC

Life Is…

Life is a highway,
If you do something wrong it will effect you

Life is a dull umbrella,
Everyone must have a rainy day

Life is a complete circle,
One day it will reach its end point

Life is a rocking guitar,
We have to make it rock

Life is a variety of candy
We can make it sweet or sour

Life is a helpful guide
It can give you directions and answers

Life is an assortment of emotions,
You can find sadness, joy, fear, love, etc.

Arianna Balceiro, Grade 5
Dante B Fascell Elementary School, FL

Music

I can't live without it.
There are many types of it.
Like rock, rap, country, reggaeton,
But there are many more types though.
To me,
There is no such thing as bad music.
My earphones and iPod are all my needs in life,
Besides family.
To you, my music may be weird,
Maybe boring or even stupid,
But to me my music is sacred,
And defines my whole life.

Patrick Lopez, Grade 6
Tequesta Trace Middle School, FL

When Will Time End

I dream of crashing
But my hear says no
I get into my car and
Remember my dream,
I called my mama to
Talk to her about it
And she says don't worry
You and your baby will be all right,
But then I get onto the highway,
Then all of a sudden a flash came upon me
And I saw my dream
All of a sudden this car hit me,
I knew my dream had already come true.

Takara Bingham, Grade 6
Philadelphia Elementary School, MS

When I Look Out My Window

When I look out my window what do I see?
A bird as beautiful as can be.
With wings long and brisk,
She glides like a flying disc.
I would love to keep her but what good would it be,
If I could not watch her glide all around me.
As I watch her fly around my home,
And wonder if she has her own.
My question is answered when I see her fly into our tree,
And that makes me very happy.
Because now I can see her beautiful flow,
Whenever I look out my window.

Taylor Rossi, Grade 6
Gold Hill Middle School, SC

A Close Encounter with a Bear

A big brown burly bear
Gave me a real scare

The bear was not close to bare
He was full of hair

Swish, there goes his claw
He missed but was sharp as a saw

Once I gathered my wits
I grinned and bared it

So I skedaddled out of there
Away from my close encounter with a bear

Collin Hutson, Grade 6
Brogden Middle School, NC

Baseball

Baseball is exciting,
Baseball is my favorite sport,
You hit the ball with a bat, you score some runs for your team.

You can get a home run,
The best,
You can get a strikeout,
The worst,
You want to get a single, double, triple, sacrifice,
But you want to at least get a hit.

Baseball can be good or bad,
Many people love this sport, I am one,
You can't always win.

Baseball is fun and all,
Baseball is the best sport of all!

Baseball is exciting and surprising as well,
I love baseball! That's all!

Andrew Marsden, Grade 4
St Thomas More School, NC

The Sky

The world was once as dark as night,
But then God said, "Let there be light!"
The light appeared; it shone so bright.
And so became the day and night.

Then God made a great big sky.
He made it wide, and clouds sail by.
Then God made a ball of light.
The yellow sun so big and bright.
And a moon and stars to shine at night.
They are such a pretty sight!

Jane Lowinski, Grade 4
Lake Park Baptist School, FL

Woody (My Dog)

Chewing wood is what he likes to do,
He also likes the cows that moo.
He has a long, cold nose,
So when he sneezes, a tornado blows.

Rose Rossell, Grade 5
North Windy Ridge School, NC

Dream

A dream lays beneath my pillow
it's very special.
It just lies there
nice and humble
while I play
in the meadow.
When night sky calls
owls hoot
and nature becomes alert.
then my Dream speaks to me
then it leaves.
and flows down the dream stream.
Then I say good night
Dream

Kenneth Harrington, Grade 6
Arlington Middle School, FL

Sadness Came Upon

That time
That day
That month and year
That last moment with her
My dear mom
My mom left
That's when the sadness came upon me
She left when I was little
And when my brother was little too
I will never forget
My dear mom
She was gone
Sadness came upon

Meranda Gomez Cochran, Grade 4
North Fayette Elementary School, GA

Me

Justin
Adventurous, sweet, helpful, protective
Brother of Stephanie, Brittany, Andreas, Thomas, Brian, Zachary, Isabel
Who loves his family, his pets, his school
Who feels uncertain, confused, uncomfortable
Who needs support, love, protection
Who fears guns, car accidents, robbers
Who gives gifts, support to others, love to others
Who would like to see my brother that is in war, go to Alabama, see the penguins
Who is the resident of Winter Garden, Florida
Carmean

Justin Carmean, Grade 5
Hope Charter School, FL

The Beagle

The beagle runs and plays and naps under a tree.
She then looks up and sees her bone. She is happy as a buzzy bee.
She picks it up and runs around and sets it where she found it.

The beagle hops up and runs in a circle. She's chasing her tail!
It's just like there's a little voice inside her saying,
"Go! Go! Go! Chase it! Chase it! Catch that tail!"

The Beagle lies back down.
She picks up her bone and chews her bone shaking her head rapidly.
She is then called inside for her meal. Then she chows down.

Katie Faber, Grade 4
Irmo Elementary School, SC

My Brother*

My brother is a huge pest,
I hope he is happy,
Because we both get the best.
He's older than me,
But not smarter,
He doesn't know the difference,
Between a flee and a bee.

He is really funny,
Though he is kind of annoying,
I'd rather have him over a bunny.
He snores in his sleep,
It sounds like he's 80,
I hope he lives that long,
He might sound like a sheep.

He gets the better piece of meat,
That's what I think,
We always get into fights,
And mostly I get beat.
The good part is he's really fun,
And great to play with
I love him, and I got him as a brother so back off he's mine I won.

Nicholas Gonzalez, Grade 5
Pinewood Acres School, FL
*Inspired by my brother

High Merit Poems – Grades 4, 5, and 6

Love That Hamster*
Love that hamster
like a pig loves to roll in mud.
I said I love that hamster
like a pig loves to roll in mud.
Love to see him alive every day
and say "You're so cute!"

He eats like a chipmunk runs for his life.
I said he eats like a chipmunk, and runs for his life.
Runs when he is scared,
when he is happy, he still runs.

His owner likes to hold him,
and pet him on the head.
I said his owner likes to hold him
likes to pet his little cute head.
I can put him away now
and I will pet him every once in a while.

Sad that he had to go away
before the right time had come.
I said it is sad that he had to go away,
before the right time had come.
He will be gone forever, and a good hamster he will always be.
Amy Saliba, Grade 5
Pinewood Acres School, FL
*Inspired by Walter Dean Myers

The Field
The poppies in the field were made of gold.
They were glowing next to the lacy, purple pillows.
People walked by and had picnics
In the numerous purple and gold blankets
That spread over the hills.
The gleaming sun shone down from the cheerful sky,
And many playful kites sailed in the wind.
Emilia Ballou, Grade 4
The Children's School at Sylvia Circle, SC

Summer
Sunflowers of yellow
Maypops are sweet
Good wonders of joy.
Great big vines at my feet
As the red roses bloom
In the hot summer sun.
I gently laugh as the wind tickles my hair.
The hot warm sun heats my sweat
As it drips down my face.
It's summertime
As I dive into the pool.
As I laugh,
Ha! Ha!
There is no more school.
Malik Lewis, Grade 5
East Marion Elementary School, MS

My Story
A tale of a young girl,
A tale of failure and glory,
Teaching, learning, hoping, finding,
This is my story.
An old worn out journal in someone else's hands
Read it! See? Now you understand.
Journaling's in my heart, just like a river dam
It's what I love, it's who I am.
A story is a lesson. It's a lose and a win.
It's a passion in performance, an adventure to begin.
So come along and you will see,
The story that's inside of me!
McKenzie Garrison, Grade 6
South Pontotoc Middle School, MS

Little Birdie in the Tree
I looked up in a tree and what did I see;
A pretty little birdie looking down at me.
I stood there and thought how nice to see;
A little birdie as free as can be.
So I looked up to see the birdie in the tree;
And I said to her fly away little bird;
Why don't you fly
high into the sky
into the sun
and have some fun
with the wind under your wings
you can fly as high as can be;
Then fly back home to your tree.
Emily Chupp, Grade 5
Ranburne Elementary School, AL

Shy Child
Shy Child, Shy Child
Come and play!
No, says Shy Child
I want to stay!
Shy Child, Shy Child
Why are you so shy?
Leave her alone, says one child
Or she will cry
If she cries, blurts another
She is not Shy Child, she is Cry Child!
Cry Child, Cry Child
Please do not cry.
Cry Child replies,
Give me a good reason why!
My reason is, I want to be your friend.
We'll be best friends till the very end!
Ok, says Cry Child, but one more thing,
What is it? What is it? I'll do anything!
Stop calling me Shy and Cry Child, if you may.
Ok, ok now let's go play!
Yasmine Fairley, Grade 6
Carver Middle School, MS

Seasons and Nature

I wonder what the birds are thinking when they sing a sweet chirp song
I hear the trees swing and sway all year long
Snow only falls in one season
Rain is all around
Summers are hot and dry I do not hear a sound
Spring is where the flowers bloom
All so sweet and lovely
Fall is where I see the colors all swarm around me
Be careful where you hack away
If a tree should fall, you must be ashamed
Remember mother earth is the spider, and we are the prey, tangled in her web of nature.

Candace Heath, Grade 6
Gold Hill Middle School, SC

Guitar Hero

Guitar Hero shreds; play rhythm, bass, or lead
You can even rock out with a six string symphony
If you miss a string, you'll still do okay
Don't get mad because it's just a game you play
Guitar Hero 3 is the best
It has better songs that put me to the test
When you hit a note, flames shoot out
It makes you rock and scream and shout
When you are playing your mind is on the game
It feels like you are about to go in the hall of fame
You're trying to get a 100% without missing a string
But if you miss it, don't worry about a thing.
When you play the game it's like you're in a band
With millions of people in the stands
Watching and cheering so very loud
It's like all you hear is the crowd
You wanna play all night long
Rocking out and playing songs
When you're playing a solo it's so fast and fun,
Your fingers hurt by the time you're done.
If you're not sure how to rock, take it from me, Everyone's a winner, it's as easy as 1,2,3.

Bailey Wittmann, Grade 4
Spruce Creek Elementary School, FL

Ocean

As the sun rose in the sky the ocean yawned and stretched to greet another day.
She slowly crept onto the shore trying not to wake the gulls.
Sailors pulled up their anchors from her deep places and began to traverse her vastness.
Before long it was noon and she began to spew out foam and roared with pride.
She began slapping the shore with her waves, at first gently.
But then in a wild fit of rage she slapped wave after wave onto the beaten up beach.
She stole more shoreline with each fit of rage as if she was in a tug of war game and the shore was losing.
As the afternoon dragged on the fit subsided and she gave up the shore.
She retreated to her place again happily rocking the children on their rafts.
She allowed the winds to blow across her warming her waters and guiding her boats.
The dolphins were leaping for joy in her warm arms, feeling very secure and happy.
She mimicked the sky tormenting and teasing it as if it was her sibling.
When the sky was blue, she became blue and when the sky sparkled she sparkled.
As the sun set in the sky she began to snore, but continued to gently rock her boats to sleep.

Megan Duffy, Grade 6
City of Pembroke Pines Charter Central Middle School, FL

My Mother

My mother's really thoughtful
She is loving to me,
She doesn't help me with my homework
But is as nice as can be.
What she does,
She does right
Sometimes I ask her for help
She doesn't because she thinks I'm bright.
I know she gets furious at me
When I don't clean my room,
She goes into the walk-in-closet
And comes back with a Swiffer vacuum.
She always nags on me
To play with my sister
She doesn't understand
She's an eavesdropping listener.
My mom she gets frustrated
Just like a mother,
It bothers me sometimes
But I still love her.
Happy Mother's Day

Gina Pribil, Grade 6
Turkey Creek Middle School, FL

Shapes

Shapes, shapes
All around
Some are up
Some are down

Look outside
Can you see?
Shapes are hiding
In the tree

Shapes, shapes
Square is one
Has four sides
It's #1

Shapes, shapes
One, two, three
Some shapes are
Even on me!

Shawn Pires, Grade 4
Egret Lake Community Elementary School, FL

The Most Important Thing

The best pet is my dog.
She is loving, caring, and she kisses you a lot.
She will lick you anytime she can.
She is outside with you, on the couch with you,
and at the bottom of your bed.

Joey Clark, Grade 6
Gold Hill Middle School, SC

The Stupendous Qualities of Mrs. Ferraro

Mrs. Ferraro is as wise as Athena,
And also as swift as a ballerina.

She is the best teacher,
(But I like to call her an "educational preacher").

She cares for us like a considerate mother,
And corrects our papers one after another!

Mrs. Ferraro dresses quite colorfully,
And smiles VERY wonderfully!

Jessica Lee, Grade 4
William S Talbot Elementary School, FL

Who I Am and What I Am Not?

I'm not a zebra
I want to explore imagination land
I want to be famous like the Queen of England
Or a bat and flap my wings and glide through the sky
Maybe a horse and run like the wind

I know what I'm going to be…me
I'm going to run at normal speed
Take a plane to fly
And pretend I'm queen of the world
And maybe I'll play animals with my friends
I am me
And…that's only what I am

Kaila Crews, Grade 6
Tarpon Springs Middle School, FL

Butterflies

Butterflies start as worms,
When they move they squirm.
They eat all kinds of leaves,
Then they get in their cocoon and believe.

In their cocoon day and night,
Waiting to see the sight.
See all the flowers,
How many hours?

In the ending,
Like a new beginning,
They grow and oh my,
Up in the sky, they fly!

Santana Moretz, Grade 5
Sharon Elementary School, NC

If

If I were a book
I'd tell many stories.
I'd let my pages flip as the wind blew by,
I'd close when night fell.

Marco Pena, Grade 4
Indian Harbour Montessori Elementary School, FL

Danger
Swim, swim, swim away
Krill shot through the sea
"Come back," the whale cried
"I want something to eat"
Madelyn Rivera, Grade 5
North Windy Ridge School, NC

Bichon Frise
Smart, fun
Playing, running, barking
Sleeping, snoring, man's best friend
My brother
Andrew Dunbar, Grade 5
Covenant Classical School, NC

The Spider
Creeping
I am a spider
Crawling
I am feared by many
Sneaking
My silk web
Creep
That I love so
Crawl
Acts as a home
Sneak
Yet I feel so alone
Being booshed by brooms
Beaten by bats
I must say it's the worst sight
My eight eyes ever did see.
Creeping
Crawling
Sneaking
Kendra MacGeorge, Grade 6
Challenger Middle School, FL

My Heap of a Jeep
Right now my Jeep
Is outside in a heap.
It's 40 years old
And it still hasn't sold.
I fixed it up to look like new
And then it sold in a day or two.
Spencer Roche, Grade 5
Olde Providence Elementary School, NC

Jim
There once was a boy named Jim
Whose dad never taught him to swim
He fell off the dock
And sunk like a rock
And that was the end of him
Lane Barry, Grade 5
Winona Elementary School, MS

Florida
F lorida is very fun
L ovable state
O h so hot
R epublican state
I nteresting
D own south of Georgia
A t the bottom of the map
Agustin Garcia, Grade 6
Tarpon Springs Middle School, FL

On the Court
On the court I don't hear my fans
I only hear my teammates
I don't think I just do it
and we win the game
Then I can hear again
The fans screaming some crying
I go home I practice and practice
I can't wait until I am
on the court again
Richard Honeycutt, Grade 4
Tabernacle Elementary School, NC

Spring
S urprises
P eter Cottontail
R abbits
I mpressed
N o school
G reen
Jesus Garcia, Grade 4
Central Park Elementary School, FL

Can You Imagine…
A bear without fur
An ocean without water

A sky without birds
A candy store without Nerds

A dog without a nose
A garden without a hose

A classroom without a teacher
A church without a preacher

A pet shop without pets
An animal hospital without a vet

The world without ice cream
Never ever having a dream

A post office without mail
A vegetable garden without snails?
Sarah Peeling, Grade 4
William S Talbot Elementary School, FL

A Hole
I feel like I'm falling falling
Falling into a deep dark hole;
with no comfort at the bottom

I feel like the hole
is towering over me as,
tall buildings over a
silent city street.

I am still falling falling
in the same
deep dark hole.
no one is there to break my fall.

It feels like the
moon has extinguished.
A dark feeling in the hole.
Brianna Fisher, Grade 5
North Windy Ridge School, NC

Colors of My Mind
Pink is the color of love.
White is the color of a dove.

Orange is a burning fire.
Purple is the color of desire.

Green is the color of the leaves on a tree.
Yellow is the color of a bumble bee.

Brown is the color of chocolate candy.
Blue makes me feel very dandy.

Red is one of the colors on the flag.
Black is the color of an oily rag.
Jensen Kotlar, Grade 6
Tequesta Trace Middle School, FL

Homework*
It stinks it smells
It gives me the chills
It has so many questions
And answers to be revealed
I wish it would just poof to infinity
So I can finally…
Oh no!
Oh no!
I have nothing to do!
There's not one thing for me to do!
There's nothing in the *world*
Fun enough for me!
I…I…I'll just…I'll just do my
H…o…m…e…w…o…r…k.
Dereck Morgado, Grade 4
Irmo Elementary School, SC
**Inspired by Jack Prelutsky*

To Get to You

Love is like a rose forever in bloom
A summer's day that never ends
A mountaintop that reaches to the heavens
If love were a river I would die to cross that river
just to get to you
If love were a mountain
I would climb to the highest peak
just to get to you
Love is like a rose forever in bloom

Kaitlin Collison, Grade 6
McRae Elementary School, FL

Kyle

He's not for me, no way Jose
he can do a triple axle
and talk in babbly basel (whatever that may be)
he's ignorant, shallow, and oh so cute
he's lovable, mean, and weird
how can he be so *wrong* but *right*
our relationship would be oh, so tight and *right*
but, *wrong*
these things I ponder
while I wonder
through my head
at night
although, cute, he may be
he is definitely *not right* for me.

Skylar Beadle Goliber, Grade 5
Hickory Day School, NC

Return*

I have seen the ruin
Yet now I see the right
I have walked within the shadow
And here I am in light
Reintroduced: fresh from the fight
society has changed
And I have changed as well
My thoughts were rearranged in a past hell
Whose memories dwell within me
These haunting treacheries of a war
Beyond my control
I return home and it's not the same
The world has changed without me
And I am left confused
I stand alone, distant, feeling rather used
As I made the ultimate sacrifice
For a country who let my grand deeds
Suffice: a payment only to return home
There and back again I was thrust
So understand I need time to let my eyes adjust
Because I'm stepping from the shadows into light

Raven Moffett, Grade 6
Trickum Middle School, GA
*In response to "Love My Rifle More Than You"
by Kayla Williams

Length

Inches, inches,
You're so small
Compared to my brother
You're like a baby doll.

Feet, feet
Where are you
Are you trying to
Measure my shoe?

Yards, yards
Where are you
Are you trying to
Measure my glue?

Miles, miles
You're so far away
You're the distance from
Jamaica to Bombay.

Krishauna Williams, Grade 4
Egret Lake Community Elementary School, FL

Pink

Pink,
It is a scorching sunburn
Sweet strawberries
The color of a blooming rose
It is the color that says
"Look at me I'm beautiful"
Pink describes the feel of a velvety blanket
That lies over my bed
Looks on a soft cashmere sweater worn in the winter
The sound of a girl stating pink is her color.
Pink. It is the color of life

Jayme Nixon, Grade 6
Arlington Middle School, FL

Be My Valentine

B oys asking girls to be their valentine,
E very girl wishing "he was mine,"

M any valentine notes being passed,
Y ou receive them very, very fast,

V alentine's Day is very fun.
A nonymous flowers and candy for everyone,
L oving, flirting, passing notes,
E veryone is wearing winter coats,
N otes are written with lots of care,
T here is puppy love in the air,
I love making chocolate hearts,
N o one likes eating the broken parts,
E njoy Valentine's Day.

Jenna-Lee Perry, Grade 6
Gold Hill Middle School, SC

It's a Hard Place to Be (Iraq)*
He's got to work all day
Ain't got no time to play
And all for a little pay
He's got to work in that sandy mess
So deep inside me I know he's the best
I know he's my father
So I know it's no bother
To work for my family
So we can live in harmony
Christopher Price, Grade 4
Pine Tree Hill Elementary School, SC
*Dedicated to Bobby Price (my dad)

Lacey
L ovely
A rtist
C aring
E ntertaining
Y earning
Lacey Holloway, Grade 4
East Jones Elementary School, MS

Chocolate
Chocolate
nice, sweet
smacking, backing, munching
candy, dessert, snack, treat
dipping, melting, dissolving
cool, awesome
chocolate
Jenny Truong, Grade 5
St Martin Upper Elementary School, MS

Horses
Horses
galloping around
hearing the wind
horses of different colors
riding
Samantha Pope, Grade 6
J Larry Newton School, AL

Skateboarding
Skateboarding is really fun
Playing games one by one

Dropping in is really hard
If you succeed you'll get far

Riding down the streets of town
Doing tricks round and round

Skateboarding is really hard
Don't give up you'll get far!!!!!
Josh Bradburn, Grade 5
North Windy Ridge School, NC

Blissful
Blissful is yellow like the sun
And also like marigolds.
It prances through my head like a deer with her fawn.
It makes me think of the time my precious baby brother was born.
It makes me feel calm — like a cool, spring day.
It makes me want to cry with joy.
Diamond Foster, Grade 5
Manchester Elementary School, NC

Ode to My Mother
Mother, oh Mother, how you treat me when I'm sick.
I feel like you're the closer you make people confess the truth.
I first saw you when I was born. You looked light skinned with brown hair
You keep me comfortable with your honesty and your jokes.
If anything ever happened to me my feelings for you would never change.
I adore you because you don't cook what you want to you ask us what we want.
Instead of me finding you, you found me.
When I'm in trouble you always figure out answers to the problem.
You take me where Dad "says" he's going to take me but doesn't.
You always keep your promises. You tell everyone the truth.
You are my mother, you gave birth to me. You bring me joy and I love you.
Jessica Green, Grade 5
Vienna Elementary School, NC

I Learned That…
I learned that nobody is perfect.
I learned that I will succeed if I try.
I learned that my parents will love me no matter what.
I learned that money isn't everything.
I learned that school is very important.
I learned that nobody will live forever.
I learned that GOD knows what is best for me even if I don't.
I learned that family and friends come first.
I learned that GOD is always there for you when you have lost hope.
I learned that my parents will encourage me to do everything I set my mind to.
I learned that life won't always be what you want.
I learned that love is very powerful.
I learned that friends are something you don't want to let go of.
I learned that everybody is different in their own special way.
I learned that everybody is unique.
I learned that someday I can make a difference.
I learned that everybody should be treated equally.
I learned that life won't always be your cup of tea.
Monica McCraw, Grade 5
Northside Elementary School, SC

Sports to Life
Sports have been a major influence in my life.
You play sports all year, till winter stops and spring is clear.
You play football, baseball till you drop and you play and play and never stop.
They say soccer is a girls sport but guys play tall, medium and short.
Some people want to go pro but usually end up with a no.
If you like sports like me then you see what I see.
Sports are my life and lets you feel free.
Blake Schmehl, Grade 6
Gold Hill Middle School, SC

You Want Me to Write a Poem?
You want me to write a poem?
No, you must be joking
I don't have any paper
My pen is dead
My head hurts
There is a bandage on my finger
I forgot my computer password
My pencil is broken
I am out of white out
I don't even know how to write a poem
Time's up? Uh oh!
All that I have written is a list of bad excuses
Philip Luther, Grade 6
Shorecrest Preparatory School, FL

The Eyes of Nature
A bird lays deep in its nest, ready to sleep.
This can only be seen by the eyes of nature.
The salty sea air, how it smells is so refreshing.
This can only be smelled by the nose of nature.
A delicious carcass dragged in from a successful hunt.
This can only be tasted by the mouth of nature.
A newborn foal, how it squeals for its mother's milk.
This can only be heard by the ears of nature.
The soft feel of a strong wolf's coat.
This can only be felt by the hands of nature.
Charlotte Thompson, Grade 6
Tomlin Middle School, FL

Where I Belong
I step on the field, and I'm where I belong.
There's no where else for me to be,
Just the nets, the soccer ball, my teammates and me.
I hear the whistle and it all falls into place.
The determination, the feelings I embrace, it overwhelms me.
But I love it all,
I can barely comprehend. I step on the field,
And it all happens again.
Gina Davis, Grade 6
Seven Springs Middle School, FL

Stars
When it is dark it gives me light
Shining brightly at midnight
Like a glowing diamond or gold
Shining my way to freedom and peace
Taking me away to my dreams and hopes
Opening my world where I can believe and wish
I can tell it my secrets
For I am sure it won't tell
Giving me confidence
Every time I feel desperate
My only companion
Kimberly Sanchez, Grade 5
Jeff Davis Elementary School, MS

I Am
I am one who likes football.
I wonder if I'll succeed.
I hear cheers through my helmet.
I see the touchdown zone.
I want to be the best I can be.
I am one who likes football.

I pretend to be a pro player.
I feel the pigskin on my hands.
I touch my soul every time I touch the field.
I worry "Am I good enough."
I cry when ever someone gets hurt.
I am one who likes football.

I understand the game.
I say someone will win today.
I dream in becoming professional.
I try my hardest.
I hope we win today.
I am one who loves football.

I will succeed!
Matt Wilson, Grade 6
Heron Creek Middle School, FL

10 Girl Scout Cookies
10 Girl Scout cookies looking divine
My dad came along now there are nine
9 Girl Scout cookies sitting on a plate
The dog came along now there are eight
8 Girl Scout cookies tasted like heaven
I would know now there are seven
7 Girl Scout cookies were all nicely fixed
They looked delicious now there are six
6 Girl Scout cookies took a milk dive
One's now in my stomach now there are five
5 Girl Scout cookies proud and having glamour
They looked so good now there are four
4 Girl Scout cookies lonely and free
My mom came and ate them now there are three
3 Girl Scout cookies had a booboo
Someone took a bite of them now there are two
2 Girl Scout cookies looking to be finished and done
Now they are and there is only one
1 Girl Scout cookie's not getting eaten and it's being stunned
Now it is gone, and there are none
Andrew Keith, Grade 6
Peachtree Charter Middle School, GA

Moon
The dark sky swallows all of
The small, shining stars twinkling brightly above.
The large, white moon that is a giant mirror,
Keeps on falling nearer and nearer.
Rebecca Skolnick, Grade 6
Pinellas County Jewish Day School, FL

Happiness Is…
Happiness is a twinkling star
that brightens the dark sky
Happiness is an animal
that comforts you when sadness comes
Happiness is a gift
from the person who cares about you
Happiness is a heart
with a warm feeling inside
Happiness is the sun
that lights your path
Happiness is an energy drink
that keeps you alive and vigorous
Happiness is a book
that brings wonder and a fairy tale
Renee Suarez, Grade 5
Dante B Fascell Elementary School, FL

Halloween
Jump scream, it's Halloween,
tick tock, it's 8 o'clock,
we all look fancy-smancy,
now we go get some candy,
tick tock, it's 10 o'clock,
jump scream, it's Halloween,
if you hear me I will groan,
I just don't want to go home
tick tock it's 12 o'clock
I go to bed and rest my head,
now only in my dream,
is it Halloween.
Savannah Plondke, Grade 5
Queen's Grant Community School, NC

Can You Imagine…
A school with no teacher
A church with no preacher

The sky with only one star
No tires on a car

Dogs with no hair
A table with no chair

Everyone's house on fire
Being the biggest liar

Everything made of rocks
Smelling dirty socks

All the pigs red instead of pink
Your house having the worst stink

Always doing math
Never finding a path?
Krystyna Malinowski, Grade 4
William S Talbot Elementary School, FL

Winter
I watch the snowflakes.
They gently drift to the ground
Like a soft blanket.
Caroline Skelton, Grade 5
Bridgeway Christian Academy, GA

Holocaust
Holocaust
Scary, massacre
Killing, gassing, shooting
Depressing, grieved, terrible, terrified
WWII
Kyle Nadler, Grade 5
Summit Hill Elementary School, GA

Nature Haikus
The peach falls faintly
A buzzing wasp flies by fast —
Stops to taste the peach

A gentle, wind blows
Rustling leaves in the peach tree
Light begins to fade

Rain begins to fall
The dirt begins to darken
Animals seek homes

Clouds clear from the sky
The sky becomes a rainbow —
The sun starts to set

Moon is now awake
She calls to her children
Asking them to come

Stars, gleaming brightly
Call to their mother the moon
Telling her they're here

The moon falls asleep
The sun shines and takes its place —
Day is here again.
Katherine Schauer, Grade 6
Bak Middle School of the Arts, FL

Girls and Boys
Girls
Unique, beautiful
Pampering, talking, laughing
Purses, make-up, sports, video games
Playing, eating, joking
Immature, cute
Boys
Janay Nichols, Grade 6
Arlington Middle School, FL

Nature
Nature is a beautiful thing
Swiftly swimming
You watch them go
Quietly, and skillfully
As they dance around you
Tickling you
As you wonder where they are
They silently slip away

Nature is a beautiful thing
Quietly, softly
You hear their song
Gently
You let the music kiss your ears
Almost silently
You hear the soprano voice
Of that one soloist
Singing their song.
Nature is a beautiful thing.
Avery Higgins, Grade 6
St John's Lutheran School, NC

Dance
I feel like I'm in the sky
Never touching the ground.
As I move using my body,
My emotions shine through.
Some people may even think I'm crazy,
"It' only a passion!" I always say.
In my head I know it's not just a passion,
It is my life. It's a dedication also.
There is only one word to describe it,
I call it "DANCE!"
Megan Archbold, Grade 6
Seven Springs Middle School, FL

My Room
This is my room
Clean for the housekeepers
All of my clothes
Are in the heapers
This is my room
The housekeepers in it
They'll be done in a flash
They'll leave in a minute
This is my room
My clothes on the floor
My bed is messed up
I drew on the door
This is my room
The next week is coming
I forgot to clean my room
And the house keepers are humming
That is my room
Sarah Klein, Grade 4
Manatee Elementary School, FL

The Bee

I was riding my bicycle, yellow and bright.
Then a speeding bullet came from my right.

I stopped in sheer fascination.
This is a phenomenon gripping the nation.

Then I saw it, as graceful as a bird,
It was a bee, I am no nerd.

Vidush Mitra, Grade 4
William S Talbot Elementary School, FL

My Life

My life is changing in front of my eyes.
It's full of sin, shame, and lies.
I watch my life transform,
Like watching a butterfly form.

My life is changing in front of my eyes.
My life is sometimes wise.
My life is tied up in knots,
Sometimes we feel like acting like little tots.

My life is changing in front of my eyes.
I might be full of sin, shame, and lies,
I'm also full of love and happiness,
Even though my life is one big mess.

Madison Winters, Grade 5
Sharon Elementary School, NC

Six Minutes

Six minutes.
Six minutes to prove I am the best.
To show how hard I worked for this moment.
Shake hands. Don't look him in the eyes. Wrestle.
Shoot first. Double leg. Takedown.
Two points, red. That's me.
Headhunt.
Less than six minutes. Hold on. Prove it.
Escape. One point, green. That's him.
Duck under. Switch. Prove it.
Throw. Fall. Pin.
Four minutes thirty-five seconds.
This minute
I am the best.

Brandon Marshall, Grade 6
McRae Elementary School, FL

Father

Fast at solving diagnostics
Always taking his time during surgery
Touching his patients and always caring for them
How caring is he.
Even if I don't see him much
Really how great can he be.

Connor Martin, Grade 5
St Thomas More School, NC

Life Is a Book

Life is a book,
every day you have to,
keep adding on. You
never know what's goin' to happen next.
It might be stupid but it's only text.

The book of your life contains many things.
It could be boring it could be interesting.
Or it could be about a bird nesting,
or a fish jumping and splashing.
or a track runner dashing.

Each chapter represents a part in your life.
From childhood on to elderly years,
the chapters capture everything from laughter to tears.
Also they capture your skills,
and always captures your thrills.

The more the chapters the longer the book.
These books always show that you've lived through it all.
They climb up with your rise and go down with your fall,
but in the end you can go back for a look.
That is why life is a book.

Willis Booth, Grade 6
J E Holmes Middle School, NC

Ode to My Sister

Sister oh sister you are so kind
You the best and I love you so much
You are there when I need you
I love riding the golf cart with you
I adore your great smile
You're a great role model and I love that
I love to play with you all the time
You are so funny and athletic
Just hanging out with you makes me happy
I know we fight sometimes but I still love you
You are one of the best in the world
I love you Christina

Michelle O'Brien, Grade 5
Vienna Elementary School, NC

Brother Joe

My brother's name is Joe
He went to a ball and wore a bow
He had to go slow
He got down low
He said, "Whoa!"
Then he said, "NO!"
Then he had to go
When he got home he made dough
Then he got on his boat and started to row
He bought a Wii and became a pro

Chelsey Daniels, Grade 5
Jeff Davis Elementary School, MS

Teenager

Soon I will be a teenager,
And drive my mother mad,
I hope I don't get grounded,
It would really make me sad.

I will try to make good choices,
And be the best that I can be,
Hold on just one second,
My mom is yelling at me!

Clean your room, make your bed,
Do your chores, use your head.
Being a teenager,
I'm starting to dread!

Samantha Matthews, Grade 6
Gold Hill Middle School, SC

So Much Horror

So much horror.
The thought, so violent, so broken.
Not right…
My father gone without a trace,
Without a mark, without a cry
Saying,
no, don't go…we need you.
Tears
Running down our faces,
blood and sweat
running down his.
Drafted into the war,
the sad, wrong, horrid chance
of never coming back.
My heart a small parcel
handed over but dropped
kisses and food to go,
memories to stay.

Journey Avritt, Grade 5
Stone Academy, SC

Spring Time

When the spring time comes,
birds and snakes fly and slither,
red flowers start to bloom
bears awaken from the winter

Samuel Still, Grade 4
PVPV/Rawlings Elementary School, FL

Youth Room

Music blaring from the stereo
Youth singing
Clapping of hands
Rhythm of drumming
Stomping feet
Doors open to go to church

Megan Pearson, Grade 6
Turkey Creek Middle School, FL

Swimming to Freedom

The water is shining,
shining,
shining,
shining.
I can see a shore in front of us. The light is dim.
The moon reflects off the water. Oars make splashes in the water.
I wondered if they were worried,
worried,
worried,
worried.
Wondered if we would get caught.
We sailed away to freedom in a skiff.
skiff,
skiff,
skiff.
I thought about my owner's family, tears dropped from Lindy's eyes.
We could hear massa coming.
coming,
coming,
coming.

Ben Putnam, Grade 4
Pinnacle Elementary School, NC

Light

As I watched day go to darkness, I lay still watching the sun set.
The birds are flying home, and the animals are all quiet. The sun is leaving!
In my heart, I begged it to come back to give everything life and hope.
To bring back its light that gives happiness to everyone.
I was all alone, but I didn't mind because it was just me and my own thoughts.
All I could think about is the sadness that came to me,
Knowing I will ever see anything again…just darkness.
I was giving my life away.
Even though the sun would come back, I couldn't wait.
I feared there would be no tomorrow.
So I thought on my own, having to wait until the sun came back the next day,
Knowing everything would be all right.

Emely Castellon, Grade 6
Freedom Middle School, FL

Books

Books are very fun to read,
They're always there in time of need.
Taking you places far, far away,
Never do they disobey.

Books can come in any size,
Big, tall, or small, they are all very wise.
They always have something to teach,
Whether it is about a person, a place, or even a peach!

So sit down today with an affable book,
If you don't like them, at least take a look.
They are not hurting you or me,
Instead, they are our friends, and will stay like that for an eternity.

Sarika Sachdeva, Grade 6
River Trail Middle School, GA

High Merit Poems – Grades 4, 5, and 6

Friends
Friends are special, important, and kind
They're always there for you standing by your side
Never giving up on you or anyone else
They're kind, nice and amazing

Never leaving you to die alone in the darkness
In heaven they will always be there with you
To protect you and love you worldwide
They will wait for you in heaven for the
Importance of your
Special, loving, and kind sweet friendship

Alexis Vangiller, Grade 5
Brooklet Elementary School, GA

What I Found in My Desk!
A tattered, torn up teddy bear,
A wrinkled old man in a chair,
My chubby, furry orange cat,
A red cockroach that's really fat,
A well-chewed piece of bubble gum,
A Halloween zombie's thumb,
A black and white spotted dog,
A slimy, red-eyed, green tree frog,
And one more thing, I must confess:
A note from teacher: "CLEAN THIS MESS!"

Brian Wiggins, Grade 4
Wellington School, FL
Patterned after "What I Found in My Desk" by Bruce Lansky

Crazy Jackie
One Monday in Illinois
I came home from school
Jackie my dog ran to me like lightning.
She loves me a lot.
I remember the time I got her.
It was at noon when I got her.
She was so cute.
I got to touch her and she licked my hand.
I knew she loved me.
So, I got her.

Erik Egly, Grade 4
Pensacola Beach Elementary School, FL

What Is Black?
Black is as quiet as a mouse.
Black is a shadowy figure in the darkness.
Black looks like a bat spreading out its wings.
Black sounds like shrieks and screams on Halloween night.
Black is a small, dark room.
Black is a piece of coal burning in ashes.
Black is ink soaking through a piece of paper.
Black creeps around in the darkness.
Black sounds as quiet as a mouse in a house of darkness.

Gloria Overman, Grade 4
Tabernacle Elementary School, NC

Making My Bed
Every morning when I awake
It is my bed that I must make

It's wrinkled, messy, and lumpy too
I changed my sheets of purple to blue

I think of putting my old, tattered blanket in the wash
But, then I decide it just needs to be tossed

The comforter must be as straight as a pin
I throw the dirty sheets in the laundry bin

I place my pillows in a neat display
I make the stuffed animals all face the same way

Everything is perfect and in order
So good, I could even bounce a quarter

And even though it is not fun
I surely relieved when the job is done

My mom comes and gives the pillows a fluff
And finally she say, "That's good enough!"

Anna Burbank, Grade 6
St Mary Magdalen Catholic School, FL

The Water Drop and the Clock
Drip, drop, plop!
That's the sound of the water drop.
Tick, tock, tick, tock!
That's the rhythm of the grand old clock.

Keeping perfect time,
Can you hear the chime?
Drip…plop!
The later and later sound of the water drop.

Plop…plop!
I can barely hear the steady water drop.
Tick, tock, tick, tock!
Still keeping perfect time, that grand old clock.

Tick, tock!
That's the last sound of the grand old clock.
…plop!
The final sound of the water drop!

Kelly Crisp, Grade 6
Boiling Springs Intermediate School, SC

Fun
Fun is doing things you like to do
Fun is running around in tennis shoes
Fun is hanging out and watching a show
You're having fun and that's all you know

Connor Ulyatt, Grade 6
Gold Hill Middle School, SC

Ideas in My Head
Ideas in my head
all jumbled about
can't think straight
head starts to hurt
figure things out
mind is clear once again
Harry Carlton, Grade 6
Tequesta Trace Middle School, FL

War
Sometimes, I think back
to the war,
with bombs exploding
all around me like
death was creeping up,
from deep unpleasant slumber.
Many times I hear a bullet
speed by faster than anything.
I'd never had the experience
of my comrades going down
right next to me.
I will never forget
the day I left.
For the first time in three years
I felt happy.
Travis Bell, Grade 6
J Larry Newton School, AL

Reading
R eading is amazing.
E verybody needs to read.
A lways read.
D elightful meanings.
I love to read.
N ever stop reading.
G reat readers equal great grades.
Allyson Baxter, Grade 4
Bostian Elementary School, NC

Friday
Friday is a blue day
The color of the sky
Friday feels like a day of playing games
It sounds like heavy metal
It smells like spring
Friday tastes like cheeseburgers
Friday is the best day of the week
Noel Cervantez, Grade 5
Vienna Elementary School, NC

Fall
yellow and red leaves
they are falling all around
fall is almost here
Adam Smith, Grade 6
Seven Springs Middle School, FL

The Eagle
In the red forest
There's a beautiful eagle
Swooping overhead
William Bollock, Grade 4
PVPV/Rawlings Elementary School, FL

Parents' Love
Parents' love is so strong
you cannot break it,
Not even when you do wrong.
Parents love you too much,
and you are too valuable
to lose the love
of your tender loving parents.
Trevin Mingo-Watts, Grade 5
North Elementary School, SC

Moonlit Day
I wake up to a
blanket of stars
and all I can
see is the
big bright
shining moon
Looking at me
Annie M. Taylor, Grade 5
North Windy Ridge School, NC

The Capybara
While walking
in the most beautiful lush
green Amazon Rainforest I hope
to see a burly dark brown capybara
with coarse fur.
As I walk
over twigs, roots, and plants
I step on bugs' exoskeletons.
Then I find
the heaviest capybara
in the muddy water.
As soon as he sees me
he goes underwater
as quick as the speed of light.
Oh what a sight!
Todd Bosarge, Grade 6
J Larry Newton School, AL

Praise the Lord
I hear church bells ringing,
And the angels singing,
It is the day He rose again,
Some do not believe in Him,
But more people do,
In my eyes He will not be forgotten.
Dustin Marsh, Grade 5
Brooklet Elementary School, GA

Moms
Moms are sweet,
Moms are neat.
Moms are great,
Don't hate them,
Appreciate them.
I love you mom!
Do you?
Jessica Lynn Collier, Grade 5
St Martin Upper Elementary School, MS

Mother
M ost caring person I know
O ne of the people that loves me best
T he best person I know
H er love is better than anyone's
E nergetic person
R esponsible person
Jazmin Henderson, Grade 6
Arnold Magnet Academy, GA

Peace
The great thing is peace
Peace makes you feel lots of love
Peace is so gentle
Cole Curis, Grade 4
St Thomas More School, NC

From a Pup to Dog
Pup
Young, restless
Biting, searching, scratching
Box, chewing toy, dog house, rope
Sleeping, playing, barking
Old, rested
Dog
Juan Duarte, Grade 6
Tequesta Trace Middle School, FL

Gone Forever
Wind on an autumn morning
Blows swiftly through
The crisp morning air.
A gentle touch
Of the sun's bright glare.

Summer fun has been unwound.
Beautiful color
Of orange, yellow and brown.

Heat was lost and cold was found.
So we wait day by day
For another day like this.
The long days like the one I had today.
Those days I will truly miss.
Marialana Kinter, Grade 4
Olde Providence Elementary School, NC

The House of the Witch
Where the witch lives is very old
dirty and dusty and covered in mold
she said that it isn't so bad
but if her mom saw it she would be mad
that house is like that all the time
but the worst part is the green slime.

Madeline Dorcely, Grade 4
Chancellor Charter School At Lantana, FL

Self-Portrait
My head is like the canopy in a tree
That has brown leaves.
My mouth is like a hole for animals to live in.
My arms are the branches.
My legs are like the roots of the tree.
My heart holds happiness that is as yellow
As the sunshine that helps this tree grow.

Maria Van Allen, Grade 4
Indian Harbour Montessori Elementary School, FL

Baby Brother
I miss you so much
I can't wait until we touch
If you're sad, I will make you glad
If you want, I can make you sweet tea
If you're crying, I know how to make you stop
If you're hungry, I can make you a bottle
I can snuggle up with you
Dear brother, I love you

Ja'Quan Perry, Grade 4
Park Ridge Elementary School, FL

The Old Man Who Lived in a Shoe
There once was a man named Stew
Who lived in a very stinky shoe
But he was very lonely
So he left to buy a pony
And the whole time the shoe cried boo, hoo

Jacob Ertzberger, Grade 5
Ranburne Elementary School, AL

Purple
What is purple? Purple is…
A newly bloomed violet in the spring breeze
Grapes freshly picked off a lingering vine.

The purple sunset dripping on the mysterious sea
Grape jelly smeared all over my younger brother's face.

A laced dress eagerly waiting for Easter Day
A plump, juicy plum on a hot summer day.

The beautiful butterfly dashing for the sunflower
The purple lipstick on my face from my aunt's kiss.

Samantha Abbott, Grade 4
Guardian Angels Catholic School, FL

What Is Winter?
Winter is feet crunching in the white snow
Winter tastes like a frozen, vanilla cappuccino
Winter smells like cookies coming out of the oven
Winter is rubbing my hand on a red silk ribbon
Winter sounds like a snowball hitting my pink coat
Winter feels like cold chills on my arms
Winter looks like a sparkly, gold Christmas tree
standing up in the living room
Winter is a pretty present in its box
Winter is like carolers singing
Do you like Winter?

Hollie Newsom, Grade 4
Tabernacle Elementary School, NC

Ode to a Race Track
Race track, oh race track, you are so big
I hear the roaring fans
I also see the blazing fast cars
I can smell the steaming hot dog
The burning hot sun hurting my face
The seats are so hot they burn my bottom off the seats
The gift shop has some great deals on all kind of stuff
I smell the rubber burning up.

Kaleb Clayton, Grade 5
Vienna Elementary School, NC

Books
How many books are there? No one knows,
but some books have cute little shows.

There are many types of books, comics and mysteries
when you go to school, you'll find books about history.

Books are expressions, from authors you see,
they wrote them for you and me to read.

Books are adventures, big or small,
you can find them in Walmart or in the mall.

I love books, they're one of the things I treasure.
How much do I love books? I can't even measure!

Quinisha Butler, Grade 5
West Marion Elementary School, MS

Soccer
Thwack! Goes the ball as I kick it down the field.
It rolls as fast as it can,
Never stopping to take a rest.
As my opponents run effortlessly after the ball,
I sprint toward the goal.
All of a sudden the ball stops.
I line it up with the goal.
Thwack! Swoosh! Goes the ball as I kick it into the net!

Libby Dewey, Grade 6
Gold Hill Middle School, SC

Spring
S winging
P laying
R unning
I n the forests
N eutralizing
G rass
Dalton Parker, Grade 4
East Jones Elementary School, MS

Cake
I dream of cake
Then I start to bake
A wonderful treat
That is oh so sweet.

I shape it and mold it
Then I fold it,
I take it out hot
And put it in a pot.

I spread blue icing on top
I feel like I will never stop
I made such an extravagant cake
That the whole world will want to bake.
Jessi Rae Varnum, Grade 6
Turkey Creek Middle School, FL

My Dad Is Tougher Than Your Dad
My dad is tougher than your dad.
When he gets up,
he eats nails and screws
for breakfast
When he goes to work,
he jumps 50 miles,
He's so strong he could
bench press 1000 pounds
when he was one year old,
When he gets home,
he boils water for his bath,
When he gets out of his bath,
he drinks 50 gallons of
Gatorade to cool down.
My dad is tougher than your dad.
Logan Elmore, Grade 5
Cool Spring Elementary School, NC

Brothers and Sisters
Brothers
Nonintelligent, stinky
Sweating, playing, procrastinating
Gross, sloppy, neat, sweet
Shopping, clothing, playing
Sophisticated, intelligent
Sisters
Lauryn M. Cardwell, Grade 5
Ranburne Elementary School, AL

My Sister Is a Sissy
My sister is a sissy,
She's afraid of bugs and rats
She's afraid of a snake quite hissy
And a friendly welcome mat.
My sister is a sissy,
She's afraid to ride rides
She's afraid of a little kissy
And a little fox hide.
I wish my sister was braver and tougher
So we could play outside
And be rougher.
Loren Jolley, Grade 6
McIntosh County Middle School, GA

The Wedding Cake
Wow look at that wedding cake
So real it's practically fake
Look at the icing
so mushy and sweet
took a bite of it
knocked me right off my feet
I had another piece
and I just realized
I made a huge mistake
I ate the piece
for the husband and wife
I'm very very sorry
that wasn't very nice
The cake was so good
I just kept going and going
and before I knew it
my belly was overflowing
maybe it was their fault
for making a good cake
and maybe next time
I won't make that mistake
Katelyn Catledge, Grade 6
Bak Middle School of the Arts, FL

The Beach
At the beach
Beneath the sun
In the water
On the shore
By my towel.
Mirian Hernandez, Grade 5
Dover Elementary School, FL

Love Life
I wish I wish I went to Paris.
I wish I wish I will get married.
I wish these wishes will come true.
I'm not going to worry
Because they will come through.
Selenia Tarver, Grade 6
Arnold Magnet Academy, GA

The Mighty Lion
While the wind blows
The mighty lion
Shouts out a furious roar
Travis Tillman, Grade 6
Seven Springs Middle School, FL

My Cleats
My cleats, my cleats
My sweaty stinky cleats.
It rained during baseball,
and now they're dirty.
I clean them after every practice,
but it's no use.
They'll never be clean.
They kill my feet
and make them ache.
I wish I had a new pair,
but it's no use,
they'll end up dirty,
just like my brand new cleats.
Jacob Dixon, Grade 5
North Windy Ridge School, NC

Time
On the wall
In the classroom
At school
Above the plug
Next to the TV
With minutes and hours.
Danielle Robbins, Grade 5
Dover Elementary School, FL

Friends Are Money
Friends are money.
Hard to get and easy to throw away.
I need more money is all they say
If you do them wrong, you'll have to pay.
Friends back you up
Money, also, is used in an emergency.
Both worth more than a crystal cup
They are the same in this way, you see.
They are both very precious
And this you will find
Depends on how you treat them
It must be well and with mind.
And if you don't care
Or you aren't always there
You might come across
A great, big tear.
So these are the words
That I think you should heed,
Friends well spent
Are something you need.
Jacob Mullins, Grade 6
J E Holmes Middle School, NC

Body Parts

This poem is about a body part
Could be the nose, lung, or heart
A foot, a finger, ear, or thigh
Spleen, gall bladder, left cheek, or eye
What an amazing array of parts you see
That make up the unique you and me
They all serve a purpose from dusk until dawn
From the smile on your face to what you sit upon
There's no better time to start
To take care of your body parts

Colby Hatten, Grade 5
Ranburne Elementary School, AL

Dylan

D is for drawing because I love to draw
Y is for yelling because I yell a lot
L is for love because I love my family
A is for attitude because I have an "Attitude"
N is for never because I never say never

Dylan Daniel, Grade 5
Ranburne Elementary School, AL

King Fisher

He is an excellent fisherman,
He loves to sit on sticks.
Have you figured out who it is?
I'll give you some hints.
He is handsome in the morning sky,
He is as blue as a light shadow,
He can dive into the water like a torpedo.
The place where I can find my friend
Is near the lake outside my house.
His eyes are like diamonds,
He flies like a plane,
And his feathers are like flowers.
Do you know who it is?
It's a King Fisher.

Jacob Horton, Grade 5
Covenant Classical School, NC

Mountains

There are big mountains.
There are small mountains.
There are hilly mountains.
There are different mountains.
There is a lot of stuff about mountains
That I want to know about.
I don't know about you but I do.
They're fun to climb.
They're fun to jump off.
There's a lot of different things
You could do on the mountains.
So why don't you try to do them all.

J. Boyd, Grade 6
St Francis Xavier Elementary School, MS

Memories

People say "you never know what you have until it's gone."
I never really believed it, until March 7, 2007
My last day in the north
I get on the bus, and sad faces stare,
I try to stay off topic, but it's hard to bear
Lots of tears and lots of hugs,
And always "I will miss you" is what I hear.
I get home boxes high,
they're packing my stuff, but it seems like my memories too.
I pack my things for my trip to Florida.
We're driving.
I know it's going to be long and boring,
But most of all sad
We get to our new house, big and full of boxes too.
I unpack my boxes
My memories aren't there
But in a way it's like a new start,
To make new friends,
And the best out of what God has planned.

Erica Stetzer, Grade 6
Lake Park Baptist School, FL

Birthdays

Birthdays are a fun affair,
Laughter fills the room.
With piñatas and some games,
There will be no gloom!

Cake and ice cream fill us up,
Even maybe pie,
Cheesecake, brownies, name your choice,
Tastes so good you'll cry!

When your date of birth comes up,
Get a little old,
Though one year adds to your age,
You're still as good as gold.

Olivia Miller, Grade 6
Providence Classical School, AL

Broken Heart

My heart is so broken
because everybody hates me
and the girl I like, she hates me too.
My classmates call me names.
I don't want to live anymore
because my heart is broken
and everybody hits on me because I am fat.
I feel like I want to beat them up
but I cannot because I will get a paddling.
Then I will be in even
bigger trouble with my Mom.
If I get into trouble I will
be unable to go to my friend's, Cody.

Donnie Thrift, Grade 5
Rock Mills Jr High School, AL

My Dog

Bandit
He is so frantic
He loves to play and sway
He loves to slip and slide

Bandit
He snoozes and slumbers
Snores and slobbers
Then finally opens his eyes

Nick Sadler, Grade 5
North Windy Ridge School, NC

The Catch

Often, when you're about to make
that perfect catch
everything gets silent.
It's just you and the ball.
Nothing else matters.
Your heart's beating
and your blood's pumping,
then, almost, almost,
the catch is good!

Drew Beeco, Grade 6
J Larry Newton School, AL

Can You Imagine…

A mall without a Claire's
Shoes not in pairs

A hospital without a nurse
A mom without a purse

Summer without fun
The sky without a sun

A restaurant without a cook
Pages without a book

A picnic on a rainy day
Flowers not blooming
in the month of May

A glass of water without a lime
A poem that doesn't rhyme

A fox that isn't sly
A kite that doesn't fly?

Morgan Brown, Grade 4
William S Talbot Elementary School, FL

Butterfly

Little butterfly
Floating in the singing breeze
Can you hear it all

Trey Kemp, Grade 5
Winona Elementary School, MS

Grandma Jan

Grandma Jan likes everything I do.
Grandma Jan loves to shop and her style is so fantastic
Grandma Jan adores puppies like I do
Grandma Jan makes the most delectable cookies
and the smell of them leads me to her warm heart and smile
Grandma Jan loves to play and party
She is a rock star
Grandma Jan always does I Spy books with me
Grandma Jan loves to do puzzles and brain teasers
and she figures them out as fast as a lion running
Grandma Jan gives me the perfect presents
Grandma Jan gives all the cool new hip stuff that I enjoy
Grandma Jan's passion is to spoil me and her dog
Grandma Jan always has her hair as perfect as a fluffy, white cloud
Grandma Jan is fond of reading magazines
The magazines she picks are on the latest fashions
Grandma Jan is always in the best mood
I have never seen her unhappy or cranky
Grandma Jan has so much in common with me
Grandma Jan is the finest person and is so full of energy

Sarah Fishel, Grade 6
Unity School, FL

Lost and Alone

The glistening emerald leaves hide me
From the agonizing heat rays
Coming from the burning sun

It's ruby trunk providing a place
For me to lean against

My weak frail legs lying on
The velvet green grass

Hours pass by
The blazing sun sets in the East
I feel an icy wind run down my spine
I see the owls come out and the blue jays go in
Then the street lights flicker on, exposing danger lurking in the dark

A twig being crunched by small feet
Breaks the silence of the night
Turns out, it was just a squirrel scurrying about
I see it trying to make its way in the world
Lost and alone…just like me

Riisa Hossein, Grade 6
Freedom Middle School, FL

Fire

Burning fire
Sparks shooting from the burning flames
Screaming people watching what they love burn down
The heat, the pain, the tears that fall, praying to God to let them live
The flames that kill

Tricia Garmager, Grade 5
The Sanibel School, FL

Contents of My Heart

Hat is black,
It is the monster lurking around the corner.

Anger is red,
It explodes out of you even when you try to stay calm.

Sorrow is blue,
It burns your heart and tears it in two.

Stress is yellow
It nags on you, and fills you with anxiety.

God is in heaven
He watches over us and takes away all these feelings.

Jesus is His Son
He is our Savior who died for us.

I am merely a boy 12 years of age still growing
My heart contains hate, anger, sorrow, stress, God, and Jesus.

Kayel Quinones, Grade 6
Tarpon Springs Middle School, FL

The Dream

I was drifting through the clouds like a bird,
The wind in my hair, the feel of the clouds on my skin.
The texture of the clouds was indescribable,
No word would fit the feel.

And then there was the freedom,
The uncontained blue sky,
I felt as free as an eagle,
For the sky never seemed to end.

As I looked down upon the land below,
I spotted tropical trees swaying in the breeze,
They seemed as if they were trying to communicate with me,
Beep! Beep! Beep!
Then it was time to return to reality.

Dara Craig, Grade 5
The Sanibel School, FL

My Life

Jared
Charming, strong, red-necky, athletic
Sibling of Jessika
Friend of Trevor
Who feels hyper and wacky
Who needs money
Who gives charity
Who fears barking squirrels
Who would like to see Heaven (but not now)
Resident of Ranburne
Brown

Jared Brown, Grade 5
Ranburne Elementary School, AL

The Old Witch's House

When you walk in the door,
you'll fall to the floor.
The floor has some dust,
that might make you bust.
Around the house,
scampered her pet mouse.
Her house was made out of stone,
and she had her own little throne.
Inside her house was all black,
to me it looked like a shack.
In her poor little room,
she had a big broom.
The big broom swept up some mice,
for a very small price.
Surrounding her house are some big trees,
that always makes her fall to her knees.

Alyssa Neill, Grade 4
Chancellor Charter School At Lantana, FL

I Am

I am Caleb and a good athlete.
I wonder why I get hungry so easily.
I hear chanting in my head.
I see me playing sports.
I want to be a champion in a sport.
I am Caleb and a good athlete.

I pretend I am a professional sports player.
I feel a famous basketball player shaking my hand.
I touch a shark.
I worry that I will lose too much in life.
I cry sometimes when I lose.
I am Caleb and a good athlete.

I understand that you can't win everything.
I say never give up.
I dream to play a professional sport when I grow up.
I try my hardest in everything I do.
I hope to do well in school and sports.
I am Caleb and a good athlete.

Caleb Sides, Grade 5
Stokesdale Elementary School, NC

Bastogne

Bullets flying in the air
No one even cared
Even if their buddy fell
For nothing went well.

Roads were what made Bastogne important
Germans charging like ants
Fighting occurred even till dawn
Ending after Germans were gone.

David Oldfather, Grade 6
Providence Classical School, AL

Nature

I sit outside on the grass.
I look and just observe, nothing else, just observe.
Nothing can stop this thing from happening.
It's nature
I suddenly turn my head to the right to spy a tree.
It's bare, I say quietly to myself.
It's just sitting there, no purpose at all, just there.
Then my focus shifts,
To the cool breeze that runs across my face.
I also notice that the sun is baking down on me like I am a cookie in the oven.
All of a sudden I feel something crawling on my leg.
As I look down, I see a tiny ant, so helpless.
What should I do? I say to myself.
So after a few seconds of thinking I decide to pick up the leaf that lay there on the ground just as dead as the tree.
I carefully but quickly pick up the leaf and scoop the feller up.
I watch the ant move about as the wind blows from side to side such a struggle for him.
I also hear a bee buzzing ever so slightly that I can hardly hear it.
As I start to get up to the sound of my mother's voice calling for dinner.
I wonder will it ever be the same.

Samantha Stilphen, Grade 5
Southern Pines Elementary School, NC

War

War, we go and fight for freedom
Moments of silence the names and ages as you read them
They go in they come out
Knowing what they're fighting for
Heads held high they march the streets
They are and will be ready to beat the war.

It gets tough and rough as it goes on
But in the end when we've won and we'll sing a victory song
The losses are great and feel like a weight on your shoulders
And your heart is fragile with pain
But as the buses pull in
And the soldiers begin to pour out like falling rain
You can't help but say thank you for bringing them home.

But where they've been they wouldn't go back again and no one would want to venture.
Guns going off "BANG," the screams of pain
The screeching of breaks and your heart beating in your throat
Running, running with all your might to get safe, to catch your breath for a moment
War is not a war of words
But a war of weapons and fighting
The war is a time bomb waiting to go off to blow up, to end the fighting.

Victoria Tronzo, Grade 6
Williston Middle School, NC

Reading and Writing

There is Scooby Doo, Nancy Drew, Dr. Seuss, but even if it's just Mother Goose…pick it up and give it a try. Now let me tell you why. Reading might be scary. There might just be a fairy, but one thing that comes to mind is the way it makes you feel every time. Whether it is happy, sad, brave, or afraid…reading can take your mind on an adventure to far off lands where dragons fly high in the sky and pirates sail the seven seas. So, whether it is a mystery, comedy, or even romance, pick it up and read. You can succeed with reading and writing.

Allyson Safrit, Grade 5
Bostian Elementary School, NC

High Merit Poems – Grades 4, 5, and 6

Between Past and Present
Arched, mossy, worn
Pillars of ancient times stand
Connecting old and modern

Fading, crumbling walls
Large tree peaks over the side
Archway to new places

Street lamps, streets
Cars parked on the new paved road
Signs leading the way

Cobblestone joins street
Crosswalk to an old archway
Up and down the steps

Pink flowers blooming
Green leaves growing on tree
Winter sleeps, spring wakes

Light, medium brown
White, beige, green, black, gray, red, pink
Colors define it

To everyone it's clear,
Archways are between past and present.
Anna Brosius, Grade 6
Woodward Academy North, GA

Love
Love
Passion, devotion
Tenderness, romantic, pleasure
Affection, attraction, attachment, delicately
Heart
Breyanna Thomas, Grade 6
Arnold Magnet Academy, GA

Mother's Day
There is someone who loves me, she is my mom
She towers over me like a big palm.
She is very calm
She is the bomb.

She loves me
She has a tissue when I sneeze
She takes me inside when she sees bees
She has a Band-Aid when I cut my knees.

She always has good news
She never ever has booze
She gives me a blanket when I snooze
She picks me up when I have the blues.
Brendan Bender, Grade 6
Turkey Creek Middle School, FL

Fletcher Allen White
Funny
Accurate
Sharp
Wishes to travel around the world
Dreams of far off galaxies
Wishes to earn as many archery trophies as his father
Who wonders what the future will be like
Who fears clowns
Who is afraid of not having friends
Who likes bacon
Who believes God is the answer
Who loves his family
Who loves fried catfish
Who loves baseball
Who plans to have a successful life
Who plans to follow his father's footsteps
Who plans to kill a big buck
This is what I am like.
Fletcher Allen White, Grade 5
Winona Elementary School, MS

Forever
I didn't think you would leave;
I can't believe you would dessert what we had!
You made me feel so sad;
You left me all alone.
I think I have shed all these tears of mine;
I wonder if you still think of me?!
The way that is was; the way it used to be.
I want you back in my arms!
No more surprises; no more alarms!
I want you to stay with me!
Why can't you just see
How perfect we are together
Forever!
Sarah Pennington, Grade 6
Scotts Creek Elementary School, NC

Baton Twirling
As I twirl,
Watch me whirl,
Spinning around,
I touch the ground,
Kicking high,
Look I can touch the sky,
I feel like I can fly,
In the sun,
I have my fun,
Now I'm almost done,
When I toss,
I have no loss,
You may clap,
For I am done,
Wasn't this fun!
Jessica Naylor, Grade 4
FSU/City of Pembroke Pines Charter Elementary School, FL

Rocks
A metamorphic rock,
Is strange to me,
It changes its form,
Through squeezing and heating!

Metamorphic rocks,
Have changed with time,
Marble and Gneiss,
Are a pretty gray kind!
Arabia Walker, Grade 4
Frank L Stanton Elementary School, GA

Waterfall
Crisp water flowing
The waterfall now falling
Crashing like a wave
Lindsay Anderson, Grade 5
Duncan Chapel Elementary School, SC

Can You Imagine…
Trees with no leaves
A hive without bees

A school with no kids
Math without grids

A party with no cake
A shed without a rake

Tests without answers
Hospitals without cancers

Pens with no ink
Vending machines with no drink

Computers without wires
Cars with no tires

No stripes on a flag
A trash can without a bag?
Dylan Maillart, Grade 4
William S Talbot Elementary School, FL

Friendship
Friendship is like two magnets.
They're hard to pull apart.

The magic in friendship is so powerful
it's like walking on water.

Once you fight, you sink,
but then you reunite and dive together
and find a valuable thing.
The jewel called friendship.
Kendall Rocco, Grade 4
Spruce Creek Elementary School, FL

Gentle Giant
Gentle giant of the deep
Dancing with a sail
Expressing peaceful harmony
By waving his prodigious tail

Leaping ever joyfully
A care not in this world
As he calls to the seven seas
The water he impearls

He must travel far up north
Many miles to go
Every mile he spreads the peace
By being more aglow

The water pulls him in and out
Like a heart that pumps inside
Very eager to reach his home
Sailing with the tide
Seidy Cabrera, Grade 5
Oliver Hoover Elementary School, FL

The Beach
The sun is so bright
I love to play in the sand
It is very warm
Skim boarding is fun to do
I love to go to the beach
Terrence Regan, Grade 4
St James Episcopal School, FL

Black
Black is dark
Black is when the clock stuck 12
Black is pure void
Black is nothingness
Black smells like rubber on a car's tires
Black tastes like licorice
Black sounds of whispers
Black looks like the night sky
Black feels like piles of dust
Black makes me feel secretive
Black is darkness
Joseph Chang, Grade 4
Olde Providence Elementary School, NC

Safety
I am traveling near and far
Going from place to place
Looking up at gigantic things
Feeling so small
Just barely missing a size 8 1/2 shoe
I made it to the ant hill safe and sound
Safe to sleep in a cozy warm bed
Amber Whitaker, Grade 6
Challenger Middle School, FL

As I Looked into Thick Darkness
As I looked into thick darkness
goose bumps ran down my legs
I felt happiness knowing we're almost
to freedom,
freedom,
freedom.
I wonder if the slave catcher will find us?
I muttered as I gently fell
asleep,
asleep,
asleep.
Timmy Eazor, Grade 4
Pinnacle Elementary School, NC

A Fairy Named Mary
There was a girl named Mary
Who looked like a fairy
Her hair was like silk
She like to drink milk
Whenever she made a mess
She needed new dress
Whenever her family wanted brunch
She always said, "No, lunch."
Then she pulled her hair
And said it's not fair
Tatiana Patton, Grade 5
Jeff Davis Elementary School, MS

My Guitar
I like to play guitar.
I want to be a star.
I like the music it makes.
It takes away heartaches.
It will take me far.
Jonathon Nugent, Grade 4
The ELLES School, FL

Rainbow Heart
My heart is a rainbow.
Filled with love,
all different colors of love,
like a crystal in the morning sun
it turns rainbow.
I hold my family close
and friends closer.
I wish I could be a better person
when things get bad.
Animals are my hideaway
when times get hard.
My heart is rainbow with love,
when I am sad my heart is blue,
when I am mad my heart is red,
but when I am surrounded by love
my heart shines the brightest of all.
Olivia Adams, Grade 5
Summit Hill Elementary School, GA

High Merit Poems – Grades 4, 5, and 6

The First Day of Autumn
Cocoa brown, firecracker red,
and jack-o'-lantern orange float through the sky.
"Crickle, crackle" leaves crunch under my feet.
I hear birds crying for spring to come back.
Look, I see a little deer prancing in the dead grass.
I feel like a stallion wanting to wander far away,
and I see bugs trying to climb the tallest tree!
It is as if the sun is ice cream
dripping all over the trees, "Drip, drip."
Then, a blizzard of leaves in the crisp wind
follows me home.
Logan White, Grade 4
Bridgeway Christian Academy, GA

With the Sun
With the sun is day and
With the moon is night.
Although they fight for time,
They will do their jobs as light and night.
They will cover the sky,
With their power of light and night.
Although moon is little and sun is big,
They have the same power for light and night.
Sun and moon are like us, we agree, we have jobs,
And we are always hurrying everywhere.
So next time you see the sun and moon,
Remember all of the people that help you.
Gian Boria, Grade 5
Eugenia B Thomas Elementary School, FL

Sleepover
It's fun to have sleepovers with friends,
We like to tell each other the new fashion trends.
We do each other's makeup,
And in the morning we don't want to wake up.
Then we're miserable when it ends.
Lauren Schafer, Grade 6
Seven Springs Middle School, FL

The Sun
The sun is so good.
I say it is a round thing
blazing very bright.
Collin Davis, Grade 4
Camden Elementary School of the Creative Arts, SC

Love
Love looks like a heart hugging the earth,
Love feels like a brand new rose,
Love smells like sweet suspense,
Love tastes like some chocolates,
Love sounds like a bird singing,
Love sings a romantic song with the bottom of her lungs,
Love dances to where she wants to go.
Krystal Jaimes, Grade 4
Tabernacle Elementary School, NC

I Do Not Understand
I do not understand
Why there's never good things on the news,
Why people see a cup half empty,
Or why there are people in this world
Who hurt innocent citizens.
But most of all I do not understand
Why the world's history was so cruel.
I do understand why we need to learn morals.
Amanda Santos, Grade 5
Oliver Hoover Elementary School, FL

Spring Flowers
I see fields of beautiful flowers.
I hear the wind rustle through the fields of flowers.
I feel the fluffy daisies near my feet.
I smell the sweet scent from the colorful flowers.
I touch the sensational fields of flowers with my hand.

Fields of beautiful flowers,
The wind rustles through the fields of flowers.
The fluffy daisies near my feet,
The sweet scent from the colorful flowers.
And touch the sensational fields of flowers with my hand.
Deepti Singam, Grade 4
Central Park Elementary School, FL

Blending into One
Diversity
What does it mean to me?
It means blending together the suburbs and the streets
Making one beat
Putting different cultures together
Making them mash
Different personalities, different backgrounds, and past
Taking something from here and there
Making it new
Diversity
What does it mean to me?
It means blending the suburbs and the streets
People from different places
With different faces making it something new
That's what diversity means to me
Taking different cultures
Blending them
And making them a version two.
Khayla Williams, Grade 6
Hand Middle School, SC

Loud
Rock and roll,
Smashing a guitar,
Turning up the volume,
And me, playing in the band.
Andre Fornes-Neuharth, Grade 4
Indian Harbour Montessori Elementary School, FL

Friendship

Friendship is pink
It smells like warm cookies
It tastes like chocolate
It sounds like laughter
It feels as soft as puppies' fur
  Friendship!

Shawna Dolzonek, Grade 6
Tarpon Springs Middle School, FL

Valentine's Day

Today is Valentine's Day
O' how I love so much
Everyone is ready for the kisses and hugs
that await them from their loved ones
Some might get a box of chocolates
or a beautiful red rose
O' how lovely Valentine's Day is
I can't wait for next year.

Zoah MacFarland, Grade 5
Trinity Lutheran School, FL

Colors Everywhere

Red chili makes my mouth burn.
Grey cement is what I see when I turn.

Lavender flowers drive me crazy.
White walls make me lazy.

Black paint is on my face.
Purple is the color of my lace.

Blue flows in the peaceful lake.
Brown is the color of a yummy cake.

Yellow is the color of a duck.
Green is the color for good luck.

Veronika Fernandez, Grade 6
Tequesta Trace Middle School, FL

Spring

S pringtime
P lay with friends
R oses are blooming
I ce cream parties
N ice animals
G reen all around

Andrew McDade, Grade 4
East Jones Elementary School, MS

Midnight

Funny
Watching birds
Loud, furry, loving
Midnight

Stephen K. Ward, Grade 5
Morgan Elementary School, NC

About Me

My hair is like the shiny silk dress my mother once wore.
My hair is the golden sun on the horizon.
My hair dances in the cool summer breeze.

My thoughts are like the sharp laws of science.
My thoughts are books of the mental library that pack themselves in the shelves.
My thoughts journey to new things like explorers that roam new lands.

My courage is like the mighty lion, strong, fearsome, and brave
My courage is the roaring storm pluming across the ocean
My courage will never crumble; it is a stone mountain towering over the rest.

Samantha Hentz, Grade 4
Queen of Angels Catholic School, GA

The Ballerina

She does her performances day and night.
When she dances she is in the spotlight.
As she dances her arms move so elegantly.
She then does a flawless quadruple pirouette.

She also plays the lovely clarinet.
She smiles like an elegant angel.
Her movements are full of grace.
The overwhelmed audience watches the angel and her perfect face.

Her cheeks were as red as roses.
Her costume was as white as snow.
She always gave a spectacular show.
As she curtsies, the audience applauds as loud as thunder.
Her name is Lena and she is a very talented ballerina.

Lena Ho, Grade 6
Freedom Middle School, FL

Utah Beach

Men run upon my shores.
Back when the water was red and the skies were filled with screams.
On my dunes and on my shores for power, money, freedom and much more.

James Foster, Grade 6
C E Williams Middle School, SC

Cleaning My Room

I do not know what is in my room, I better pick up a bristly old broom.
There might be disgusting brown mold. For all I know we might be doomed.
Old and ripped up clothes are on the floor, I guess I had better clean them up.
Ratty old toys are on the floor, I had better pick those up at the store.
My shiny blue iPod is missing. I could have sworn I left it here.
My rooms is a mess. Oh dear!
Disgusting, slimy bugs might be on the floor. I can't even walk to open the door!
In the end, I must be working hard. My room now is cleaned!
I am so happy my clothes are cleaned up!
The bugs all died. The toys are put away.
I am finally up ride! I guess God is on my side.
See, it all worked out in the end.
My room is now cleaned and this poem now ends.

Amanda Berg, Grade 6
St Mary Magdalen Catholic School, FL

Movies

My family is a movie:
My dad is the script,
meant to be followed
and not be the follower.
My mom is the producer,
making sure that everyone follows the script
and keeps everything in line.
Copper, my puppy, is the film,
he is funny, he is sad, he is romantic
and he is happy.
I am the screen,
on which the film is played.
I am used throughout the whole world
and without the screen
the film would never be shown.
The screen would be nothing
without the film, the script, and the producer.

Susanna Belt, Grade 5
FSU/City of Pembroke Pines Charter Elementary School, FL

Stephanie

Athletic, responsible, fair, and loving,
Daughter of Alvaro and Sonia.
Lover of soccer, milk chocolate, and dogs
Who feels happiness when playing with dogs, glad
When Carolina wins, and joy when getting good grades.
Who needs love, privacy, and fresh air.
Who gives hugs, love, and kisses.
Who fears lions, stingrays, and sharks.
Who would like to see no homework,
no tests, and no more diseases.
Residential of Four Oaks,
Luna

Stephanie Luna, Grade 5
Four Oaks Elementary School, NC

DyneQua Davis

I'm kind to people.
I think I'm smart.
I'm 10 years old
Wishes to be a millionaire.
Dream to be a singer.
Wants to be a teacher like Mrs. DeNoon and Mrs. Dees
Wonders will I achieve.
I'm really afraid of dogs.
My baby brother is scared of loud things.
I like to sing.
I believe I can do anything I put my mind to.
I love my Mom, Dad, baby brother, Auntie, and Grandparents.
I plan on moving when I'm 18 to 20.
I am also planning on moving to Tennessee.
I'm also planning on having a two story house.
Last but not least, I hope to have at least a little money.

DyneQua Davis, Grade 5
Winona Elementary School, MS

My Wonderful World*

If I were in charge of the world,
I'd make summer vacation longer.

If I were in charge of the world,
I'd elect a proper president.

If I were in charge of the world,
I'd allow children to eat ice cream like pigs.

If I were in charge of the world,
I'd stop world hunger.

If I were in charge of the world,
I'd make a room full of popcorn. Pop!

If I were in charge of the world,
I'd make more churches.

If I were in charge of the world,
I'd stop drug dealing everywhere.

If I were in charge of the world,
I'd end this poem right now.

Matthew Hallman, Grade 4
Irmo Elementary School, SC
*Inspired by Judith Viorst

Jogging in the Night

Jogging in the night, running downtown,
the full moon in the sky, birds chirping in the trees,
cars flying by, crowds at the concert,
lights turning off, feel the ocean breeze,
Jogging in the night

John Farese, Grade 6
Shorecrest Preparatory School, FL

What Is Poetry

What is poetry
Poetry is the people,
The whole nation
Of people,
It's just every day,
While the kids play outside,
All their little games they don't have the same,
To them it's just easy to imagine
And let all their dreams out,
Make me want to scream
out all my pain,
it's just a shame
but I have no one to blame,
for my mistakes,
I take it and I learn,
Then I go on with my life without living with fear,
I live life with care

Donneisha Smith, Grade 6
Varsity Lakes Middle School, FL

Why I Love My Mom
I love my mom
She is nice and sweet
And very, very neat
She's there through the thick and thin
She is there to the end.
If I am lost,
And do not know where to go
She will lead me down the right road.
That is why I love my mom!
Sabeth Hunt, Grade 6
Saint Pauls Middle School, NC

Her
Sitting at my desk
five minutes till the bell
afraid of going home
to whatever might happen

getting off the bus
walking into a door of fear
expecting the unexpected
of what she might do

dinner in silence
a glare in the eye
no love for me
just want to cry

going to bed that night
I didn't know it would be my last
now I live in a better place
with her out of my fear
Connor Callais, Grade 6
Chapin Middle School, SC

Easter Bunny
Easter Bunny
cuddly, furry
hopping, eating, sleeping
Hop, hop, hop away
Peter Cottontail
Taylor Jurgrau, Grade 4
Central Park Elementary School, FL

Serenity
You gave me wings,
You made me soar.
Through your heart I
fly once more.

Secret strength,
Inside of me,
Is based on you —
serenity
Shannon Cherney, Grade 6
North Myrtle Beach Middle School, SC

Springtime
S ummer's not far away
P ut on your rain coats
R ain rain go away
I ce has melted away
N o place like the outdoors
G reat weather
T ime to wear shorts again
I 'm going to go outside
M any places to go in good weather
E venings have more daylight
John Haymond Turley, Grade 5
Queen's Grant Community School, NC

Easter Bunny
Funny, furry
Hopping, running, munching
At the top of the pile
Peter Cottontail
Adam Koppel, Grade 4
Central Park Elementary School, FL

Raindrops on My Tiny Window
Gloomy, moist, nothing to do,
the clouds hang over the little town
like a warm cozy blanket.
Tick-tock the sound of the old clock
made a pattern of ticks and tocks
in the old rugged room.
Thunder crashed and
lightning glowed and flashed
in the dark gloomy night.
I sit there alone and bored
like a guitar that hasn't
been played in a million years.
Again I sit there bored and nothing to do
on this boring gloomy and tiring day.
Maya Shuler, Grade 4
St Thomas More School, NC

Life
Life is tough.
Life is long.
Life seems never ending,
But we all soon will know,
That life is shorter than it seems.
So live life good,
For soon you will see
Life is fading away.
Live your own life for no one
Can replace it.
It is yours to live and create.
Be good to yourself and
Others, for if you do your
Life will be happy forever.
Allison Daneault, Grade 5
Our Lady of Fatima School, MS

Darkness
Though I pray at night
My weary soul still weeps with pain
So I roll over on my side
And try to dream of peace and happiness
But all I get is grief and sadness
Savannah Rose Holshouser, Grade 5
Morgan Elementary School, NC

Peace
Peace is a thing that everyone needs
Peace is loving, it does good deeds
Peace is showing, peace is knowing
Peace brings peace to everything
Katy McNamara, Grade 4
St Thomas More School, NC

The Storm
The storm is a lion,
Lashing and slashing,
At anything in the way.
Come as it may or waiting at bay,
Now it is here bashing away.

Pelting rain on the windowpane,
The storm is making gain.
Vicious and violent,
Tearing and tyrant,
Through the hills and plains.

Lightning flashing,
And thunder crashing,
As if in a battlefield.
It continues through the day.
The giant storm is here to stay.

As the battle ends,
The lion's hunger thins.
The wind subsides,
And the lion hides,
Back in his den.
Tyler Flint, Grade 6
J E Holmes Middle School, NC

Marine Life
Awesome aquarium
Fish, dolphins, and sea turtles
Scuba divers and sharks
All swimming together
In a great big school
Super shows
Orcas, seals and penguins
Trainers and treats
All jumping together
Getting the crowd wet.
Nico Sepulveda, Grade 6
Tequesta Trace Middle School, FL

My Flower School
Can you imagine a huge garden?
Made of different kinds of flowers
like jasmine, roses, lilies and sunflowers,
when I think of that, I remember my school
full of unique flowers that represent each of us,
each with our own personalities and bright colors,
when I think of that I am proud to grow in my flower school.
Maria Bozo, Grade 4
FSU/City of Pembroke Pines Charter Elementary School, FL

Sisters
S weet as blueberry pie,
I ncredibly cute to me and my friends,
S poiled rotten,
T hinking they're funny,
E ven though they're whiney,
R emember you are the one they look up to,
S ometimes completely annoying.
Brittany Parker, Grade 6
Arnold Magnet Academy, GA

The Wolf Pack
I'm a warm blooded mammal.
The pack I live in is territorial.
In my pack I'm the alpha.
I'm above beta and omega.
Our large teeth help us as a predator.
We usually make our catch but sometimes we are failure.
We see a gun made for me.
The pack runs into the dens.
Cyrique McClellan, Grade 5
Hall Fletcher Elementary School, NC

Allie
Allie
Pretty
Loving
Imaginative
Wishes to be a teacher
Dreams of being famous
Wants to get a good education
Who wonders what a Liger is
Who fears spiders
Who is afraid of heights
Who likes dancing
Who believes everyone is equal
Who loves singing
Who loves babysitting
Who loves her family
Who loves to swim
Who plans to be wealthy
Who plans to have children
Who plans to pass 5th grade
Who is thankful to God for all His blessings
Allie Wilson, Grade 5
Winona Elementary School, MS

Students
Students students working hard
to make their grades go up.
Students students doing a test
to make their teachers happy!
Students students eating to get their energy.
Paul Pham, Grade 5
Queen's Grant Community School, NC

Cats
Cats are really very cool,
But they may not like the swimming pool!
If you have a nasty rat,
You should call the trusty cat!
They can be fat,
Or wear a hat.
They don't have flaws,
But be careful of their claws!
They have soft-colored fur,
A cat is right for a him or her.
Kaley Tolbert, Grade 5
Poinciana Elementary School, FL

Black
Black is the night of the new moon
Black is the death and decay
Black is the darkness of the devil's heart
Black is the shadows of the night
Black will squeeze you like an anaconda tightening its grip
Black is the color of evil
Black is my friend
Julie Olson, Grade 6
Westview Middle School, SC

Weak White
White is weak.
Not bold like the other colors.
She always seems to need help.
She likes to speak Spanish, she calls red rojo.

Vanilla sundaes are her favorite.
She loves puppies.
And in the wintertime she has snowball fights too.

You couldn't pay her a million dollars to eat tofu.
The same things with sour cream.
She likes sheep.
And she really wants a poodle named Noodle.

She has a ship named La Blanco
For some reason she is always using a Kleenex
Her favorite candy is big fluffy marshmallows.
And she loves watching clouds go by.
Her house is white too.
Julianna Wall, Grade 4
Youngsville Elementary School, NC

Games

Eyes widen
Thumb twitches
People laugh
People cry
People lose
People win
Hands pressing
TV is on
One word
Game over!

Richard Hoeun, Grade 6
Arlington Middle School, FL

I Am

I am smart and independent.
I wonder about the world.
I hear teachers talking.
I see Tia Byrd.
I want a cell phone.
I am smart and independent.

I pretend to be a singer.
I feel lots of emotions in my body.
I touch my mechanical pencil.
I worry about my granddaddy.
I cry for my grandma.
I am smart and independent.

I understand people's problems.
I say people who believe can achieve.
I dream about fun stuff and parties.
I try to make good grades.
I hope to be on *American Idol*.
I am smart and independent.

Taliah Taylor, Grade 6
North Myrtle Beach Middle School, SC

The Waves

They're powerful
Drumming against the shore
Their scent makes me feel excited
Blue tides

Christianna Messinger, Grade 5
The Sanibel School, FL

A Long Flight

Sometimes, when we're on a long flight
and we've played cards and talked,
we usually have one layover
when we have to run for the next flight.
Then we board again and watch a movie
and listen to music
until we finally land
and we're at our destination.

Foster Hemphill, Grade 6
J Larry Newton School, AL

Dreaming

Dreaming is a world full of life, mysteries, fun and beautiful things
It doesn't matter whether you're asleep or awake,
You're escaping from the outside world,
You're going into your imagination
Secrets and memories.

Alisha Patel, Grade 6
St John's Lutheran School, NC

Just One Last Time

Have you ever had a sad moment that has occurred in your family?
My grandfather was part of one in my family,
It all started out on a sunny day on 9/11/02 when I
Was at my friend Paul's birthday party.
And my dad came and picked me up
Because when I stared at a clover,
I knew the party was over.
When I got into the car nothing seemed right
I asked my dad what was wrong and he whispered
"Your grandfather had died today because he woke up,
Hit his head on the nightstand, and never woke up."
I myself personally thought it was a joke,
But when I saw my grandmother, I began to choke.
All the way home everyone mourned
But, when we got home I took my anger and sadness out on a tree,
And my dad asked why I was so mad, and I said because,
I did not get to tell him I love him
"Just one last time."

Robby Barr, Grade 6
Lake Park Baptist School, FL

I Fight for My Country

If I don't come back from this war,
I will still be a part of my wife and kids' minds and hearts.
I want to be myself, so I am going to show them what I am made of.
I will fight through every trap and every soldier I come up against.
I will come out alive from this war.
I will show them what I am made of.
I fight for my country.

I am down to one last breath, but I tell myself I can do it,
So I fight and fight until I win.
So, I fight for my country, for you,
So I can come home to you.
I can do anything I want to,
But I just fight for my country.
Yea!

Jacob T., Grade 5
Grandfather Academy, NC

The Biggest Snowball

The biggest snowball I ever did see was done by me,
It squished and squashed as it rolled along and it pished and poshed as it came along,
It went up high, way taller than me and was as wide as a million peas,
Now it rolled along just like I said and then it ran down a hill toward town.

Blake Johnson, Grade 4
St Thomas More School, NC

My Deepest Fear
Expectations hover over you
Like a deep dark cloud
If you live up to them
You'll surely be proud

But if you don't
You're a loser a failure a clown
You're surely to be frowned upon
for not going up
but heading down

My deepest fear is not of
monsters, aliens or any other scary stuff
but of myself
not being good enough
Francesca Levy, Grade 6
City of Pembroke Pines Charter Central Middle School, FL

I Am
I am a child.
I wonder about my future.
I hear children are cool.
I want to see love in the world.
I am a child.

I pretend things do not bother me.
I feel good when things go well.
I touch my Bible and,
I worry about people around the world.
I pray for those who are hurt.
I am a child.

I understand life is sometimes hard.
I say I will try my best.
I dream of peaceful life for everyone.
I try to make life better for everyone.
I hope things will always go well.
Elizabeth Humphries, Grade 6
Boiling Springs Intermediate School, SC

The Ugly Witch
I met a witch
that fell in a ditch.
She loves chocolate candy
and her brother's name is Andy.
Her name is Vicky
and she's always picky.
Her fingernails are hot pink
and she always gives you a wink.
She likes flying her broom
in a zoom.
She likes to smell daisy's
but she's always lazy.
Djwaidah Dieudonne, Grade 4
Chancellor Charter School At Lantana, FL

Wild and Free
Horses, horses running wild and free,
What would happen if they see me?

Mane and tail whipping, streaming, flying.
They just keep on trying,

Trying to outrun each other.
Having a race with their brother.

Colt, stallion, mare, and filly,
All together acting silly.

Majestic creatures,
With amazing features.

Horses, horses running wild and free,
Free, free they will always be.
Brittany Bivins, Grade 6
Gold Hill Middle School, SC

My Ice Cream Cone
My Ice cream cone is a giant snow hill.
I would rather eat it than any other meal.
It is as white as a cloud and as sweet as my mother.
Every time I eat one I want another.
My ice cream cone is like a snowball.
I can't get enough of it at all.
Julie King, Grade 5
CrossPointe Christian Academy, GA

Colors of the World
White is a symbol of love,
Gray are the feathers of a dove.

Green are the leaves on a tree in spring,
Blue is the sky that makes me want to sing.

Orange is like the skin of a sweet potato,
Red is like a fresh picked tomato.

Pink is like a little bunny's nose,
Yellow is the sun as it rose.

Black is the sky on a rainy day,
Purple are the flowers that bloom in May.
Angeli Marinace, Grade 6
Tequesta Trace Middle School, FL

Red
Red looks like a stripe on the American flag.
Red sounds like the popping and crackling fire in the fireplace.
Red smells like the fresh picked red apples from the orchard.
Red tastes like the cherry tomatoes in my fresh garden salad.
Red feels like a warm and loving hug after a long busy day.
Zoe Bona, Grade 4
Guardian Angels Catholic School, FL

July
July is red, white, and blue
The color of fireworks
It feels hot and cool
It sounds like kids playing
It smells like the pool
It tastes like lemonade
Hot, cool, and fun month.
Caroline Waters, Grade 5
Vienna Elementary School, NC

Bird/Tree
Bird
Beautiful, colorful
Pooping, flying, eating
Robin, humming bird, oak, magnolia
Growing, living, shading
Rough, green
Tree
Kaitlyn Reed, Grade 5
Dover Elementary School, FL

Zoo
I love the zoo.
It is exciting fun.
I would like to go,
With you.

On a bright sunny day,
We will come.
We will see the animals,
And feed a few.

Most of the animals,
Are mammals.
After we see them all at the zoo,
I will leave with you.
Savannah Willis, Grade 4
Bayshore Christian School, FL

Red
The color red
Makes me get
Out of bed
And ready set
And go.

It makes me feel sad
And bad
And mad
All at the same bad time.

The color reminds me of NC State
And makes me elaborate
And demonstrate.
Nathan Moose, Grade 5
East Albemarle Elementary School, NC

Spring
Every day in spring
I will dance
I will sing
With my friend Chance
Karrizma Hood, Grade 6
Arnold Magnet Academy, GA

My House
My house is made of wood
        p to the attic
and when I go u
it is *scary*
but when I go d
      o
       w
        n to my room
it is cozy
Sara Swayze, Grade 4
Spruce Creek Elementary School, FL

Ice Cream
An ice
cream cone is
so sweet and
it is so wonderful
to eat you
would probably
get sick
if you
ate too
many!
Tori Romero, Grade 5
St Martin Upper Elementary School, MS

Circle
I feel so empty deep inside.
I feel like only half a circle.
I can't find my other half.
I wonder where could it be.

I search and search and what do I find?
I find nothing I'm looking for.
Did I lose it? I ask myself.
Did I ever have my other half?

What does it look like?
I hope that it comes back.
I search all over, up and down
Side to side and all around.

I figured out about my other half.
It is the love of my life.
I stop searching, hoping I will find him.
Will he come to me, hopefully?
GeeKeyvia McCain, Grade 5
North Elementary School, SC

Spring
Each spring we hear the birds sing,
We also hear church bells ring.
Leaves fall from tall trees,
We also hear the buzzing of bumblebees.

People go to the park and play,
Next door in the field horses neigh.
Spring is a time where life begins,
It's a time to start over again.

Children go to the park and play,
They also go for a nice long hike.
We girls go to the mall,
Boys go and play ball.

We ride a car to school,
And act so totally cool.
We get to go out,
Also we go roam about.
Krystal Medlin, Grade 5
Sharon Elementary School, NC

Hannah Grant
H orses are my favorite animal
A nd I love to swim in my pool
N ow that I'm older I'm changing
N ow I still love horses
A nd I love to play volleyball
H ey that's just me being me

G reat grades I have
R unning around the court
A nd showing my horse will soon start
N ow that I'm older I have changed
T he year is almost over,
    so now I will change some more
Hannah Grant, Grade 6
Tarpon Springs Middle School, FL

My Life
My life is an easy come easy go
Nothing major nothing small
Just nice and simple…just easy go
Nice and quiet nothing happening
Not poor Not rich
Just easy come easy go…
It's all the same-o same-o…
It's just like any other life
Just not spoiled rot…
I take life by the hand
Don't waste my time away…
I praise God every day…
Go to church
It's just an easy come easy go life
Jennifer Marie McAllister, Grade 6
Philadelphia Elementary School, MS

When Spring Is Near

The children come out of their homes to play,
Birds come out and start to sing,
Snow starts to move out of trees' ways,
And rabbits start to hop in the sunny days.

The snow falls off branches and goes away,
Grass becomes green instead of brown,
Animals come out and start to say,
"What a wonderful town!"

All of this happens when spring is near,
A time of joy, happiness, and cheer.

Ashima Varma, Grade 5
Buies Creek Elementary School, NC

Summer Spirits

The crisp summer air comes to greet you at the door.
It's happy to see you more and more.
As you're walking to the bus stop,
You don't even realize what the spirits are trying to tell you.
They are trying to tell you about something that you'll try today
that may end your young life the wrong way.
The spirits are trying to tell you about drugs.
You don't listen because you want to be cool.
You just floof it off and sit at your stool.
You don't know what's going to happen.
You will end up in the emergency room, fighting for your life.
You think you should have listened.
Then everything goes dark.

Christen Vencil, Grade 6
McRae Elementary School, FL

The German Shepherd and I

One day my dad had bought me a pretty German Shepherd.
It was pretty and had silky fur the same color
As a Milky Way and he had a black outline.
Sometimes the dog chased me
Like he's the predator and I'm the prey.
He likes to come outside and play.
I loved him because he listened.
He was very polite. If someone hit me,
He might bite.
When he died, I cried.
You can see the patches under my eyes.
I missed Floppy from the day he died.

Quitman Smith, Grade 5
East Marion Elementary School, MS

Beach

B eneath my toes warm sand lies
E ncircling them in a comfortable blanket
A s I step onto the glowing sand
C rowned and adorned with colorful umbrellas
H iding people in cool, dark shade.

Rachel Watjen, Grade 6
Boiling Springs Intermediate School, SC

Sports

I like football, how about you?
I like baseball and basketball too.
Not all sports are cool and fun,
But most of them I love a ton.
Football's my favorite for many different reasons.
The number one rule is to stay tough all season.
I love sports and you should too.
Try some of them, you may like a few.

Avery Welch, Grade 5
Calusa Elementary School, FL

Spring

Spring is a season, one of four.
Happiness fills my soul more and more.

I play softball during this time.
I can't wait 'til the final chime.

If the groundhog sees his shadow, I am glad.
But if he doesn't, I am very, very sad.

Watch all the beautiful flowers bloom.
You can smell their fragrances fill the room.

I find joy in all of spring's new things,
Especially birds, when they spread their wings.

Maddie Mohr, Grade 6
Gold Hill Middle School, SC

Summer's Nature

Summertime is so much fun,
Playing games in the sun.
Catching fish every day,
In my backyard by the bay.

Dolphin and manatee swimming by,
Watching the pelicans as they fly.
Mullets jumping way up high,
Nature's so beautiful, it makes me sigh.

Hunter Morris, Grade 4
Indian Harbour Montessori Elementary School, FL

David Field

David
Grandfather
Strong, caring, smart, fun to be with
Lover of math, family, and his pool
Who believes my room is always messy
Who wants me to be successful, smart, and to be clean
Who uses his knowledge, patience, and his money
Who gives his time, money, and love
Who says, "Go clean up that room"
Field

Patrick Field, Grade 6
Newport Middle School, NC

Ode to My Cello

Beautifully covered
In high-gloss varnish,
It glistens and sparkles
In the light.
It's made of dark oak.
I watch as the bow
Glides up and down
On tensioned strings.
And listen as
The notes merge out
Of the "f" hole.
I am so grateful
For all it has done.
It has successfully
Brought me through
An honors orchestra
Audition.
It sits there begging
To be played.
And its wish becomes
My command.

Clayton Odom, Grade 6
CrossRoads Middle School, SC

Perfect or Not?

In this little world of mine,
It seems like everything is quite fine.
But take a closer look,
and you will see,
That everything doesn't fit quite perfectly.
Working harder and harder every day
Wishing I could just run away
Time going by too slowly
Nothing to do but cry
Sitting in my room
Just wanting to die
Wishing for a better life each day
Nothing left to do but pray
while time just fades away

Mikayla Coleman, Grade 5
St Martin Upper Elementary School, MS

A New Friend

It was a nice day
I went to school
I met a girl
Her name was Isabella
She is a beautiful girl
She asked me something
She said she wanted something
She said she wanted to be my friend
I was very happy
I did not know what to say
So, I just said that would be fine

Shelby Christensen, Grade 4
Pensacola Beach Elementary School, FL

Sierra

Sierra
Highlighter
Loud, bright,
Lover of all things truly funny, chocolate, and beavers,
Who believes quiet is an insult,
Who wants a more creative world, attention, and to be heard,
Who uses he mind, nerve, and outdoor voice indoors,
Who gives insults a dozen, complaints a million, and headaches to one and all,
Who says "If you aren't laughing you're not living it!"
Austin

Sierra Austin, Grade 6
Broad Creek Middle School, NC

Feelings

I am tall. But not at all.
I feel like crying but I am dying.
I do not know what to do I am so confused.
It makes me want to scream and my theme is green.
When I go to the beach I feel so asleep.
My lunch is such a bunch.
When I read a book I don't want to look.
When my backpack is jumpy I feel so lumpy.
I don't feel right I feel so out of sight.
My brain is shaped like a cane.
For goodness sake I have a headache.
When people keep talking I feel like I'm not walking.
All I had for lunch was bread all I can hear is an echo in my head.
All I said is leave me something I read.
I feel so lazy like a daisy.
While I am walking down a lonely road I feel like my head is about to explode.
My head is rolling and I am just not flowing.
When my mom leaves and I wave I feel like I am trapped in a cave.
In the day I feel so afraid
In my world it is always night I am always searching for that white, bright light.

Zahrea Small, Grade 5
Bethune Elementary School, FL

Tornadoes

Tornadoes are twisty they ruined everyone's homes.
Everyone takes cover when there's a tornado.
Tornadoes are very dangerous.
They can destroy food stores and restaurants.
Everyone has to eat uncooked food while the tornado is continuing to destroy homes.

Nana Ramirez, Grade 5
Hope Charter School, FL

Go with the Flow

Sometimes things don't go your way,
but you know you'll do better the next day.
Just go with the flow and see, you'll know,
when the time comes for you to shine.
And when you succeed all you need to be is a good sport
and not to brag in front of others and don't nag your sister or brother.
Be a role model as I'm trying to say, don't be mean to others and go your own way.

Clare Doyle, Grade 4
St Thomas More School, NC

High Merit Poems – Grades 4, 5, and 6

Ode to Gracie

Gracie's fur is as white as snow,
her ears as soft as down,
her brown eyes simply glow.
She's the cutest dog in town.

When we feed her
she gets in a really good mood
and can't wait until she can chow down
on her delicious bowl of food.

She gets dirtier than a pig,
but we don't mind.
We just wash her up
and make her shine.

Gracie is very playful;
she loves to chase a ball.
We give her lots of exercise
by chasing her down the hall.

Gracie is as fast as lightning.
She might could beat a horse,
but that's not why we love her, of course.
We love her because she is our dog, Gracie.

Matthew Jackson, Grade 6
CrossRoads Middle School, SC

Basketball

I love to play basketball
With my friend Paul
I also play with Mark
When I go to Osprey Park
I love being on the court
Because it is my favorite sport.

Saad Akhtar, Grade 4
The Muslim Academy of Greater Orlando, FL

Matt

He's always loving
He's always caring
But sometimes he's a little daring
He takes a nap every once in awhile
So when he wakes up he'll have a giant smile
He's cute and sweet in every way
That's what makes it a beautiful day
He's thoughtful and generous
That's no doubt
Although sometimes he will pout
If you get to know him, he's really funny
Even if it's not sunny
My brother loves me with all his heart
But even though we argue and fight
Our love for each other will always be bright

Hali Wilson, Grade 5
Ranburne Elementary School, AL

Horses

Horses are everything to me.
They say Hi, by breathing into each others nose.
I rinse them down with a hose.
Sometimes they make mean faces.
But they are still my favorite.

Andrea L. Barrick, Grade 4
Spruce Creek Elementary School, FL

In the Park

In Columbia Friendship Park
With every last person glaring at me
I was bouncing around with my legs crossed
Hopeful for a bathroom

I spotted my mother coming toward me
Skiiing across the steep wet grounds
But by the time she reached me
It was too late

I could feel it running down my legs
And I could hear the immense laughter
Even my little brother
Couldn't stop himself from grinning

When everything finally stopped
I didn't know what to do, so I ran…
Through the park…
Across the street…
And behind the bank.

And all I could think about
Was the embarrassment.

Kellé Thigpen, Grade 5
East Marion Elementary School, MS

Blue

Have you ever smelled, tasted, heard, seen, and felt
Blue?

It smells like the wind blowing to you.
Like the wind coming from the waves.
Also the smell of fresh blueberries.

It tastes like fresh blueberries.
The tastes of chlorine water while swimming.

It sounds like waves from the ocean splashing.
The sound of the ocean roaring.

It looks like many colors of the world.
It looks like the sky.
It looks like the ocean.

To me the color blue makes me feel peaceful.

Aerial Jones, Grade 6
Arlington Middle School, FL

The Sky
The early morning sunshine awoke me
From my deep sleep under the
Glistening moonlight.

The stars were shining bright
Beside the moon, until the sun
Pushed the moon and stars aside.

Before I knew it, the white clouds
Joined the sun and they became one.
The baby blue sky made me want to
Go back to sleep.

I was up and I could see
My shadow while picking wild flowers.
I heard wood peckers pecking
In trees to find their breakfast.

I look up to see
A glimmering waterfall
Looking back at me.
Emily Estermyer, Grade 5
Eastside Elementary School, GA

Shopping
I went to the store.
I had 100 dollars.
I left the place broke.
Logan Peeples, Grade 5
Winona Elementary School, MS

The Worst Dinner I Ever Ate
The worst dinner I ever ate
Spaghetti and meatballs on my date

It was so bad
It made you mad

Their spinach was so scary
And don't forget it was hairy

But what about the potatoes
They were covered in tomatoes
Wyatt Phillips, Grade 6
Gold Hill Middle School, SC

Life
You've always heard the saying,
"Use your time wisely"
Because each minute, each day,
Are so precious and unpredictable.
Each mistake is a step closer to death,
But take a risk, take a chance
Because life is shorter than it appears.
Jasmine Bui, Grade 6
Gold Hill Middle School, SC

My Mom
Today is my mother's birthday
I love her very deeply
Her birthday is April Fool's Day
Today she was dressed very neatly

She is very kind to me
I love her and she loves me
For the FCAT, she gave me tea
She will heal my injured knee

She is very nice and sweet
My mom is nice to my sister and I
She always makes me good food to eat
My mom always gives us pie

I love my mom very much
After school, to see her I will rush
Cullen Smith, Grade 4
PVPV/Rawlings Elementary School, FL

Snow
The snow falls all around,
Dancing gracefully to the ground.
Pure, feathery, soft yet bitter,
The snow falls without even a pitter.
As it very slowly flies,
It turns, swoops, dips, and dives;
It's as joyful as the sunrise,
And as intricate as dirty lies.
The snow falls all around,
But it never, ever makes a sound.
Kevin Berry, Grade 5
Summit Hill Elementary School, GA

Peaceful
Clouds up in the sky
Birds flying side to side
The silence in the air
Leaves changing color green and red

The wetness in the grass
The water in the pool
Pictures in my head
There's more than a few

The sound of the waves
As they crash on the shore
I love the way you sing to me
And there's even more

The cry of a new born baby
You can tell when it's near
You always want to get away
Even when you say it's okay
Caitlin Elias, Grade 5
Orlando Junior Academy, FL

Mrs. Ferraro
Mrs. Ferraro is a great teacher.
She probably is a good dancer.
She is very pretty.
Her favorite character is Betty.
She loves to teach reading.
Her favorite subject is writing.
She never makes jokes.
She loves to drink Coke.
She loves to go to mall.
And loves to watch football.
She is very funny.
Her favorite animal is a bunny.
Jina Kim, Grade 4
William S Talbot Elementary School, FL

Easter Bunny
Furry, cuddly
Hopping, jumping, giving
Help kids have fun.
Peter Cottontail
Ethan Saffer, Grade 4
Central Park Elementary School, FL

Whatif?*
Last night, while I lay thinking here,
Some Whatifs crawled inside my ear
and pranced and partied all night long
and sang their same old whatif song.
Whatif they close the school ?
Whatif I drowned in the swimming pool?
Whatif I can't sing anymore?
Whatif I become poor?
Whatif I never learned to ride a bike?
Whatif I get lost on a hike?
Whatif my parents went on a strike?
Whatif my dog runs away?
Whatif I become a great shame?
Tia Sinatra, Grade 6
Challenger Middle School, FL
*Patterned after Shel Silverstein's
"What If"

My Brother and I
My brother and I were having fun
Playing in the sun.

He tried to jump in the air as a frog,
But he was a hog!

On our way to bed,
Tyler hit his head.
The next day
We went to play
In the hay!
Nicholas Threatte, Grade 4
Edwards Elementary School, SC

High Merit Poems – Grades 4, 5, and 6

Can You Imagine…
A life without a dog
Not wanting to eat your favorite food like a hog

When you're hurt not yelling OWE
Riding in a car through the Panama Canal

Football without a referee
American not a free country

A tree with no leaves
A beehive without bees

The world without air
Or a hamster with no hair

A beach with no sand
Somebody without a hand

A car with no wheels
People without heels?

Chandler Coons, Grade 4
William S Talbot Elementary School, FL

Shoes
Big shoes
Small shoes
Running shoes
Walking shoes
High Heel shoes
Tall shoes
Lots of different shoes
Ballet flats and
Cowgirl boots
Lots of different shoes

Rachel Gatewood, Grade 6
St Francis Xavier Elementary School, MS

My Day
Every time I want to play.
  my mother says another day.
Every time I get a sore
  I turn around and get sore
    some more
When I got my special bear
  And I found a slight tear
It grew and grew and grew some more
  They wouldn't take it at the corner store.
Homework time! I told my mom I couldn't
  Surprise! she said, "Okay you shouldn't!"
I screamed! I shouted! I want some cocoa
  My father said, "Oh! dear, she's gone loco!"
Night time! Now I have to rest my head
  So that means it's time for bed.
    Nighty-night!

Rae-Shawn Wiggles, Grade 5
Wynnebrook Elementary School, FL

Cats
I know one animal
That is not dog nor hamster.
It's a warm soft cat.
Sometimes I think of being a cat
That is as orange as a
Carved pumpkin on Halloween,
In the jet black sky.
I wish I was a cat
Cuddling with a human
And feeling as warm as the hot yellow sun,
I wish I was a cat that is eating
Munchy, crunchy tasty cat food
That tastes like tuna fish.
And if I was a cat
I would cuddle up with my kittens and
Sleep like a calm snowy white lamb.
If I were a cat I would sit on my
Owner's lap
And purr, purr, purr!

Wilbert Galletti, Grade 4
Julian D Parker School of Science, Math & Technology, FL

Iraq
A place where it gives you violent chills.
A place where soldiers climb gravel hills.
They're on the lookout, trying to stay safe.
The explosions scare even the brave.
So while you're at home in your peaceful life,
Think about those who keep that alive.

Daniel Zimmermann, Grade 4
Olde Providence Elementary School, NC

I Am
I am your friend
I wonder what it would be like if the universe ended.
I hear the silence of God and what he speaks
I see life and afterlife surrounding us.
I want to be your hero because…
I am your friend.

I pretend I am empowered
I feel greater than life
I touch every source
I worry about cancellation
I cry when you cry because…
I am your friend.

I understand why people get upset
I say we shouldn't spend our lives in a deep depression.
I dream about the world's unknown.
I try to lead the world away from danger
I hope that you are glad to be here because…
I am your friend.

Melody Bateman, Grade 6
Heron Creek Middle School, FL

The Sounds of Earth

Listen to the sounds of Earth
The birds singing melodies that please the world
The trees whispering words of gossip as the wind darts across fields of flowers
The animals gathering food to save during the cold winter's worst
The rivers running through the land as a life supply to an abundance of living creatures
So next time you go out into that beautiful world, that astonishing world, that remarkable world
Next time,
Listen to the sounds of Earth.

Eric Hipp, Grade 6
Tarpon Springs Middle School, FL

I'll Always Remember

I'll always remember my grandparent's home, the smell of things baking when I walk through the door
My nana's hug is a warm cozy blanket, my papa's smile is as bright as the sun

They have no rules for me, time doesn't matter
My nana spoils me with terrific tasty treats, my papa is so funny, he always makes me laugh

I love when they take me to the park to play, we walk and play sports and sit in the sun
My nana tells me stories about when she was young, my papa teaches me soccer skills he learned as a boy

We stay up late playing cards at the table, I help Papa fix things around the house
I help Nana baking cookies and scones, we have so much fun that the time goes so fast

The smell of the turkey cooking on Thanksgiving Day, the beautiful lights at Christmas shining like stars
Green all around for St. Patrick's Day, they make holidays special in so many ways

I feel love and joy when I'm always there, Nana sneaks me money as she hugs me goodbye
Papa stands in the driveway and waves as I leave, I'll always remember my grandparent's home

Matthew Digney, Grade 6
Unity School, FL

Yellow

Yellow are the daisies that are blooming in my front yard. Yellow is my umbrella that shields me from the rain. Yellow is my lunch box holding all my delicious foods. Yellow is the sun sparkling at the beautiful beach. Yellow is the popcorn popping in the microwave. Yellow are the stars twinkling as I fall asleep. Yellow is the glowing smile on everyone's face!

Lindsey Cariello, Grade 4
Guardian Angels Catholic School, FL

Life

Day by day it fades, day by day it comes back. Day by day childhood is gone for one!
We watch it come and go we watch it rise we watch it go we watch it come and go.
But when you grow older childhood goes it doesn't last long does it.
How long was your childhood?
Life is short…
        SO LIVE TO LIVE!

So be a kid and…
        live to live!

Have some fun and play around…
        BE A KID!

While it lasts…

Hailey Arceneaux, Grade 4
Virginia A Boone Highland Oaks Elementary School, FL

Monday Night Football

Late at night the football game was played.
By very large men who were very well paid.
The visiting team had been perfect up till now,
The home team tried to stop them somehow.
As the Patriots' offense marched down the field,
The Ravens defense refused to yield.
Suddenly the game winning catch was made,
The roar of the stadium began to fade.
Despite their best efforts Baltimore had failed,
And once again the New England Patriots prevailed!

Reuben Siegman, Grade 6
Pinellas County Jewish Day School, FL

Sadness Is…

Sadness is a steep canyon,
   and falling to the extreme darkness.
Sadness is an eroded rock,
   worn away to nothing.
Sadness is a broken toy,
   does nothing but remain quiet and still.
Sadness is a pen with no ink,
   no color inside but a hollow space.
Sadness is a dark room,
   penetrating a quiet empty worn chilly space.
Sadness is a ripped paper,
   not usable and torn in half.
Sadness is the deep sea,
   drowning on rough hard ocean water depths.

Paulo-Emmanuel D. Subido, Grade 5
Dante B Fascell Elementary School, FL

The Fallen Brother

On February 27, 2007, one year ago,
A day that changed the Spartanburg County and Duncan Police
   Departments
Forever, when an officer
Was killed in the line of fire.
While making a quick go,
At attempting
A confrontation
When he was slowed down by a .38 caliber,
And held by a brother not knowing what would transpire.

Jonathan Scott, Grade 6
Camperdown Academy, SC

Parties

P laying with friends and family
A joyful time
R eceiving and giving gifts
T alking and meeting new people
I ce cream and cake
E njoying fun with your friends
S miling because you're having fun

Koury Eargle, Grade 6
St Francis Xavier Elementary School, MS

I Am

I am funny and cool.
I wonder who is going to laugh next.
I hear laughs around me.
I see the weirdest things.
I want to make everyone laugh.
I am funny and cool.

I pretend to be a comedian.
I feel happy every time I hear a laugh.
I touch the hot air of laughs around me.
I worry without me, the world would be dull.
I cry because I laugh so hard.
I am funny and cool.

I understand the true meaning of funny.
I say the funniest things.
I dream to make the dull people laugh.
I try day after day after day to make people laugh.
I am funny and cool.

Steve Pierre-Louis, Grade 6
Heron Creek Middle School, FL

School

School is as horrifying as frankenstein
With moist air and lightless sky
Thunder roaring as loud as a lion
Black molded windows and rusted old doors
Big long hallways with flickering light bulbs
A cafeteria with cells as a dungeon
Disgusting food that looks like earthworms
And teachers as dead as mummies

Emmanuel Talledo, Grade 6
Freedom Middle School, FL

The Dog and the Frog

The Dog was walking along and met a frog
He was on a log
The Dog was assisted by the frog through the fog
Then they came to a bog
There was a hog standing next to the bog
They were helped through the bog by the hog
Then it was so late, they had to build a fire.
That night, there was a lot of fog.
With the fire, they created smog.

Wailes Kemp, Grade 6
St Francis Xavier Elementary School, MS

The Earth

There are stars and there are cars.
There is the moon and there are raccoons.
The night sky is black and the sea is blue.
There are trucks and there are ducks.
There are frogs and there are dogs.
That is the Earth.

Carlisle Koestler, Grade 6
St Francis Xavier Elementary School, MS

Numbers, Numbers, Everywhere!

Number, numbers everywhere
1, 2, 3, over there.

4, 5, 6 always clicks
7, 8, 9 trying to climb.

Numbers, numbers, everywhere
1, 2, 3, over there.

10, 11, 12 ring the bell.
13, 14, 15 is trying to get with 16.
16 is a teen
And is always mean.

Numbers, numbers, everywhere
1, 2, 3, over there.

Alaysia Strong, Grade 4
Edwards Elementary School, SC

Without Friends

I would be lost without a beat
Bored without a tune
Dancing with two left feet
Weaving without a loom

I would be a flower without petals
A fire without a flame
A car without metals
A party to which nobody came

I would be a puzzle missing a piece
A bird feeder without a seed
A Thanksgiving without a feast
A horse without a lead

Sydney Sovern, Grade 6
Gold Hill Middle School, SC

Being Almost to Freedom

It was quiet
not even a sound was made.
The light was shining
brightly into the room
onto me.
It was good to have,
our own comfortable bed and pillow.
Comfortable bed and pillow,
comfortable bed and pillow,
how was it to be a slave
and to be whipped?
I feel happy to be almost to freedom,
to have somewhere to stay that is soft,
not a lumpy bed,
that is made out of straw,
I'm almost to freedom.

Bryson Love, Grade 4
Pinnacle Elementary School, NC

Crazy Kitty

My kitty is crazy, he eats baby food, out of a can.
He loves to be by people especially a man.
He puts his motor on, falls fast asleep listening to noises of many sheep.
He wakes up to a spoon in a can.
He is a crazy kitty, who eats like a man.
My kitty is sweet, my kitty is neat,
but when it comes to food he is in a hungry mood.
My kitty is testy, but he is the besty

Danielle Edwards, Grade 4
Spruce Creek Elementary School, FL

Theron, What a Guy!

I remember the days when everybody yelled
"Theron, what a guy!"
I remember the days when people said, "I love you."
Theron, what a guy!
I remember when people said, "I like your pants!"
Theron, what a guy!
I remember when people said I was cool
Theron, what a guy!
I remember when people said, "That boy has Coogi shirts!"
Theron, what a guy!
I remember when people said, "I like your hair."
Theron, what a guy!
I remember when people said, "That boy is funny."
Theron, what a guy!
I remember when people said, "That boy is spoiled."
Theron, what a guy!
I remember when people said, "That boy only wears J's and Wills!"
Theron, Theron, what a guy you are!
Theron, what a guy!

Theron Reddy, Grade 6
Westview Middle School, SC

Peace

Peace is the sound of the war ending in Iraq.
It is the sight of the sun gazing upon the ocean.
The taste of clean water in Africa is peace.
Peace is the color of blue in the pool at summer time.
It is the voice of Martin Luther King Jr. giving his "I Have a Dream" speech.
The touch of a new fallen snow in winter is peace.
New cut grass is the smell of peace after a drought.
Peace is happiness.

Maggie Laura Carter, Grade 4
Wrights Mill Road Elementary School, AL

Smart Sallie

Smart Sallie sat sad singing a song of misery.
She sat sobbing in a room until she saw a saint.
And she said Smart Sallie why are you sitting in a room full of sad and sobbing?

She couldn't help but smile in a way that was friendly and sweet.
The saint said now get up and listen to those sweet sounding birds and hear my words.
Smart Sallie saw the saint and listened and got an A.

Jordan Gantt, Grade 5
Brooklet Elementary School, GA

In His Kingdom

A veil of despair encases my soul,
Shadowing bliss, the anguish unrolls,
Even the sky is a smear of gray wool,
The sole witness to the tears I release
An incoming flood washing 'way ease.
But as a tear stings on my cheek,
A fiery star shoots 'cross the bleak.
And now my soul appears to speak
When he's in view.
My heart's anew.
Spirit just flew.
In his kingdom. Let the page turn.
Let the waves churn today.
In his kingdom. Where my heart soars.
Where the ocean roars each day.
In his kingdom.
In an altered world, I fly on wings unfurled at bay.
But only in his kingdom, where heart's desires sing from.
I was so wrong. My heart sings a song to be,
Eternally
In his kingdom.

Sarah Butler, Grade 6
Champion Preparatory Academy, FL

October

October is orange and black
The colors of fall and night
October feels like leaves brushing against you
It sounds like scary movies
It smells like pumpkin pie
It tastes like melted chocolate
October seems like it lasts forever

Allison Irwin, Grade 5
Vienna Elementary School, NC

The Girl

As her eyes shine like the stars above;
I gaze at her with deep compassion,
Wondering how lucky I am to have such a beautiful girl.
Though I enjoy this I question myself,
Why did she pick me?
I'm no different from anyone else,
Was it love at first sight?
Or were we meant to be?

Dakota Efird, Grade 6
Albemarle Middle School, NC

Pizza Tastes Good

Pizza is a food and it tastes good
I would eat every slice in the world if I could
I eat with my hand and not with the sand
I think it tastes best when I don't make a mess
The cheesy sauce melts in my mouth
I could eat it in the north, east, west, or south

Stervensky Prospere, Grade 4
Park Ridge Elementary School, FL

No Present

I got nothing for my birthday.
I got nothing for Christmas.
Nothing for Halloween
Nothing for Easter
Nothing for Thanksgiving
Nothing for Valentine's Day
But you know what's even better?
It's not the first time it happened.

Dylan Dixon, Grade 4
Clearview Avenue Elementary School, FL

The Really Awesome Witch!

I know a funny witch
that fell in a ditch.
She has a black hat
and a weird black cat.
She has a t-shirt that is black
she has a boyfriend named Jack!
Her legs are very super silly long
and she also likes King Kong.
Her feet are really big
and her cat can really dig.

Parker Lennertz, Grade 4
Chancellor Charter School At Lantana, FL

Sports

Amber
Athlete
Lover of soccer, kickball, and my daddy
Who believes that boyfriends are a waste of time
Who wants to win the rest of my games
Who uses sportsmanship, time, and speed
Who gives words of advice, books, and clothes
Who says "Be nice, be quiet, and go away"
Autry

Amber Autry, Grade 6
Broad Creek Middle School, NC

Her?

Intelligent.
She's smart as a dictionary.
Reminding me of my own mother,
Strong and, caring.
Every day she is near me,
Yet she is blind.
She doesn't know of my love.
It's as if she's never known me.
I disappear in her eyes.
When I read my stories all I can do is think about her.
I can't concentrate, my grades have fallen.
And, it's all her fault!
No matter what she does, I will always forgive her.
I think I'm love sick.

Andrew Diaz, Grade 4
Virginia A Boone Highland Oaks Elementary School, FL

Rachel White
Rachel
Brunette, crafty, creative
Sibling of Jordan
Lover of animals
Who fears roaches
Who needs high speed internet
Who gives cards to the elderly
Who would like to see Australia
Resident of GA
White
Rachel White, Grade 6
Pulaski County Middle School, GA

Can You Imagine…
A pencil with no lead
A hotel that does not have a bed

A library with no books
A state with no crooks

A television with no shows
A town with no crows

A mommy with no hugs
A lake with no bugs

A dinner with no food
Doing something
when you're not in the mood

A school with no teachers
A forest without scary creatures

Vermont with no bears
A mom that never cares?
Alex Chase, Grade 4
William S Talbot Elementary School, FL

My Mom and Dad Are Madly in Love
My Mom and Dad
Are madly in love
No matter what
They will not shove

When my Mom and Dad
Have a date
My Mom and Dad
Come home late

When my dad
Gives Mom a flower
She kisses him
For an hour
Angela Moulton, Grade 4
Freeport Elementary School, FL

Friends
Friends are the people you care about,
They're always there for you,
Make you happy when you're sad,
Never turn their backs on you
Not letting you down.
Friends are almost like family,
Helping you with your problems,
Making sure you're OK.
They spend so much time with you,
They can never be replaced,
Physically, or in your heart.
Friends are special,
So don't let a friend go,
Because you'll never be able,
To replace them.
Not now, not ever.
Jonna Leigh Nance, Grade 5
Grays Chapel Elementary School, NC

Holocaust
Holocaust
Dreadful, ghastly
Dispirit, fishearten, vatastrophe
Dismay, outrage, devastation, havoc
Holocaust
Lee McClellan, Grade 5
Summit Hill Elementary School, GA

The Colors of My World
Red is the color of my hair.
Pink pajamas are fun to wear.

Green as the grass in my yard.
Black as an ace on a playing card.

White is the moon as I sleep at night.
Purple is the color of my brand new kite.

Yellow lollipops are fun to eat.
Brown chocolate milk just can't be beat.

Silver coins are nice and shiny.
Gray mice are very tiny.
Brooke Kramer, Grade 6
Tequesta Trace Middle School, FL

Daytime's Night
Daytime
Bright, blinding
Changing, moving, working
Cloud, sun, moon, stars
Sleeping, snoring, dreaming
Dark, gloomy
Nighttime
Danny Ramsland, Grade 6
Seven Springs Middle School, FL

Summertime
The blazing sun,
The open pool,
Cruises and bike rides,
All are mine to enjoy.

School's out,
The sun's out,
Camp out,
Lawnmower out too.

A hike in the woods,
A dip in the pool,
A lawn to mow,
A couple of dollars will do.
Blake Silver, Grade 4
Providence Classical School, AL

Imagine Colors
Brown is the color of tree bark.
Black is the color of when it gets dark.

Pink is the color of a princess crown.
Cream is the color of a wedding gown.

Yellow is the color of Winnie the Pooh.
White is the color of Elmer's glue.

Red is the color of a hot fire.
Silver is the color of an electric wire.

Purple is the color of a beautiful flower.
Gold is the color of the Eiffel Tower.
Hannah Glick, Grade 6
Tequesta Trace Middle School, FL

My Goats
Oh, I love my goats!
I really, really do.
We started out with thirteen,
and now we have sixty-two!
Feeding them is a lot of work,
but it gets the job done.
I know this sounds crazy,
but it's actually pretty fun.
Garrett Sellers, Grade 5
Tuscaloosa Academy, AL

Johnny
J oyful
O bey
H andsome
N oisy
N asty
Y oung
Johnny Brown, Grade 4
East Jones Elementary School, MS

Among My Thoughts
As the journey begins,
you will find a mystery unfound in your mind.
A thought within you, and a thought among you,
you think of a moment a moment of pride,
a moment that makes you want to cry.
I make my thought a thought I bought,
a thought of sadness that I've got.

Chelsea Grace Gillette, Grade 5
Queen's Grant Community School, NC

The Anything Door
I can I will.
I can find something awesome in each day.
I can be better.
you can be a better person.
you will not be bad.
you can be the best person you can be.
you can do anything you put your mind to.
I will be respectful.
I can be trustworthy.
you can be fair.
you will be loved.
you will be responsible.
you are all the best.
We can all post the fact because
We're all in it together.

Nathan Linhthasack, Grade 4
Clearview Avenue Elementary School, FL

Why Do Things Happen?
Why do things happen?
Things happen for a reason, but why
Do they happen the way they do?
My dad used to say things happen for a reason.

My mother says things happen for a reason, because
God's trying to tell me something good.
I guess that's why things happen.
It happens for a reason.

Leyshaun Davis, Grade 6
Philadelphia Elementary School, MS

A Rose
A rose so red
A rose so soft
Growing so high above the moss
It's beautiful in its texture
It grows for its name
I remember how high a rose became
It was so beautiful nobody could draw it
They gazed in awe as they saw it
They smiled and clapped for the winning flower
I was the champ at least for the hour

Jessica McQuaig, Grade 5
Carter Community Charter, NC

Georgia
Georgia, oh Georgia
How you are on my mind
I think and think of you
All the time
But now it's time to go deep inside
So go to Six Flags
And take a ride
It is beautiful
Looking at all the sights
So you better be tall
And reach the height

In the neighborhood people say hello
But in the projects, speakers thumping "acapello"
Going to school
Taking a dip in the pool
Although we are in a drought
I don't have a doubt
Going to the Dome
Is like taking a trip to Rome
That was awesome how the Hawk flew by
But it is time to go. See you later. Bye!

Tiara Whitfield, Grade 6
Academy of Lithonia Charter School, GA

My Family
Family is forever
Mine is the best ever

They'll always be there for me
I'll always try to be the person they expect me to be

I love them so much
It's like they have the special touch

I have Abbie, Mom and Dad
And Rollie, they are all so rad

They always help me in everything I do
When I say thank you they say, "I did it just for you"

I have to admit they are the best
I am so glad that I was this blessed

Hailey Williams, Grade 6
Brogden Middle School, NC

The Alley Cat
There was a cat that was very mean
Nobody knew why he was mean except me
He was mean because he was very hungry
"Leave him alone!" my friends yelled
As I walked up to him with my tuna in my hand
I set it on the ground as I watched him eat that tuna
We became friends

Meghan Forgy, Grade 4
Spruce Creek Elementary School, FL

Freedom

F ighting for liberty
R ights
E verlasting independence
E agles
D eclaration of Independence
O verseas men
M onuments and memorials

Blake O'Leary, Grade 5
Bramlett Elementary School, GA

Humor

Laugh
Snicker
Giggle
Tickle
Ha ha
Ho ho
Humor is fun, but it's just begun.
Belly laugh
Chuckle, chuckle
Humor is something everyone needs.
It leads to joy.
Let's laugh. Oh, boy!
Tee hee
Tee hee
Laughing is cool, but you might drool.
Join the fun and laugh with me.
Giggle, giggle
Hee, hee

Zachary Torricelli, Grade 5
Our Lady of Fatima School, MS

The Performance

The eyes
They stare
You have a need
I have a need
To dazzle
They stare
I impress
They're amazed
They watch again
And again
I feel the need
Again I must
The pressure
To do better
Better than the last
To amuse
To fascinate
I may do something stupid
That I may regret
But still I accomplish
As the eyes stare

Kiersten Schmidt, Grade 6
Seven Springs Middle School, FL

Winter

Winter sounds like Christmas carols.
Winter tastes like delicious candy canes.
Winter smells like fresh homemade chocolate chip Christmas cookies.
Winter looks like mouth-watering chocolate chip cookies.
Winter feels like she just gave her mom a dozen presents.
Winter is the touch of a prickly Christmas tree.
Winter is a gleaming Christmas tree.
Winter is as cold as chocolate ice cream.
Winter skis like an ice princess.
Winter is glorious.

Jennifer Lowder, Grade 4
Tabernacle Elementary School, NC

I'm Talking Quiet!

I'm talking quiet!
I'm talking soft!
I'm talking silent, placid, calm!
I'm talking smoothed, peaceful, murmured, hushed!
I'm talking uninterrupted, serene, muttered, muted, restrained!
I'm talking understated, subdued, unobtrusive, mumbled, tranquil, no noise!
I'm talking calmed down, muffled, voiceless, speechless!
I'm talking quiet!

Victoria Badgett, Grade 4
Wellington School, FL

My Dreams Always Go Down the Drain

I feel lifeless, useless, ugly, alone, solo, and dreamless.
People like me need their dreams to survive those cold careless nights.
But unlike anyone and everyone, I always have my dreams slip away from beneath me
And I feel like I can't even breathe.
This feeling is not a pleasure but my dreams are a treasure
That is always just out of reach.
The beach is somewhere where I can relax and dream of my dreams,
When I'm there I'm no one else but me.
This feels great, but when I step back into reality
All those special moments of the beach and my dreams drift away
To be saved for another day.
But what if I don't want to wait for that day to arrive?
What if I've been torn so many times that I can't make it to that day?
And I just slowly fade
Along the way?
My dreams are going down the drain.
Will I soon follow?

Kaelyn Drake, Grade 6
Freedom Middle School, FL

Cures for a Boring School Day

Transform my desk into an arcade.
Build a track in the center of the classroom and race around the room.
Transform my desk into a Ferrari.
Transform my desk into a plane and fly to Canada.
Use my desk for karate practice.
Break a monkey-shaped piñata and eat all the candy.
Make a 2,000 fit party popper and fill it with caramel.

Joel Hernandez II, Grade 4
Wellington School, FL

Tigers

Giant and fluffy
Graceful abandoned feline
Hunting at dark night

Nick Kokenzie, Grade 6
City of Pembroke Pines Charter Central Middle School, FL

Spring

What's spring?
   beautiful, and lovely weather
   time for birds to fly
   new animals entering the world
   picnic lunches at the park
   no school, and a time to play
   riding your horse through the valley
   dipping, and diving into lakes and pools
   is a time for friends to play.
That's spring!

Christina Conrad, Grade 6
Turkey Creek Middle School, FL

My Best Friend

When I come home from school,
When I'm sick,
When I'm really mad,
When I don't want to go to school,
When I don't want to talk to anyone,
I know I will always have my best friend,
Even if I lose every friend at school.
My friend and I spend a lot of time together
Like going fishing, or running around the neighborhood
or killing a snake, or swimming in the lake,
or just playing around.
Me and my best friend always have good times, my dog.

Sam Andrews, Grade 6
St Francis Xavier Elementary School, MS

Shooting Stars

Sometimes I see you, sometimes I do not
Sometimes there's many, sometimes there's not

Oh so high up in the sky
You give great shimmer by and by

You reveal yourself to us at night
Oh what a glorious sight

Your constellations can be hard to find
Gazing at you helps me to unwind

Some are big, some are small
And sometimes you can even fall

And if you see it, quick, make a wish
'Cause I'm a shooting star, not a silly fish

Jessi Varner, Grade 6
Boiling Springs Intermediate School, SC

About Me

My hair is as blond as champagne,
My eyes, people want more,
My teeth are as white as fresh fallen snow,
And my voice is to die for.

My personality is as sweet as a newborn neonate,
My athletic side is a tiger waiting to pounce on its prey,
My girlie side is like I am 100% girl and nothing else.

My clothes are as cute as an infant's bottom,
My shoes are big balls of cuteness,
And my accessories are like clouds in the colorful sky.

Cierra Crowe, Grade 5
Brooklet Elementary School, GA

Rain

Rain is tapping on the window.
I wonder when it will go.

It begins to drop,
to the ground with a plop.

It runs down hills,
like a drink when it spills.

It flows into streams,
very quickly, it seems.

It begins to flood,
like a puddle of mud.

Be glad when it goes away,
because it might come back some day.

Robert Liberty, Grade 6
Boiling Springs Intermediate School, SC

The Girl

Day by day night by night
Angels have you in their sight
My love for you is like a wolf's bite
And dare I say
I will always be by your side
Your eyes are like currents of fresh water
And you're as beautiful as the sun when it sets
You are the only one who can get me up when I'm down
My heart feels pierced when you're around
Not butterflies but bubbles of joy are in
I watch you like the lion
Watches the antelope spring
Fully in the cool air,
But not for such reason
I love you,
The one person I won't have to prove.

Jessica West, Grade 6
McRae Elementary School, FL

My Grandparents
What are grandparents?
A free hug
someone to watch you
A free history lesson
someone to ask about your day.

A ride home from school
Someone to cook for you
A phone call at 9:30 to see if you're ok,

That's a grandparent!
Riley Kerwin, Grade 6
Turkey Creek Middle School, FL

If Only I Knew
If only I knew why the sky is blue
Or why the stars are yellow

If only I knew why birds say coo
Or why the plants have dew

If only I knew why the grass is green
Or why I love jelly beans

If only I knew why I love you
Or why you love me too
Krista Tagaras, Grade 6
Tarpon Springs Middle School, FL

Hot Shot
The crowd is cheering
The crowd is screaming
With only twelve seconds
On the game clock
The team has the ball
Down by two
They pass the ball
To their best player
Alex Walker
With nine seconds
Ticking on the clock
At two
Alex shoots a three
The crowd goes silent
He makes the three
Yeah!
He wins the game
Alex Walker, Grade 6
Shorecrest Preparatory School, FL

Iceland
Iceland has puffins
That give their food to their young
Iceland is the best
Lindsay Smith, Grade 6
St Petersburg Christian School, FL

Games
Games
fun, intense
running, hitting, catching
Play hard or go home
Baseball
Jarrett Thompson, Grade 5
Queen's Grant Community School, NC

Love
A person will love you forever,
never let you go.
They will never want to lose you
if they love you so!
Alison D. Smith, Grade 5
Morgan Elementary School, NC

Frog
Jumping, jumping, jump
It leaps like a fast airplane
Falling in water
Swimming down, down to darkness
Up, up again in the air
Ian O'Brien, Grade 4
Pensacola Beach Elementary School, FL

Tick, Tock
Tick, tock
goes the clock
as I watch
and wait.

The bell is about to ring,
it's almost time to go.
Can I listen any longer?
I think the answer's no.

I rush out the door
and tell my teacher bye.
Finally I get home
I tell my parents hi.
Caroline Lalla, Grade 5
North Elementary School, SC

A Beautiful Color
A red rose on a warm spring day
Sparks flying from a hot blazing fire
Fireworks crackling through the night
A cardinal singing with all its might
How you feel when you get a sunburn
When you eat a bitter apple
Smelling an eye-watering onion
The idea of a wicked plot
How you feel on Valentine's day
As bright as a light bulb
Garrett Thigpen, Grade 5
Covenant Classical School, NC

Blue Moon
Does my black storm sing silent
Upon fast wind; along blazing lightning
Sailing with the night sky inside the
Blue Moon
Chloe Lilly, Grade 5
North Windy Ridge School, NC

Being Happy
Sounds like you're in a peaceful place
Looks like a place in the sky
Tastes like a sweet pineapple
Feels like a comfy bed
Smells like a grilled chicken
It must be peaceful.
Tylar East, Grade 5
Ranburne Elementary School, AL

The Moon and the Star
There has never been a couple
Like the moon and the star
A couple since the beginning of time
They represent how true love
Is supposed to be.
Now I understand why couples
Like to take a walk in the moonlight
So they can be moonstruck
With their great feeling of love
To have the feeling of always
Being together forever
Like the moon and the star
Tavijae Lee, Grade 4
Stone Academy, SC

I Am
I am smart and funny
I wonder who killed the Iceman
I hear chatter
I see people laughing
I want to go home and get on youtube
I am smart and funny

I pretend life is really funny
I feel people around me laughing
I touch the air as I am talking
I worry when I say something wrong
I cry when people are mad at me
I am smart and funny

I understand I'm not the smartest,
Nor funniest person
I say that I could be
I try to become that
I hope I will
I am smart and funny
Zack Fischer, Grade 6
Heron Creek Middle School, FL

High Merit Poems – Grades 4, 5, and 6

The Constant Fear
The constant fear in the pale pale night
  Will things ever be the same
    Will the pain ever go away
      Will the heartache ever end
        All the questions dead ends
          Only time can tell
            Only time can mend my broken heart
Ali Sage, Grade 6
Seven Springs Middle School, FL

Rainy Day
Rainy day, please go away.
I will hate this day if you don't go away.
The clouds are black and it is really windy.
I'm about to get mad when I am usually friendly.
It is really muddy and it is really wet.
It's not going to stop raining, I know and I bet.
It has stopped raining, and the clouds have cleared up.
I thought I was dreaming, oh, I almost gave up.
The rain has stopped, so I yelled, "Yeah!"
But the next morning I woke up.
It was another rainy day.
Demario Bagley, Grade 6
Carter Community Charter, NC

My Dog Annie
My dog Annie loves to be outside
When I open the door, it's like she's being pulled by a tide.
"Run, run," she seems to say.
"Stop!" I cry, hoping attention she will pay.
She runs through our yard and stops at the sidewalk,
Then comes another dog who just wants to talk.
Sniff and sniff in circles they go,
Me catching up, saying "Annie, girl, no!"
Soon they are done and she sits in the grass,
She's hoping the time will not quickly pass.
Ten minutes later I'm on top of the driveway
Saying, "Annie come here," she still has attention to pay.
I run up behind her, I pet her and sit,
I know she's hoping I will not soon quit.
We go inside so slow and so steady,
But then she spots the neighbor's dog, Teddy.
Caroline Gibbs, Grade 5
Sabal Point Elementary School, FL

Volleyball
Volleyball
Awesome, fun
Bumps, sets, spikes
I love volleyball a lot
Serves, blocks, digs
Athletic, amazing
Volleyball
Stephanie Kidd, Grade 6
Challenger K8 School of Science and Mathematics, FL

Lucky Christmas
Freezing breeze in the air.
Cold snow falling from the sky
wet and mushy.
Arctic fox crossing my yard.
Putting the bow on top of the Christmas tree.
Building a snowman with my bare hands.
Sledding down the snowy white hill.
Drinking hot chocolate
getting warm from the snow.
A snow owl coming to my window.
Watching the snow fall on Christmas Eve.
Watching the snow freeze
before it hits the ground.
Sedona Quesenberry, Grade 4
Tabernacle Elementary School, NC

Summer
Summer
Hot, sunny
Sweltering, blistering, scorching
Flowers, lawnmowers, snowman, snow shovel
Freezing, snowing, sleeting
Cold, dreary
Winter
Aaron Cabe, Grade 6
Scotts Creek Elementary School, NC

The Rainbow
Red is the color of my sister's cheeks.
Purple flowers will bloom in a few weeks.

Pink is the color that I like.
Blue is the color of my bike.

Gray is a bore.
White is the bird that soars.

Yellow is the burning sun.
Tan is the color of my toasted bun.

Gold makes a lovely wedding ring.
Orange is my bell that goes ding.
Nathlie Leal, Grade 6
Tequesta Trace Middle School, FL

Trash
I don't like taking out the trash.
When I do it I try to dash.
Because the trash is smelly and stinky
I ship it away in a dingy.
Because sometimes it gets very large
I store it on a little barge.
Sometimes when I take out the trash
I'll accidentally drop it and some things will smash.
Drew Sheldon, Grade 6
St Mary Magdalen Catholic School, FL

Special Gifts

Sometimes, when I'm not looking
the perfect picture
comes into my camera.
It's always a surprise each time.
I review the frames,
catching nature off guard,
a sleeping kitty
or a breathtaking sunset;
special gifts.

Madeleine Huhn, Grade 6
J Larry Newton School, AL

Day's End

Sun starts to set
It starts to get late
My friends start to leave one by one
Soon they have all gone home
I get very depressed
my parents call
I tell them I will go
I start walking home
I mourn over the day's end

Luis Granados, Grade 6
Tequesta Trace Middle School, FL

The Noise

A noise in the dark
A noise in the light
Bothers no one now
Higher and higher!
Still no one hears
Silence now
Everyone notices
Now this is silence!
The rain has left
Let us all hear

Anais Ball-Gonzalez, Grade 6
Tequesta Trace Middle School, FL

Let's Get Together

Together we stand
Divided we fall
So let's stick together
Despite it all.
When one is down
Then all are down.
If she's a storyteller
And he's a yeller
Just 'cause we look alike
Doesn't mean we are.
I may be colored
You may not be
As long as we stick together
Friends we will be.

Kristin Henry, Grade 6
Hand Middle School, SC

Music

Music is a song of
emotion and passion.
It takes steps
but easy to do.
You need the passion
and a little bit of rhythm too.
Music expresses feelings.
Music changes just like a feeling.
Once you think something
then your mind goes into a daze.
The emotion can build
and start flowing like a hurricane.
It goes till the emotions explode
and music comes out of your mouth
from your soul.

Sheree Simon, Grade 5
Forestville Road Elementary School, NC

In the Snow

In the snow here and there
Snow is falling everywhere.
Will it stick? Will it stay?
Will we get time to play?

Make a snowman fat and round,
Until he melts back to the ground.

Run and jump, laugh and play
Dodging snowballs all day.
Colder and colder as I get,
It's time for some hot chocolate.

Darnell Hall, Grade 5
Our Lady of Fatima School, MS

Brothers and Sisters

Brothers
mean, rough
annoying, confusing, unsupporting
cars, cards, shopping mall, phone
loving, caring, unconfusing
nice, supportive
Sisters

Lynzee Turner, Grade 5
Ranburne Elementary School, AL

Spring

Spring is here.
The flowers are blooming.
The birds are chirping.
You feel like you could float away!
The air is warmer.
The sun is shining.
It's such a beautiful day!
Spring is here.

Vanessa Hensley, Grade 5
North Windy Ridge School, NC

I Am

I am responsible and kind
I wonder what I had for homework
I hear a lion roaring at me
I see my future being bright
I want a laptop
I am responsible and kind

I pretend to be a college graduate
I feel needles poking at me
I touch the top of a mountain
I worry that I will get a C in school
I cry because my sister hits me
I am responsible and kind

I understand school and life
I say that I will be successful in life
I dream of me making money
I try to make the world a better place
I hope for world peace
I am responsible and kind

Sarah Plott, Grade 5
Stokesdale Elementary School, NC

The Waterfall

Pouring, falling, dripping
waterfall
peacefully roars
in a secret forest

Suzanna Neal, Grade 4
PVPV/Rawlings Elementary School, FL

Eyes

Your eyes are like bright sapphires
Your voice is like a bird's sweet song
Your hair shimmers like the setting sun
Reflecting off smooth water
I love you so but do you love me

Matthew Hobbs, Grade 6
Shorecrest Preparatory School, FL

Danger!

There's a pony,
There's a hare,
Oh my gosh,
there's a bear!
A chill runs down my spine
my chances look thinner than twine.
Could this be it?
I start to think
when I turn, I'm surprised
It's gone!
Now I'm out of breath
but why should I care?
Since I've just cheated death!

Megan Cummings, Grade 6
McRae Elementary School, FL

What Do You Do
What do you do
When a tornado is coming?
What do you do
When the humming birds start humming?
What do you do
When you make a mistake?
What do you do
When your heart breaks?
What do you do
When the kids are at play?
I Pray.

Bridgett Anderson, Grade 5
CrossPointe Christian Academy, GA

Overslept
The clock struck ten,
Right when I dropped my pen.
I'm finally done writing this poem,
Making rhymes is much easier at home.
I'm so tired, I think I'm going to be dead.
I'm going to sleep in, if I don't go to bed.
What is that noise so early in the morning?
It's my alarm clock, it's so annoying.
What time is it, seven, oh no my poem is due at eight!
I need to hurry up, I haven't even ate!
How am I going to get to school?
Maybe I could cut through the bushes by the pool.
Seven thirty, I'm going to make it! Wait where's my poem?
I left it at my house, need to hurry back home.
Finally, I made it to school, I'm just in time!
I hope you like how I rhyme.
What, did it wrong! Please don't give me detention.
Next time, I'll pay more attention.

Garrison Brockway, Grade 6
Gold Hill Middle School, SC

Rainbows
Rainbows sparkle in the light.
Rainbows are colorful in every way.
Rainbows sit by the sun every few days.
If you watch you will see the beauty of a rainbow.
After that you can thank me.

Marianna Santostefano, Grade 4
Spruce Creek Elementary School, FL

Surfer
There once was a surfer named Gary Gray
who liked to surf on big waves all day

It did not matter rain or shine
all he said is that wave is mine

Until he met hit match you see
now he surfs among the heavenly

Ben Golden, Grade 6
Pinellas County Jewish Day School, FL

Shopping
I love you.
I can't wait to swipe that debit card.
I can't wait to sign my name.
I love trying on those shoes.
I love going into the dressing room.
Nike, Pacsun, Abercrombi, American Eagle.
I love shopping and I always will.

Brai Royer, Grade 5
Pensacola Beach Elementary School, FL

I Fly in the Wind
I am a baseball, always soaring through the air
I am lightning, I move really quick
I am the road, I get driven on every day
I am a mouse, I am very sneaky
I am a knot, I get tangled up all the time
I am a boat, I sail on the water
I am a camera, I picture stuff in my head
I am a plane, I fly in the wind

Alan Johnson, Grade 5
Four Oaks Elementary School, NC

Pitching
The nice leather on my hands.
Me walking onto the mound.
I am in my stretch, strike one.
The next pitch, strike two.
That pitch was sizzling like bacon on a pan.
I am on fire.
It is time to unleash the beast.
Strike three, you're out.

Josh Lamb, Grade 6
Seven Springs Middle School, FL

Success
Do you want success
and beat the rest?
Or do you want to be the best?
It's up to you
Don't live in a shoe,
Be happy with what you,
CHOOSE!!!

Success, Success,
oh, I want to be the best,
oh, I don't want to live in a shoe!
Oh how about you?!

Do you want Success
and beat the rest?
Or do you want to be the best

I KNOW I DO!!!

Shoshana Huayllas, Grade 4
Clearview Avenue Elementary School, FL

Puppies

P layful
U nlikely to know what they're doing
P erfect
P lain funny
I n their own style
E very pup is different
S ometimes a pain in the neck

Alexandria Passamonte, Grade 4
Spruce Creek Elementary School, FL

Mountains Far and Near

Mountains far and mountains near
Come closer, let me hear
Your animals frisking about
And the splashing of the trout.
Mountains far and mountains near
Come closer still so I can hear
The rustling of your leaves about
And the music of my ear
From mountains far and mountains near.

Koehna Jordan, Grade 4
Life Community Academy, NC

Hunting

Hunting…
    Such a wonderful sport!
However,
    some people might give it a retort!
I think they might be vegetarians
    But still I want to begin…
        Hunting!

Dakota Anders, Grade 6
Scotts Creek Elementary School, NC

Oreo the Puppy

A puppy was in a pet store
It was a cute one too
I wanted it so bad that
I begged and begged 100 times

It was like an Oreo cookie
And it made me hungry
So I went to a store
And got a chocolate cookie

The puppy wanted some too
So I gave it some cookie
I didn't see the sign that said
Do not feed animals

I got the puppy
Because they caught me
I named it Oreo
Because it would only eat Oreo cookies.

Bethany McKenzie, Grade 5
West Marion Elementary School, MS

The Best Buddy Ever*

My buddy is my dog and my life…
Every time I think about him, he brightens me just right!
His white and brown fur shines as the sun reflects on it…
As his fur flies when the wind hits it and his joyful grin brightens my DAY!
My other half is my life my life is my other.
My other half is my dog and he's my LIFE!

Ayauna Mitchell, Grade 6
Gold Hill Middle School, SC
**R.I.P. Bo-Bo Dickerson (I miss you)*

I Don't Understand

I don't understand
    why sometimes kids and adults are mean to me
    why some people treat others badly
    why kids drop out of school.

Bust most of all
    why family members you love have to die
    why individuals have to suffer
    why strangers have to steal and ruin their lives by doing drugs.

What I understand most is
    why kids go to school
    why I enjoy being myself
    why I love my family.

Jose Catarino, Grade 6
Turkey Creek Middle School, FL

Shay

Shay
Singer
Sweet, outgoing, caring, and interesting
Lover of singing, animals, and friends
Who believes everyone can succeed in their dreams
Who wants a loving family, to go to college, and a singing career
Who uses support, care, and love
Who gives good advice, songs to the world, and a great performance
Who says don't be afraid to speak your mind
Coolican

Shay Coolican, Grade 6
Broad Creek Middle School, NC

I Am From…

I am from wind whistling through the window screen
From running around the kitchen getting Mom to scare my hiccups away
From the old fence in our backyard
From good times with my friends
From the warm cookie smell when I get home
From my car bed
From banging pots and pans
From singing songs in the car
From crying at Stephanie's funeral
I love where I am from
I love it

Lakeland Jackson, Grade 4
Settles Bridge Elementary School, GA

High Merit Poems – Grades 4, 5, and 6

The Flea
There once was a flea, jumping through the sky
Leaping onto others way up high
He bites and is greedy like a hog
His favorite home is on my dog
I'm going to the store to make him go "Bye, Bye!"
Izayah Thomas, Grade 5
Manchester Elementary School, NC

The Shot
Duke is known for their amazing shot,
on that day Christian Laettner was hot.

2.1 seconds were left on the clock,
Grant Hill was the one with the rock.

Grant was determined when he went to make the throw,
Kentucky hated their equal foe.

No one knew how the game was going to finish,
But Kentucky's dominance was about to diminish.

The turnaround jumper fell right in,
Duke had just had one of its greatest wins.

The clock finally ticked zero,
Christian Laettner was made Duke's hero.

That game was one of the best played,
But that shot was the greatest made.
Cameron McNeill, Grade 6
Brogden Middle School, NC

The Door
This is a large, black door.
Now, what could it be for?
Might there be a secret meeting inside?
Not by any laws do these people abide.
There may be a large debate going on.
Who knows? These people might talk until dawn.
What country is this large door in?
Possibly in one where not many have been.
There might be a child resting his head
Sleeping peacefully inside his own bed.
This could be the door to an old church.
On the top of the roof some birds might perch.
I wonder who made this door so elegant?
Through this door many things have been sent.
There are many uses for such a door
For entering and exiting and much more.
Whatever it's for it, for as long as it's there
People will see it and always stare.
And people will think, this is a large, black door,
And once they go in, they will know what it's for.
A.J. Cole, Grade 6
Woodward Academy North, GA

The Tall Grandfather Clock
The tall grandfather clock is ticking and tocking,
ticking and tocking,
ticking through the hot day and the cold night.
It's saying good morning, good day, and good night
to you and to me.
Damien Ahrens, Grade 5
North Windy Ridge School, NC

Cat Conference
The cats get together
To talk about the weather
And the new things in their neighborhood

"Meow, purr, mew, so what else is new?
Have you seen the new bird bath? The water's very blue!"

These cats, not very good,
Are elegant and suave, acting as only a cat should.

They come from all around, some Persian, some Siamese.
They eat a dinner of tuna, potatoes, and peas.

But as if out of nowhere, dogs come to disrupt!
Hissing and spitting is heard, and the cats leave abrupt.

Yet this is not the end of the cat conference,
Their meeting is just starting to commence.

"Meow, purr, mew, so what else is new?
Have you seen the new bird bath? The water's really blue!"
Henry Black, Grade 6
St John's Lutheran School, NC

Football
When I play football
I feel the wind trying to slow me down
My heart pounds as I thunder through the field
Though they try to make me yield
The feeling that you get when you make a touchdown
Is extraordinary
You hear the crowd yelling out your name
Yah Tucker, Yah Tucker
It hurts my ears
As I take a player down the ground shakes
I can make out his pain
Winning is like nothing else in the world
When I'm at quarterback I throw the ball hard
Whoosh, it rockets through the air to the wide receiver
Crack, crack
I can hear the defensive players' helmets bust
As they tumble to the ground
It's not just winning
It's the rush
I'm not just a kid I'm a football player
Tucker Sanders, Grade 6
Williston Middle School, NC

Holocaust
Hearing the train coming
To pick us up 6 million Jews
To be taken to our death
Never to see light again
The Nazis split us up
The weak the strong
The weak to be killed right along
The strong to be at labor long
The hospital will lie so you die
Because we have no hope
We the survivors
Who are our teachers must tell all
Never to forget
This tragic event
Samantha Medoff, Grade 6
Tequesta Trace Middle School, FL

Night Sky
Twinkling and shining stars
in a dark night sky
happy,
hugging these two,
finally together again
the stars shine like lightning bugs
guiding us north to freedom.
Stephanie Duncan, Grade 4
Pinnacle Elementary School, NC

Savana
Savana skipped and scanned
As she ran down the school hallway,
If I may say, I am quicker than a cat
I am faster than a rat,
I ran on the road to school,
Help me, help me
A phogowoonshologo passed!
It's chasing me!
Help me, help me!
Sara Ellis, Grade 4
Barnardsville Elementary School, NC

Spring Joys
Spring joys
Flowers, rainbows
Growing, smiling, singing
Blossoms reaching up to the sky
Artwork
Cassie Bright, Grade 5
Bridgeway Christian Academy, GA

Everlasting Japan
Its culture moves me
Its days are everlasting
My heart will love it
Leah Kihumba, Grade 6
St Petersburg Christian School, FL

Spring
Flowers, flowers everywhere,
Come outside breathe fresh air.
Not too cold, not too hot,
Go outside and play a lot.
Better than all the seasons,
for lots, and lots, and lots
of reasons.
Samantha Sheir, Grade 4
Central Park Elementary School, FL

Bob
There once was a dog named Bob
Who only sat and sobbed
His old girlfriend came in
And kicked him in the shin
And said, "Get over it, you old dog."
Will Baughn, Grade 5
Ranburne Elementary School, AL

School
School is where I learn all day.
School is where I am all day.
School is where I go to shine,
Make good grades then climb
Up to seventh grade!
Jessica Schweiger, Grade 6
Statesville Middle School, NC

Darkness Is…
A huge black pit
Everywhere God's light doesn't shine
A huge black hole in space
My burning black soul
The dark shadow that follows you
Jordan Basye, Grade 6
Arlington Middle School, FL

Bunnies
B eautiful
U sually active
N ever very bad
N ice
I nnocent
E ats sometimes
S leeps a lot
Sara Costner, Grade 4
Spruce Creek Elementary School, FL

Spring
I see Easter eggs,
I hear bees buzzing,
I feel wind blowing,
I smell spring air,
I touch spring flowers.
Cierra Jankie, Grade 4
Central Park Elementary School, FL

Can You Imagine…
A turtle with hair
A zoo without a bear

A camel wearing eye liner
A mine without a single miner

The Gators without a quarterback
A human without a back

Football without a ball
New York without a mall

A dog that doesn't bark
The sky never dark

An animal without foes
A human without toes

The world without time
A couplet that doesn't rhyme?
Sona Thakur, Grade 4
William S Talbot Elementary School, FL

The African Plains
An amazing sunrise
Marks the start to a new day
A buffalo gets up from its resting place
Sniffing the air for signs of his race
The canaries sing great songs,
"Briight, briight"
They sing happily,
As the cheetahs
Search below for vulnerable prey
Rudy Zindel, Grade 5
Rosarian Academy, FL

Fishing
Last night I set up my fishing pole;
Tomorrow I will go to a fishing hole.
I've got four rods and reels;
I use them to catch electric eels!
Today I put on my waders
I might go hook a hunting alligator
I used a fly to catch a rainbow trout!
I did it without a doubt!
Seth Sloan, Grade 6
Scotts Creek Elementary School, NC

Cheer
C heer stunts are fun.
H ave fun to learn
E arn medals when we win.
E ager to do something
R ace out to begin.
Destin Calhoun, Grade 4
East Jones Elementary School, MS

High Merit Poems – Grades 4, 5, and 6

Brothers

I'm the youngest of four brothers.
Other than Sam, Dave and Abe,
There are no others.

We used to do everything together,
No matter how bad the weather.
It could have rained or snowed,
But we went always down the road.

A lot of time has passed,
Since we last had a blast.
Each does his own thing,
Even in the spring.

Arie Akinin, Grade 4
Virginia A Boone Highland Oaks Elementary School, FL

Food Fight

Flicking peas and pizza in the face,
And peaches on my new white pants.
Milk in the eyes
And green beans on my nicest shirt
Everybody yelling and screaming and shouting out loud.
Food Fight.
We all go to lunch detention.
And never get to eat or drink those foods again.

Tyson Whiddon, Grade 4
Freeport Elementary School, FL

The Girl Who Kissed the Moon Goodbye*

Way up high, in the sparkly place, I can fly.
Where no one is sad.
Where the flowers smell like honey.
Where my family will stay with me forever.

Where there'll be peace forever.
But I am in a smoky village.
Soldiers in black suits jump around chasing.
I am alone.
Smoke comes out of a chimney. A lot of smoke.
People with stars come in…and out comes smoke.

Where's the world of peace? Not here.
I am scared.
Soldiers grab me.
They stick a star on me and throw me on a train.

I escape. I rip my star off and fall to the ground.
A man gets beaten to the ground. Dead.
My heart stops. The moon is sad.

Where is the place of honey?
Not here.
No one is here. I kiss the moon goodbye.

Shoshana LeVine, Grade 5
Pinellas County Jewish Day School, FL
*Inspired by "Number the Stars" by Lois Lowry

My Dog

There are many types of dogs,
Some are short and some are tall,
But the dog I have is the best of all

She loves to run and fetch a ball,
And if in the mood will give you her paw.

She spends her day a most puppies do
By playing with socks, and somebody's shoe,
But when I get home she's always there because
She knows I really care.

Seeing her at first can be quiet a surprise,
She's a bit unusual beginning with size.

Her eyes are brown, her face a bit flat, and
Pointy ears, which make her look like a rat.

My day is made when I give her a hug, because
She is my Chihuahua Pug.

Mel Staton, Grade 6
Chapin Middle School, SC

Fruit

Fruit's so yummy
They're so sweet, sour, or bitter
So good, so juicy, delicious, and wonderful
The nutrients flow through our tummies like a wavy river
So marvelous

They're so healthy
Fruit gives me an energy boost
Fruit is so bright and colorful, red, green, blue, and pink
Fruit fills up my belly on a bright blue beautiful sunny day
Grapes, pears, and plums

Kelsey Congress, Grade 5
The Sanibel School, FL

The Shark

A shark is like a torpedo, streaming through the night,
It's teeth are sharp as knives, gleaming in the light.
It's fins are like sails, cutting through the air,
It's attitude is strong, fierce like a bear.
It's eyes are like black pearls, fierce and dark as night,
It's diet is enough to cause anyone some fright.
It's body is strong and grey, it's bulk like a tank,
It's sides are strong as steel; it has the strongest flank.
It's the ruler of the sea; all the fish will flee.
Yet it should not be put in captivity,
It should be free to roam the sea,
And yet we humans think that we
Have the right to rule whatever we see.
Why can't humans be humans and let nature be?

Andrew Zidek, Grade 6
Challenger Middle School, FL

Hoof Beat

"Clop, clop, clop" the rhythmic thunder of hooves kicking up dirt behind me.
"Clop, clop, clop" down the dirt path.
"Clop, clop, clop" through the wide open field.
"Clop, clop, clop" up the hills.
"Clop, clop" to freedom.
"Clop, clop, clop" away from the fighting.
"Clop, clop, clop" away from the stress.
"Clop, clop, clop" wind whipping mane and hair, blowing away all fear.
"Clop, clop, clop" all worries.
"Clop, clop, clop" and then I wake up.
Back to reality.
Back to the stress, and fighting, and fear.
My body remains here in the swirling tornado of life,
But my heart belongs in the saddle beating to the steady beat of hooves pounding the earth.
Spirit soaring through the wind blowing our hair, free.

Madison Coghan, Grade 6
Martinez Middle School, FL

The Beach

I see the sun setting over the crystal clear waters. The colors outrages-orange, tickle-me-pink, and electric-yellow shoot out of the bright, round sun, hovering over the salty Atlantic Ocean. I spot the seagulls, the color of pearl white. CAW! CAW! One sails over to a spot in the water. All of a sudden, SWOOSH! He swoops down like a hawk, begins splashing it's wings, and soars up into the sky with its catch of the day. I climb up a sand dune to receive a closer view. BLECH! Sand splashed in my mouth. I begin to watch the horizon, ready to doze off into a dream. A wonderful, wonderful dream.

Valerie Mosser, Grade 4
Coral Park Elementary School, FL

Florida

Florida is very exciting and it is unique from other states.
It is the most beautiful state I know because of all the gorgeous palm trees.
One of the things that I think is one of the best parts of Florida is, its theme park Walt Disney World.
It is the second Walt Disney World in all of the United States!!!!!
Florida is very humid in the sun! But I still have fun!!
Florida has a colony named St. Augustine, it is the oldest colony in all of America.
This is why I think Florida is very special to me.

Jonathan Harris, Grade 4
FSU/City of Pembroke Pines Charter Elementary School, FL

I Learned That…

I learned that my parents care about me.
I learned that life always takes you somewhere where you didn't expect to go.
I learned that two heads are better than one.
I learned that two wrongs make a right.
I learned that friendship can only go so far, but love will last forever.
I learned to accept people for who they are no matter how they look.
I learned to take life as it is.
I learned to never give up no matter how hard it looks.
I learned to say thank you for everything I receive.
I learned that school will get you far in life.
I learned to never pick on people.
I learned to always try something new.
I learned that brothers may be annoying, but they love and care about you.
I learned that teachers are not here to befriend me, but to get me ready for the real world.
I learned that family, friends, and teachers are here for one reason, for my well being.

Denitra Jackson, Grade 5
Northside Elementary School, SC

When My Brother Went to College
On this day I'm feeling sad
Nothing is going right
My mind is blocked
So I can't think
My heart just stopped
And I can't feel a thing
I start to weep
And then I say
I'm gonna sleep this day away
And there I go off to bed
Turn off the light and lay my head
So peaceful and quiet my room is
And I twist and roll till I go to sleep
When I wake up as alive as alive can be
I look back at the past and say oh poor me
My brother just left for college
And I'm still here so sad and lonely
With no one to talk to or play with
Sometimes I cry but I always know
He's coming back soon to visit and love.

Carolina Zindel, Grade 5
Rosarian Academy, FL

World War I
Boom! Bam! Shoot 'em. Run.
This war ain't no fun.
Try not to get struck. Hurry up. DUCK.
Nationalism is what started this crazy war.
I hope it all walks out the door.
Men fighting for land.
Yeah, I get it
You wanted more land
Fight for it?
Come on man?

Kiaundria Truesdale, Grade 5
North Elementary School, SC

Be Myself*
When I'm by myself and close my eyes
I dream about the galaxy floating by.

I dream about playing baseball on all the planets
And hitting a homerun clear to Atlantis!

I go crazy like I've just won the World Series…
My dreams float in space and everything varies.

In my dreams I visit the Milky Way,
I eat and drink everything…every day!

I love the wonderful world of my dreams,
That's where I create all sorts of schemes!

Sean Hutchison, Grade 4
Irmo Elementary School, SC
*Inspired by Eloise Greenfield

Behind the Castle Door
A beautiful stone and iron door.
Who lives behind it?
A Princess and many more,
Servants, maids, and even cooks.
A Princess named Belle,
And servants who will come,
If she gives a yell.
What Belle says always goes.
Tonight there is going to be a ball.
People all running all around the place,
Putting down carpet so no one falls.
Everyone is oh so busy.
The cooks are making delicious food.
The servants are doing Belle's hair.
The maids are making sure everything looks good,
And Belle is getting dressed in her gown.
Now guests are arriving in groups of four.
The cars are unloading.
Now more and more and more,
And now the castle door is closing.

Grace Broadbent, Grade 6
Woodward Academy North, GA

Lake
L ounge around the lake awhile
A ct out something so someone can guess what I am!
K neel down to find clams!
E at lots of ice cream!

Allyson Myrick, Grade 4
East Jones Elementary School, MS

Memories of a Soldier
Sustained
Suspended
In the high, beautiful blue sky above,
Serving for my country

Dodging missiles
Shooting them
War is a death trap

These memories of mine, are my very best of all.
Memories of the high, beautiful sky

Memories of losses,
Memories of wins

Memories of men who are no longer with us

I fought for our justice
I fought for our rights

I am a soldier
These are my memories.

Marissa Rahn, Grade 6
Seven Springs Middle School, FL

The Baseball Bat
I wait patiently in the dugout
I cannot wait until someone uses me
Finally someone grabs me on the rubber
I swing through the air
I missed
I swing again
I feel something hit me
I hit the ground hard
I go back to the dugout

Jace Amberson, Grade 4
Pensacola Beach Elementary School, FL

Bandit
He may be chunky and frisky,
He's also very light.
He's covered in the wonderful colors,
Black and light white.
He eats so much he's getting fat,
Even though he is my cat.
He plays all the time he is very fun,
When it comes to cats,
My cat Bandit is number one.

Brian Cox, Grade 6
Tarpon Springs Middle School, FL

Funeral
My eyes stare down
On your sleeping face
And all the awakened flowers
That surround you in their vase

As all the people leave
I don't move from my spot
Just thinking where you'd be
Cause it is where I'm not

All my salty tears
Stream out from my eyes
Their taste isn't the first
But this event is a surprise

I can't wait for the day
I see you smile and grin
I can't wait for the day
I see you again.

Taylor Harrison, Grade 6
Chapin Middle School, SC

Mellow
Mellow is blue
It smells like a pine forest
It tastes like chocolate cake
It sounds like soothing music
It feels like a sunset at the beach

Jason Bernstein, Grade 6
Tarpon Springs Middle School, FL

Happiness
Happiness is the sight of people smiling on their birthdays.
Kids laughing while playing a game of tag is the sound of happiness.
Happiness feels like helping someone in need.
A big chunk of cake tastes like happiness.
Happiness smells like flowers being given to you after a day of hard work.

Nicole Roberts, Grade 4
Wrights Mill Road Elementary School, AL

Kittens
To some people, a baby chick is very cute, and even a furry rabbit.
I would have to agree.
To people who like to jump, a kitten is like a football player
Trying to catch the ball.
But to me, a little midnight black-and-white kitten
That likes to jump on the couch to watch a movie with you,
Purring like a car engine,
Is the most wonderful thing in the whole world.
Oh, kittens that are mine — Ruffy and Twinkle — warm my heart
In the morning, and in the night.
Meow!

Kayla Porter, Grade 4
Julian D Parker School of Science, Math & Technology, FL

Sensing Nature
Listening to the pleasant sound of a spring nearby.
Feeling the most sensitive touch of the wind.
Leaves soaring through the sky.
I walk so calmly through the woods.
Hearing the peaceful sound of birds chirping up high.
Squirrels in the canopy bouncing from branch to branch.
The sweet smell of gorgeous flowers surround me.
The warm, bright sun floods through the woods.
As I walk, I see, I hear, and smell the way nature is and how wonderful it can be.

Davin McGee, Grade 6
McRae Elementary School, FL

The Soccer Game
One morning on a hot summer day,
there is a soccer game that I will play.
This game is really fun,
when there is a bright shining sun.
There are teammates that can be friends,
right after the soccer season ends.
Today is a big soccer game that's going to be tough,
and it's also going to be very very rough.
This game is the soccer tournament and is really really big,
after this game I'm going to smell like a pig!
There is a trophy that you can get,
if you have more points for the game to set.
There is one more goal that my team needs to make,
and I have to make it for goodness sake!
I made the goal and I won the game, now I feel better and not the same.
When I come home with my trophy to keep
I went to bed with a good night sleep.

Shiv Bhakta, Grade 5
Our Lady of Fatima School, MS

Dragon's Morning

The sun has risen and seems to say:
Get up, it's the start of a new day.
In its cave the dragon wakes,
Stands up and starts to stretch and shake.
He walks outside and flexes his wings,
Listening quietly as a small bird sings.
In a burst of air he's off,
Down below a squirrel scoffs.
Up and up the dragon flies,
Soaring through the morning skies.

Veronika Cesar, Grade 6
Freedom Middle School, FL

First Time Fishing

My brothers, cousin, and I went fishing.
The ride was like picking cotton from a field;
Yeah, it was boring.
It was the longest hour ever.
When we got to the lake,
We were the only people fishing.
My paw-paw caught a fish
As big as his head
But threw it back.
Everybody got a fish, but me.
They talked about me the whole time.
The hook got stuck in my head.
My blood was red as a chili pepper.
Every bait I got the fish ate in one bite!
The trip was like our football games.
It was fun!

Jaron Anderson, Grade 5
East Marion Elementary School, MS

Let Freedom Ring

Freedom yells at the top of her lungs
Freedom feels like justice in war
Freedom sounds like a bell ringing
Freedom marches like a soldier going off to war
Freedom moves like an eagle soaring in the sky
Freedom is like a 21 gun salute
Freedom doesn't look back
She is not afraid

Hannah Staley, Grade 4
Tabernacle Elementary School, NC

Thinking of You

Thinking of you wherever you are.
We pray for our sorrows to end
And hope our hearts blend.
Now I will step forward to realize this wish.
And who knows maybe starting a new journey
may not be so hard or it already began.
There are many worlds but they all share the same sky —
ONE SKY, ONE DESTINY

Kaishanna Young, Grade 6
Philadelphia Elementary School, MS

The Sun

When the sun is up
I like the light
because it is bright.
When it's light
I feel happy
when it's gone
I feel sad.
When I fall asleep
and wake up again
I become happy once again.

Mathew Maldonado, Grade 5
Eugenia B Thomas Elementary School, FL

Rollercoaster Ride

Waiting in line for thirty minutes now,
Can't wait to get up front and sit down,
Sitting down no floor under me,
My aunt and my brother right beside me,

Going up that hill steep as could be,
Looking down to see everyone looking at me,
Two hundred and ten feet up in the air,
Dropping ninety degrees straight down I wouldn't dare,

Ahhhh is all you could hear,
While we sat and rode the ride of fear,
Going up another hill this one not as high,
Going over water and getting splashed right in the eye,

Twisting and turning in the air,
People screaming like wild animals everywhere,
Slowing down and touching the ground,
When we stopped it made a screeching sound,
But it was a blast,
I wish it could last.

Rena Poulson, Grade 6
Williston Middle School, NC

4th of July

I remember on the 4th of July.
We seen the beautiful fireworks up in the sky
But an accident happened.
A firework went off
And hit my brother in the eye.

We went to the mall.
My family bought it all.
We went to a lot of places.
We had a ball.

We were on the way home.
My cousin named Rhome
Was getting on my nerves singing a song.

Jalon Anderson, Grade 5
East Marion Elementary School, MS

Football
F earless
O ffenses
O r
T ough
B litzing
A nd
L inebackers vs
L inemen
Joshua Bar-Haim, Grade 4
Prince Avenue Christian School, GA

Love
Love is good
Love is thoughtful
Love is what you get
From your family and friends
Treavor Windsor, Grade 5
Rock Mills Jr High School, AL

Flowers
F lowers
L ittle flowers
O range flowers
W hite flowers
E ven pink flowers
R ed flowers
S unflowers
Jasmine McGill, Grade 4
East Jones Elementary School, MS

Nightmare
N ight is when it happens
I nteresting like two headed turtles
G ross as broccoli
H orror like scary movies
T orture like being grounded
M urder like mystery stories
A wful like my handwriting
R IP as put on graves
E vil as bulldogs
Ricardo Araujo, Grade 6
Tarpon Springs Middle School, FL

Blooming Flowers
I see blooming flowers
I hear a rustle
I feel wind in my hair
I smell roses
I touch the blooming daisies
Blooming flowers
A rustle
Wind in my hair
Roses
The blooming daisies
Jordyn Sanchez, Grade 4
Central Park Elementary School, FL

Wind
I am the wind blowing through your hair
Brushing soft on skin so fair
I whistle filling streets with fright
Extra eerie in the dark of night

My cold breeze shall make you shiver
Chills up your spine to make you quiver
You inhale my sweet refreshing breeze
Unlock the door with frozen keys

Bird wings rest upon my shoulder
They fly south as I get colder
Hurricanes twirl in the palm of my hand
I also bring grief across the land…
Ava Pasnon, Grade 6
Bak Middle School of the Arts, FL

Time
Time is ticking
Time is clicking
Time is wasting
Time is racing
Time is spinning
Time is winning
Time is going
Time is flowing
Time.
What else could you say about it?
You will all see in good time.
Trace Guy, Grade 4
Pine Tree Hill Elementary School, SC

The Bomb
It was in the low fifties,
and I was up to bat.
My friend Logan Hollyman was pitching,
and he was in his groove.
The first pitch was a ball,
but the next pitch was a strike
that I fouled off.
"I'm not going to strike out." I told him.
I got ready
for the next pitch.
It was my favorite pitch
which was high and outside,
and that's when I swung.
It was a great swing.
I used all my hips,
and hit it right on the barrel of the bat.
The ball went sky high,
and I started jogging to first base.
Because as soon as I hit it
I knew it would be my
first homerun!
Ben Lowinski, Grade 6
Lake Park Baptist School, FL

Raining
Beating on my window
It plays a lovely tune

But changes mood
Screams to the sky
Fighting with the thunder

Fades away
Leaves for awhile
To greet another town.
Leah Wilkerson, Grade 6
St John's Lutheran School, NC

Not Enough Time
There isn't enough time in the world
For me to do a thing.
I will often be finishing up something,
When the bell decides to ring.

It really annoys me
That time can't wait on you.
If only they could invent something
That's totally brand new.

Oh, how I hate the days flying by,
If only they could be longer.
I see my free time vanishing,
How could the day get any wronger.

I try my hardest to beat time
At its own game.
I find that it's impossible,
Because it fades as quickly as it came.
Jenna French, Grade 6
J E Holmes Middle School, NC

Spring
Slowly it creeps in:
The plants growing,
The flowers blooming,
And smiles bright!

Slowly it creeps in:
The rains falling,
The birds calling,
It's just right
  Spring!
Tiffany Reid, Grade 4
Central Park Elementary School, FL

Bluebird in the Sky
Bluebird in the sky
With a bright beak and long wings
In the afternoon.
Rebecca Young, Grade 6
Tequesta Trace Middle School, FL

High Merit Poems – Grades 4, 5, and 6

Feelings of Winter
I love the feeling of waking up
And seeing an amazing white blanket outside my window.
Chills run down my spine
Stumbling downstairs, slipping on jackets, slipping on coats,
Throwing snowballs with all my friends
Getting hit…my legs, my toes
White fluffy flakes going to and through my throat
But getting a huge taste of hot cocoa
Is the best feeling ever.
Tanner Hall, Grade 4
Sharon Elementary School, GA

In the Morning
When the sun shines bright,
the morning turns light.
I like it when it's not dark as night.
I see the houses, it's a great sight.

I start the day with a morning yawn,
and see the sun brighter than dawn.
I see my cat, his eyes dark as a fawn,
then I take him outside to play in the lawn.

I eat breakfast with my mom and dad,
feeling happy, better than sad.
My sister comes down looking mad,
so we cheer her up with a morning chat.

This is how my morning is,
sometimes different, like screaming kids.
I like the mornings I would say,
but I like it better than the rest of the day.
Melissa Santiago, Grade 5
Manchester Elementary School, NC

Walking with You
On this night, the stars so bright,
I'm walking with you through this heavenly light.

The pearly gates show when we are together,
I would walk the line for you, despite the weather.

As we walk these streets of gold,
The feeling grows, as I'm told.

A never ending love,
Floating as gently as a dove.

So as the night is fading,
I can't stop saying.

Life is love and love is life.
So I've enjoyed walking with you on this heavenly night.
Bradley Hughes, Grade 6
Brogden Middle School, NC

Cats
To me, cats are best.
They know when to play and know when to rest.

Cats can be hyper or they can be lazy.
They can be named Razor or Daisy.

Some can be clingy.
With tails that are stringy.

Some may break apart.
With an independent heart.

Some live in the wild.
Some play with a child.

Whether born lazy or meant to roam,
Cats are the greatest, free or at home.
Hayley Morrison, Grade 6
Boiling Springs Intermediate School, SC

My Grandma, My Hero
Whether in heaven or on earth
My grandma had always been there for me
She loved all of us,
My dog, my sister, and especially me
I cherish the time I spent with her
Our best memory is playing cards together
Either Old Maid or Rummy
Rummy was our favorite
We laugh half the time
Because I was always winning
Grandma was smart,
Sweet, and supportive
She was pretty like a butterfly
She was a prize fighter
Especially when she started to get sick
Now she is gone,
But she will always be there for me
My grandma, my hero
Nick Callaway, Grade 6
Unity School, FL

Love Always Has Its Way
Love is like a rose
It is elegant and beautiful
But it also has thorns
That can hurt you real badly
Love can be like choosing a puppy
You want the cutest one
But that one is just not right
For some reason you want the one no one wants
And it is the perfect match
Love is your personal roller coaster
So enjoy the ride
Hallie Wheeler, Grade 6
McRae Elementary School, FL

Hunter
I run though the Savannah
I walk through the tall grass
I stock my prey
I leap to the ground
Yummm!
That was a good meal
Then I sniff the air
My mane blows in the wind.
Lexi McNamara, Grade 4
Pensacola Beach Elementary School, FL

I Keep Moving Along
I am a diary; Secrets are kept in me
I am a flower; I'm very delicate
I am the rain; I fall from the sky
I am the wind; I like to breeze through
I am instructions; easy to understand
I am a pencil; always being held

I am a camera; I get the picture
I am the ocean; I keep moving along
Kayla McLamb, Grade 5
Four Oaks Elementary School, NC

God Is
God is love.
He cherishes us from above.
He wakes us up every day.
To carry us through a stormy way.
Alexius Jefferson, Grade 5
West Marion Elementary School, MS

Keys
keys
  jingling
    by the
      music
      of the
      wind
      unlocking
      unseen
        things
     keys
      have
      mysteries
     inside their
    silver, copper
      coats
   keys dangling
       on
   a key ring
    waiting,
  waiting, waiting
   for someone.
Amy Poe, Grade 4
Stone Academy, SC

Nimisha
Like a rose, blooming all around me, bursting out ideas.
Like a giraffe, I stand up for myself straight, tall, and elegant
Like the colors light pink and yellow
at times I am caring, generous, and elegant and at other times,
I shine bright all around me as a hyper excited leader
Like Jell-O, I am noisy and nothing can get past me for I know everything
Like a straightener, I flatten out everyone's problems like a helper
Like a pearl, always trying to be perfect and doing my best every chance I get
Like a Z-3 BMW, I zoom through most of all my obstacles and problems
And like a notebook, I save all my remarkable thoughts
and open like a roaring mouth to share it with everyone
Nimisha Vasandani, Grade 5
Sharon Elementary School, GA

You Light Up My Life
You light up the room when that's just what it needs.
You light up my world when everything seems gray.
You light up my life when everything's gone wrong.
And all it takes is one look my way to let me know everything's okay.
Elizabeth Henley, Grade 6
St Francis Xavier Elementary School, MS

Can You Imagine?
Can you imagine?
A night with no frights? A day with no fights?
Can you imagine?
A life with no loops? A government with no troops?
Can you imagine?
If Earth was actually heaven? If there was no 9/11?
Can you imagine?
If there was no such thing as a nightmare? If evil was rare?
Well it's not rare. Evil is everywhere.
Can you only imagine?
Can you only imagine?
Well I can only imagine.
The world is a complex place. There is only one human race.
One day the world will change
One day, you'll see! But that person who changes it, won't be you or me.
It will be the Creator, that we cannot see.
I know that all sounds quite odd, but that my friend *is*, yes God.
Andrea E. Rivera-Velazquez, Grade 6
Tarpon Springs Middle School, FL

Winter
Winter jumps for joy like a little kid getting a gift.
Winter is toys pleading to play with girls and boys on Christmas Day.
Winter is hot chocolate running down my throat making me warm.
Winter is fresh, warm cookies waiting to be eaten.
Winter feels heartwarming by giving people gifts.
Winter is kids laughing while playing in the snow.
Winter is a snowman coming to life when you put on his top hat.
Winter is a crystal snowflake falling from the sky to tell you winter is here.
Winter is a snowman dancing around.
Winter is tiny pieces of ice making you shiver.
Michaela Dawkins, Grade 4
Tabernacle Elementary School, NC

Pink

Pink is like a bunny jumping in meadows full of flowers.
Pink is like a pink ribbon in a little girl's hair.
Pink tastes like a sugary cherry.
Pink is like a humming bird singing on a tree.
Pink smells like a rose that's ready to be picked.
Pink is a new baby sister that was just born.
Pink is a butterfly.
Pink is like a light shade of red.
Pink is like a cranberry.
Pink is a mermaid and her hair cascading over her shoulders.

Aidee Tejeda-Manzano, Grade 4
Tabernacle Elementary School, NC

Me!!

Kristen
Fun
Hyper, athletic, outgoing, sister
Lover of dogs, sports, friends
Who believes in Santa/Easter Bunny/Tooth Fairy
Who wants friends, happiness, no drama
Who uses good advice, friends, the computer
Who gives joy, peace, presents
Who says, "one man's trash is another man's treasure"
Baker

Kristen Baker, Grade 6
Broad Creek Middle School, NC

What a Day

an island with a cool breeze sitting there waiting
the sweet smell of ocean mist goes across my face
the sound of fish jumping for their survival and their first meal
the sun just peeking over the horizon
shadows in the water disappear into the deeper parts
all the corals start to bloom into their gorgeous figures
even sharks go to their cold places
hermit crabs start to run
you hear the pitter patter of the crabs' claws
now the sun is lowering down to the horizon
what a day in chub cay bahamas

Taylor Wolf, Grade 6
Shorecrest Preparatory School, FL

Spring

Spring is in the air,
Flowers are blooming everywhere,
Bright colors of yellow, pink, and green fill the air,
The sun begins to shine brightly and the weather is fair,
Birds are singing a happy song,
While the days grow long,
Butterflies flutter all around,
Seldom landing on the ground,
While children prance round and round!
Yes, spring is my favorite time of the year!
It brings a lot of cheer!

Kyle Cox, Grade 5
Tuscaloosa Academy, AL

Peace Is a Violin

Peace is a violin.
I woke up on a snowy, white winter day
Snow blanketed the ground, icicles hung on trees
Like still stalactites cold to the touch.
I took out the violin and
Filled the air with a song of
Peace.

Love is a viola.
I flung open the door on Valentine's Eve
Present in one hand, viola in the other.
I lay the present on soft snow,
Took out the viola and filled the sky with
A sweet song of
Love.

Hope is a violoncello.
I was in a memorial for people who left us
Seven years ago, on 9/11.
I think back to that fateful day,
Remembering all those who left,
Took out the violoncello and filled the world with
A sweet song of hope.

Nemi Kalio, Grade 6
R D and Euzelle P Smith Middle School, NC

This Guy with Me

Oh how he looks at me romantic,
I am really starting to panic.
Is he coming over here with a rose,
Or is he going to propose?

He's the most handsome man I've ever seen
And he looks like a colorful beam.
He said, "My heart will mend,
Will you be my girlfriend?"

It was such a beautiful sight
So the whole day was bright.
I know it's just around the bend,
But that's the end

Michelle Le, Grade 5
St Martin Upper Elementary School, MS

Washing the Car

Soon I will be washing my mother's dirty car
Directly under the shining star
The soap suds are coming toward my feet
While the sun brings the blazing heat
I have a soaking soap rag in my hand
While I listen to my favorite band.
Once I finish this painstaking chore
My body feels so very sore

Shandy Sulen, Grade 6
St Mary Magdalen Catholic School, FL

An Ode to Books
A book is a loyal friend.
Books tell jokes.
Books make you laugh,
Books make you sad,
Or make you jolly.
But a book too is a loyal friend,
That doesn't tell lies,
Or tell secrets.
A book is someone I can talk to,
Books relate to me,
They never hurt my feelings.
That's why a books is a loyal friend.
Diane Hall, Grade 5
Sharon Elementary School, NC

Plies
P retty down to earth
L ikes to go to church
I ntelligent towards family
E xcellent rapper
S tays in touch with his mother
Chelsea Bryson, Grade 6
Arnold Magnet Academy, GA

Pretty Little Petals
From stem to stem
they pick me all day.
With my pretty little
petals I can float away.
Alexis Gunning, Grade 6
Milwee Middle School, FL

I'm From
I'm from a state
where it snows every
winter and you don't
have to dress heavily
I'm from
I'm from a place
where you can
play soccer in the
house
I'm from
I'm from a town
so small it seems
like it is an inch
long
I'm from
I'm from a house
where you can
blow up your dad's
room and get away
with it
I'm from
Grayson R. Guiney, Grade 4
Irmo Elementary School, SC

Jaquavious
Cute
Kind
Smart
Wishes to be a NFL player
Dreams of being successful
Wants to pass 5th grade
Who wonders about life in ten years
Who fears dying
Who is afraid of God
Who likes sports
Who believes in world peace
Who loves football
Who loves people
Who loves ELA
Who loves science
Who loves math
Who loves babies
Who plans to save the homeless
Who plans to retire from the NFL at 40
Who plans to die at 110
This is my dream, what's yours?
Jaquavious Forrest, Grade 5
Winona Elementary School, MS

Rabbit
Rabbit
Furry, creatures
Fat fluffy little tails
Bouncing, cozy, fluffy, cotton
Cuddly
Chantal White, Grade 6
Arnold Magnet Academy, GA

Moving
When you move,
It's hard to get in the groove.
The moving trucks come,
But you're glad when it's done.
Everyone cries,
Almost like someone dies.
You're covered in boxes,
And you look like oxes.
When you change your school,
You look real uncool.
You get a new room,
It's like your dungeon of doom.
You beg to go back today,
But you know there's no way.
You have to be befriended,
I'd rather be suspended!
You have new teachers,
That smell like old sneakers.
Now it gets better,
And you send your friends a letter.
Emily Denmeade, Grade 6
Gold Hill Middle School, SC

Books Are Adventures
Books are adventures
written down.
Sometimes they make you
sad and frown.

You can climb up a mountain,
dive through the sea,
or be a movie star on TV.
Now how exciting would that be?

Reading makes you
think great thoughts.
So read some books…
lots and lots!
Reading can take you there.
Books can take you anywhere!
Cameron Wilson, Grade 5
Bostian Elementary School, NC

Hatred
Hate is the color black
Hate is a feeling that can come back

Once you start to hate
You can never relate
To anything good

But everyone should
Be able to love

But hate is a curse
That isn't that good
Jake Timpanaro, Grade 6
Tarpon Springs Middle School, FL

Valentine's Day
Valentine's Day is here with
lot's of sweets
and treats

I like the sweets.
I like the treats.
I love to eat them all.

When they get here I scream yes.
I eat them one by one
here they go 1…2…3…4.
Ashley Ward, Grade 5
Buies Creek Elementary School, NC

The Beach
Gorgeous palm trees sway
Water ripples on the shore
Sand slides on the bay
Aidan Bermingham, Grade 4
St Thomas More School, NC

Dismissal

The students were bored with show and tell,
They could hardly wait for the ringing of the bell;
They were looking at the clock
Watching it go tick, tock.
When the bell finally rang,
They acted like a bunch of orangutans.
The kids ran to their lockers,
There were a bunch of talkers.
The kids turned on their cell phones,
Then I heard some big groans,
Because their batteries died,
Some kids even cried.
Up ahead I see the door ajar,
I also see the buses afar;
I walk onto the bus
And there was a bunch of fuss.
Alas the day is over,
Time to go see my dog Rover.

Sarah Herb, Grade 6
Kernan Middle School, FL

Stars

When the sun goes down,
The moon comes up.
The stars are bright,
They make people wake at night.
That only happens when
The sun goes down and the moon comes up!

Kimberlie Nivard, Grade 5
Wynnebrook Elementary School, FL

Where Does the Music Come From

Where does the music come from
Away from my breath does it form
Will happiness show
Will eternal love grow
Where does the music come from
Does it come from the nightingale's song
Will it prosper all the year long
From the river mist swirling
Or the wind that is roaring
Calling on for the snow
Where does the music come from
The autumn-like trees that tower above
Harps strumming away
Until the break of the dawning day
Beyond the waning of the silver white moon
Drifting from the foggy black gloom
Where does the music come from
The glistening of the jewel-like stars
Or the dreams of a sleeping child afar
But now I know and I will always tell it apart
For the music it comes from the heart

Margaret Taylor, Grade 6
Shannon Forest Christian School, SC

Spring

Spring, spring, spring is here,
What a beautiful thing to hear.
Hear the wind blowing, sun
Shining, and flowers sprouting.

Spring, spring, what a pretty thing,
Hear the birds chirping
Their songs in the meadow of green.

Spring, spring, spring is here,
Let me hear a hooray because school is not here!

Spring, spring, spring is here,
Did you forget Easter is near?

Spring, spring, what a beautiful sight,
Of the wolf howling under the moonlight.

Spring, spring, what a dreadful night,
Did you forget it's the last day of spring,
What a terrible night.

Jennifer Miller, Grade 4
Central Park Elementary School, FL

Calm

Butterfly fluttering
Around a field of flowers,
Sucking sweet nectar.
Sunshine pouring down on his wings,
And me, sleeping on the grass below.

Nikolai Chenet, Grade 4
Indian Harbour Montessori Elementary School, FL

I Am

I am special and nice
I wonder if I will ever be a millionaire
I hear the muffling sound of a convertible
I see my pop coming from heaven to see me
I want to see my pop again
I am special and nice

I pretend my sister is always nice
I feel very mad at my sister all the time
I touch my pop's hand when he comes to see me
I worry that I will never see my pop again
I cry when I think of pop
I am special and nice

I understand he is in a better place
I say it is my fault for what happened
I dream he makes it to heaven
I try to imagine that he is in a better place
I hope no one goes through what he went through
I am special and nice

Erica Marshall, Grade 5
Stokesdale Elementary School, NC

The Wild Cat
I hear a disturbance in the air
There is a pounce and then a glare
Then a flash of gleaming teeth
The angry creature starts to seethe
The creature missed its prey
The mouse had run away
So it tries and tries again
Then it returns to its den
It finally caught some food
To bring home to its brood
Emma Bogerd, Grade 6
Brogden Middle School, NC

My Special Tree
A 60 year old Ficus
Grows on my property
Let me tell you why
It's so special to me
Among the big roots
That hang down to the ground
A jungle like club house
Is what I have found
Whenever my friends
Would come over to play
We'd have great fun
For most of the day
Destiny Kosloske, Grade 5
The Sanibel School, FL

France
France the beautiful.
The Eiffel Tower I see.
When will I see France?
Aaliyah Gordon, Grade 6
St Petersburg Christian School, FL

Lion
See the lion stalk the boar,
Swiftly moving from tree to tree.
Getting closer, and closer still.
Closing in on its prey.
The boar, unsuspecting.
The lion so close to its tasty treat.
The boar is gone.
Dante Alvarado, Grade 5
Rosarian Academy, FL

The Moon
The moon is such a beautiful sight
sitting in the sky all night
It's here for everyone to see
it seems like
someone is sitting on it having tea
Oh, what a sight to see!
Jason Jensen, Grade 4
Pine Tree Hill Elementary School, SC

Always Us
I want to yell, "Please don't let me go!"
I need you in my arms tonight.
I want you to hold me tight
And keep me safe from all.
I'll never let go!
That's a promise...
'Til the end,
Always,
Us.
Haley Hemmit, Grade 6
Corkscrew Middle School, FL

Boris
Boris never liked spelling bees
He couldn't even spell trees
Websters and Thesaurus
Were never for Boris
He'd rather be eating green peas
Anna Destino, Grade 5
North Windy Ridge School, NC

Sit Down Stay
Sit Down Stay
I hear it every day
I'm just a simple dog
And I simply can't obey
Sit Down Stay
Why do you taunt me so
Sit Down Stay
Why do you mock me so
Sit Down Stay
Oh, just please go away!
Adrianna Rose Young, Grade 4
Lynn Fanning Elementary School, AL

The Forest
A beautiful sight
I see the cold water creek
It has rocks in it
Hidden back in the forest
Where the leaves rustle softly
Lee Morris, Grade 4
St James Episcopal School, FL

Spring Leaves
Spring leaves are green
Fall ones are not
Spring leaves can truly be seen
As fall leaves will rot.

Spring leaves grow
Fall leaves die
On spring leaves I see no snow
When fall is over, its leaves start to cry.
Shayla Lee, Grade 4
Aulander Elementary School, NC

Butterflies
Gentle butterflies
Graceful and very gorgeous
Flying in the air
Kayla Futrell, Grade 6
Arnold Magnet Academy, GA

Spring
Spring is the best time of year,
Everyone is full of cheer!
Birds chirping, children laughing
Rain falling, flowers blooming
So much fun in the sun!
Rachel Derrickson, Grade 4
Moyock Elementary School, NC

Maria
My closest friend.
My loving sister.
As she can't speak or walk.
I still love her.

I love her
I love her with all my heart.
She doesn't live with me.

I wish she could talk
And have fun.
But she can't.

So I still love her.
My sister
Maria.
Nicole David, Grade 5
Buies Creek Elementary School, NC

Sick
Sick! Sick! Sick I tell you!
I've got a boo-boo!
AHH! AHHH! AHHH-CHOO!!
I'm even coughing too!

Twisted ankle!! Bloody nose!!
What happens next?!
Only the Lord knows!!!

Check my temp!!
Is it too hot or too cool?!
Do you think I'm sick enough
To STAY out of school?!

Say!! Say!!
What do you say?!!
A teacher work day?!
Never mind...Can I go play?
Jordan Rogers, Grade 5
Morgan Elementary School, NC

The Deep Blue Sea

Down I go into this deep blue sea
Swimming towards the reef
Where the fish roam free
Dolphins, whales, and amazing creatures
A funny faced fish with amazing features
I turn around to see a shark
And I scare him away when I make a dog's bark
Then I swim up to shore to look at the land
I saw trash thrown by mean men

Isabella Larsen and Katie Zaeh, Grade 4
Settles Bridge Elementary School, GA

Someone Else

What do you do when you're feeling low,
When someone lets you go?

What do you do when they're gone,
And you just can't move on?

What do you do when they pass you by,
And you just want to cry?

You just keep moving through the throng,
Because someone else will come along.

Mallory Crimi, Grade 6
Gold Hill Middle School, SC

If You Were at the Alamo

If you were at the Alamo,
You could see Santa Ana's death flag in the sky
You could hear bullets whizzing by.

BOOM! BANG! Crash! Clang! Go the cannon balls
Little children frightened with their dolls.

Jerk of your musket flying back
Bruises all over you blue and black.

Guns firing, cannons thundering, bullets bursting by
"Remember the Alamo!" the Texans loudly cried.

The Texans fought as brave as a lion
"Remember the Alamo!" the Texans were cryin'.

Those words are what ended it all.

Micah Monticello, Grade 5
Covenant Classical School, NC

Attention or Detention

Attention! Attention! Give attention to me;
Attention! Attention! Just listen I plea
If you don't pay attention,
I'll give you detention!
So, please give your attention to me!

Jon Paul Smith, Grade 5
Foundation Christian Academy, FL

Seasons

Spring is warm with lots of fur
The allergies make your eyes water with blur
Pack away those jackets and gloves
Waiting to see those peaceful doves
Everything that a little kid loves
Playing in the park until it turns dark
Summer is toasty, roasty, and hot
Tanning of your body and banning of your crock pot
You go to the pool so you can stay cool
Fall is cool with turkey and pie
Your weight starts going up higher than high
The stuffing is good my oh my
Then you think why the turkey
Makes you feel drowsy
Winter is cold with freezing and sneezing.
Drinking a mug full of hot cocoa
And hoping no one will go loco
Snowflakes fall from the sky to the ground
Passing those cookies around and around
Then spring again

Myranda Richards, Grade 6
McRae Elementary School, FL

Wind

Wind, Wind.
Blow, Blow.
How far will it go?
I don't know how far it will go.
Just wind, wind…please blow.

Blake Hudson, Grade 6
St Francis Xavier Elementary School, MS

Sadness Is…

Sadness is a rainy day,
That interrupts your soccer game.

Sadness is running out of gas,
And not being able to make to school on time.

Sadness is your dog,
Huffing and puffing with his head down.

Sadness is a horrible dream,
Always wanting it to stop.

Sadness is losing your phone,
Not able to keep contact with your family.

Sadness is your grandmother,
At the funeral in a coffin.

Sadness is your homework,
Getting lost and getting a bad grade.

Christian Armendariz, Grade 4
Dante B Fascell Elementary School, FL

Mama

My mama is the best
She helps me when I'm sick
She comforts me when I'm down
And helps me get the winning crown
My mama is the best
She does anything for me
She would run a hundred miles
To see me smile
My mama is the best!

Liz Eslick, Grade 4
Edwards Elementary School, SC

Dreams

Slowly drifting and falling
Into sweet and peaceful sleep
And when the time is right
A tiny being must creep
From the inner workings of your soul
Into your blissful sleep
To stride into your quiet thoughts
Without making a peep
It works slowly within you
To make your sleeping life
Into a moving picture
Filled with happiness and no strife
This joyous little creature
With a smile that always beams
That makes your night's rest happy
Is none other than a dream

Fernanda Arnay, Grade 6
Varsity Lakes Middle School, FL

Bffs

Bffs are what you call one of a kind.
Bffs are what some people want to find.
Bffs are there for you!
Bffs keep you up when you got the flu!
Bffs help you through the day!
Bffs are there when you want to play!
Bffs tell you what boys to choose.
Bffs tell which ones to lose!
Bffs are soo cool.
Bffs like to throw each other in the pool!
LBD is what you call bffs.
We will never let go till we're very old!
People say friends come and go!
But we care and go with the flow!

Bridget Barahona, Grade 6
Challenger Middle School, FL

Lilly

My Lilly is white
She sits on my lap and sleeps
Puppies are cuties.

Maya Westby, Grade 6
Hope Charter School, FL

When the Wind Blows

When the wind blows, great things can happen.
People can be cooled off or warmed up, when the wind blows.
When the wind blows, leaves are picked off of the tree tops, and
seedlings can be carried for great distances.
People can fly kites and sail boats, when the wind blows.

When the wind blows in the summer the air is hot and sticky,
scorching the ice cream right off the cone.
But when the wind blows in the winter air is cold, and howls
through the leafless trees, the cold air is like a freezing knife blade
that cuts through your clothes and gives you the shivers.

But the wind of fall and spring are more calm, and soothing.
In the fall, when the wind blows, the garnet and gold colored
leaves are pushed off of the treetops and left to float down and
litter the ground.
In the spring, the warm wind rustles the newly grown grass, as the tiny
green leaves start to unfold and unravel themselves, amongst the
worn outstretching branches of the giant tree.

Matthew Drennan, Grade 6
Chapin Middle School, SC

Painting the Sunset

The sun, so beautifully
placed on the horizon
with great care
not to disturb the other colors
on the canvas of sky.

Orange, red, yellow, pink
with splotches of blue
dot the scene in the air.

An artist of wondrous talent
must spend years to spread the colors on the expanse of air.
Yet every afternoon the different images just appear in the atmosphere.

Many can try to catch the beauty of the sunset.
But when none but God can place the masterpieces upon the horizon,
you must stop trying to capture it.
Appreciate the mysterious marvelous creation of God,
for tomorrow brings a new one.

Cameron Daly, Grade 6
Chapin Middle School, SC

Like a Bird

You think of each day just slowly passing by
Sometimes I just want to run away, get out of there, and fly
I wish I were a bird sometimes and could just spread my wings
My feelings are too delicate though, I feel like I'm attached to the thinnest string
Who knows when the string will snap?
But I hope when it does, I will bounce back
Your feelings are the most important things
So fly your way out and spread your wings!

Alexis Martinez, Grade 6
Freedom Middle School, FL

Sisters
Sisters can be weird sometimes a lot
But mine's the weirdest without a thought
She drinks raw eggs
She plays with her deformed head
She picks her guitar with her toes
And out the silly music flows
Her favorite show is *Blues Clues*
She even does weird dance moves
She licks herself like a cat
Her favorite animal is a bat
I could name things all day
But I'm not going to do that, no way
This is good-bye I have to go do chores
She's outside making beetle bug s'mores
Charlotte Rowe, Grade 5
West Lake Elementary School, NC

The Big One That Got Away
What a beautiful day to be outside to fish!
I rush to the creek where I throw my line in deep;
Hoping to snag the big ole' trout!
With the worms and the corn I have lying about
I wait with anticipation to feel that tug on my line!
Without hesitation, I will pull that trout
Free from the water it lived in!
I wait and wait until that magic moment arrives!
The jerk, the pull, with excitement!
Then...all of a sudden, my line went "snap"
Like a twig! What frustration! What anger!
This is the day that the *big one* got away!
Jared Buchanon, Grade 6
Scotts Creek Elementary School, NC

Hello Kitty
My favorite cat is Hello Kitty
She is very small, friendly, and pretty
She always looks good, especially in pink
Some people don't, but that's what I think
Janeen Garib, Grade 4
Muslim Academy of Greater Orlando, FL

My Name
Maya
Friend
Happy, caring, funny, strange
Lover of animals, talking, my family
Who believes in caring for all creatures
Who wants happiness, world peace, and nature to thrive
Who uses money for charity, time to help others,
sympathy for times of grief
Who gives food, solutions, and help
Who says to believe that God will always guide you
Mathews
Maya Mathews, Grade 6
Broad Creek Middle School, NC

The Sun and the Moon
The sun glows and is very bright
Seems like an everlasting light.
When the sun is bright all is well
He always leaves us with stories to tell.

When the sun goes down all is black
Not even a glow through anywhere.
There's one thing the sun and moon share
Both their lights shine through any crack.

When the sun comes up it's orange and pink
What a sight to see, we won't blink.
The sun goes up the moon goes down,
It lights up our hometown.
Barak Pizzuto, Grade 5
Sharon Elementary School, NC

My School
Oh how I love my school.
It has books, teachers, and more.
You can make friends and have classes like math and reading.
When you graduate school you will miss everything.
Nathan Borders, Grade 5
Rock Mills Jr High School, AL

BFFAE
My BFFAE
Is Mary —

She loves to play all day
She flies a kite
She is very nice

Although I am sad to say
She's moving away

I will still keep in touch
We will very much

I hope this is not the end
We will still be close friends
Camille Bexley, Grade 6
St Francis Xavier Elementary School, MS

Daufuskie
D aufuskie is the best
A n awesome place to be
U nbelievable beauty
F un on the beach
U nusual sights
S chool is fun on the island
K ids collect shells
I t's an island
E xtremely small
Emily Lofton, Grade 5
Daufuskie Island Elementary School, SC

My Brother
My brother is everything,
Nice, kind, and super funny,
He's very helpful and understanding,
Every day he is cheerful,
He can get annoying after awhile,
But I love him.
Katie Blackwelder, Grade 6
Gold Hill Middle School, SC

The Magic of Morning
When the world awakens,
all is beautiful.
A new light shines anew,
the early call of the songbird chimes,
a dreamer's wish is born.
Hear the wind salute the morning,
like a soldier of nature,
standing at ready.
The sun makes its return,
for it's glorious arrival,
and this is the magic of morning.
Hayden Crowley, Grade 6
Heritage Middle School, GA

Stars
Stars
Bright, wonderful
Shine, light, shoot
All of them twinkle at night.
Big Dipper
Matilde Velasco, Grade 5
Dover Elementary School, FL

The Hummingbird
To watch a hummingbird fly
Is such a beautiful sight
To see him fly effortlessly
In the bright sunlight

To listen to a hummingbird sing
Is such a wonderful sound
To hear the clear, sweet notes
Going up and down
Becca Bonham, Grade 6
Chapin Middle School, SC

Misery
Trouble breaks out
They're calling my mom
She gets mad at me
She asks to speak with me
She threatens to ground me
When I get home, it's misery.
Mykel Ashman, Grade 6
Tequesta Trace Middle School, FL

Spring
S pring is when
all is at **P** eace and all
is t **R** anquil
the birds s **I** ng their happy songs
with **N** everending
G race
Patrick O'Donnell, Grade 5
St Thomas More School, NC

Springing to Life
Everything blooming,
Warm weather booming.
Little flower buds,
Tons of delicious spuds.
Warm breezes,
No winter freezes.
Birds chirping,
Little kids slurping.
This is my favorite season,
Except for the sneezin'.
Bridget Luckie, Grade 6
Gold Hill Middle School, SC

When I'm by Myself*
When I'm by myself
and I close my eyes
I'm a dog ready to bark
I'm a TV ready to be watched
I'm a clock ticking
I'm a book ready to be published
I'm a floor ready to be walked on
I'm a pencil ready to be sharpened
And when I open my eyes
What I care to be is me.
Anna Masse, Grade 4
Irmo Elementary School, SC
*Inspired by Eloise Greenfield

War
War, the technology, the good, the bad,
Helping scaring away enemies,
The people who lose are mad,
Fighting side by side with buddies.
People dying,
There is no winning in killing,
People crying,
A puddle made by tears is filling.
Bad guys always lose,
Good guys always win,
While losing bad guys snooze,
Good guys are eating out of tin.
People filled with terror,
Bad guys winning is very, very rare.
Jacob Doyle, Grade 4
PVPV/Rawlings Elementary School, FL

Can You Imagine?
Limeade without lime
Words that don't rhyme

Tables on the ceiling
Having no feelings

Houses without walls
Sports without balls

Having no pains
Knowing no names

Markers without ink
Having never to blink

Having no worries
No ice cream flurries

Lions without manes
Having no brains?
Kyle Rubin, Grade 4
William S Talbot Elementary School, FL

Seasons Pass
Winter
Playing in the snow
Until it melts away
Spring
Snow replaced by flowers
A picnic in the park
Summer
Warmer weather
Swimming in a pool
Fall
The leaves fall off the trees
Raking into piles.
Winter again.
Fred Marro, Grade 5
Rosarian Academy, FL

The Grand Canyon
G igantic
R ock
A wesome
N ice place to visit
D eep

C ool
A dry place
N avajos live there
Y ou can white-water raft
O ld
N atural
Luke Mikszta, Grade 4
St Thomas More School, NC

Fall

Rich-color leaves fall down from trees
   You feel a delightful breeze
Red, orange, yellow and brown
   There will be no reason to have a frown
Playing in piles of fallen leaves
   Bring delight for you and me
This season comes once a year
   So dream of fall every year

Kenneth Rivera, Grade 5
Wynnebrook Elementary School, FL

Anger

Anger is burnt black
It smells like overcooked toast
It tastes like a flaming wing burning your mouth
It sounds like scorching fires
It feels like the devil has come upon you

Kyle Foley, Grade 6
Tarpon Springs Middle School, FL

No Place for Hate

School is a wonderful place,
Where we practice daily not to hate.
Bullies try to frighten me,
But I walk away.
Whenever there is a fight,
Hitting and punching,
Never makes the situation right.
I will settle the fight in a healthful way.
Say no to the person, and then walk away.

If the situation heats up more,
Ask a parent, guardian, or adult for help,
That will even the score!
School is wonderful place,
Where we practice not to hate!

Tykirea Duggan, Grade 5
Frank L Stanton Elementary School, GA

Houses

Houses are special places,
Even though they have different faces.
Some are massive and some are petite,
Some are modest and some are neat.

What goes on inside a house?
Sometimes it's noisy; sometimes it's as quiet as a mouse.
Cooking, cleaning, laughing, playing,
Homework, TV, sleeping, praying.

Your house's looks are not the key;
The important thing is what you cannot see.
Is there love and is there fun?
If there is, you're a lucky one!

Maggie Emery, Grade 5
Sharon Elementary School, NC

My Not So Good Bike Ride

I was riding on a very long hike,
On my crooked, out-of-line bike.
Dad said, "I was slick,"
Bro said, "Try a trick!"
Then I landed on a "came-out-of-nowhere" spike!!

Kezia Domond, Grade 4
Pelican Marsh Elementary School, FL

The Red Sox

The Red Sox are so cool
In baseball they rule
They can beat the Yankees in a home run duel
They can turn games into a rout
And they can strike people out
When the Red Sox are mentioned people get up and shout
LET'S GO RED SOX!!

Wally Wibowo, Grade 6
St Francis Xavier Elementary School, MS

Autumn

Wind blowing steadily through the trees
Making each delicate leaf fall like feather to the ground
Red, brown, yellow, and orange
Red like roses on Valentine's
Brown like bark on a tree
Yellow like the sun on a summer's day
And orange like a flower blowing in the breeze
When you see these things you know that autumn has arrived

Peyton Sarko, Grade 6
Gold Hill Middle School, SC

Shekeydrah

Cool
Funny
Friendly
Wishes to save the animals in Antarctica
Dreams of becoming a choreographer
Wants to make more friends
Who wonders if the world is ending
Who fears nothing at all
Who is afraid of bumble bees
Who likes to watch TV
Who believes Expo markers smell funny
Who loves the bright sunlight
Who loves the dark cold nights
Who loves to make good grades
Who loves to dance
Who plans to be rich, who plans to be famous
Who plans to own a dance club
Everyone wishes, dreams, wants, wonders,
   fears, likes, believes, loves, and plans.
Even the author of this story,
Shekeydrah Robinson.

Shekeydrah Robinson, Grade 5
Winona Elementary School, MS

Such Simple Words

You said those words and my heart stopped.
I felt a horribly despondent feeling spread throughout my body.
My cheeks were red my eyes didn't move and a nervous tingle shivered down my spine.
Such simple words could hurt me so why would you say it?
I thought you had a burning love for me sparkling in your eyes.
To my surprise your heart is ice cold.
Everything around me faded to black, all the sounds became white noise.
Four gray dull cement walls formed a room and I was trapped inside.
There I stood in the cold, dark room, imprisoned abandoned and alone.
Such simple words could hurt me so. Why would you say it?
I gave you my heart in all hopes and you crushed it without a care, and then you laughed.
I should have opened my eyes to see that you didn't care.

Jasmin Ramirez, Grade 6
Freedom Middle School, FL

The Widow and the Boy

One day a woman was walking on the side of the road broken hearted.
Her husband had just died from a harmful illness.

When she was walking from the wake she saw a small boy.
The small boy was holding a sign that said help! The woman
went by the boy and said what do you need help with?
The little boy looked shocked and said money.
Then the woman looked at the small boy and said come live
with me I have a lot of money.

The first night that the boy spent the night was very happy. When everybody
was asleep he heard noise. He went downstairs and he saw the wife and husband.
the woman had passed away during the night.

The small boy went to the woman's room and read her will. When he read it
his frown turned up. The woman gave the boy the money and the house. At the wake
the people in her family buried them next to each other. After the wake the boy turned to say
one last goodbye. He saw the couple dancing together on their graves.

Holly Mallet, Grade 5
St Martin Upper Elementary School, MS

Sunday Mornings with My Grandpa

Every Sunday morning at around 9 o'clock
I hear the creak of the front door my dog barks his loud ruff
He is as happy as when you see all of your presents on your birthday.
Even though it awakens me I still have great enthusiasm.
I know when I arrive downstairs there will be a giant, delicious cookie
The size of the moon and a man who loves me more than anything waiting to see me.
It is my grandpa. My grandpa brings me a delicious breakfast every Sunday morning.
He brings eggs as yellow as the sun and salami as delicious as warm, freshly baked brownies
We also walk my dog, Koda, together. On our walks around the block,
While my dog is running happily down the street, we talk about all the news that week,
And what we look forward to the next. Once we arrive back at my house,
I start munching on my giant cookie.
Sometimes, my grandpa even brings his racecar driving suit and helmet.
If I am lucky enough, I may get to try it on.
Then it is time for Grandpa to say goodbye and his most famous saying,
"Grandpa's history and the rest is a mystery." I know he loves me and I love him.

Alexa Kimmel, Grade 6
Unity School, FL

Mother Nature's Daughter
Autumn has worked her charms yet again.
Memories whoosh around in your head.
You see ancient worlds just waiting to be explored.
You hear the leaves rustling in the light breeze.
You are at peace.
The leaves reveal their hidden beauty
of starlit orange, chestnut brown, sunny lemon.
Their masks blow off.
Mother Nature has put on her flowing gown,
dripping with rubies, sapphires, diamonds,
in honor of your favorite season.
Fall.

Kate Ruelle, Grade 5
Bridgeway Christian Academy, GA

A Witch or Wizard's Pet
If I were a witch or wizard,
I would make a lizard
my pet.
He could survive a blizzard
and I would feed him gizzard.
He could eat a hummingbird,
or maybe one-thirds.
But he can't eat too big of a bird,
blimy, that's just absurd.
He's dotted with black dots and has green eyes,
oh! How big they are in size!
He's black and has no teeth,
and he chews on cleats,
for he's not neat
He can be, for a long time, asleep,
for he is, every day, lazy and beat.
His favorite food is meat,
he goes out in the heat.
That's my lizards personality,
because that's his specialty!

Nicholas Otranto, Grade 4
Chancellor Charter School At Lantana, FL

Bunker Hill
Bunker hill, Bunker hill over those bumpy hills
bombs and gunshots just flying in the air.

There lay the dead and some are half alive,
but the proudest of all are the ones still alive.

We fight for you, we fight for you "oh" yes we do
for your freedom and for your death.
Sometimes we may not always win
but at least we always tried our best.

Oho that flag that beautiful flag
it stands there for freedom and our death.

Madison Jenkins, Grade 5
Queen's Grant Community School, NC

Dori and the Mouse
Dori the cat lived in a warm house.
Everything was perfect, except for the mouse.
She had a clean bathroom and a soft, fluffy bed,
And wonderful owners who kept her fed.

The mouse was a pest; he made so much noise,
And continued to steal all of Dori's toys.
She began to think of what she could do,
"There's got to be some way to get rid of you!"

"I could chase him around until he drops,
Or into a corner where my owner keeps the mop."
Finally she decided to open the door,
The mouse ran out and was no more!

Haley Stallings, Grade 6
Providence Classical School, AL

War
many people met a fate that they did not want
they were proud and vain
their families never got to say goodbye
to see the color of their eyes
even if they begged them not to go — to be careful
though it brings sorrow to some people
it brings happiness to other people
this is what happens in war

Clayton Cravey, Grade 6
Shorecrest Preparatory School, FL

Georgia
Georgia is my home state
Where I live
Where I abide
Where others come to thrive

Home to many that we know
Those that want to glow
Others that happen to fall
And don't do anything at all

There is the Live Oak Tree where the dogs might pee
Here is the Cherokee Rose striking a pose
O look at the boy trying to reach the Peach
I want to go swimming at the beach

Flying in the sky is the brown thrasher
Flirting with other birds like a masher
Can you see the honeybee acting like a flee
Buzzing around here and there just to get a glare

Look is that a hog
No it's a Green Tree Frog
I hope that I made you smile
See you in a little while!!

Brianna Smith, Grade 6
Academy of Lithonia Charter School, GA

Candy

Lollipop! Lollipop!
Hershey bar! Hershey bar!
Yum Yum Yum!
I want Toostie Rolls,
Candy corn,
Carmel Toffee,
Laffy Taffy!
All I want
for dinner
is…
CANDY!

Kendall Marsh, Grade 4
Garrison Jones Elementary School, FL

Penguins

Small baby penguin
Parading in the cold air
Having a great time
Other penguins come to join
Loving cuddly sweet creatures

Caroline Votaw, Grade 4
St James Episcopal School, FL

A Chip on Your Shoulder

Have you ever
felt that your body
was being tipped over?

like it's a struggle
just to do one simple
thing?

No one was willing
to offer you a helping
hand.

Then at once you
just went crazy,
depression was in
your system.

So you gave up on
all your hopes and
dreams and now
you're over.

Shania Knight, Grade 5
Buies Creek Elementary School, NC

Monster Truck

Big Foot 5
Drives over crashed cars
Every single week
At arenas and dirt tracks
For the money and it is Big Foot's job

Robbie Ashby, Grade 5
Morgan Elementary School, NC

Minty or Moses

Harriet Tubman, the abolitionist
Which means by white people she was never kissed
She was born in Dorchester County many people say
I'm sure when she lived there she didn't like it that way
Her family called her Minty we never knew why
But with authors these days it could be just a lie
Her head got hit with a two pound weight, probably really hard
No wonder she got bad grades on her report card
She hardly recovered from an attack of measles and bronchitis
But with her strength we knew that she was going to fight it
She helped more than 300 slaves to freedom, we know that for a fact
Even though she did this her whole life, she hardly ever packed
Now people called her Moses, now we know why
Like the Bible character, she would never, ever cry
Even though her life went from slave to runaway, she had to die one day, some day
She died on on March 10, 1913, if we could only beg if she were alive
Pretty, pretty please?

Shannon Stubbs, Grade 4
Panther Run Elementary School, FL

Sport

hay batta, hay batta swing.
strike one after the pitcher threw.
the baseball bat cracked as loud as thunder.
the ball went flying as it was going out of the park.
crack, crack, crack the game is on as the other team players were sad,
as the game kept getting bad for them.

Andrew Rheinheimer, Grade 6
Challenger Middle School, FL

Friends Forever

Friends bring you near the light
Even though if it's so dim or so bright.

Friends are your angels wherever you go,
Even though if you're so fast or so slow.

Friends are your memories you cherish forever.
Those were the times you spent together.

Friends are your prayers you keep in mind,
A friend so great and a friend so kind.

Friends are the life that you keep in your heart,
They'll always keep ending and they'll always start.

Friends are light, your angels, the memories, your prayers, and your heart,
But, don't forget to put these things in your shopping cart.

Without a friend, what would you do?
So start finding a friend, 'til the day is through!

But at the end, when the day is through
Just remember, you've also been a dear good friend to all of us, too.!

Maria Villamor, Grade 5
Windsor Elementary School, NC

I Am

I am a girl who fell for that one boy.
I wonder if he still loves me.
I hear my heart beat for him.
I want him to want me.
I am a girl who fell for that one boy.

I pretend I am fine when I'm not.
I feel sad but I know everything will be fine.
I touch my face and wash away the tears.
I worry about my friends.
I cry when I am sad.
I am strong and weak.

I understand my friends and family.
I say everything will be fine when I don't know.
I dream about my future.
I try to let him go but I can't.
I hope I will get him back.
I am me and only me, no more, no less.

Esmeralda Campos, Grade 6
Heron Creek Middle School, FL

Flowers

Flowers are works of art,
Their beauty flows into our heart.
Lilies, daisies, also roses,
They all strike beautiful poses.
Colors of them are unique,
Their beauty and physique.
Lilies are spring's gift to earth
Artists have portrayed them since birth.
Roses are so delicate and versatile,
When painted on canvas their beauty is immeasurable.
Daisies are so playful and fun,
Ladies in portraits surrounded by tons.
In a field of fresh blooming flowers,
An artist could get lost painting for hours.
The beauty, the texture, the colors, the smells,
If only a canvas these things would tell.
The joy that is felt when receiving flowers
No artist can capture though painting for hours.
A variety of flowers are present in many ways,
On the canvas of life from birth to the grave.

Alyssa Horton, Grade 6
J E Holmes Middle School, NC

The Lady in the Chair

The lady in the chair is very special to me.
Who may you think of this lady to be?
Who more than Grandmama Frances?
She can hardly speak
With the cancer she is weak.
But I see her as a key, the key to my heart
Where she will always be.

Lyndsey Pulliam, Grade 4
Settles Bridge Elementary School, GA

Starry Night

It was a starry night,
and I was flying my kite,
when I saw a bare spot in the sky.
It was like the stars that had been there
had run away when they got much too shy.
I took one more look above my head,
at the moon shining down on me.
And I finally realized that this was the most beautiful sight,
and that anyone would be lucky to see.

Katie Selby, Grade 6
Seven Springs Middle School, FL

A Bold Move

It was a cold, sunny day in Snowshoe, West Virginia,
and I was ready for a good day of snowboarding.
Today would be the day that I attempt my very first rail!
As I approached the Terrain Park,
I spotted the perfect rail for me.
It was a one foot thick, six feet long box rail
that I approached at a very slow speed.
I jumped, turned my board,
and landed on the rail.
My board slipped,
and I landed on my back.
I slid across the rail
and fell at the end of it.
I got up slowly,
and realized that it didn't hurt very much.
The next time I ride a rail,
I will not turn my board sideways on it.

Paul Schumacher, Grade 6
Lake Park Baptist School, FL

The Coral Reef

The coral reef is such a pretty sight
It's off of Australia's coast
The colors are beautiful and oh, so bright
Its fish are colored the most

It is inhabited with millions of fish
The plants sway slowly
Just to see it is my wish
Some look like ravioli

The coral is filled with tons of colors
It's beautiful and constantly in motion
The colors make everything look much duller
The coral reef brightens the ocean

Sending scuba divers to the lab,
Making boaters stop in wonder
From clownfish to crabs
Is the great coral reef from the land of "Down under!"

Kennedy Byrd, Grade 6
Boiling Springs Intermediate School, SC

My Hamster

My hamster is cuddly,
He is very soft.
Whenever I watch him,
He goes into his loft.

He runs very fast on his wheel.
He keeps me up all night,
My mom doesn't like it so much,
So my mom and I will fight.

Emily Gell, Grade 4
Chancellor Charter School At Lantana, FL

The Wind

The wind is everywhere.
The wind is an unexpected visitor.
The wind shapes sand dunes like a child playing with clay.
The wind licks my cheek when it's raining.
The wind is a towel for the plants.
The wind is a wolf howling outside my window.
The wind is a savage warrior destroying houses.
The wind is everywhere.

Rafael Campana, Grade 5
Oliver Hoover Elementary School, FL

Spirit Door

This door holds many memories inside
Where all of the gloom and fear abides.
From the outside a breeze blows by.
It's devious, misdirected, bitter, and wry.
Its blackness sets a formidable tone.
It gradually creaked open with a groan.
Its bleak feeling gave off an uncanny sense.
The silence was leading to suspense.
I trudged in; soon the door was sealed.
Then what was inside was certainly revealed.
The desolate stretch was filled with fear.
Malicious spirits roam about here.
The spirits mourn on this woeful day.
All of my thoughts just whittled away.
They hoped for release right out that door,
But they were invisible; they couldn't do much more.
I finally fled this dreadful enclosure.
I shielded my eyes due to the sun's exposure.
I'm glad I do not have to go through their pain.
If you go back to the door, their spirits still remain.

Amy Gorowitz, Grade 6
Woodward Academy North, GA

The Flag

The flag has red and white stripes
and a blue square.
And stars that shine
like the sun.

Christian Flick, Grade 4
Camden Elementary School of the Creative Arts, SC

The Witch Named Mary

The witch is old,
her heart seems cold.
Her hair looks like mold,
but she has lots of gold.
She's not pretty, but has a cute kitty.
She has a wart,
the size of an airport.
Instead of shampoo,
she uses crazy glue.
She is wild,
like a child.
"Ahhh!" he screams
as she lets out her steam.
She may be a freak,
but she is very unique.
Her face is like a Halloween mask,
and she smells like gas.

Shenelle Schnegelberger, Grade 4
Chancellor Charter School At Lantana, FL

Grandma

She didn't go anywhere just back in my heart,
She has just been there from the start.
Even though she is off this Earth,
She has been there since my birth.
My only memory of her is her fabulous art.

Alex Hinkle, Grade 6
Seven Springs Middle School, FL

Adventure Across the Earth

My horse stops by a willow tree
To see the children run with glee
The white butterflies skip across the grass
As they try to talk to me.

I hear a sound, a very loud sound
And my horse hurries off the mound.
Pebbles and leaves jump beyond our way
As his feet fly off the ground.

We stop by a cabin, dark and gray
And a villager walks past our way.
Orange, yellow and pink flowers he is watering
Which smell like springtime in May.

I whip my horse and he begins to trot
And then I spot a castle in a shock.
It has a bridge and a king and queen
But the flowers in the front will rot.

Now there is some time I have to make
So my horse scampers beyond a lake.
'Twas a dream this was to be
As I begin my morning wake.

Gabrielle Argimón, Grade 5
Pinewood Acres School, FL

School Is Fun

School, school we learn and play,
Teachers teach us every day.
There's Mrs. Corsbie, Mrs. Brown, Mrs. Howell, too,
Mrs. Tyson, Mrs. Tedford, Mrs. Goggans, Mrs. McGough.
There's history, math, reading, too,
English, science, spelling, what's new?
School is cool, school is fun,
So let's go and get our work done!

Jessica Spain, Grade 5
Haleyville Elementary School, AL

Jasmine Is Cool

Jasmine is cool and she really loves school
Mrs. Blue is her teacher and she rules
Mrs. Graham is reading and Jasmine is succeeding

Jasmine is smart
And not tart
Jasmine is nice
And afraid of mice

Jasmine knows all the states
I think
That's why she carries crates

Jasmine can read a book
Jasmine caught a fish on a hook
Jasmine is short
And can shoot on a basketball court

Jasmine Benson, Grade 5
East Albemarle Elementary School, NC

I Am Myself

I am kind and sweet
I wonder what's going to happen in life
I hear a ghost in the basement
I see a fight every day
I want a group of friends without drama
I am kind and sweet

I pretend to be shy
I feel scared about spiders
I touch my heart with my hand
I worry about my family
I cry when I'm sad
I am kind and sweet.

I understand there's drama
I say just walk away
I dream to live a happy life
I try to have a positive attitude
I hope my friends will always be there for me
I am kind and sweet.

Paige Harriman, Grade 6
Tarpon Springs Middle School, FL

Past, Present, Future

Don't fear the future
It has to come.
Don't dread the past it already happened.
Live in the present you're in it now.
Enjoy it.

Christa Santiago, Grade 6
Holy Name of Jesus School, FL

Autumn

Autumn, Autumn drift and wander.
Wave your branches around me.
Spread your leaves of auburn, marigold, and ruby
throughout the forest.
Throw warm splatters of paint,
the colors of mahogany, oak, and maple.
Show me the trees' treasures.
Light the way for a lost star of color
to flow through the treetops.
Become a dream,
like the love of a young child.

Kaley Hecht, Grade 4
Bridgeway Christian Academy, GA

Receiving

Receiving, catching, and passing.
It gives you an unexplainable amount of strength and courage.
It makes you want to run right through someone.
Passing also gives you an uncontrollable amount of courage.
It makes you feel like you can pass 1,000 yards.
I am strong, I am legend, I can pass 1,000 yards.
I am uncontrollable.

Danney Fritch, Grade 6
McRae Elementary School, FL

Restaurant

Good smells traveling everywhere,
Going from room to room.
People eating hastily,
Others waiting to consume.

Waiters dashing from place to place,
Acting like it's a race.
More and more people coming in,
Waiting to see their grin.

Cooks in the kitchen making food,
So good they won't get sued.
Making concoctions very fast.
Hoping they won't get sassed.

Eating where there are five stars,
Is like going to Mars.
Sometimes they have their bad days,
But most they're all the craze.

Hannah Turner, Grade 6
Boiling Springs Intermediate School, SC

My Favorite Dog
They come in black, brown, and yellow,
Stronger than the strongest fellow.
Yellow, yellow,
Sweet and mellow.
Brown, brown,
Great for town.
Black, black,
Playing out back.
Labrador, Labrador,
I will love you forevermore.
Kirsten Sanchez, Grade 5
Poinciana Elementary School, FL

War
War is such a terrible thing,
and it won't prove that one is king.
People think it solves our fights,
but it only makes no rights.
War goes on and is with us now,
let's not make it an honorable bow.
Thomas Kendrick, Grade 6
Holy Name of Jesus School, FL

What Makes a Cryer
Something stronger than light
Something stronger than fire
Something stronger than might
Something stronger than a liar
And this is what makes a cryer
Madeline Robb, Grade 6
H J MacDonald Middle School, NC

The Big Brown Bear
There once was a big brown bear.
Who never really seemed to care.
He had no money.
He stole some honey.
That was not very fair.
Lauren Pearson, Grade 5
Winona Elementary School, MS

Moms
Moms do everything
so here's a thank you
for all you do.
You cook and clean,
I'm surprised you're not mean.
You do laundry and dishes,
a genie should give you three wishes.
You're always so nice,
but I don't like your red beans and rice.
You love me and I love you,
so thanks for all you do!
Chloe Thomas, Grade 5
Allatoona Elementary School, GA

Darkness
Darkness
Crawling over the sky,
Flooding cities and towns,
It's always there,
Lurking in the closets or under the bed.

Darkness
There are secrets in the dark,
Waiting to be discovered.
Listening to the silence.
For sounds that can be heard.

Darkness
The only way to escape it,
The only way to lose it,
Is to let out the light in you,
Or…turn on a light.
Michael McLamb, Grade 6
Tarpon Springs Middle School, FL

My Dog Poppy
My dog is Poppy
Her ears very floppy

She's tan and white
But does not bite

She plays around
And then lays down

She goes to sleep
And doesn't make a peep

She wakes up
What a cute little pup
Luke Beecher, Grade 6
Tarpon Springs Middle School, FL

Can You See the Colors I See?
Peach is the color of your heel
Orange is the color of an orange peel

Red is the color of the skin of an apple
White is the color of a wedding chapel

Blue is the color of a lake
Brown is the color of a chocolate cake

Yellow is the color of the sun
Tan is the color of a bun

Black makes me want to go to bed
Grey is the color of lead
Jared Blumberg, Grade 6
Tequesta Trace Middle School, FL

Friend
F is fight for you
R is reason with you
I is I love you
E is enjoy the laughter we have
N is never ending friendship we share
D is deserve a friend just like you
Gracie Powell, Grade 6
Gold Hill Middle School, SC

Winter
Winter is like an icicle
drip from a tree.
Winter is a snowman
looking at me.
Winter is like my hands
warming over a fire.
Winter is like singing in a
beautiful church choir.
Winter is like the smell and
taste of a Christmas ham.
Winter is like a Christmas
tree falling down BAM!
Winter is like the touch of
Christmas essence.
Winter is a happy feeling
of looking at my family.
Winter is like the love coming
from my heart.
Winter is like opening up
presents go on and start.
Destiny Deweese, Grade 4
Tabernacle Elementary School, NC

Singing
Singing makes me happy;
I do it for the fun.
Singing is my life;
I can sing while I run!

I sing about my feelings;
Sometimes I don't know I'm singing!
It's like a curse,
But I don't want it to go away!

I want to be a singer
So everyone can enjoy my singing.
I want everyone to know one thing;
Is it that Brittany Moore can sing!

I will sing and sing
Until my heart gives out!
But I will keep on singing,
Even as I enter the gates of heaven!
Brittany Moore, Grade 6
Scotts Creek Elementary School, NC

Why Do We Wonder?

I wonder about people,
how were they made?
I wonder about frogs and their big leaping legs
but the one question that won't comply
Why do we wonder,
a question I can't deny

Zachary Sommers, Grade 4
Clearview Avenue Elementary School, FL

Dylan

My brother is like ice cream,
Both sweet and hard.
His taste is changing every day.
When people are near he acts so sweet,
But with me he is both kind and strict.
His sweet voice may make you real happy,
But when you are with him you're in a for a big surprise.
He will take you along for a fun ride.

Amanda Glass, Grade 6
Mount Zion Christian School, SC

A Day in the Swamp

The sun rose in the morning
Made everything alive and shone down light on the Micanopy
Fish alive and deer come to the river like a magnet
Black Bears chase the fish and they catch the fish
The crocodile with its secrecy swims along
With nightfall falling the deer burrows
And the bear goes to its den
The fish go in hiding
The hunters come out
Except for in Canada, it's illegal to hunt with a flashlight
BANG!
He comes to the river
Picks up his deer and goes home
Smelling like blood
Through the forest waiting for tomorrow morning

Zachary Burns, Grade 6
McRae Elementary School, FL

Seashore

I love the seashore.
It has mushy sand.
I love the cold water on my feet.
I think that is the best kind of land.
I love jumping in the water,
Sometimes I even leap.
I love picking up shells.
There are so many different kinds of them.
Sometimes there are jelly fish that have
Washed upon the shore,
They feel like ice pack gels.
So, there are so many different kinds of things
On the seashore.

Elaine Biedenharn, Grade 6
St Francis Xavier Elementary School, MS

Ode to Caroline

Caroline, oh Caroline, you are so kind,
You give me snacks when I am starving.
You wear funky red glasses and have blonde hair,
You tell me funny things through out the day.
We met in the beginning of the year
In Mr. Vorbroker's 5th grade class.
You and I have the same personalities
We both like animals, shopping, and boys.
When I don't know something in math,
You are always there to help me,
If I'm sick you take care of me just like my mother,
I am so glad to have a friend like you,
Oh Caroline, you are a true friend.

Sarah Mouna, Grade 5
Vienna Elementary School, NC

Mother's Day

I bought my mom a pot of gold
Which was full of love
The bowl was very bright and bold
She wondered what it was made of.

I bought her a pearl
That she will enjoy
She twirled and swirled
When she got it she went "Oh Boy!"

My mom is my friend
She is knocking on the door
She likes me to lend
She has presents but she still wants more.

My mom is a star
I gave her a ring
She has come very far
In everything.

My mom likes green
I just wanted to say
She can be a queen
Happy Mother's Day.

Abigail Castillo, Grade 6
Turkey Creek Middle School, FL

Stranded!

S and everywhere
T rees as far as the eye can see
R ocks so sharp touching them will make you bleed
A nacondas in the bed
N ever going to see civilization again
D on't know how long I'll survive
E verywhere looks as scary as can be
D eath is all I see

Zachary Mayer, Grade 5
Rosarian Academy, FL

Skate
S kateboarding
K ick flip
A wesome
T ricks
E xciting

Devon Scott, Grade 4
Spruce Creek Elementary School, FL

Jonathan
HIs hair so soft,
Like fluffy marshmallows,
On a cloud.
His beady eyes
Sparkle
When he laughs
Out loud.
His small nose that
Squints up when
He smells the aroma
Of cookies baking.
His mouth without
Teeth that drools
When he opens
And takes food in.
His soft and glowing
Skin with
An innocent face you'll
Never get tired of
Looking at.

Calista Wilson, Grade 6
J E Holmes Middle School, NC

I'm So Curious
I'm so curious
Sometimes I sit in the window
Wondering if I am ever going
To see you again
I have a lot of bad days
Dad please come
And see me
I'm so curious as to when
I'll see you again.

Jonnay Wilbon, Grade 5
Minor Elementary School, AL

Washing My Dog
I grab the hose
turn it on
see my dog, all wet
and grimey
the soap in my hand is slimy
I scrub the dirt off her fur,
then I turn the water on,
and the dirt is gone!

Olivia Friloux, Grade 6
St Mary Magdalen Catholic School, FL

One Pie of a Kind…Duh, Duh, Duh
Hot apple pie rough and round
crisp and golden brown
as it wobbly comes out of the oven
the apples inside are rectangular and topped with sugar and cinnamon

Apple pie…Out in a hot summer's day,
very stickily sliding around on your plate.

Apple pie is marvelously topped with just whipped cream
but luxuriously topped with whipped cream and vanilla bean ice-cream,
on a hot summer's day
apple pie is soft as a bird's wing
and as hot as the sun as I eat it.
pie a food for people not pets,
The pie walked right into my mouth!
MMM…MMM…GOOD! CRUNCH!

Sara Banyard, Grade 4
Irmo Elementary School, SC

Dark Blue
Dark blue is intense
It sounds like the rippling, calm river
It smells like fresh picked orchids
It tastes like cool, refreshing blueberries on a summer day
It looks like the deep, mysterious ocean where anything can happen
It feels like silky velvet
Dark blue is intense

Jessi Rowe, Grade 6
City of Pembroke Pines Charter Central Middle School, FL

The Origin
Yes you've heard of it just in a different way,
you plug in your headphones to your iPod and press play
and you think you have found it you're right…partially

If you think that's the only music you are partially wrong!!
Just look around and music is everywhere look at any persons face
and music is there, look at any thing, see and listen

Music is my brain is music is the world (world)
Music is visual and oral in the world life is music video
itself art jumping out at me like "a tiger pouncing on PPRREEYY"
but eye (i) (I) enjoy it the inspiration of music is what keeps people
(homo sapiens) going every day,

I (i)f music is stuck in your head let it stay and flourish
and allow love of life enter and live (already!!) and you will not
be disappointed (give it some tea, too) you must not be
disappointed (!) by the origin of wonder (entertainment)
and interest because you thrive (survive) on wonder
and interest don't be troubled or worried if you don't have
music to enjoy and appreciate because it can grown on itself
(gets some music!) and survive and (feed) off of your heart
and blend with amazement as the origin of all wonder!(?)

James Wenz, Grade 6
Shorecrest Preparatory School, FL

High Merit Poems – Grades 4, 5, and 6

Love

Love me truly,
Love me so
Love me, love me
Love my soul
I'm so good
I'm so great
I'll give you dollar
If you make
Me a delicious,
Mouth-watering,
Strawberry
Pineapple shake
If that is all it takes.

Khandis Gordon, Grade 4
Julian D Parker School of Science, Math & Technology, FL

I Dance to Music!!!

I dance to music,
twist, turn, and shake.
Dancing is an expression,
A feeling I can't escape.

I move to the beat
And wiggle in the streets.
I tap my feet and study the rhythm
of the beat.

this music I hear right now in my ear,
Sounds so mysterious, so wondrous, and so mystic!
Let's all share this time to dance in a bind.

I LOVE TO DANCE!!!
Twist, turn and shake. Everyone can do it.
Dancing is just as easy as a piece of cake.
So…please don't hate because I can dance and you can't.

Ajare' Y. Norman, Grade 6
Philadelphia Elementary School, MS

Tim Valone's Cell Phone

There once was a man named Tim Valone
Who was obsessed with his new cell phone.
He was always on a call, day and night
Talking to his friends, Bob, John, and Dwight.

Then one day when he was giving a ring
To his mother, then happened a terrible thing.
His cell phone grew right on to his ear
And his screeching mother's voice was all he could hear.

So from then on, he heard her nag.
Yes, forever he listened to that old hag.
And today Tim's cell phone is still stuck to his head.
I bet it'll still be there long after he's dead.

Lucy Fuller, Grade 6
Challenger K8 School of Science and Mathematics, FL

My Dream Girl

Her eyes crystal blue
Staring at me like X-rays
A beautiful smile illuminated her face
Teeth lined like a well mannered marching band
Shining like the sun itself
Her hair flowing like the ocean
Brown like melted milk chocolate
Her body perfect like Heaven itself
Her Heart even more beautiful
She is surely my dream Girl.

Dylan Brandrick, Grade 6
McRae Elementary School, FL

My Way or Hit the Highway

Once so graceful
The clicking sound of a new bike.
The squeaking brakes come to a stop.
Wait! Listen closely.
Can you hear it?
The sound of nails scratching on the chalkboard.
I look up and down
Nothing. I didn't see it…yet.
That beautiful clicking noise has stopped.
All of the sudden,
It feels like the world has stopped…
1! 2! 3! Down for the count.
So blurry. Can't seem to find
My vision so dirty and I am whirly.
I must've made a mistake.

Daniel Branch, Grade 5
East Marion Elementary School, MS

The Boy Named Zack

I told this boy who I once knew,
"I have some powers. You believe me, don't you?"
But he chuckled and laughed until he started to cry.
He said, "Show me. Show me. I want to see you try."
I waved my hand good-bye to him.
I said, "Wocko, Wicko, Wacko, and Wim."
Zap! He was gone and never came back.
That's what happened to the boy named Zack.

Kiana Morgan, Grade 4
West Bertie Elementary School, NC

My Dog Named Tanner

His bark is like an alarm,
telling burglars to go away.
His howl sounds like the wind
during a winter night in Chicago.
His hair covers him like a blanket
for an orphan in the cold.
His bite could puncture a brick wall.
His face is the god of everything beautiful.
That is my dog named Tanner.

Christian Wilson, Grade 6
J Larry Newton School, AL

The Ocean
The sun shines on me
The waves touch my feet gently
I smell salty breeze
The world is joyful near me
The ocean is my home always
Carly Ascik, Grade 4
St James Episcopal School, FL

Food
Food
Delicious and good
Loving that food
Health foods,
Diet foods,
Junk foods,
Sweet foods,
Lovin' that
Good smellin'
Never failin'
Out of this world
Food
Hannah Whitehead, Grade 5
St Martin Upper Elementary School, MS

Holocaust
Holocaust
Dreadful, horrifying
Fighting, killing, attacking
It was so sad.
World War II
Leobardo Martinez, Grade 5
Dover Elementary School, FL

Kayla
Cute
Lovable
Happy
Wishes to see her daddy again
Dreams of being a basketball player
Wants to go to Heaven
Who wonders what color God is
Who fears God
Who is afraid of snakes and spiders
Who likes boys
Who believes in God
Who loves God
Who loves my mother
Who loves my daddy
Who loves all my family and friends
Who plans to go to college
Who plans to go to heaven
Who plans to get married and have kids
Now you know a little about me.
Kayla Jones, Grade 5
Winona Elementary School, MS

Volleyball
Fun sport
Bump, set and spike
Is an aggressive sport
Bumping the balls over the net
Winners
Andrea Espinoza, Grade 6
St Mark's Lutheran School, FL

Sleeping
Near the forest
Below the moon
Under the sky
In a tree
To sleep.
Cassandra Bueno, Grade 5
Dover Elementary School, FL

An Artist's View
I am daydreaming.
About my life-fulfilling dream.
Here I am, a girl with a special eye.
I could brush the blue-stained sky.
I make my way into a path of light,
Gazing into an artist's sight.
I swish slightly on the board,
My paintbrush is like a sword.
All alone,
Me, myself, and I,
As I wake into the world.
I am daydreaming.
Kennedy Gilbert, Grade 5
Oakland Elementary School, SC

Ode to Lovers
When lovers love
They find someone
To love and believe in.
People vision their
Lover in their mind
All the time.
You have someone
To share your
Thoughts with.
Your lover will help
You with your problems.
You will have things in common.
Your lover will be there
When you're going through rough times.
Your lover will share
Happy times with you.
When lovers love
They find someone
To love and believe in.
Carissa Moose, Grade 5
Sharon Elementary School, NC

There Once Was a Dog Named Spot
There once was a dog named spot
He liked to eat a lot
His favorite food was a tater tot
One time his tot was too hot
Because he cooked them in a crock pot
Zana Dodson, Grade 5
Ranburne Elementary School, AL

A Free Spirit
A horse, a shadow, now wind, now rain,
Galloping as if to run off a biting pain,
But then again how smoothly she goes,
And how her mane and tail flows,
Reaching, stretching towards the sky,
Like she is about to fly,
Her eyes so big, her heart so full,
Traveling with nature's pull.
Clare Jamieson, Grade 5
Summit Hill Elementary School, GA

Some People Are
Some people are funny,
some are scary,
some are friends,
some are mean,
some are best friends,
some are married,
some are boyfriends and girlfriends,
but my favorite of all
is best friends.
Jordan Jenkins, Grade 5
West Marion Elementary School, MS

Comedy/Drama
Comedy
Funny, lighthearted
Laughing, chuckling, smiling
Entertaining, enjoyable, serious, grim
Fighting, romancing, storytelling
Tragedy, heartbreak
Drama
David Greenberg, Grade 6
Pinellas County Jewish Day School, FL

Dogs
Some are mean and bark
Others like to hide in the dark
Some are nice and listen
Some are scared and frightened
I don't like most dogs
Some are fat as logs
They run and catch
When you throw something they fetch
Luke Abrigo, Grade 6
Gold Hill Middle School, SC

Lucky

My dog Lucky is so nice,
His fur is like the color of ice.
He likes to run and chase squirrels,
But he does not like girls.
I love my dog Lucky so much,
Because his fur is so soft, it's nice to touch.

Cooper Musgrove, Grade 6
Gold Hill Middle School, SC

Lightning Strike

You never know when lightning will strike
but when it does you'll have a fright.
You'll know when it strikes because
there is a bright light at night.

Jules Pierre Hopkins, Grade 5
Our Lady of Fatima School, MS

The Message

I wait and I wait for a full moon night and day,
Or for the stars to be aligned just the right way
For in the deepest as deep would want to go,
I wait for the message,
But still receive a no.
For as long as I could want to go,
None will ever know.
As long as I can wait,
I'll search for that message no matter how long it would take.

Jashea Cannady, Grade 6
Kernan Middle School, FL

Orange

Orange moves like the breeze
Orange speaks like a firecracker
He is a fox sneaking across the snow
He is the rarest sunset in the sky
He is the rarest gem on the land
Orange is the color of the sunset upon us
He is like a tiger lily in the wind
He is like a beautiful bonfire out in the wilderness.

Kyle Skeen, Grade 4
Tabernacle Elementary School, NC

Daydreaming or Not

In my dreams, daydreaming or not
I don't know why but it seems to happen often
Knowing it happens it's very hard not to do so
Sometimes it's light
Sometimes it's dark
But most of all it's dramatic
Most of the time it's in action
Other times it's just being lazy
Doing things that seem impossible
But in the morning when I wake up I realize…
Nothing is impossible, daydreaming or not

Ka'Travia Wright, Grade 6
Brogden Middle School, NC

Best Friends

I'm in here with you.
You are in here with me.
We are in this classroom like a happy family.
If I leave will you follow me?
Or come to another classroom with me,
If I leave the school will you sit on the stool and cry,
And forget that you and I,
Are best friends.

Asya Beckley, Grade 5
Minor Elementary School, AL

I Am Hurricane

I am Hurricane
As you walk along the ocean
You hear my destruction
I set my hunt in motion
The more I smash, the more infuriated I get
With every hustle and bustle, the more real my threat
All the wind and rain
The flooding, the horrid pain

Everyone was crying
And people were dying
The lost of mortality
Comprehend this nightmare, it's reality
It all happened so fast
Don't you wish this was the past?
A coffin may be your cast
At last…

I came twirling in, smashing everything in my path
You want to hear my laugh?
You'll hear it in my aftermath
Feel free to be at peace, but don't rest
Because you haven't seen my best

Chloe Gonzalez, Grade 6
Freedom Middle School, FL

Rainbows of the World

Yellow seems like the bright sun
Brown is the top of a bun

Red is when blood meets the heart
Black is when you throw a dart

Blueberries are delicious to eat
Green is my little baby seat

Gold is the color that kings own
Orange on the street are the bright cones

White seems to be everywhere, in the streets, in the air
Pink seems to mean that you just care

Juan Ortega, Grade 6
Tequesta Trace Middle School, FL

Wind
The wind dancing through the leaves
Peaceful at the journey's end
Whistling through the trees beyond
As soundless as a sleeping child
Adam Martoccia, Grade 6
Gold Hill Middle School, SC

PawPaw
P erfect man
A lways was my hero
W onderful, helpful, fellow
P owerful
A nimal lover
W ell known as Kendall
Victoria Greer, Grade 5
Elba Elementary School, AL

The Jewel Thief
Grab your money from its spot,
Keep it by your side;
Lock your doors and hide your kids,
Jewel Thief's right outside!

He has come to take away
All your prized possessions.
Call a person really quick
To teach the thief lessons.

Suddenly a noise is heard,
Quick! Run to the door.
OMG! It's Superman,
Thieves will be no more!

He saved you and all your things.
Yay for Superman!
Robbers now are history,
Let's give him a hand!
Monica Underwood, Grade 6
Providence Classical School, AL

Springtime
Animals are waking
From a long winter's nap.
What time could it be?
Flowers are blooming
And the trees drip sap.
What time could it be?
A bunny frolics
From its mother's lap.
What time could it be?
Mustangs will gallop
Across the map.
What time could it be?
Springtime!
Mia Ravaschieri, Grade 5
Rosarian Academy, FL

The Three Key Words
Love, peace, harmony, the three key words to a happy life.
Without these three words you will not live a happy, whole and complete life.
So remember to keep these words in mind.
Arianna Poteet, Grade 4
Spruce Creek Elementary School, FL

Good Friends and Bad Friends
Bad friends will turn you down when you are in need.
Bad friends will turn their backs on you.
Bad friends will forget about you.
Bad friends will treat you like dirt.
Bad friends will make fun of you to make them look good and you horrible.

Good friends will lift you up in spirit.
Good friends will not leave you stranded.
Good friends will stay by your side.
Good friends will help you out in time of need.
Good friends defend you when people make fun of you.
Good friends will stick with you until the end.
A good friend will not cut you out of anything.
My good friend is Jesus. I hope He's yours too.
Amelia Proctor, Grade 6
Bessie Allen Preparatory School, AL

Beach
Cool breeze brushes in my hair, sun beats down on my cheeks,
On the shore, I watch the children play in the surf
The sand is hot at first but then cool as I walk to the ocean water.
The beach is my home, my love, and it's beautiful.
Tori Moore, Grade 4
Spruce Creek Elementary School, FL

My Country
I love my country, it has lots of palm trees.
I love my country, it has lots of mountains.
I love my country, it had lots of fountains.
I love my country, it has lots of people who dress their best.
I love my country, it has lots of fruits and gardens
I love my country, it has lots of places where kids run with smiles on their faces.
I love my country, it has music flowing through the air.
I love my country, everyone is fair and cares.
I love my country, the sports they do I must say they are hard to play.
I love my country, where people are sweet.
I love my country, where there is lots of treats.
I love my country, it has lots of trains.
I love my country, when it rains.
I love my country, where people like to ride bikes.
I love my country, where people like to hike.
I love its big blue sky and its far horizons.
I love my country at night.
I love my country at night, when people sleep there's not a peep.
I love my country at night, when the stars shine bright.
I love my country at night, when the animals dance under the moon's light.
I love my country, Colombia.
Maria Osorio, Grade 4
FSU/City of Pembroke Pines Charter Elementary School, FL

Darkness

She sits alone in the darkness,
Hot tears dripping down her face.
She hears the rain outside
Slowly falling to the ground.
She feels alone and quiet.
She doesn't know where to go.
Her heart hurts like a big balloon
That has burst and fallen apart.
To her she has disappeared.
She's lost. She is heartbroken.
She is weary and blue.
She sits alone in the darkness and cries.

Dorothy Jane Modla, Grade 4
The Children's School at Sylvia Circle, SC

Valentine Crush

I had a Valentine crush.
He was so cute.
I wrote him a letter.
And didn't want anyone to know my pain.
He read the letter to see if he knew, but I zoomed down the hall
leaving nothing at all.
I got a text message on my phone it said,
"I know what you wrote, I know who you like
and I'm going to tell your crush tonight!!!"

Alena Wash, Grade 6
Philadelphia Elementary School, MS

Looking Through the Glass

I'm looking at myself in the mirror,
I see things you don't see.
I'm looking at myself in the mirror,
And these are the things that I see:

I see brown eyes that are looking in the future.
They see who I want to be.
A daycare owner,
That's who I want to be.

I see a nose that is sniffing,
Things to tears and smiles.
I'll do anything to smell happiness
Even if I go one hundred miles.

I see a mouth that is cheering on people,
Laughing, encouraging
This mouth sometimes gets in trouble
But that's OK, it's me.

You're looking at me on this paper,
Now you know what was never seen.
You're looking at me on this paper,
And this poem was written by a pre-teen.

Tatyana Gaines, Grade 5
Oakland Elementary School, SC

first kiss

love is that tingle in your stomach
that gives you a cold shiver
the face on the moon that lights up the night
love tastes like warm chocolate
running down your throat
love is the sound of a cascading river
flowing down a path
the feel of a star grasped in your hand
love floats
in all of your dreams
love is your heart pounding
on your very first kiss
love is the flame
that lights your way through darkness
love is the whisper of the wind
that gives you a quiver
love swirls into a pink heart that you treasure forever

Cheyanne Reese, Grade 4
Tabernacle Elementary School, NC

No

I didn't want to hear it,
all I could hear were those terrifying words.
I ran, ran until I reached the pond.
From then on, I tried to convince myself
that it wasn't true.
My dad came rushing up.
He held me, and I cried,
for my aunt had passed away late afternoon.

Maddie Mateer, Grade 5
Pensacola Beach Elementary School, FL

My Grandmother

She was my mentor, my love, and my guide.
She told me every thing would be all right.
She said be brave in all that you do,
And never let any one walk all over you.
She loved me in such a way
That brought sunshine to my rainy day.
She told me to believe and to have faith in tomorrow,
Even if it brought upon sorrow.
She was the perfect role model,
She was my grandmother,
Whom I loved as much as my mother.
Though she is gone now her words are still with me,
Her spirit will always lie within me.
I love her so dearly,
As she loves me,
Even though my eyes cannot see.
She is my hero the one who I believe in
She is the sunshine when I feel as though I cannot win.
All I can say is that I miss her,
But I am glad that she is happy,
For that is what is best.

Meredith Mauldin, Grade 6
Immaculate Conception School, MS

School

Six forty five I arise
Brush the sleep from my eyes
Ooh I don't think it's cool
Oh my another day of school
Thinking of school
I'm no fool
I wish I was swimming in my pool
But you know
I have to go
To a place which will shape my world
I'd rather go to school than to be a fool

Kishon Austrie, Grade 6
Gold Hill Middle School, SC

The Statue of Liberty

Stands so bright.
Represents what's right.
Doesn't go down without
A fight.
She makes things right.
She is in our sight.
For she will always be
Our light.

Ashley King, Grade 6
Rock Mills Jr High School, AL

Wild Wolves

Wild wolves
running free
barking and growling
sunset comes
they vanish
I never see…
the wild wolves

Kristina Brennan, Grade 6
Tequesta Trace Middle School, FL

Life Is Like a Step

Step, step, step

It took me a while
Before I realized
That life is like a step

You start from the bottom
And reach to the top
Like summer to autumn
The cycle never stops

It may be rough
You'll be put through the test
Be tough
Because life is like a step

Raphael Lowe, Grade 6
Brogden Middle School, NC

I Am Kailey

I am a bowler, I am a star.
I wonder why the world is round.
I hear birds chirping in a tree.
I see people dancing happily.
I want that toy in the store.
I am a bowler, I am a star.

I pretend to be a girly person.
I feel like I have a hole in my heart.
I touch my dad's heart, with love.
I worry that I will not do well on tests.
I cry when I hurt.
I am a bowler, I am a star.

I understand why we have friends.
I say I don't, but I really do.
I dream of everyone having
    the same amount of happiness and joy.
I try to have faith in all of my friends.
I hope that I did well on FCAT.
I am a bowler, I am a star.

Kailey Theodore, Grade 6
Tarpon Springs Middle School, FL

The Hurricane

Hurricane Wilma
family, pets, and I were scared
hamsters got frightened
bird stopped chirping

thunder and lightning
flashlights
apartment filled with darkness
candles help us to find our way

next day power is back
faced tones of fears
hoped and prayed

Julia Suglia, Grade 5
Rosarian Academy, FL

The Whiteness of Snow

Snow falling
Trees going dormant
Galoshes' tracks
Schools closing
Warm fuzzy mittens
A vast white world
Hot cocoa by the fire
Snowballs flying
Sledding down the biggest hill in town
The sun peeks out
All melts away

Trey Langston, Grade 6
Turkey Creek Middle School, FL

I Am…

I am sane but crazy
I wonder about war
I hear baby cries
I see planes over head
I want peace
I am sane but crazy
I pretend I am a soldier
I feel hopeful
I touch air
I worry that war will never end
I cry over death
I am sane but crazy.
I understand the world is in trouble
I say good can help
I dream I am a peace maker
I try to bring forgiveness
I hope for a better world
I am sane but crazy!

Ashley Nazario, Grade 6
Heron Creek Middle School, FL

Dipping to Freedom

The Big Dipper
with shining dots
shining in the sky
a peaceful darkness
a drink gourd that points to freedom
what an amazing sight
I feel peaceful
peaceful
peaceful
with those stars of bright
leading me.

Matthew Dills, Grade 4
Pinnacle Elementary School, NC

Peace

God of grace Lord of kings,
Set me free of evil things.
Thank You Lord for being king.
I will praise You Lord when I sing.
And I see God and I feel love,
I see Him in the sky above.

Aleah Morrison, Grade 5
Sharon Elementary School, NC

Friend

F riendship
R espectful
I ndivisible
E ncouraging
N egotiative
D ependable

Jamin Johnson, Grade 4
St Helena Elementary School, SC

Sharks
Sharks are really cool
Swimming graceful animals
Swirling, soft and calm

Ariana Fornes-Neuharth, Grade 4
Indian Harbour Montessori Elementary School, FL

Summer
Summer,
When the days are long
Summer,
You just can't go wrong
Take a rest under the shade of a tree
Or go on Lake Murray and water ski
Summer,
I take off my shirt and jump in the pool
The water feels so refreshing and cool
Summer,
Back yard baseball and riding bikes
Go firefly catching on a warm summer night.
Summer

Coleman Weldon, Grade 6
Chapin Middle School, SC

Life
One new birth,
thousands of new possibilities.
New ideas, new dreams.

Starts as tiny as dust,
then grows into a blooming flower.

Simple ingredients in life's recipe:
sweetness, care, and kindness
cook into a young child,
unaware, young, and pure.

Then slowly, slowly,
the bud blooms into a beautiful flower.
Thousands of petals,
each a new possibility,
growing, caring, sharing…

Until at long last,
they each develop into one glorious dream,
showing the world what it can do.

Mallory Duffield, Grade 6
Trickum Middle School, GA

Barthlemew
There once was a man named Barthlemew
Who always wanted to follow you
He was very nice
And ate a lot of rice
He has a friend named Sue

Kasey Kemmerlin, Grade 5
Ranburne Elementary School, AL

My Family
I love my family
My family loves me
I used to play with my niece and nephew each day
I hope I will see them again someday
My mother and father liked to buy me things
Now I have nowhere to put them
When I was short, my sisters made fun of me
Now I'm tall — they don't mess with me
They joke around to make me laugh
My cousins are funny, so funny
When I'm sad, they make me happy
My grandmother likes to buy me things
I also thank her because if it weren't for her
None of this would ever happen

Jesse Ramirez, Grade 6
Statesville Middle School, NC

Hiccups
Hiccups don't know how I got 'em.
What should I do?
Honk, honk. honk
That's me thinking what to do,
Honk, honk
Try to scare them away?,
Or try to drink lots of water?
Honk,
I'll just make sure I don't scatter.
Maybe lay down,
Or go to sleep,
That's what I'll do,
You should see,
I wait one minute,
two minutes,
Still waiting,
Honk, honk
later another five minutes,
Burp!!
What happened?
No more hiccups!!!

Vivian Acosta, Grade 5
Eugenia B Thomas Elementary School, FL

Squishy and Me
Squishy oh Squishy you are the best
We sit and gaze at the sunset
My dog's name is Squishy because she loves to cuddle.
Her favorite game is jumping in puddles
I can remember when she was a pup
She used to drink right out of my cup
My Squishy is nice, not mean at all
She even likes chasing a muddy soccer ball
She makes me happy, she makes me smile
Now its off to the park, so we can play for a while!

Antares Lance, Grade 5
North Windy Ridge School, NC

I Am From...

I am from the dewy grass in the morning.
I am from walking in to the barn and seeing all of the cute horse's heads.
I am from my best friend Anna.
I am from looking into the ocean, and thinking that I just watched a big yellow fish go by.

Emily Nicoletti, Grade 4
Settles Bridge Elementary School, GA

Our Love

"I loved you once, I loved twice," that's all I have to say.
No matter how much others try, there is nothing that can stop me from loving you.
I know that I love you so much and want the whole world to know.
I dream that you would hold my hand and love me the way I love you.
As we walk side by side sharing through the path of love and our age, as we grow older our love gets stronger.
But all I have in my heart is the love I have for you, and the first words I told you is "I love you."
To me those words are stronger, as we walk through the path of love.
We get older, but at the end we die loving each other.

Selene Evangelista, Grade 6
Statesville Middle School, NC

Love

You think you know what love is, till you come to that one day, for that one moment you're in peace, or love as they call it. Then, something happens. It's like a mirror shattering upon your feet. You bleed, and you can't stand any longer because of the pain you feel. But you don't just feel it on the outside, but on the inside too. You cry, but you know that there is nothing left to cry about. So, you move on from what you thought was love, and you never seem to find the answer as to why you were even crying in the first place. Soon, it all seems as if it were a dream, but you still remember the day you felt the pain you were going through. As you move on wondering why they call it love, you ask yourself "how can they call it love if it ends up killing people in their mind and soul?"

Jasmine Bryant, Grade 6
Seven Springs Middle School, FL

The Heavenly Forest

The mystic forest, like a home to me showed me its pleasant sights:
A small stream, like a conversing group, babbled to the wind.
A moss-covered boulder, shelter-of-all, hosted a fox and her cubs.
A rushing waterfall, fit for an opera, sang to the scorching sun.
Royal birds singing, nature's brass trumpets, talked of the wonders they have seen.
Scented pine trees, potpourri to the nose, reached to fill my nostrils with its fragrance.
Perfumed wildflowers, sugar-sweet, took me with them to their aroma-filled world.
The plant tainted wind, like fresh-cut grass, revealed the dew dropped landscape.
The blood-red raspberries, pockets of joy, stained my fingers.
The trodden earth, the organic road, dampened my feet as I walked.
Nature's rhythmical heartbeat, the core of all existence, has and will beat steadily, creating life.

Devin Zwolski, Grade 6
Santa Rosa Christian Academy, FL

Dreams

Dreams are the sound of an athlete crossing the finish line in the Olympics.
It is the smell of chlorine in the water as you reach the pool for the National Championship.
The feel of dreams is getting to shake the president's hand on your birthday.
The puppy that you've always wanted that you received is the sight of dreams.
It tastes like a giant cake on your fourth birthday you thought your parents would never buy.
Dreams are the color of yellow for all of the excitement and achievements you've made.

Taylor Coe, Grade 4
Wrights Mill Road Elementary School, AL

What Spring Break Is For

Spring Break is a time for breaking,
Not for doing chores like leaf raking.
We should be playing with hula-hoops.
Not doing math with triangles and quadroopaloops.
We should be outside having fun,
Like swimming under the golden sun.
But anyway, we want to say thanks,
To all of the parents that let us play with tanks,
For bringing us to Disneyland,
But mostly for being our friends.

Anna Griffin, Grade 5
St Thomas More School, NC

Weather

Weather is both angelic and devilish,
much like a golden lion.
It might bring a luminous day,
or maybe the trees will shiver in distress.

It might exterminate or eradicate.
It is not tame like a dog,
but unpredictable like a courageous eagle.
It can deliver a healing water
or shoot down a destructive light show.

It may whisper in your ear
or suffer a booming tantrum.
It might bring a cerulean sky
or turn this terrestrial sphere
into a nebulous camouflage.

Joseph Shomar, Grade 5
Oliver Hoover Elementary School, FL

Life

Life is very crazy
Every single day
It also gets quiet hazy
And you don't know what to say

People walk in the street
And try not to get hit
Children complain about their feet
And their parents have a fit

People go to school or work
But it's really just the same
'Cause sometimes your boss is a jerk
And your friends can act real lame

Do you want to stay a baby
Or grow up to be old
Life is very crazy
For that's what I was told

Kaleb Elliott, Grade 6
Boiling Springs Intermediate School, SC

The Dog on the Corner

Sitting there,
Waiting for attention.
Waiting to be fed, to be groomed.
Waiting to be played with, and walked.

He remembers when he was a puppy,
When he danced happily around his owner's home.
He used to have a belly full of puppy chow.
Now, all that's inside of his belly is nothing.
All he is now is skin and bones.

He sits on the corner, watching people walk by.
Singing to people, begging for food.
He notices car horns beeping,
And hears the songs that the birds are tweeting.
Look at his eyes and listen to their question:
What did I do wrong, what did I do to deserve this torture?

Now he sits there chained to a fence,
Instead of roaming free like he should.
Years pass by as the dog sits on the corner.
He gets older and weaker, then dies.
Watch as the dog lies on the corner.

Kaelah Bowers, Grade 6
CrossRoads Middle School, SC

The Test

All tumbles and jumbles,
knots and thoughts are
stirred up in my mind.
My heart is beating up a mess.
Oh gosh I should have studied more for this test.

How will I do?
Will my parents say I'm proud of you?
Will that dreaded mark be on my test?
A C, or even a D?

Finally I find the answers in my brain.
I scribble them down and turn my test in.

Hey, I got an A!
I shouldn't be all that worried about nothing.
Hip hip hooray! Book the marching band!

Catherine Benedict, Grade 4
The Westminster Schools, GA

Self-Portrait

My hair is wild like the sea.
My nostrils are like two caves.
My fingers are like slithering snakes.
My bottom lip is a speed bump.
My heart holds the song of the wilderness,
That is as colorful as autumn leaves.

Jesse Bennett, Grade 4
Indian Harbour Montessori Elementary School, FL

Flowers

Flowers… red, pink, yellow
they are so sweet and very mellow
As they may look like a clone
They each have a mind of their own.

The flowers look nice and fresh in spring
As if they are about to sing
Although in the winter they die out
In the spring they come about.

Sunny Ross, Grade 6
Chapin Middle School, SC

Silly Brother

I know I love my mother
I have a little brother
He was kind but then in time
He was as silly as a hen

Isaiah Adams, Grade 6
Arnold Magnet Academy, GA

Golf

G olf is a great sport.
O bviously it looks easy.
L eave your anger at home
F orget bad habits.

Robert Pfeiffer, Grade 6
Seven Springs Middle School, FL

Kitties

S weet like a cake
P retty as a feather
R eally really cuddly
I s soft as a pillow
T hinks like a cat
Z ingy
Y ours truly, Spritzy

Jonathan Conrad, Grade 4
Prince Avenue Christian School, GA

Candy

Candy is sweet,
it sends tingles to my feet.
Candy is tart,
it sends love to my heart.

Candy is so tasty
it makes my head go crazy.
Candy is so creamy
it makes me go dreamy.

Candy is so crunchy
it makes me have the munchies.
Candy is
oh so dandy.

Amber Beasley, Grade 5
Buies Creek Elementary School, NC

The World

The world is like school, you learn a lot of things from it.
You learn what is wrong and right.
There are all kinds of ethnic groups in the world, just like school.
The world is an education for you.
The world is like a school, you know what to do.

Breonna Atwater, Grade 6
Brogden Middle School, NC

Life

Many people take life for granted,
but they don't realize how precious life is.
They say that they don't like what they have,
or they want something they don't have.
They never are thankful for what they do have.
They just want more.

People who have been struck by disasters who were just like us.
But now they are left with nothing but the clothes on their backs.
They are forced to try to pick up the scraps and try to start all over again.
Without even a few dollars to spare.

Many of us think disasters such as fires could never happen to us.
Disasters can happen to anyone.
Some people lose family in disasters.
Some say they bring it on themselves.
Say they deserved it.
No one deserves to dies.
No one deserves to have their life taken away.

Jesse Huskins, Grade 6
Saint Pauls Middle School, NC

We Are Connected

We are all different, but we are all connected
Although we may have different personalities, accents, hair and skin color
We are all connected.

Everyone has a trait in them different from anyone else in the world
No one in the world is the same
But we are all connected.

If we are cut, the blood is always red
We all make mistakes
We all have feelings
We are all human
We are diverse
But in all that diversity
We are all connected.

No matter how much you look alike
We are all different
You can never change it
When you die there will never again be someone just like you
We are all different
We are all connected.

William Bloch, Grade 6
Hand Middle School, SC

Staples

The water was warm and sunny,
and it was a perfect day to go to the beach.
We went snorkeling by the rocks,
on the small beach.
Then we went on the big beach.
With a skim board,
our snorkels and masks,
we went swimming.
BAAAAAAAAAAAMMM!!!
Something had hit me in the head.
It was the skim board.
I came back to the small beach with my hand on my head.
My dad took me to the hospital.
When we got in the doctor said one word,
"STAPLES."
He numbed my head,
then went "CLANK, CLANK, CLANK."
I went back to the beach that same day,
with 7 staples in my head.

Riley Otowchits, Grade 6
Lake Park Baptist School, FL

Dazzling Love

The blooming season of love,
Two by two fly the dazzling dove,
There are many stunning colors of spring,
A man presents the first engagement ring.

Everyone knows that love is in the air,
You might feel passion and care,
No one can hide the beauty of the season,
I guess spring is the reason,
For love.

Katelyn Gano, Grade 6
Gold Hill Middle School, SC

All About Friends

Friends can be anything,
Some stick to you like static cling.

They're all over there's all kinds,
Which ones you want make up your mind.

Not just any friend I say,
The kind that makes a cheery day.

Maybe of the Einstein sort,
Maybe from the feline port.

Or maybe the ones close to you,
Whom if you'd lost you'd be so blue.

If you don't listen to me,
Just get one yourself and see!!!

Tabatha Cross, Grade 6
Boiling Springs Intermediate School, SC

Twenty Years from Now

I wonder, I wonder
Where will I live
Will I have a head full of hair?
Will my arms be loaded with kids?

I wonder, I wonder
Will I live with my mom
Will I live with my aunt
At a hotel?
Or maybe an apartment
Will I have a big mansion?

I wonder, I wonder
Will my hair be orange, yellow, brown, or green?
Or will it be in between

I wonder, I wonder
Will I have kids
Maybe a boy, or maybe a girl.
One, two, three, four,
I only want one
So I am not always bored
But will I really want to play
Hide and seek in the dark.

Haile Foskey, Grade 4
Clearview Avenue Elementary School, FL

Spring

As the wind blows the blossoms sway in the sun
As the sun sets the dandelions roar their loudest
As the moon shines little flower buds sleep
Hoping one day they will be as free as the roses
As the sun rises the birds chirp in the cloudy gray sky
As the rain falls there are puddles for you and I "splash"
The rain has stopped and the moon shines just right
The stars twinkle as the daffodils and tulips sing and dance
For the rain has come again
As I get into bed I hear the flowers sing
My favorite lullaby so I can go to sleep
Goodnight flowers I will soon hear your song again

Cecilia Ross, Grade 6
Williston Middle School, NC

Colors of Me

At times I am black,
    Black, like the trickle of rain in the forever night sky,
    And a lone cricket chirping in the dark.
At times I am blue,
    Blue, like the roaring of waves in the dusk sunset,
    A random sailor trying to find a way.
At times I am green,
    Green, like the thriving grass in a summer field,
    An elderly chipmunk knowing every cranny in the world.

Andrew Gallagher, Grade 5
Sharon Elementary School, GA

When I Look in Your Eyes
When I look in your eyes
I see tears falling inside,
I see your past filled with sadness,
But you try to hide it

Your face looks angry
But inside you are sad,
It's like you were hiding
Most of your life, your past

When I look in your eyes,
I see hurricanes, thunder, and rain,
I try to look harder,
And what I see is mostly pain

I know you are a good person
So I'll try to look harder
And I know I will find
The real you that is hiding.
Sofia Schwarzenberg, Grade 6
Tequesta Trace Middle School, FL

Eric/Noe
Eric
Shy, timid
Irritating, helping, caring
Brother, friend, brother, soccer player
Bonding, entertaining, running
Talkative, Mohawk-man
Noe
Noe Salmeron, Grade 5
Dover Elementary School, FL

Tennis Ball
I glide through the air
I get whacked with a tennis racket
I go up in the air
I come back down
Sometimes I get missed
Then I lay there on the ground
Then someone comes and picks me up
Then I go in the air again
Anna Larsen, Grade 4
Pensacola Beach Elementary School, FL

Madison
M adison
A ugust
D ependable
I ntelligent
S weet
O n fire!
N ice
Madison Gatlin, Grade 4
East Jones Elementary School, MS

School
School can be hard
School can be fun
I love when we
Can play games,
Run, and have fun.
Cameron Foxworth, Grade 5
West Marion Elementary School, MS

An Amazing Sunset
A crimson sphere
Creeping slowly down from the heavens
Just like an angel
Passing leisurely through the air
As time swiftly goes by.

When darkness enshrouds me,
I say good night to the crimson angel
Until the next twilight
When the cycle repeats itself
Just like nature intended.
Hunter Rodriguez, Grade 5
Oliver Hoover Elementary School, FL

I Wish Upon a Shooting Star
I wish upon a shooting star
That I might go really far

To Africa and villages there
To help children breathe safe air

I want to give them a future bright
I want to teach them of the light

I wish upon a shooting star
That I might go really far

Living in a star-studded dream
Standing on stage, I am supreme

Dancing to the rhythm and the beat
As the audience sits in their seats

I wish upon a shooting star
That I might go really far

On the red carpet I want to stand
That is my dream that is my plan

Standing in front of all my fans
Smiling and shaking hands

I wish upon a shooting star
That I might go really far
Kristen Tuttle, Grade 6
Home School, GA

Smart Car
I will step
Into a Smart Car
That is my very own.
This car is something special
That has become well-known.

Everyone has one,
This wonderful,
Self-driving car.
You program it
And then it lifts up
Towards the sun.

It heads to
Your destination
Faster and safer than
The cars on the ground.
Its motor runs smooth,
Barely making a sound.
Liana Philpott, Grade 6
J E Holmes Middle School, NC

Lady on the Bus
On the bus,
in a seat,
Rosa Parks
is who will be.
A tired woman,
who was black,
told by a white man
"to the back."
"No" she said,
turning pale.
Then she went
straight to jail.
Hannah Britt, Grade 6
Saint Pauls Middle School, NC

Witch's Brew
Some mummy dust
A werewolf eye
A pony's head
Our school's chicken pot pie

A dead tree's limb
Some old chunky milk
A dusty, dusty skull
A spider's silk

A frog's gut
A doggie's tail
I'm sure this brew
Will not fail
Raleigh Cassada, Grade 5
Summit Hill Elementary School, GA

Sports

Sports are fun; they are cool.
They are also interesting.
Sports are hard to do when you do not practice.
So work hard and you will get better at it.

Trenton Hill, Grade 5
Rock Mills Jr High School, AL

Wave Song

You listen, you hear,
The sounds of the beach, crash, bang, peck-peck
The sandpiper rapidly searches for food.
Neptune, the god of the waves and sea,
Watching over his children, the fish.
The unnatural:
Fishing boats,
Nets raking up fish like leaves in the fall.
The supernatural:
Sharks of the deep slither like a snake in the garden,
Born free now to be eaten by GUY HARVEY and ANDE.
Crunch the sand,
The texture and the mood of the beach.
Skates and rays hover over the bottom like a UFO.
The sound of nature is the
Wave Song.

Stevie Marinak, Grade 6
Gulf Stream School, FL

The Talking Dog

There once was a dog named Paul.
He was a magic, talking dog.
There was a man named Ben
Who found Paul lost in a dead end.

While walking down the street,
Ben thought he heard Paul speak.
Ben said, "Excuse me. What did you say?"
Paul said, "How are you doing today?"

A talking dog! I must be sick!
Or someone's playing a real mean trick.

Daryen Wilson, Grade 5
East Marion Elementary School, MS

Dream Live On

Roses are red violets are blue
dreams are real and here is my proof
like Martin Luther King Jr.
had a dream that black people
and white people would be treated equally
and his dream came true so yours can too!
In your heart real dreams live
Or some die away a dream is a
dream dead or alive.

Antwon Wright, Grade 5
Four Oaks Elementary School, NC

Santa's Hat

Christmas tastes like hot cocoa
being sipped up everywhere
It smells like cookies just coming out
of the oven at the bakery
It feels like a Christmas present
that you are tearing apart to
figure out what it is
Christmas feels like not being able to
go to sleep at night
It sounds a lot like Christmas
carols being sung in the winter snow
Christmas looks like
an angel on the top of a tree
Christmas is a full moon in the
dark black sky filled with snowflakes
Christmas is like a Christmas tree out in the
winter snow
Snow is like a
blanket pulling itself over the earth
Christmas is my
favorite time of the year!!!

Joshua Hamby, Grade 4
Tabernacle Elementary School, NC

My Friend, the Dog

My friend, the dog is very fun.
We play all day and we like to run.
My friend, the dog is very fair,
We play games by my rules and he doesn't care.
My friend, the dog is very smart
And my friend, the dog has a great heart.
I love my friend the dog, I don't know if you care,
But my friend the dog is always there.

Barrett Teller, Grade 6
St Francis Xavier Elementary School, MS

My Name

L oyal
I nspiring
N atural
D ifferent
S assy
E xcellent
Y oung

Lindsey May, Grade 6
St Francis Xavier Elementary School, MS

Yellow

Yellow feels like spring
It sounds like the buzz of bumble bees
Yellow smells like fragrant sunflowers
It tastes like a cool glass of lemonade
Yellow looks like the burning sun
It feels like the fur of a Labrador Retriever

Jonah Wichterich, Grade 6
City of Pembroke Pines Charter High School, FL

A Writer
Peter
Writes stories
Every day
On the playground
Because he is a good writer.
Dashon Floyd, Grade 4
St Helena Elementary School, SC

Shampoo
I sit in a bottle,
Brand new,
Shiny and squeaky,
They pour me out,
Rub me it their filth.

Then let me free fall,
Down the drain,
That dark, slimy hole,
where all the excess hair goes.

I squirm around,
Covered in your filth.

A turn here,
A big drop here,
Will it ever stop?

I finally stop,
In a smelly stream,
Now down a grate,
Into a gruesome pool.
Eli Vestal, Grade 6
J E Holmes Middle School, NC

Summer
Summer is a great part of the year!
It has beautiful flowers
And wonderful birds
Summer is great!

Although it is hot,
You can make a great big splash!
The water is cool in the pool.
Summer is great!

Summer is loads of fun,
Although I hate to go to bed!
I wish summer would never end!
Summer is great!

Summer is awesome
Because I can play football
I like to tackle.
Football — my favorite game!
Russell LaCoe, Grade 6
Scotts Creek Elementary School, NC

Happy Is…
Happy is a smile upon your pretty little face.
Happy is you blowing out candles on your cake.
Happy is when you get a fluffy little puppy licking your face.
Happy is when you turn double digits.
Happy is when you have a snow day and no school.
Happy is when your mean parents are away and you have no rules.
Happy is when you move schools and make new friends.
Happy is when there is a friend there ready to lend you a hand.
Neely Jones, Grade 5
Northside Elementary School, SC

Kayla Hunter
Kayla
Sister
Caring, nice, helpful, smart
Lover of my family, nature, and art
Who believes God loves everyone
Who wants a D.S., peace on earth, and to go to college
Who uses love, knowledge, and what I know to teach my brother
Who gives knowledge to my brother, use to my parents,
and respect to my teachers
Who says, "It's not what you look like, it's what's on the inside"
Hunter
Kayla Hunter, Grade 6
Newport Middle School, NC

Love Is…
Love is the sweetness between the flowers and the bees.
Love is the friendship that my mom gives me.
Love is what I give to my friends and family.
Love is the connection of the trees and the ground.
Love is the care for your country.
Love is the one thing that comes from our heart.
Love is what I put in my family roots.
Love is what a child gives to their favorite toy.
Love is what has made me faithful.
Love is all the strength I have in me.
Love is the trust in someone.
Love is what we give to life until our death is near.
Love is what someone gives when they are ready.
Love is when the mama bird is looking for something to feed her baby.
Love is just one kiss away.
Love is the tears of someone.
Love can be found anywhere at any time.
Karla Torres, Grade 5
Northside Elementary School, SC

Untitled
Spaghetti is my favorite meal.
The way the noodles drool onto the plate.
The sauce kisses the noodles to give it flavor.
The meatballs run onto the plate to make the meal.
The parmesan cheese dances on top to make the meal complete.
And ready to eat.
Neil Nowall, Grade 6
Challenger Middle School, FL

Hearts

Hearts, hearts, I love hearts,
Valentine's day, marriage day, and even Christmas
Those parts have a lot of hearts
And every day you have to have a heart.

Peyton Taylor, Grade 5
Queen's Grant Community School, NC

Caitlyn

Caitlyn Alexandra Castille
Creative
Friendly
Athletic
Wishes to live a happy life
Dreams of becoming an Olympic softball player
Wants to become a neonatal nurse
Who wonders what heaven is like
Who fears snakes
Who's afraid of failure
Who likes softball
Who believes in God
Who loves Jesus Christ
Who loves animals
Who loves family
Who loves friends
Who plans to have a job
Who plans to live a Christian life
Who plans to have a family
These are the things that make me who I am

Caitlyn Alexandra Castille, Grade 5
Winona Elementary School, MS

Girl Scouts

I am a girl scout
I am honest and fair
Friendly and caring
Helpful and considerate
I am responsible for what I say and do
I respect myself and others and my authorities
I use my resources wisely and to make the world a better place
I am a girl scout!

Chelsea Pittman, Grade 6
Tarpon Springs Middle School, FL

What Is White?

White, tastes like vanilla ice cream
White, is like touching a snowman
White, is the sight of clouds
White, is like a baseball flying
White, is the moon in sight
White, is as beautiful as flower
White, is a light
White, is as white as a white tiger
White, is the paper we write on
White, is like a t-shirt blowing in the wind

Andrew Hettinger, Grade 4
Tabernacle Elementary School, NC

The Stare of the Grave

Between your eyes your beauty lies
Your choice lays within your voice
I looked up beautiful in the dictionary
What I came upon
was your name
Printed in a frame
Then, when I went to see your answer
As well to lay my eyes on you
My heart fell to see you
With yet another lover
As my heart sank my mind went blank
As I dropped to my knees to cry
my heart said vengeance to those whom fly
While I sit and cry
Then as I turned my head
All my heart converged to hatred
And I gave a deathly stare…
The stare of the grave.

Triston LaMon, Grade 6
McRae Elementary School, FL

I Am

I am responsible and valued
I wonder if war will ever halt in its tracks
I hear the thundering of the waves
I see me flooring a Ferrari convertible
I want a billion dollars to give to charity
I am responsible and valued

I pretend to be a street racer
I feel sadness for orphans
I touch excellent work and awesome grades
I worry about black holes
I cry when I lose something special
I am responsible and valued

I understand that I'm not so arrogant
I say Michael Vick is a horrible crook
I dream of being a super sports star
I try my best in athletic games
I hope poachers won't wipe away our animals
I am responsible and valued

Boris Abreu, Grade 5
Sharon Elementary School, GA

July 4th

July 4th is red
The color of fireworks bursting
July 4th feels like a party that never stops
It sounds like people oohing, aahing the fireworks
It smells like Bar-B-Q cooking
It tastes like hot dogs and hamburgers just off the grill
July 4th, it's sad that it only happens once a year.

Tori Atkins, Grade 5
Vienna Elementary School, NC

Flowers
Never before
Have I noticed
The quiet dignities
And colorful personalities,
Of a flower.

The chrysanthemum,
Speaks to me in playful tones,
"Come, come, admire me!"
It says.

The dignified rose,
Bows its scarlet petals
As I skip past.

And the spontaneous dandelion,
Bobbing in the breeze,
Awaiting its time to be whisked away
By the wind.
Sabina Meschke, Grade 6
Bak Middle School of the Arts, FL

Nature
I love this thing called nature.
I don't know why I love it.
But once I get on the subject,
I can't stop thinking of it.
I love nature!
I like to listen to nature.
Sometimes it causes laughter.
The birds in the air,
Their whistles I share.
I love nature!
The sound I hear
A song or two
A roar from a bear
That I hear in the air
Oh, I love nature!
How can it be?
Now can you see?
I love nature.
Natalie Fontaine, Grade 4
Lake Park Baptist School, FL

Little Fairy
Little fairy! Little fairy!
Living in a wall
Getting chased by Captain Hook
And all
Dancing on your bed
Jumping up and down
Flying overhead
Without a single sound
Breanna Johnson, Grade 4
Freeport Elementary School, FL

Rain
Rain, rain stay and play
Rain, rain don't go away.
Rain falls on trees and makes them grow
Rain falls on rivers to make them flow.
So rain you can't go,
We need you to help our earth grow.
Kayleigh Haskin, Grade 5
Allatoona Elementary School, GA

Japanese Hornet
As black as midnight
As yellow as the sun
Wings as delicate as a swan
A stinger as painful as a knife in my back
That is a Japanese Hornet.
Caleb Hicks, Grade 5
Covenant Classical School, NC

My Dog Named Darby
I have a dog
Her name is Darby,
I love her dearly
And she's my darling.
She's black
And that's a fact,
She's two
But she acts brand new.
She loves to jump
She loves to play,
She loves to play all day.
She loves to lick
She gives all the love she can,
She's very frisky
And she loves to frolic, too.
She loves to cuddle
She also loves to snuggle,
She loves to burrow, too.
She sleeps at people's feet
She has big brown eyes
As cute as pie.
Elizabeth Meadows, Grade 5
Northside Methodist Church School, AL

Jethro
It was two years ago
When my mom and dad told me
Our dog died
I burst into tears
I cried for a whole day
I could still feel his fur
He was my first dog
He died at the vet
I was the last one to know
Jacob Baldwin, Grade 4
Pensacola Beach Elementary School, FL

The Stars That Lead to Freedom
The stars are shining
in the dark like
angels
angels
angels
looking
over the Earth
Lindy is happy
to see her father again
Lindy says Papa
in a laughing voice
it sounded so loving
the way she loved him
when will this family go to freedom
Skyler Martinez, Grade 4
Pinnacle Elementary School, NC

Reed S. Rushing
Athletic
Smart
Patient
Wishes to become a pro soccer player
Dreams of saving lives
Wants to live long
Who wonders what heaven is like
Who fears torture
Who is afraid of death
Who likes to play sports
Who believes in God
Who loves his family
Who loves to play soccer
Who loves music
Who loves God
Who plans to have a good life
Who plans to play pro soccer
Who plans to go to heaven
This poem describes me
Reed S. Rushing, Grade 5
Winona Elementary School, MS

My Treehouse
My treehouse is my special place.
I go there to find peace and quiet.
When I need to get away,
I climb the ladder.
To uncover a world unknown,
I'll sit on my window seat
and gaze at the starts all night.
After homework,
I run to the treehouse and daydream.
My treehouse is my special place
where I go every day.
You will see me there every afternoon.
Taylor Michelle Felton, Grade 6
Saint Pauls Middle School, NC

A Figment of Imagination

standing at a dead end
knowing you're in my presence makes me feel content
but not being assured that you're not focusing on just me
sends a wave of selfishness over my head
knocking me back
hesitant to take one more step
towards the rest of what this world has to offer

clutching on to sweet dreams
we know won't come true
we'll jump
never looking back
knowing what we had was a good thing

holding on tight to what we know and believe
we try to explain what's unexplainable
hoping to reach to the core of hearts
to trust us when we say
it's never too late to continue on
through a journey that you've all ready made it this far through

Hannah Singley, Grade 6
Chapin Middle School, SC

So Many Sports

Baseball is a sport I've yet to play.
Maybe I'll get a chance to try it next May.
Before the game, I'll check my laces.
I'll make sure they're tied, so I can run the bases.

Basketball is a super-fast sport.
I like the way I dribble up and down the court.
I like slam dunks and taking it to the hoop.
I even like doing the alley-oop!!

Soccer is a sport full of many kicks.
I'm even learning to do a few fancy footwork tricks.
Playing goalie is the best of all.
It's fun to see how many times I can block the ball.

Football is a sport I'd like to play all day.
I'd be a defensive end, blitzing away.
If I make enough sacks, while the scouts are watching me,
maybe one day I'll play for Tennessee!!!!

Jacob Anderson, Grade 5
North Windy Ridge School, NC

Chores

Whenever I do chores, they make me say EWH!
Cleaning dishes, doing laundry, and even dog poo.
Our dishes can fill up San Francisco Bay.
My laundry, getting out of it, no way!
You're lucky I would say;
To a kid who doesn't have to do chores any day!

DaraGracen Adams, Grade 4
Edwards Elementary School, SC

Family

I love my brother dearly,
I don't like it when he gets all teary.
He's really cool. He loves to go to school.
He's so much fun,
You should see him run.

My sisters are cool.
When they were babies, they would drool.
I love them a lot. Look, they're in a flowerpot.
My sisters are funny,
One of them hops like a bunny.

My dad rules! He is so cool.
He can skateboard and wakeboard. He can cook.
I guess he can even read a book.
He likes to fish.
I'm his wish.

My mom cares. She fixes peoples hair.
She's a good cook. She reads the beauty book.
She likes flashy things. She has a diamond ring.
She is very funny.
She even calls me honey.

Chandler Cauthen, Grade 5
North Elementary School, SC

Hannah

H elps others when in need
A chieves her goals
N ever talks that much during class
N ever forgets her homework so far this year
A lways helping others
H opes to make all A's on her report card

Hannah Sullivant, Grade 5
Winona Elementary School, MS

Shadow

I see my shadow during the day,
Right beside me it will always stay.

It follows me wherever I go,
Running, dancing, fast and slow.

I jump, I step, I twirl around,
And my shadow does it without a sound.

When the sun goes down my shadow grows,
Stretching and stretching, still touching my toes.

But when the long day turns to night,
My shadow hides out of sight.

The sun comes up and my shadow appears,
And I play the long day with my shadow staying near.

Sarah Greene, Grade 6
Boiling Springs Intermediate School, SC

Cousins Forever
A cousin, a cousin,
A few or a dozen.
People to get excited about seeing,
I think it's a wonderful greeting.
Friends forever, a gift from God,
We all are just some peas in a pod.
Riley Patterson, Grade 4
St Thomas More School, NC

Cruise Ship
Cruise ship cutting through ocean blue
Dolphins cavorting as they view
They watch me as I recreate
They watch me as I luxuriate

I wonder what the dolphins think
When the ship passes in a blink
Oh, how the ship must entice
On it's way to paradise

From high atop my balcony
Breezes blowing most zesty
The air so warm and cottony soft
Loving every moment upon my loft
Pierson Haines, Grade 6
Chapin Middle School, SC

I See People
I see people
gathered around a campfire
laughin' and singin'
dark as the trees at night
fire gleaming in the air
so warm and cuddly
they were laughin' and singin'
fire poppin'
I thinkin' about freedom
are they?
I feelin'
like a bag of ashes
I'm so hot
serious faces
serious faces
serious faces
as they think about freedom.
Jonathan Byars, Grade 4
Pinnacle Elementary School, NC

I Am a Flower
I am beautiful
My colors are loud
My stem stands tall and proud
I have leaves as bright as me
I am a glamorous flower
Kiley Stromberg, Grade 5
Pensacola Beach Elementary School, FL

True and Fake Friends
True friends will catch you when you fall.
They may be short or they may be tall.
Some friends are true and others are fake,
Fake friends like to your face and behind your back, spit on your name,
True friends will bake you a cake.
Fake people barely even know your name,
True friends will always keep your secrets,
While fake friends won't care, so they will tell your secrets.
You should always be able to count on true friends,
Because if you can't, then maybe it should be the end,
So hopefully you won't and don't have any fake friends,
If you do that lets you know that anyone can pretend.
Samantha Harrell, Grade 6
Albemarle School, NC

I'm Talking Crazy!
I'm talking crazy!
I'm talking insane!
I'm talking kooky, loony, bonkers, bizarre!
I'm talking wild, weird, extreme, outrageous!
I'm talking senseless, ridiculous, odd, silly, mad!
I'm talking zany, unwise, foolish, passionate, eccentric, outlandish!
I'm talking wacky, goofy, comical, clownish, scatterbrained, unbalanced, fanatical!
I'm talking CRAZY!
Sashinya DeSilva, Grade 4
Wellington School, FL

Nature's Wonders
The clouds are bunnies' tails, spun of pure cotton,
Mother Nature itself, should never be forgotten,
The trees are gentle waves in a peaceful, unknown sea
The wind whistles a message saying "Don't forget me,"
The rain is a sign from the heavens above,
Then, out of the blue comes a beautiful, white dove,
The eagle is a butterfly, waiting to open its new wings of glory,
The star has shone on so many things it just has to tell its story,
The wolf is an endless sky of beauty, just hidden in a dark shell,
The birds that chirp all day and night are nature's wonderful bell,
The rocks all around us are masses of beauty, just misunderstood,
Who would have thought our world was so beautiful, most people never could.
Serina Scott, Grade 5
Brooklet Elementary School, GA

Sweet Treats
Candy canes, lollipops,
suckers and more
I see all of that as I walk through the door
cakes and cookies sit on the table
ice cream and brownies are out in the stable
I look at the labels and they say sugar free
but I wonder why all of these kids are jumping up and down pulling on me?
messing up the house dirtying up the floor
I hate it all I can't take it anymore
no more sweet treats no more no more!
Najja Simpson, Grade 5
Clay Home School, FL

Migration
So bright yet weak are the sounds of night,
While white gleaming gown-like figures
Fly over the water like a cheetah with wings,
Graceful swans flying above the moonlit sky,
Go far away from their summer's home,
To go to an unknown place much warmer than before,
They fly south every year and back in the spring to start again.
Adrian Kant, Grade 6
Shorecrest Preparatory School, FL

The Rollercoaster Ride
Up and down and all around
Jerking swaying from side to side
Screaming and yelling through the bends
When suddenly the ride comes to the end
You stumble back and forth as you depart
It's over, let's go again to the start
Justin Montgomery, Grade 5
East Marion Elementary School, MS

The Mountains
Above me,
A sky of purples, pinks, and blues.
A lady hands me hot chocolate
It is as if a piece of heaven
Has landed in the cup in my hands.
I hear the sounds of a train,
Rumbling on its rusty track.
I am starting to feel the freeze,
Seeping into my wool jacket.
The hot air from my breath
Making a puff of cold air in front of my face.
Trees swaying to the rhythm of the wind.
The sun has gone down,
And time for me to step into the cabin,
'Til tomorrow, tomorrow in the mountains.
Lauren Velez, Grade 6
Seven Springs Middle School, FL

Shopping
Shopping is not like a sport
It's not something you can play on a court.
I like to go shopping; it's really fun to me
There's so much to do and so much to see.
I love to shop, day and night,
And even if there is no light.
Shopping here, shopping there,
Making everyone stop and stare.
Shopping shopping all the time,
It will cost way more than a dime.
Charging up the credit card
But don't worry it's not hard.
I love to shop all day long,
And I don't think it's wrong.
Courtney Horton, Grade 6
Boiling Springs Intermediate School, SC

Martin Luther King Jr.
Martin Luther King Jr.
a black, powerful man
He wanted freedom for everyone
He wanted to take a stand

He preached and preached all day
and at night he preached and prayed
Preached for black rights until he died
He passed away we still thank him till this day
Elizabeth Vargas, Grade 6
Saint Pauls Middle School, NC

Chocolate Is a Taste of Heaven in Your Mouth
Chocolate is like a taste of heaven in your mouth.
Stop crying and sit down in your house.
Pray and believe in what you want.
You don't have to cry all night to see your blessing.
God hears you in the night,
So heaven is a piece of chocolate,
Because God is so good like chocolate,
So keep eating heaven.
Jay West, Grade 6
Mount Zion Christian School, SC

In the Jungle
Walking through the jungle
animals furiously scatter
to find their homes.
Trees swaying in the wind,
missing branches fallen
around me.
Beautiful flowers with the smell seeping into my skin,
the smell of misty rain.
I inhale the sweet nectar of the blooms.
A chipmunk scurries around to find some food.
I drop a walnut.
He thanks me by coming and playing with me.
See what he has been through.
They make their new homes, find their families,
say goodbye.
The sweet smell of my mom's cooking.
Feel the warmth of my mom's arms
around me.
Can't wait to go back to the jungle tomorrow.
Callie Glover, Grade 5
Summit Hill Elementary School, GA

Life
Life is a journey we all must take
Full of obstacles and tough choices to make.

Sometimes we win and sometimes we lose,
It all depends on the pathways we choose.
Hailee Garren, Grade 6
St John's Lutheran School, NC

My Cat Stricklin

My cat is as furry as a teddy bear.
As striped as a zebra.
He runs as fast as a cheetah.
His eyes are bluer than the sky.
With claws sharper than a knife.
His purrrrs are sweeter than chocolate.
Thank you Santa for giving us Stricklin.

Cassidy Davis, Grade 4
Edwards Elementary School, SC

Leaf

Off the tree
Passed the bush
Between the houses
Underneath the clouds
Without any sound
Over the grass
Above the cars
Through the wind
Beyond the ground
Across the streets
Down out of the sky
Out of the wind
Along the grass
Onto the dirt
Outside the house
Near the tree
By the bush
Without flight

Cody Shockley, Grade 6
J E Holmes Middle School, NC

Ballerina

As the pitter-patter
Of light footsteps
Paint a picture on the stage,
This certain person takes me far
Into a time of king and page.

She dances oh so softly,
Like clouds floating in the air.
So delicate, so intricate,
You feel like you are there.

This is a special woman,
This one in arabesque.
She is living the greatest dream,
The one that I like best.

This single ballerina,
In rond de jambe en l'air,
Is a whisper of a feather,
Floating upon air.

Peri Imler, Grade 6
Gold Hill Middle School, SC

Bailey

B ashful
A thletic
I ntelligent
L oving
E ager
Y oungest

Bailey Thorton, Grade 4
East Jones Elementary School, MS

Ashley

A thletic
S hopper
H opeful
L adybug
E nliven
Y oungest

Ashley Hutchins, Grade 4
East Jones Elementary School, MS

Gone

I remember it like it was yesterday.
The day that I lost someone important
That day I felt alone, sad, and angry
That I couldn't stop it from happening.

I used to go visit him
We would have so much fun.
I didn't think
He would go that soon.
All of the many hours
We watched TV together
Were all gone.

I wasn't that old then
But I remember him.
He would give me stuff
From the 60's.
Now I feel bad that
I don't have many of them.

I know he's gone
To a better place.
But I will always remember
Him in my heart.

Matthew Moore, Grade 6
J E Holmes Middle School, NC

Cougar

Animal
Loud, tan
Speeding, eating, jumping
What a cool pet!
Cougar

Gavino Ibarra, Grade 5
Dover Elementary School, FL

Baseball

Spring is here
baseball is near.

The sweat rolling
down my face,
feeling the stitched
in my hand, the
ring of my bat
in my hand.

Those are just
a few things
that are near.

Zachary Hobbs, Grade 5
Buies Creek Elementary School, NC

The Sun and Moon

The sun and the moon, they dance
around and around in a trance
up and down
without a sound
turning around while they prance

Suzette Soule, Grade 5
North Windy Ridge School, NC

Daffodils

I meander through a garden of daffodils
Smell the essence of thunder and rain
As I walk past the field of flowers
Spring is in bloom
And winter has dissolved
Oh, how I do adore spring

Jade Caswell, Grade 6
Shorecrest Preparatory School, FL

Spring

S crumptious
P owerful
R adical
I nteresting
N ice
G rand

Cecilia Lopez, Grade 4
Coldwater Elementary School, AL

Guitars

G reat
U nusual
I mpossible
T itles
A wesome
R oars
S ongs

Michael Frantz, Grade 4
Spruce Creek Elementary School, FL

High Merit Poems – Grades 4, 5, and 6

Between
I'm too good to be bad,
But too bad to be good.
I don't keep track of fads
Like most people would.
I get sad; I get mad.
(That's when I'm not glad
For the things that I have)
I'm not conceited.
I'm no angel.
I can achieve it,
But only when I'm able.
Good times fly by, just like the bad ones.
These things happen,
I have got to move on.
I'm too good to be bad, too bad to be good,
But things end up like the stories say they should.
No matter where I go, you can always find me
Where I will always be: somewhere in-between
All of life's crazy schemes —
The same place I've always been,
The same way I'll always be.

Regina Andreoni, Grade 6
St Thomas More School, NC

Snow Feels Too…
Swishing, whirling, swirling, falling snow
Sticking, freezing, calming, melting snow
Sparkling, swishing snow
Snow feels calm, cold, excited, and scared
It bounces in the wind
WHOOSH!
And swoops down from the sky
SWISH!
Snow is as blurry as a camera lens when it is wet
Snow tastes like clear crisp frozen water
Except when it is yellow
Snow makes me feel happy and
G
R
A
C
E
F
U
L

Emma Applegate, Grade 4
Sharon Elementary School, GA

If
If I were the color pink,
I'd be on flowers and in the sky at sunset.
I'd have very many shades, and
I'd bring color to our world.

Jeannine Widere, Grade 4
Indian Harbour Montessori Elementary School, FL

To Be a Dolphin
Dolphins can swim as fast as trains,
Flipping through the sky with the rain.
Darting around the ocean blue
Like water bugs with a cool sensation.

All day long they twitter and twist
And all night long they sleep in peace
When they wake they start to play
Tag and chase and hide all day.

At dusk, when the sea is black from the reflection of
the sky, they tell stories
Of sea gods and water heroes
Then settle to rest.

Matthew T. Lutts, Grade 6
Chapin Middle School, SC

Pictures
Pictures, pictures everywhere
There's one here, there's one there.
Open your eyes to see that there's a picture inside of me
Pictures show your true color and they also last forever.
When you look at a picture, what do you see?
Shapes, lines, curves, action, creativity
Someone's life and much more
Nice friends, nice family, don't you see
A beautiful picture for you and me
Deep down inside, your heart is
A picture showing who you really are
So now, we all know pictures are special.

Kiyhanna Hall, Grade 4
Windsor Elementary School, NC

Chris Paul
There once was a dude named Chris Paul
His fade away was off the wall.
He has got mad skills,
Which helps him pay bills.
The game he plays is basketball.

Jonathan Jones Jr., Grade 6
Lake Park Baptist School, FL

Friends
Do you have friends that are the best?
Do you have friends north, south, east, and west?

Do you have 1,2,3, or more?
Or do you have friends galore?

Are all your friends super kind?
Are they intelligent or are they a bit behind?

Do you have friends around the globe?
If you do, do they wear a robe?

Lydia Yang, Grade 4
William S Talbot Elementary School, FL

Sparta

The sky was grey.
The Persians, they wanted to slay.
The Persians said, "Bow down!"
"To our god and pray!"
Sparta did not obey.
Sparta ran halfway.
Persia ran halfway.
They started to fight straight away,
In the war brothers were slain.
Wars were won and lost.
They fought in the frost.
Sparta was double crossed.
They would win at any cost!
Sparta went to Nirvana when they lost.
But though they died,
They can say they tried.

Griffin Beckham, Grade 6
Camperdown Academy, SC

Mad Waters

Anger
screaming, hitting
swinging, crying, stomping
raging, forging, releasing, venting
rolling, swelling, knocking
crashing, beating
Waves

Cheyenne Smith, Grade 5
Ranburne Elementary School, AL

School

School is the place we love
It's where we learn and study
It's where we meet friends and buddies
It's where we find paper and pencils
It's where we draw with stencils
School is the place we love
Pre-k thru twelfth that's the rest
Some kids love the test
Others would just rather rest
School well we think it's bad
Most of us are very sad

Courtney Lee, Grade 6
Arnold Magnet Academy, GA

Valentine's Day

Hugs　　　　　Kisses
The best　valentines　kind
Love　　　　　　　sharing
Cheer　　　　　　fantastic
Cool　　　　　　flower
Awesome giving
Happiness
Love

Caitlin Bryant, Grade 5
Buies Creek Elementary School, NC

My Stinky Little Brother

My stinky little brother mostly makes me happy, but sometimes he makes me sad.
Sometimes because of him I tend to turn red and get very mad.
I love my brother, I really do!
It's just that my brother hits, kicks, and punches me too!
My brother is a total mess,
and he normally makes me really, really stressed.
But sometimes I feel happy when my brother is nice to me.
Nice is the way I want him to be.
I love it when he hugs me and kisses me at night.
Then I hug him really intensely tight.
Now it is time to go, so have a good day.
My brother is being kind to me, no way, no way!

Mallory McGee, Grade 4
Monarch Elementary School, SC

Moonlight

I see you almost every day
You sparkle like water droplets on a swan
Your magnificent glow leaves me speechless
You are the halo from an angel from heaven
Even though you are a rock,
I see you as a star I can gaze at
You are a light bulb that never burns out
You are the fireworks display on the Fourth of July,
But you are on all the time
Your beams of light are like a party,
That brings fun and merriment to the night
When you rise into the sky your elegant rays of light rouse all creatures
When humans see you they think sleep,
But I stay up and watch as your vibrant display fades into oblivion.

Corrine Borsch, Grade 6
Tarpon Springs Middle School, FL

I Am

I am fast and a horse lover.
I wonder what it feels like to run in the wind.
I hear a horse whinnying loudly.
I see a horse running in a meadow.
I want a horse that is black, white, and brown named Copper.
I am fast and a horse lover.

I pretend I am the world champion barrel racer.
I feel excited about the horse show.
I touch the soft fur on the horse's neck.
I worry that I might fall off.
I cry when my horse hurts itself.
I am fast and a horse lover.

I understand that the horses are fast.
I say horses are smart.
I dream of a beautiful black, white, and brown horse named Copper.
I try to beat a girl named Becca on a horse.
I hope I get a horse.
I am fast and a horse lover.

Caitlin Horner, Grade 6
Heron Creek Middle School, FL

High Merit Poems – Grades 4, 5, and 6

The Spotted Rhino
The spotted rhino grazing in a field,
Dancing all around with diamonds hanging from his ears.
Music played from far, far away,
Coming from the city of Musical May.
The rhino's spots jumped off his back,
Trying to catch up with the sounds smack, knack, whack.
His tears smashed like broken eggs on the ground,
Nowhere in sight could the spots be found.
The spots still traveling at lightning speed,
Like hungry wild buffalo in a stampede.
His twinky nose picked up their trail,
Moving his short legs slow as a snail.
Chasing his spots through the jungle way,
Heading to the so-called city of Musical May.
The spots arrived for the rhythmic sounds,
Swinging and swaying to the music all around.
"Get on my back" the rhino called,
The spots turned and said, "Hold on wait, we're having a ball."
Racing through the crowd around them,
One by one back onto him
His mission fulfilled now back home for more thrills.
Emily Shae Flynt, Grade 4
Grays Chapel Elementary School, NC

Friendship
Friendship can come with a lot of regrets!
If you get in fights you can work through them.
What if your friends are not true to you?
Even though they can be back stabbers
You just have to forgive them sometimes!
Hopefully all your friends are true.
That way you'll never be blue.
Chanda Stiwinter, Grade 6
Scotts Creek Elementary School, NC

The Horsey Way
horse can neigh, but they can't dance
they can run, they can trot, and they can prance
they don't get pimples
they don't get dimples
they can be pretty loud
but they make you proud
there are Andalusians, Paso Finos, and Haflingers
all of them hooves, but no fingers
they eat hay
they have nothing to pay
they give lessons
all in different sessions
you can tie them down
or ride them to town
they are so adorable
and very huggable
they like to lick my hand with their tongues
oh, I can love horses all day long!
Kimberly Picado, Grade 6
Challenger Middle School, FL

Hockey
I wish I could play hockey
Like Sidney Crosby
And I dream I could play in the NHL
I am in the right position at the right time
Putting pucks in the net like it is 600 ft. wide
I used to pass the net and miss the puck coming across
But now I have found his mental picture of the ice
I seem to get three points per game
But I'm really just a 12 year old boy
Who is playing his favorite game of hockey.
Zack Mitchell, Grade 6
Shorecrest Preparatory School, FL

Autumn's Serenity
"Swish, swish," bright and colorful leaves fall from the trees.
Serenity fills the forest.
"Rustle, rustle," whisper the trees swaying in the wind,
Bursting colors everywhere:
Auburn, maroon, orange, and red.
"Crackle, crackle," the bushes move as small animals
Make their commute around the forest.
The forest shows an expression of hope
To everyone who passes through it.
Fall, give me joy.
Put together the pieces of your inviting puzzle.
"Splatter, splatter, pitter-patter," the raindrops
Dance in the sky of abundance.
"Rush, Rush," go the animals running to find shelter.
"Splash," the rain lands on the leaves making a calming noise.
As the forest becomes dark, the animals settle down for sleep.
The trees stop whispering.
The heavy rain becomes a drizzle.
The moon comes into clear view,
And everything becomes deathly silent until morning.
Haley Clark, Grade 5
Bridgeway Christian Academy, GA

Grandmother's Love
What happens to someone who you love,
When you really love them,
And then they leave you alone,
So you think to yourself,
who's going to be able to sit me down
And have a talk with me when times get rough,
I thought they would be here forever,
but that was just a dream,
love means a lot,
It depends on how far you take it,
Your spirit is still here,
Although your body is gone
Every day I say a prayer
Just for you.
Briona Lawrence, Grade 5
Minor Elementary School, AL

Weather

The rain softly spoke to me through pits and pats. It said, "No playing today but maybe another day."
The snow softly lands on the icy land. Children jump for joy and yell, "Snow!"
Hail comes down in icy chunks, big as softballs. You don't dare step outside or else you could get hit.
The sun shoots golden rays to let us know that it is day. It helps you see.
Hurry quick it is soon to be dark. Spend your daytime wisely.

Sean Purner, Grade 4
St Thomas More School, NC

Man's Best Companion

There are dogs that are cute, there are dogs that are dashing,
Some dog's when they pant, you see their teeth flashing.
There are small terriers; there are big Great Danes,
And the stray dogs you see through your window panes.
And some dogs' barks are very queer, no matter how beautiful they may appear,
Some might yap; or occasionally growl, and at night, sometimes even howl.
The colors of dogs are interesting too, from black to the color of bamboo,
Dogs are so many colors I can't name them all, let's just say, they're every color you see at the mall.
Dogs are everywhere; you see pictures too, you can usually find them in a zoo.
Wolves are also related you know, they hunt in packs; trudging through snow,
They have thick fur, so they don't say "burr."
That's why in the summer dogs sit over a vent, or sit in the shade while you're in your tent.
When you are in trouble, they'll come "on the double"
But they're never too big to cuddle, and when they're in a muddle,
Think, "At least they can't fire a cannon."
They are always happy to be your companion.

Abby Ojeda, Grade 5
Ojeda Academy, NC

I Love Spring

The spring is here thank the Lord
Hayden twits when the sun raises and sleeps when the fun dies
Every bird twits and flies while every dog barks and runs
My dog and I went to the doggy park and saw the birds making their nest
You may not like spring that much, but it is the best time of the year for me
I sat in a tree just seating and seating until I saw a woodpecker higher in the tree
I was walking on the sidewalk when I saw a turtle in the road I named him Fred the turtle
But, until next year I have to suffer until next spring

Brandon Bailey, Grade 5
Palmetto Christian Academy, SC

The Otter Was After the Fish

The otter was after the fish.
The starved aquatic mammal could finally snack on its prey.
It swam and swam but the scaly victim seemed farther moment after moment.
The otter was after the fish.
As they both raced, they both were tiring out.
Hunger kept the otter going and fear kept the fish fleeing for its life!
The otter was after the fish.
After a while the otter was gathering ideas of doubts for survival.
"What if I never eat again? Or maybe my life isn't worth anything to anyone!" he thought.
The otter was after the fish.
All of a sudden the otter told himself "Those are lies! How can I even come up with such dumbfounded ideas?"
So the otter gave one last burst of speed and agility.
The otter had caught the fish.

Gabriel Lopez, Grade 6
Freedom Middle School, FL

Waldo

I once met Waldo who is a fat cat
I gave him a really cool hat

And on this really cool hat
There is a black bat

Waldo is full of joy
When he is playing with his toy

Waldo likes to sit on his blue mat
This is where I go over and give him a pat

While I am giving him a pat
I tell him he is a great cat

Playing with Waldo I really enjoy
Even though he is a boy

I have a brown chair and this is where I sat
Until Waldo brought me a big rat

Now I have no place to chat
And it is all thanks to Waldo that fat cat

Sara Shelton, Grade 4
Spruce Creek Elementary School, FL

Gram

My gram is sweet.
My gram is kind.
She will do anything for you.
Her smile shows love.
Her eyes show joy.
There is nothing to prove.
She's the best gram in the world,
I love her so.
She loves me too.
Sometimes she gets mad at me,
But that never changes our love between us.

Kristian Walker, Grade 5
Ranburne Elementary School, AL

Running

He's running down the field
Other teams cower at the mere sight of him
He's smashing through the other team
He's on the move
And he'll let us know by the roar of helmets crashing
Men jumping on his back only to hi the dirt
With the fear of losing their lives
Now we see him in a suit photographed with his trophy
He's holding the Heisman as a sophomore
He's Tim Tebow

Colton Mayo, Grade 6
Shorecrest Preparatory School, FL

Measurement

Inches are so very small
Like bugs and tiny seats,
When they become bigger,
They will turn into feet.

Feet are so very big
Like a keyboard or briefcase
And when it becomes 3 feet
Yards will take its place.

Yards are so very tall
Like doors or crocodiles
And when combined 1,760 yards
Will turn into miles.

Miles are humongous
Like roads or streets
And now I'm done
With this rhyming sheet.

Kirver Garcia, Grade 4
Egret Lake Community Elementary School, FL

The Love of a Mother

When I thought I didn't need you, you were there
When I did need you, you were there
When I cried, you were there
When I laughed, you were there
When my heart was broken, you were there
So on this day I just want to say thank you
For giving me a chance to know
The love of a mother
Thank you for having me in your life
I love you in so many ways that words could never say
You were always there

Justine Durley, Grade 6
Ethline R Williams Preparatory School, FL

Gardener Snakes

As nice as a caterpillar and as green as an apple
you are a gardener snake.
You can help people with bugs and get a good menu
So go and help gardeners.

James Neal, Grade 5
St Martin Upper Elementary School, MS

It Can

It can pick you up set you down.
Toss you up and throw you down.
Make you cry.
Make you wanna die.
Can make you smile, laugh too, and live to see it through.
To me it is sad sometimes glad.
whether it's short or long
It was life all along.

Jessica Hylton, Grade 6
McRae Elementary School, FL

Corey

C ares about people
O rganized with things
R espectful
E xcellent at sports
Y ear is what it takes to see me again

Corey Stewart, Grade 5
Winona Elementary School, MS

The Difference

Boy
Fun, clever
Running, playing, sleeping
Homosapien, man, woman, queen
Shopping, showing, living
Pretty, smart
Girl

Dylan Rupert, Grade 6
Tequesta Trace Middle School, FL

My Unexpected Day

I heard my tummy rumble,
I got on my bike and took a ride,
I hit a rock and took a tumble,
I scraped my knee and cried.

A car came by and splash,
I got soaked all over!
Splish splash!
It started to rain and I found a clover.

The rain stopped,
And I was happy.
I went hop and got a pop,
My day was happy

Madi Weigel, Grade 5
The Sanibel School, FL

Song of the Bird

The song of the bird,
oh what does it mean?
Is it a sign of happiness,
or of sorrow unseen?

He sings softly to me,
his voice so meek,
sitting up there
on his wooden seat.

His body, a work of art,
his colors so bright.
Off he flies into the night.
As he sings his mysterious melody
I wonder, is he calling to me?

Courtney Amick, Grade 6
Chapin Middle School, SC

Manata Ray

Gliding by the shore
As graceful as a dolphin
Catching schools of krill
Being loved by beach goers
Winding down for the warm night

Shane Imm, Grade 4
Pensacola Beach Elementary School, FL

Kiki

Kiki
Small and furry
Playing, watching, and sleeping
She is so very cute
Kitten

Luke Harrison, Grade 5
Winona Elementary School, MS

Good Guys or Bad Guys

Superhero
Honored, good
Flying, saving, running
Brave, secret, minion, doom
Destroying, inventing, plotting
Hateful, evil
Villain

Andy Therathanakorn, Grade 6
Tequesta Trace Middle School, FL

Writing for School

I need an idea that's really funny
It's not like I'm getting any money
I'm just doing it for school
It has to be cool
Or else everyone will think I'm a dummy

Chase Daniels, Grade 6
B'nai Shalom Day School, NC

Sea Music

Whoosh, whoosh, go the waves
Can't you hear the breeze whistling?
Swish, choom, whoosh
Can you feel the sun?
The ocean changing shades
Can you feel the rush?
Wave language
The flapping of a bird's wings overhead
Hehehe! Goes the dolphin
An ocean band
Spreading its talent
Can't you feel the water rising?
I do.
A flood of white caps, trying to reach up
Sea music.

Amy Churbuck, Grade 6
Gulf Stream School, FL

Still Standing Tall

Although they talk about me,
I'm still standing tall,

They might despise me but
I'm not going to fall,
I'm going to still *stand tall*,

Some might put me down but
I'm *never* going to fall,
Because God had blessed me not to fall,
I'm still Standing Tall!

TreVion Garrison, Grade 5
Minor Elementary School, AL

Who Is This Person?

As I look back on Christmas day
I see a familiar face.
This face brings Exultation
To my heart.
Who is this person?
This person has immense
Round emerald eyes.
His hair is pearly,
Stubby, and smooth.
His skin is a warm color.
Who is this person?
His smile stretches
Surrounding his face.
His eyes are a
Vibrant rainbow.
Who is this person?
Suddenly my mind
Sparks like fire.
Who is this person?
It's my Grandpa, of course!

Max Fields, Grade 6
Unity School, FL

Football

Football is one of my all time sports.
I love to tackle and hit.
I used to play sports of all sorts.

I enjoy them a bit.
Football gives me great joy.
It is a very rough and tough sport.
Knocking people around like a toy.

Knocking me down takes a fort.
Wolfpack is my favorite college team.
They are a hard team to beat.
Winning makes the fans gleam.
Other teams can't take the heat.

Tyler Snook, Grade 5
Sharon Elementary School, NC

High Merit Poems – Grades 4, 5, and 6

Winter's Wonders

I wonder what it's like,
To ride a bike,
In winter's hard snowfalls.
To glide on ice,
Like rolling dice,
And see snowmen's faces glow.
To sled down a hill
In winter's freezing chill,
And hear the sound of children's laughter.
Oh, the thrill of winter's wonders!

Kyle Brooks, Grade 6
Gold Hill Middle School, SC

Spring

Yellow, green, pink, orange, and blue,
These are the colors of the changing season;
Flowers are blooming and dazzling,
while trees are grand;
Everything colorful and awake;
People starting to get out,
New growth in every hidden corner of the earth,
Gentle showers bring the buds to bloom,
Try the honeysuckles here and there,
Savor the honey all day long;
Keep on playing — don't go!
Stay in spring alongside me.
Climb the trees,
Eat popsicles all day,
Smell the fresh cut grass,
Swing from a tire on a tree;
All living things come alive!

Eryn Wood, Grade 5
JJ Jones Intermediate School, NC

Birthdays

Birthdays are full of surprises
Especially when you open the door and everyone rises.
The day belongs to you
So it's up to you on what to do.

First you plan to eat the cake
Which was a huge mistake.
Then you open the presents wrapped with big bows,
As soon as you see it your face just glows!

After the presents you plan to go to the mall
That seemed to last not long at all.
You bought shoes, clothes, toys and more
What else could you wish for?

The party is over and you had your day
You really don't want it to go away.
Just wait until next year
And you will be celebrated with another cheer.

Angela Kay, Grade 6
Boiling Springs Intermediate School, SC

How I Think Winter

When I think about winter
And how the winds blow
I think about how much fun I have in the snow
As I fly like a dart, barely touching the land
Over seas of soft snow like dunes of sand
Thick wool socks with boots and skis
With layer upon layer so that I won't freeze
After crunching and slushing and snowball fighting
A cup of hot cocoa would sure be inviting
When I think about winter
And how the winds blow
I think about how much fun I have in the snow

Chance Simmons, Grade 6
Williston Middle School, NC

Summer

Summer is a time where a lot of people have fun,
Some of the people relax in the sun.
Some of the people take a vacation,
To a spot to have relaxation.

We can go and play sports,
Or go outside to play in our shorts.
I love summer so much,
But I still wonder why it goes by in a rush.

Mason Joel Nance, Grade 4
Grays Chapel Elementary School, NC

Our Days

Some days are good
Some days are bad
Some days are happy
Some days are sad
Some days are windy
Some days are not
Some days are cold
Some days are hot
But, they will repeat themselves
Whether I like it or not!

Sahar Jan, Grade 4
The Muslim Academy of Greater Orlando, FL

What's Love?...

What is love I don't know.
There is the one from family
like your moms, dads, uncles and brothers
grandparents, cousins, aunts and sisters.

Then there's love from your mate and date,
and love you give your children
the truth is love is all those things.
Someone to care for you.

Alfredo Altnor, Grade 6
Brogden Middle School, NC

Friendship

What is friendship?
Friendship is being able to trust them
keeping secrets quiet
knowing they are there for you
fighting and telling them you're sorry
always hanging out
being there when they are sad
never lying to them

That's friendship!

Kaitlyn Sullivent, Grade 6
Turkey Creek Middle School, FL

Winter Love

Winter, you go by as fast as a dove
But you are awesome thus is love
Some people want you to be shoved
Out of my life all lonely
You are truly the apple of
My life
I love
you

Jackie Parsons, Grade 4
Sangaree Intermediate School, SC

South Carolina

From the mountains
To the sea,
South Carolina
Is the place to be!

Playing in the BIG erupting waves
To hiking in the mountains,
South Carolina
Rocks, as you can see!

Columbia, the capital,
The State House is the key.
Fort Sumter, Fort Moultrie —
South Carolina has your history!

South Carolina is my favorite state,
I hope you're not late!

Ella Clayton, Grade 4
Irmo Elementary School, SC

What Is Love?

Love is like hugs and kisses
It is the amazing scent of roses
It feels like the stickiness of chocolates
Love tastes like silky smooth chocolates
It sounds like candy hearts rattling
She speaks by saying, "I love you"
Love moves romantically

Victoria Tuttle, Grade 4
Tabernacle Elementary School, NC

The Peaceful Ocean

The ocean,
Salty, slow, and silent
Waves crashing upon shore,
Like little volcanoes erupting.

The wind blows whoosh, whoosh,
It sends chills down my back
And gets sand in my dark brown eyes.

I pick shells in the bright sunlight
Colors of white, black, purple and so many more
I look in each one just to make sure there's not a…
PEARL!

Now I look up in the sky I see colors of red, blue, and purple.
It looks like layers of icing on a cake,
I wish it could stay forever but slowly it gets dark.
Like the colors I slowly go to sleep.

Zainab Bhagat, Grade 4
Irmo Elementary School, SC

Tsunami

It came in the deathly fright of night,
Showering the scent of casualties around the village
But a light guided me through pain and suffering.
The anguish of thousands of people weighed heavily down on me
The phone stood in front of me,
Had I the strength to reach it in time?
Yes…

Boats broke through the wall of water.
We are the people climbing the wall of sorrow and pain…not water.
Stuck between the tunnel of death
We fight for life, God gives us the life
Using our power for the strife
Rescued at last from this time
Leaving all the other people behind
They were thrown in a ditch
For me, it was a deed of a terrorist
Showing us the evil
Weighing down like a seesaw
And the souls dash away like geese
During the *Tsunami*…

Brandon Cordova, Grade 5
Oliver Hoover Elementary School, FL

St. Patrick's Day

St. Patrick's Day is green
The color of shamrocks and grapes
St. Patrick's Day feels like sneaky Leprechauns lurking all around
It sounds like giggling little people up and down
It smells like green spring grass growing
St. Patrick's Day tastes like green sweet treats
St. Patrick's Day begins spring break retreat

Brianna Pilcher, Grade 5
Vienna Elementary School, NC

High Merit Poems – Grades 4, 5, and 6

Heaven on Earth
Her voice is sweet and faint
Like an angel's
Her eyes are blue and large
Like the ocean
Her hair is blonde and soft
Like a polar bears fur
She is shy and innocent
Like a baby bluebird
She acts like a saint, my guardian angel
And she is what she seems, nothing fake, all authentic
She's my guardian angel watching over me

She's like my second shield, tough and protective
She shoos away my fears when I'm confronted with danger
She's there to lend a hand when I have fallen down
She cheers me up when I am sorrowful
And she is what she seems, nothing fake, all authentic
She's my guardian angel watching over me
Kelly Izquierdo, Grade 5
Oliver Hoover Elementary School, FL

Paul Revere
I woke up one morning just to hear,
The soldiers fighting with lots of fear,
I saw the flag swaying from side to side,
It made me remember the story of Paul Revere's ride,
The ride was hard and long,
Maybe while he was riding he made up a song,
It could be short and mellow,
Maybe it would sound as good as a cello.
Ashley Streitman, Grade 5
Queen's Grant Community School, NC

Sea Music
Waves are crashing onto the shore,
but not just any shore,
the beach shore.
It has that salty smell;
it is also the smell of fresh air.
It is so relaxing.
You get to wash all your troubles away.
The beach is a magical place.
You can do a lot of things.
You can swim, fish, and catch the fish in the ocean.
You could also boat,
or surf the magical waves.
It is amazing what you can find
treasure to an old shoe in the blue.
I wonder how it would be if
you could live in the ocean.
It would be awesome adventures
to explore the wonders of the ocean.
Grant Schultz, Grade 6
Gulf Stream School, FL

Big White Round Clock
Tick tock, tick tock
There goes that big, white, round clock.
One, two, three, four, five, six, seven, eight, nine ten.
Now you got it, go again.
When the clock strikes three
Out of school Yippee!
When the clock strikes four,
It's time for more!
When the clock strikes five.
It's time to say "goodbye."
Megan Michele Rogers, Grade 4
Lake Park Baptist School, FL

Junk Foods
Junk food is really what I like
I eat and eat with all my might.
I know they can be really bad
Being fat would make me sad.

There is a wild variety
From tacos to french fries
If you added them all together
They would pile to the skies

There's salty there's spicy
There's tangy, there's sweet.
Compared to fancy food
They cannot compete.

They're just good to eat
While you ride on the street.
Trace Witt, Grade 6
Boiling Springs Intermediate School, SC

I Am
I am finally awake from the sleep filled night.
I wonder if anyone's awake.
I hear the bees buzzing outside my window.
I see the sun rising above the grass.
I want to go pick the beautiful flowers.
I am finally awake from the sleep filled night.

I pretend to smell the beautiful flowers.
I feel the warmth of the sun come in my window.
I touch the cold fog on my window.
I worry my brothers will come and bug me.
I cry when I am sad.
I am finally awake from the sleep filled night.

I understand that it's still early.
I say the sunrise looks beautiful.
I dream of what the sunset will look like.
I hope someone will wake up soon.
I am finally awake from the sleep filled night.
Sammy Senter, Grade 6
Heron Creek Middle School, FL

Friends

Friends are like flowers
each time I'll pick you
Friends are forever
especially you!
You're engraved in my heart
forever and a day
Together,
Forever,
In my heart you will stay!

Your eyes are like stars,
Stand out from a mile
You always cheer me up
With your smile!
Hand to hand,
Heart to heart,
Together,
Forever,
We'll never spread apart!

Anna Combs, Grade 4
Stone Academy, SC

Today I Will

Today I will let my imagination go,
Here, then there,
To and fro.
Today I let my imagination go,
It went to California, flying high.
If you see it, say "Hi."
It went to the North Pole.
If it saw Santa, it said, "Hello,"
And gave him my dream of a dirt bike.

Clint Sweatman, Grade 4
Cool Spring Elementary School, NC

Dawn

I see the red giant coming from the hills
In it's orange cover.

I hear the song of the birds
Coming from the trees.

I smell the peaches
From our giant peach tree.

I taste the drips of water
From last night's shower.

I feel the chill from the wind
When I step out my door.

That is why I enjoy
A fine summer dawn.

Dalen White, Grade 4
Foster Park Elementary School, SC

Burning Love

In my heart, you are mine,
I'll Love you until the end of time.
In the morning, I want you in my arms,
but for now, you are my charm.
I will love you forever and a day,
even if they say nay.
Our love is so pure as a dove,
now, I grant you my love.

Amber Perdue, Grade 6
Rosenwald Middle School, FL

I Am

I am amazing and artistic.
I wonder about my grandmother.
I hear the birds chirping.
I see a rainbow.
I want to be a nurse.
I am amazing and artistic.

I pretend I'm on top of the world.
I feel wonderful.
I touch a unicorn.
I worry about my mom.
I cry when I'm hurt.
I am amazing and artistic.

I understand my feelings.
I say to be yourself.
I dream of being a princess.
I try to believe in myself.
I hope I can be an artist someday.
I am amazing and artistic.

Kameron Bullard, Grade 5
Stokesdale Elementary School, NC

Courtney

C lever
O utstanding
U nderstanding
R eader
T alented
N eat
E ncouraging
Y oung

Courtney Fenwick, Grade 4
Spruce Creek Elementary School, FL

Hearts

The beautiful hearts
Are falling from the sky
From God's home
During the month of February
Because people are sharing love.

Aaliyah Haynes, Grade 4
St Helena Elementary School, SC

Edwona Burt

Silly
Loving
Smart
Wishing to be famous
Dreaming to be a teacher
Want to always succeed
Wonder what I'll be when I'm grown
Fears things I really can't stand
Afraid of God…
Believe I can do whatever I want…
Love my mom, dad, brother, granny…
Plans to finish high school, college,
And get my teaching license…
Now you know a little about me.

Edwona Burt, Grade 5
Winona Elementary School, MS

Love

To some people it's wonderful
To some people it's horrible
To some people it's sweet as candy
To others contagious as a germ
Some people call it romance
Some people call it destiny
I call it love

Timothy Temmerman, Grade 6
Tarpon Springs Middle School, FL

Spring Is…

spring is
beautiful butterflies
frilly flowers
fresh green leaves on the trees
sparkling rainbows
green grass
wondrous sunsets
new born babies
chipmunks and squirrels waking up
that's what I think of spring

Alec Farson, Grade 6
McRae Elementary School, FL

Stay in School

Roses are red
Violets are blue
You should stay in school.

Because things you don't know
Can be something to stop you
From getting the good job you want
In your bright future
You will be able to look back and say
I'm glad I stayed in school.

Ahija Spivey, Grade 4
Windsor Elementary School, NC

High Merit Poems – Grades 4, 5, and 6

My Journey Home
Like the windy, crystal blue river
through the green, lush forest
around the steep, rocky hill
down the steepest mountain
around the swerving corner
through the desert field
down through the canyons of the far
through the tiger's terrain
swept through the crystal river
down through the green hollow
through the tornadoes of Alabama
down through the city of the night
like the wind being swept off your feet
through the farms where cattle live
also through the terrains where the lion is
walking along the shores of the ocean
through the crystal caves
down through the meadows
what lies ahead
is my cottage in the forest.

Nicole Straka, Grade 6
McRae Elementary School, FL

I Am
I am eccentric and sweet
I wonder what the future holds for me
I hear babies crying helplessly to their mothers
I see birds flying through the horizon
I want to know what people think of me
I am eccentric and sweet

I pretend to know what I'm talking about
I feel butterflies in my stomach as if I'm on a roller coaster
I touch the clouds up in the beautiful light blue sky
I cry when someone whom I love is hurt inside and out
I am eccentric and sweet

I understand that God is always with us
I say never to hate just to dislike
I dream about heaven and what it's like
I hope that one day everyone will be free
I am eccentric and sweet

Carissa Perry-Smith, Grade 6
City of Pembroke Pines Charter Central Middle School, FL

Folding Clothes
When the time comes, I always know,
Indeed it's my turn to fold the clothes.
It's really not that hard, I do exaggerate,
It's really just the long sleeve shirts that I simply hate.
Usually, I only have to fold all of my clothes,
Other times I have to fold the whole entire load!
Although this job can be boring it's also kind of fun,
At times it can be hard, but it's only hard when you get tons.

Henry Torres, Grade 6
St Mary Magdalen Catholic School, FL

Dark and Stormy Night
It was a dark and stormy night,
I went into the house creak, creak,
My throat was dry and tight,
I felt very, very, meek.

There were slimy monsters everywhere,
That was the last place I'd want to be,
The witches whistled through the air,
There were strange creatures following me.

I see a spine-chilling, white and wispy ghost,
Oh no! I let out a horrifying scream!
He wants to haunt me the most!
But it is just a dream.

Tanay Singh, Grade 4
Irmo Elementary School, SC

I Am the Prince
Tossing and turning
Thoughts racing through my head
I still feel the fire burning
As I lay vulnerably in bed.

I shut my eyes wearily.
She is probably just another pretender
But I try to think happily,
Maybe she will be sweet and tender.

Suddenly I hear a groan.
I rush into her room to sneak a glimpse of her.
I think to myself someday
She could be sitting on the throne.

She looks at me and says, "Help sir."
She says she can't sleep.
I stop and think, I make a big leap,
I show a wink.

I rush to my room cheerfully singing.
I found my new wife.
As many thoughts are ringing.
I now know who I am living with for the rest of my life.

Sydnie Newman, Grade 5
Olde Providence Elementary School, NC

School Days
School days
Wake up in the morning
Don't want to go
But Mom comes and says, "Get up!"
I go to school, study, learn, and work
I come back. I can't wait until I come back

Alejandro Aguayo, Grade 6
Tequesta Trace Middle School, FL

Possibility

If the world would realize
that we should stop smoking
and polluting our world
then there's a possibility

If the U.S. would realize
that war is not the solution
for every disagreement
then there's a possibility

If Florida would realize
that we locals don't live
in fantasy land like Disney
then there's a possibility

If we are all wishing
to go to heaven
then there's a possibility

Sam Tenorio, Grade 5
Orlando Junior Academy, FL

Spring

Spring is all types of colors
All beautiful blending together
It feels like heat rising from a volcano
Spring sounds like the chirp of Heaven
It smells like fresh fruit
It tastes like apples
Spring starts the hotness of the year.

Garrett Jacobs, Grade 5
Vienna Elementary School, NC

Green

Spring is here.
Happiness is everywhere.
Warm days fair.
Of course, no despair.
The look of fun.
Children here they come.
The feel of water flow
No one can tell me not to have fun, no!
The taste of pollen.
From the flower it's fallen.
Friends talking is the sound
The words they come in pounds.
The smell of fresh air.
Like I said, no despair.

Taylor Holland, Grade 6
Arlington Middle School, FL

Gentle Puppies

Gentle puppy bites
Rough and dangerous creature
Moves slowly through town

Shavaunte Pippins, Grade 6
Arnold Magnet Academy, GA

Georgia Is

Georgia is warm like the beaches of Florida
Georgia is beautiful like a garden of flowers

Georgia is tough like the strength of steel
Georgia is peaceful like a humble bumblebee

Georgia is dangerous only sometimes anyway
Georgia is the state of the peach that falls on Happy New Year's Day

Georgia is unpredictable when it comes to weather sometimes
Georgia is my favorite state but not all people think that way

Georgia has great colleges like Spelman and Morehouse
Georgia is where I was born and where I will stay

Georgia is my home that I love dearly
Georgia is everything at least that's what I think

Clarke Powell, Grade 6
Academy of Lithonia Charter School, GA

Whatif*

Last night, while I lay thinking some whatifs crawled inside my ear
It pranced and danced all night long and sang the old whatif song
Whatif I was blue?
Whatif I was a shoe?
Whatif I was a car?
Whatif I was a yellow star?
Whatif I was not able to play?
Whatif I was born in may?
Whatif I was a ball?
Whatif I was a doll?
Everything seems swell, and then the night time whatif strikes again.

Autumn Llorens, Grade 6
Challenger Middle School, FL
*Patterned after "Whatif" by Shel Silverstein

The Strongest Person I Know

My grandma Nanny is the strongest person I know
She is bullet proof glass, unbreakable
Whether it's getting burned doing the thing he loves — cooking
Or trying to keep her heart as healthy as a baby
She will never give up

My Nanny is the strongest person I know
When everyone was crying in the hospital thinking and feeling the worst
I kept thinking, "I don't know why they're crying,
I know my Nanny will be okay."

I begin to think about the great memories we share
The cooking, enjoying a good show, and sitting out back watching the waves hit the seawall
I admire Nanny because she will never stop fighting and never give up
My nanny is as strong as a bull
That is why I love my grandma Nanny!

Christian Mauro, Grade 6
Unity School, FL

High Merit Poems – Grades 4, 5, and 6

Forgotten Loved Ones

The loved ones are always special
Because they are loved ones.
People who are loved by different people
Are special because they are loved ones.

I am looking for a loved one
Because I don't have a loved one right now.
But I'll keep looking for a loved one
Because they are special.

Is that a loved one?
I need to find one
Because if I don't,
I'll never see him.

Adrien Pacheco, Grade 4
Bayshore Christian School, FL

Ferret

Crack! Crack! Crack!
What was that!
Maybe it was a giant elephant
Are you sure?
Open up the kitchen door
I see the shadow in the night
Go back inside and get a flashlight
What should we do while we wait?
Should we run like the wind
Or should we crouch like a pin
No! But wait, the shadow is moving
I think it might be twilight oozing
To my surprise it was not
A great big, fat parrot
But a small, cuddly ferret
Whose skin was his umbrella in the cold rain
Which helps keep his fur unstained
Whoosh, the ferret ran away

Leila Glover, Grade 6
Brogden Middle School, NC

I Wonder

I wonder about my life…
I'm only ten right now.
How tall will I be?
Will I be cute as a flamingo?
Will I go to college
And be a famous mathematician?
Will I have a great future
And have a million dollars?
Will I remember my teacher and classmates?
And will I wonder what they're doing?
Will I ever see them again?
I wonder.

Tuh'nesia Stephens, Grade 4
Clearview Avenue Elementary School, FL

Kit Kat

Kit Kat is what they call me
At nights, I look inside of me.
Right when I go to bed I hear, "Get up, Karli!"

I let my friends brag about something,
I'll have something to brag about too.
It's where I am now in GT, the coolest place to be.

And I want to be a teacher
To make money for DS games.
I want to go to college — Lander University,
And I have a great grade tree.

And learn about science and how it works,
I want to get a college degree,
And learn about smartness in me.

I have two sisters and one brother.
I also want to be just like my sister, Shannon.
She has the perfect life.

Karli Andrews, Grade 5
Oakland Elementary School, SC

Three Years

Hiding my feelings from everyone.
Pretending as if it never happened.
Knowing I would be broken;
Like a mirror hurdling to the floor.
With millions of pieces of what could have been.
How could you?
Why did you do it anyway?
You could've just killed me then and there.
You took my heart and left me bleeding.
And now I'm here with only old memories,
And stitches over the empty space in my chest.
If only it wasn't *Life*.

Alexis Velez, Grade 6
Freedom Middle School, FL

Wonderful Colors

Brown are the leaves in the winter
Red is the blood that comes from my splinter.

Blue are the sheets on my bed
Grey is the color of pencil's lead.

Yellow are the stripes on the backs of bees
Green are the plants and the trees.

Orange like a basketball
Tan just like the paint on my wall.

Black just like a large tower
Pink just like a blossomed flower.

David Goldwyn, Grade 6
Tequesta Trace Middle School, FL

Best Friends!
Best friends are people who are kind,
Best friends are people who care,
Best friend stick together,
Best friends share,
Best friends are the best.
They like each other for who they are.
They're nice to each other,
No matter how small,
And no matter how tall,
And no matter how skinny,
And no matter how fat.
Best friends stick like a ball and bat,
If they move to another state,
They'll be in your heart,
Forever to stay.
Ashley Knight, Grade 4
Freeport Elementary School, FL

Stars
Stars are bright
through the night
as they twinkle and shine
like a pretty little dime
oh how I love the stars at night.
Allie Singley, Grade 5
West Marion Elementary School, MS

Life
Life moves one
Like several trees swaying in the wind.

All the way from that little acorn.
We live life.

We live in a society
Where if one of us falls, we all fall.

For every branch we have
Is just a memory,

And we usually forget
That little acorn we used to be.
Alex Umstead, Grade 6
Brogden Middle School, NC

My Love
You were standin' there,
Nothing to do,
When you came over here,
I turned blue,
I couldn't move,
I couldn't speak,
Until the day that our eyes will meet.
Kim Carter, Grade 6
McRae Elementary School, FL

My Daddy
My daddy was great.
My daddy was funny.
He never did anything mean to me.
But now I know it was time for good bye.
How I miss him.
It makes me cry
But now I know he is in a better place.
He is in my heart to stay
And no one can take that away.
Casey Hunt, Grade 5
West Marion Elementary School, MS

Springtime
I see the clouds up above,
I hear the trees blowing,
I feel the wind against me,
I smell the morning air,
I touch the flowers below,
The clouds up above,
The trees blowing,
The cool wind against me,
The morning air,
The flowers below.
Jocelyn Cohen, Grade 4
Central Park Elementary School, FL

Dragon Fly
Zipping through the morning light,
Buzzing with great delight,
High up flying in the sky,
The trees I will go flying by,
Because I am a dragon fly.
Bailey Storms, Grade 5
Montessori Community School, NC

Flowers
Flowers all around,
on the ground,
You can spot them in all colors,
red, white, blue, green,
on and on,
you want to quilt a cover
with colors of joy,
smells of happiness,
and ground of beauty,
bugs from all around
lay to sleep,
kids give them to
their parents,
and then a smile
as wide as the world,
flowers are nature
beauty and more!
Heather Daly, Grade 5
North Windy Ridge School, NC

Surprised
Surprised is a volcano of colors
It sounds like an explosion of cheers
It feels like everyone is looking at you
It smells like happy on a plate
It tastes like pudding.
Emily Cline, Grade 5
Vienna Elementary School, NC

The Monster Under My Bed
I have a monster under my bed.
His name is Fred, and he loves bread.
He wears a hat
That feels like a furry brown cat.
He has a friend her name is Jane
And she lives in the trash can.
She's mostly sleepy and very creepy.
You should see Fred, but give him bread
And he'll might not eat you.
Bailey Giles, Grade 5
West Marion Elementary School, MS

God's Love
In the darkness is
God's light shining for all who
Seek His loving heart.
Samuel Pickerign, Grade 4
Bridgeway Christian Academy, GA

Deep
bubbles rising
water heavy
above me
blurred sun
below
darkness

as I sink
darkness
rises

bottom
black
pitch black
nothing
Adam Brower-Lingsch, Grade 4
Stone Academy, SC

Rain
Rain
Wet and clear
Splashes on the ground
Loud and fast
Rain is one of nature's wonders.
Matthew Noble, Grade 5
Our Lady of Fatima School, MS

Brothers

Although we are different
I want you to know I love you brother.
And I still do
Even though you hit me when you feel like it
We still love each other.

Devin Lenox, Grade 5
Trinity Lutheran School, FL

A Garden Full of Colors

Pink, purple, blue, yellow, orange, green, red
You spin into spring
Adoring its beautiful but fragile
Works of art

Red, pink, purple, blue, yellow, orange, green
You feel their velvety petals
Smell the fresh dirt
After a rainfall

Green, red, pink, purple, blue, yellow, orange
You hear the bees lazily buzzing along
Working to their own song
You can almost taste the honey
Sweet, sticky, orange-gold honey

Orange, green, red, pink, purple, blue, yellow
Sweetly looking up at you
As if saying
"How do you do?"

Yellow, orange, green, red, pink, purple, blue
I love gardens
How 'bout you

Leah Jones, Grade 6
St John's Lutheran School, NC

Busy Bees

As I was wandering through the meadows
I spied a bee buzzing from flower to flower
Collecting golden nectar
For the rest of the hive.
When it flew closer, its minute wings cast buzzing
Into my ears.
Being as minuscule as it appears
The black and yellow yellow jacket works to its limits
Soaring from flower to flower
Helping them, too.
As it makes its retreat to its hive
The yellow jacket brings the collected nectar
To the rest of the busy bees
To make honey,
A luscious treat from hither to yon.
Who knew such a small creature
Had so much to do?

Thomas Morin, Grade 4
Indian Trace Elementary School, FL

Flowers Are Like Life

Flowers are like life
Sensitive and delicate to the touch
Can be altered or changed by much

Life is graceful and elegant
But here is a helpful hint
Do not be so eager to bud
Or pity, you may be a dud

Any careless person can take a life away
But it takes a true person to bloom and stay
You can wither or weep your life away
Or you can sing a mid-summer night's song

But both life and flowers must die
So go on, don't run away
And don't you dare cry or be shy
Make the most of your life before it wilts away

Devin Shackelford, Grade 6
Peachtree Charter Middle School, GA

Dustin

Dustin
Nice, smart, strong, excitable
sibling of RozLynn
friend of Nathan, Trevor, Jacob, and Dylan S
who feels worried
who needs money and horses
who gives pencils
who would like to see Rodney Atkins
Resident of Muscadine, AL
"Three D"

Dustin D. Davis, Grade 5
Ranburne Elementary School, AL

Friends

They know what to do,
they're called friends and I'll show you.
They help you when you're mad or have a tear in your eye,
they will make you happy with an apple cream pie.
Just hold on girl I'm on the way,
to help you make your day.

Alyssa DiCristo, Grade 5
Queen's Grant Community School, NC

A Farmer Named Boo

There once was a farmer named Boo
His favorite color was blue
He loved to visit the cows and owls every day.
So he would say hay.
The cows would moo and the owls would hoo.
So Boo always knew those cows and owls loved him too.

Jacob Michael, Grade 5
Queen's Grant Community School, NC

Nature's Emotions

The moon and stars,
Are blowing at me.
The wind's whisking sand,
Off the shore of the sea.
Thunder is coming,
I think the sun's mad.
Rain's coming too,
I think the clouds are sad.
The sea level's rising
Higher and higher,
While the wind and the rain
stop the rage of a fire.
A tornado zooms by,
Trying to finish it's marathon.
I think the finish line's
somewhere in Oregon.
The prize is the loss,
of people so dear.
You better watch out,
A hurricane's near!

Jennifer Egbebike, Grade 6
St Kevin Catholic School, FL

My Brother

My brother is annoying
Each and every day
Even though all he wants
To do is play

He'll go into my room
He'll throw away my stuff
When I don't want to play
Each and every day

He'll get mad and sad
Each and every day
When I don't want to play
Each and every day

My brother is annoying
Each and every day
But I love him with all my heart
When we do play each and every day

Samantha Schmidt, Grade 5
Brooklet Elementary School, GA

Father

F antastic
A lways there for me
T errific in many ways
H umorous
E vangelist
R eal deal

Jonathan Crownover, Grade 5
Ranburne Elementary School, AL

Rainy Day

Rainy day,
Rainy day,
Such fun to play!
Jump in puddles, I may.
Go splish, go splash, I'll say
Rainy day!
Rainy day!

Alyssa Graham, Grade 4
Immaculate Conception School, MS

Beach Music

This sea: Always the noise of the
Water splashing and sizzling,
When it goes back out to open ocean

This sand: bang and smash
When you print your feet into the sand

These shells: jangle and swish
Every which way like the rush in a mall
During a holiday

This sky: roars with engine sounds
From the mysterious helicopters
Hidden behind the clouds
Which are as white as a sheep's wool

These boats: And always the noise
Bang Rumble Sizzle.
Beach Music.

Adam DeVita, Grade 6
Gulf Stream School, FL

The Beach

The beach is warm,
The sand is hot and smooth
The water is making waves,
And there are people walking.

I play in the ocean,
Boogie in the waves with rhythm,
Jump over waves and dive for joy,
Yum, trailers with beach food.

I build sand castles so high,
Sometimes touching the sky,
I fly kites in the ocean,
Then play volleyball with friends.

My friends throw sand on me,
I jump in the ocean to clean off,
Only five minutes left to play,
Wish I could stay.

Ashlei Barnes, Grade 5
North Elementary School, SC

Rapid Kite

I fly rapidly in the deep blue sky,
For I view the world from 100 feet.
The wind is my power,
For I stay in one place.
I can be different colors and shapes.

Tyler Christensen, Grade 5
Pensacola Beach Elementary School, FL

Neighborhood

Neighborhood fun
There's Katie, Holly,
Julia, and Danielle
Or Hannah Montana
Monkey, froggy
And Ronald
I'm the clown named BOZO
We are all famous for different reasons
That's how we receive our names
Which are then used forever
We wear our friendship necklaces
to show our friendship
That is the joy of the
Neighborhood

Victoria Bang, Grade 6
Shorecrest Preparatory School, FL

Basketball

Right now basketball is me
The ball like my head
Zooming past my opponents

My body like the goal
Standing up straight and tall
A beast in the paint

My arms the sidelines
Nothing gets them
Without getting called
Swish

Stephen Mininni, Grade 6
St John's Lutheran School, NC

I Wish

I wish I could
   go back in time
   to look and find a button
   to take me back in time
I hope and pray
   for my life to change
Then, again,
   I am at rest
   looking down, feeling blessed
I just wish…

Andesha Williams, Grade 5
Wynnebrook Elementary School, FL

Oceans

Waves washing on the shores,
The ocean is something I cannot ignore.

Twinkling water as far as the eye can see,
I wonder how deep the ocean can be.

Waves tumbling upon the sand,
Water splashing on my hand.

I listen to the seagulls passing by,
I look to find the wonderful, blue sea sky.

Seashells washing up on the beach,
The entire ocean is my reach.

Britney Balmer, Grade 6
Brogden Middle School, NC

I Am

I am a person who likes basketball.
I wonder why coaches get so mad
If you don't do something right.
I hear the net go swoosh, swoosh, swoosh.
I see my teammates do an awesome job.
I want to make it to the NBA.
I am a person who likes basketball.

I pretend to get hurt when I am really not.
I feel the intensity of the games.
I touch the basketball and it is cold.
I worry we will lose.
I cry when I am really hurt,
I am a person who likes basketball.

I understand that we won't always win.
I saw we can get a good record.
I dream to win a championship.
I try to do my best.
I hope to win every game.
I am a person who likes basketball.

Jimmy Pierce, Grade 6
Heron Creek Middle School, FL

I Am What I Am

I am the ocean that sways across the coast
I am the man that gives the people hope
I am the One who created land, man, and beast
No one can sit down in my seat
As I take the throne with authority
I still come out with immunity
Forever more still living
Come on, let's go, time is ticking
I am what I am

Cameron Roosevelt Southerland, Grade 5
Carter Community Charter, NC

Making Beds

Early this morning
I got out of bed
And quickly made the bedspread.
I straightened the green sheets
Then fluffed up the thin pillows
Pushed open the heavy windows
And looked at the green willows
Back to the bed
Pulled up the thick comforter.
Pillows are placed
In a particular space
Now for the final act
The Grandfather pillow for my back.
Last but not least, my green fleece
And the stuffed animals that are a showpiece.

Samantha Bendfeldt, Grade 6
St Mary Magdalen Catholic School, FL

I Am

I am smart and good at hockey
I wonder if I can score
I hear the cheer
I see the score board
I want to win the game
I am smart and good at hockey
I pretend I'm alone and in the ZONE
I feel the pressure
I touch the puck with my stick
I worry that I will miss
I cry whether I win or lose
I am smart and good at hockey
I understand the consequence if I miss
I say "I can do it" in my mind
I dream of winning the championship
I try real hard
I hope I make it
I am smart and good at hockey!!!

Austin Thurow, Grade 6
Heron Creek Middle School, FL

The Sun

The sun is a beautiful part of nature.
Without it, the world would have no excitement;
No brightness to lay
Like a fresh blanket over the world.
A truly amazing force it is.
You can't look at it,
But you still know of its beauty.
It never gets tired, even as it sets,
Illuminating more of the world.
Don't forget that when the sun goes away,
Hidden behind some clouds,
The sun is always there,
Lighting up the world.

Olivia Blair, Grade 6
CrossRoads Middle School, SC

Trooper (My Dog)
T roublesome
R idiculously funny
O n the go and
O n our couch
P ep-filled
E ver so happy and
R eady to love

Rachel Brannen, Grade 4
Prince Avenue Christian School, GA

Tree Frogs
Tree Frogs hop, hop, hop
Through the forest at night.
Looking for the morning light.
Finding a way to escape the night.

Emily Burnette, Grade 5
North Windy Ridge School, NC

Diversity
To me, diversity means
That everyone is the same inside.
We all may have
Different skin color,
But everyone has a heart,
Everyone has a type of blood,
And everyone has a life to live.
Everyone was created by God,
Therefore, we are all the same,
Inside, outside, and all around,
We are all the same.
This is what diversity means to me.

Clarissa Gaither, Grade 6
Hand Middle School, SC

As You See
A pencil and a piece of paper
Is what you need to write a poem
It is not as easy as you see,
You need to be a bumble bee.

You could fly through the sky,
And hide in you hive,
But it is not as easy as you see.
You have to see the big huge sea.

You need to feed the fish,
And surf the best,
But it is not as easy as you see,
You have to write a poem you see.

You need a pencil and paper,
And be a bumble bee,
And see the big huge sea,
And then it is easy, as you see.

John Spisak, Grade 6
Gold Hill Middle School, SC

Sixth Grade
I would rather be home
Than bullies, homework, and principles!
I'd rather go outside and play
Than detention, oss, and iss!
I would rather play video games than listen to teachers get on me!
But I would go to see the friends I have.

Trevin Bryson, Grade 6
Scotts Creek Elementary School, NC

New Year's Resolution
Bounce bounce dribble dribble swish
For the New Year this is my wish
Each time I handle a basketball
I hear the cling clang of the net and that's all
As the crowd yells for me
I am a frog when I jump and then I dunk
Then my team begins to sense the sweet smell of victory
In baseball I will let out all my anger as the ball draws near
It will get what it expects as I hit it then it flies with the air
But sports are not my only desire to improve upon this year
I want to control my temper which can get red hot and cause fear
I want to be calm and easy going and not to let some things bother me
In 2008 I want to be fair
Like the wind that blows the air we will all get a share
I want to shine in every way
Like the sun does every day
I want to be better in school
And to be friendly among my peers which is cool
These are my resolutions for this year and I hope that they all will come true
I have 365 days to work on it I am going to make mine come true
Well how about you

Tyler Davis, Grade 5
Waccamaw Elementary School, SC

The Circle of Life
The circle of life is living and dying
and it happens again and again.
It goes baby, child to teen
and by the time you are an adult there are many sights that you have seen.
The circle of life goes around and around
all life has it even has the crickets that make a wonderful sound.

Theodore Bilden, Grade 4
St Thomas More School, NC

What It Is
Sometimes, wants are more than needs.
We can't always think of the right thing.
Nevertheless, one thing for sure is love.
Most people want a good person in their lives to look after them,
to care and to love them.
However, that is not true with all.
So next time you see someone that cares for you say…
"I love you," and brighten up their day!

Ashley Dupper, Grade 6
The Good Shepherd Day School, FL

I Have Lots of Fans

I am an encyclopedia, full of great knowledge
I am the grass, smooth with a little edge.
I am a guardian angel, always watching people
I am a book, full of words and pictures
I am a word, easy to understand
I am a rose, nice and elegant
I am a paper, easy to tear
I am a movie star, I have lots of fans

Nykia Walker, Grade 5
Four Oaks Elementary School, NC

Red

Red is a spring rose,
It's a mint,
The color red is a strawberry,
Cheeks are red, dog tongues are red,
It tastes like a red juicy apple,
In winter red is angry,
Slushies taste as sweet as red,
Darkness is red,
Red rolls down a traffic light,
Red jumps in grass.

Red is for love,
It does not need help with homework,
Red wraps itself around us,
It's as huge as Clifford,
Red has long skinny legs like a lizard,
Red is cute as some puppy eyes.
Whenever red plays with his friend her face turns red.
She is hot as an oven.
Red loves pets.

Katlyn Evans, Grade 4
Youngsville Elementary School, NC

Summer Vacation

F-cats are over and spring is here
We are almost at the end of another school year
Time for friends, family, and fun
Going to the beach and spending some time in the sun
Taking a vacation and going in the pool
No more getting up early and going to school
I'll be counting down the days of another year end
Until next school year and I'll start all over again!

Nicole Pignataro, Grade 4
Spruce Creek Elementary School, FL

Sports

Sports are awesome
Football, baseball, basketball
Swoosh! Home run! Touchdown! Goal!
Sports are enjoyable
My favorite sports are basketball, baseball, football, and soccer
Home run! Hooray!

Joshua Congress, Grade 5
The Sanibel School, FL

Ode to Jevanté's Skateboard

She waits in silence,
Torn up from grinding.
Then, she gets picked up,
Bursting with joy
About to be ridden.
At last, she is on the road.
Sun shining down on her griptape.
Sparkling beautifully like a diamond.

After a long day, she is put back.
I am in bed thinking about her.
Lying in darkness, wishing I could ride her.
I try to sneak out to ride the beauty,
But my mom catches me.

Finally, it is day.
Back to riding my trustworthy board.
Day turns to night,
And my mom calls me in.
After dinner, I get ready for bed.
Again, in darkness,
Lying in torture,
Still wanting to ride.

Jevanté Gross, Grade 6
CrossRoads Middle School, SC

My Mom

My mom is a very happy person,
She's polite, friendly, and never fearsome.
I know she'd do anything for me,
She's as gentle as a butterfly and as busy as a bee.
She's extremely courageous,
Her love is contagious.
She's as sweet as candy,
She's very handy.
She's the best mom ever,
I wouldn't want to lose her,
NEVER!

Bayley Corder, Grade 5
Grays Chapel Elementary School, NC

Rain

Rain, rain never stays
it comes and goes those rainy days.
they are my favorite
you hear the rain
plopping down on the ground.
when it comes I always say you're the best but you never stay.
I think of God pouring water from a jug
when it hits the floor it goes plop.
Rain, rain I'll never forget you
you can come and go but you're the best.

Kayla Edmondson, Grade 5
Orlando Junior Academy, FL

Forgotten
A jacket thrust into a dark and forgotten closet,
while the mind of a human was being filled with other thoughts.
Pushing the jacket further away from existence and the hopefulness was being
drawn from the mentality of the jacket because of its yearning to be worn one more time
and the feeling to be wanted, to be loved, and not to be forgotten but the human mind keeps pushing
the jacket away into the darkness of space
always to be forgotten
and never to be
remembered.

Lucas Owens, Grade 4
Madison Cross Roads Elementary School, AL

Reading
I could read all day on a hot summer's day. I would not go to sleep until the moon comes up. As the wind is blowing, my pages will still flutter like the butterflies I have been reading about. I would wake up the next morning with the book in my lap. I will go outside and sit in the swing. As I turn the pages, the knowledge pours into my mind as I learn about the birds that fly around me. Reading has made me so happy…I think with all my new knowledge, I will let my mind soar some more…

Alex Allen, Grade 5
Bostian Elementary School, NC

Brown
Brown is the coffee beans being ground and crushed. It is the construction workers splattering copper paint on a new building. It is the grande two no fat latté being served to a thirsty customer. It is the Hershey's chocolate bar smooth and creamy on my tongue. Brown is the fur on my dog as he chews on his bone. Brown is the dirt smeared on my toes as I play.

Caroline Ward, Grade 4
Guardian Angels Catholic School, FL

The Prettiest Garden in the World
Memories, memories flashing by my eyes. Got it…this one!

I remember the scent of the flowers; bluebells, pink pansies, and yellow honeysuckles, walking through the front door.
I remember going out on the porch, looking out; the thrilling feeling of being on top of the world,
hearing Nana's little pit patting feet on the white tile.
I remember feeling I don't ever want to leave, the feeling of being in heaven.
I remember taking out the striped lawn chairs, leaning back, and Nana sitting with her perfect posture, as straight as a stick.
I remember helping Nana get poppy seed bagels ready and pouring lemonade, the color of the sun.
I remember crying because Sam died that day and Nana saying, "He's always with us."
I remember the sweet tastes of the fruit of Nana's garden and the laughing fit everyone had
when I bit into the luscious orange and it squirted juice at me.
I remember the silent tears of happiness, of joy, and the sadness of a death.
I remember falling asleep to the lullaby of the wind in my ears and the wind wrapping me in a blanket of love.
I remember most of all: the garden and Nana.

Ilana Nutovits, Grade 6
Unity School, FL

The Summer Picnic
I went on a summer picnic with my family and guess what I saw,
Plenty of delicious food prepared by my ma.
Apples here and sandwiches there lots of food everywhere.
The sun shined bright as I bit into a delicious egg white. Then my mom said it was time for dessert.
When we finished dessert everything was at its best, everything except my messy shirt.
As we started to leave I started to get sad. Then guess what I found, a shiny dime
And said why am I sad, just wait until next time.

Stephen Alexander, Grade 5
Our Lady of Fatima School, MS

Puerto Rico

Puerto Rico beautiful island
It has little frogs that sing a lullaby when you rest
It is rich and pretty
It has many fields
It has colorful flowers
It is very small
It is very beautiful and pretty
It is filled with life

Antonio Wallace, Grade 6
Challenger Middle School, FL

The Whispering Waves

The whispering waves,
Whisper wisely.
They whack the seashore and boats,
As they whisper wise words.
These wistful waves whisper,
As they shimmer in the sunlight.
Waves whisper to each other as they travel.
Their whispers wisp through the wind,
Speaking of whereabouts of other waves.
The wise waves will whisper endlessly.

Sofia Calvo, Grade 4
St Thomas More School, NC

Teacher

You are the best teacher I've ever known
You're a princess and you are royalty

Even though you are royalty
You still mean everything to me

Your long, brown, beautiful hair
Sends me through heaven's air

Your amazing eyes are even better than angel's
Your face sends me through space

Even though you are my teacher
You are the second most important woman to me

Cyrus Knighton, Grade 4
Park Ridge Elementary School, FL

Dragons

Dragons are scary creatures that fly through the sky
until the 500th year they will never die.

With wings of silver and gold
and lots of legends have been told.

If you don't believe me
find the dragons and then you will see.

William Doyle, Grade 6
McRae Elementary School, FL

Waves

Waves, as blue as the summer sky,
Soak her clothed legs at a silent hour of night.
Whoosh, whoosh, she's never tired of the willing sound.
Will she ever turn back home,
Will she ever get bored of the wave's beauty?
All now was quiet, her favorite way.
Day was going to bring loud kids and mad parents,
But now, now was calm.
Stars, as shiny and bright as her loving eyes,
Dance in the clouds with beauty.
The moon is a beauty guiding her this night.
Day is soon, calm would end,
Just as the night shall end at day.

Caitlin Bitting, Grade 4
The Children's School at Sylvia Circle, SC

It Was You

You had to go. Don't you know.
I miss you a lot.
Paw paw, you were a very courteous man.
I look up in the night sky;
The stars shining so bright.
I start to think of you.
Is it really true?
Remember how we went to the fields.
We had so much fun in the blazing hot sun.
Now it's all gone and I am very alone.
I am empty now, somehow.
I weep and grieve as a stupendous
Pool of tears fill the floor.
I get up and go to the front door.
I see you fly by in the dark night's sky.
You are an angel now.
I will see your face in the graceful place!

Angel Lynn Goldman, Grade 5
East Marion Elementary School, MS

Choices

Your voice makes all of the choices…
Some choices are good ones,
Other choices are bad ones.
Still other choices are sad ones…

I hope today that my voice makes
Smart, thoughtful, kind, and
Honest choices — all day long…
And for every day of my life!

Drico Toles, Grade 4
Clearview Avenue Elementary School, FL

A Waterfall

A waterfall is like God's tears,
Full of joy, wonder, and sweetness,
Yet, also full of sorrow and great years of weeping.

Caleb Reider, Grade 6
Mount Zion Christian School, SC

Mom

My mother is kind.
Always loving.
Giving what she can.
Helping me with anything and everything.
Always exciting me with everything.
Gets what I need as soon as she can.
That's my loving caring mother.
Lindsay Rhoden, Grade 5
Ranburne Elementary School, AL

Silver

Silver
The color that brightly gleams
Through the whispers of gentle streams
The color of the night
The moon and star that shine so bright
Cold, the color of metal chains
The color of blades inflicting pain
The color of jewelry often worn
Breakfast cutlery in the morn
The color of a coin to make a wish
The flowing scales of a wading fish
The slippery grip of a metal rod
Silver, the sweat upon your bod
Unique, the silver flames of a fire
The fresh new rim of a tire
The color goes back through history
Fluorescent silver on a key
Silver the feather of a dove
Silver the color that I love
Isaiah Anthony, Grade 6
Arlington Middle School, FL

Beauty in Sorrow

Beauty in Sorrow
A pain in the soul
Wait till the 'morrow
See what it holds

Waiting is painful
This I know true
Wait till the 'morrow
The end will renew

Walk down the path
Help on the way
these familiar faces
Keep evil at bay

Sorrowless Beauty
A soul without pain
This is the 'morrow
See what I gain
Nora Holihan, Grade 6
Milwee Middle School, FL

Ballet

Ballet is graceful
Ballet is fun
You wear pink slippers
But you never ever run.

You always wear tutus
You never wear pants
And all you want to do
Is dance, dance, dance.
Bayley Dawson, Grade 5
Colerain Elementary School, NC

Death

death
painful, horrible
crying, mourning, burying
strong, unstoppable, kind, sweet
breathing, running, playing
wonderful, refreshing
life
Stephen Vaye, Grade 6
Arlington Middle School, FL

If I Had the Power to Change

If I had the power to change
believe me I would rearrange
the concept of war
would be no more
If I had the power to change

If I had the power to change
different ways would not be so strange
Everyone would get along
no opinions would be wrong
If I had the power to change

If I had the power to change
My changes would be so wide ranged
Anyone who was sick
would heal very quick
If I had the power to change
Alexis Keith, Grade 6
Chapin Middle School, SC

Miracles Happen

Miracles happen here and there.
Miracles happen everywhere.
Miracles happen in the dawn of the day.
Miracles happen as small children play.
Miracles happen in the dark of the night.
Miracles happen right in our sight.
Miracles happen here and there.
Miracles happen everywhere.
Cameron Brooke Higgason, Grade 6
Philadelphia Elementary School, MS

Fire Red

Red is a fire, red is part of
the American Flag
it is a warm color,
red is lava
this color is evil.

Red looks good on shirts
and it is nasty and mad,
it is wonderful on cars and
bright in the sun
in the afternoon.
Fredrick Dunston, Grade 4
Youngsville Elementary School, NC

The Lake

Sitting under the sun I bake
here on this big beautiful lake.
I feel the cool breeze
while my body lies at ease

I jump in the sparkling water
while the gleaming sun gets hotter.
I sit in the burning hot seat
while I dip my steaming feet.

As I lay and jump and sit
I know I never want to leave it.
Brittany Franceschina, Grade 6
Chapin Middle School, SC

On a Winter's Day

On a winter's day snow
is like cotton falling
to the colorless earth.
My feet and hands like tons of ice.
On a cold winter's day a
blanket of snow rests delicately
on a tree's branches like
feathers falling to the soft grass.
On a winter's day hibernating animals
sleep like lifeless rocks…
On a winter's day.
Adrianna Keene, Grade 5
Four Oaks Elementary School, NC

Jackson

J ack
A thletic
C olton
K ind
S loppy
O bedient
N ice
Jackson Hill, Grade 4
East Jones Elementary School, MS

In the Dark
I walk out at night and it is so dark,
But I can see lights they are shining so bright
It's like you're holding a diamond up to the sun.

It's so bright and beautiful that I'm not glum.
I can hear sounds like crickets and frogs
It's like a zoo,

But why ruin the moment by talking to you.

Victoria Bullen, Grade 5
Brooklet Elementary School, GA

My Greatest Pain
I was running in the yard.
Then I got tackled by my cousin.
I fell on my elbow.
As I continued to lay in the yard,
I could feel about a million eyes looking at me.
The pain rushing through my elbow
Got worse and worse
As I got weaker and weaker.
I was still as a stone
While I lay in the yard
Crying out for help.
Then suddenly I was lifted by my father
And rushed to a hospital.

Prescott Waller, Grade 5
East Marion Elementary School, MS

The Morning Sun
The morning sun is bright
It has a lot of light.
The sun helps plants grow
and stay healthy.
The sun helps with growing
a beautiful rose.
The sun is
the most wonderful thing
in the world.

Wayne Summerset, Grade 4
Julian D Parker School of Science, Math & Technology, FL

James
James
Helpful, nice, talkative, active
Son of Joe
Lover of Debbie, Destine, and Joe
Who feels sad, mad and happy
Who needs a fish, cat and dogs
Who fears the dark, woods, and snakes
Who gives fish, shoes, and toys
Who would like to see my bike, cat and dog
Resident of South Carolina
Driessen

James Driessen, Grade 4
St Helena Elementary School, SC

Jeffery
JEFFERY

Funny, crazy, athletic, and nice
Brother of Ebony
Who loves basketball, girls, and money
Who feels happy when playing basketball
Who needs money, girls, and love
Who gives love and friendship
Who wants to visit New Orleans, France, and New York
Who fears death
Resident of Columbus, GA

WALTON

Jeffery Walton, Grade 6
Arnold Magnet Academy, GA

My Brother Played Baseball
My big brother played baseball
To me he is the best of all
He plays with me and my cousins
Every time he bats he hits a dozen
He helps us with our throws and swings
Even though he thinks he's a king
He hung up his uniform
and as you can see it's been torn
He runs really really fast
You know he won't come in last
His senior year they were great
They went all the way and won state
That's why my big brother is good as you can see
I love him and he loves me

Christen Shirey, Grade 5
Ranburne Elementary School, AL

The Chilly Summer Night
On that chilly summer night,
my mom was rollerblading with no one in sight.
Coming out of our development,
she was half way to the main road,
when she tripped on a crack and fell on the pavement.
She lay there spellbound not knowing what happened,
but all she knew was the pain in her back.
A car pulled up and asked if she needed help.
She said no, but really meant yes.
After a while she got up,
and slowly started to walk home.
She walked inside crying, wincing in pain,
saying I think I broke my back.
She was rushed to the hospital,
but I never knew,
that my mom had broke her back,
on that chilly summer night.

Christian Nereau, Grade 6
Lake Park Baptist School, FL

A Rainy Day!
Gray skies,
Wet air,
Oops there goes my hair.
First it's straight,
Then turned curly
Oh no now it's frizzy.
Here it comes
A little rumble
A streak of light
Drip drop,
Pitter patter,
Splitter splatter
It's a rainy day.

Ashely Cisco, Grade 6
Gold Hill Middle School, SC

Chasing My Dreams
Here I sit
Giving up
Dreams to fulfill
Goals to reach
I need to stop sitting here
And chase my dreams
With all my might I will succeed

Wesley G. Smith, Grade 6
Philadelphia Elementary School, MS

Small Wonders
a tiny weed
sways nervously at the slightest breeze
bent in places
the loveliest colors of lilac and white
so small you can't feel it
small wonders await you every day

a tiny white flower engulfed in grass
hairs on her petals
five stamens — all white
small wonders await you every day

a small red rock
half hidden in sand
picked it up
will keep
small wonders await you every day

Clare Reid, Grade 5
Sharon Elementary School, GA

Mangos
Mangos are juicy and sweet
Their taste cannot be beat
Mangos are tropical
Their taste is phenomenal
That's why mangos are so neat

Bryan Broadhurst, Grade 5
North Windy Ridge School, NC

Spring Break
S pecial memories and happy times will behold you during Spring Break
P eople run through flower meadows
R ainy season is here once more
I t will be a time of great fun and laughter
N o one will sit still during Spring Break
G rowing flowers welcome blossoming flowers

B e happy and spontaneous during Spring Break
R elaxing is the main reason for Spring Break
E ach family does something different and special
A flower will blossom
K indness will lead to joyful times during Spring Break

Tierra Knight, Grade 6
Perquimans County Middle School, NC

Beach Music
I hear the sand speak
It crinkles,
and the ocean saying *whoosh, wish, wash,*
and the wind *wooooshiii.*
I see the footprints of a person who has been here a while ago.
I see a boat that probably has many miles to go before they sleep.
Seaweed washes up on shore
like yesterday's trash.
The shells were probably inhabited long ago,
until the predator ate whatever animal was in it.
The seeds will soon blossom,
into a beautiful tree.
That is the music of the beach.

Chandler Zombek, Grade 6
Gulf Stream School, FL

I Am
I am happy and funny
I wonder if I will pass fifth grade
I hear music in my head
I see a unicorn rushing through the clouds
I want to make it to middle school
I am happy and funny

I pretend I travel around the world
I feel wind going through my body
I touch the sky
I worry about when I get a test I get frustrated and don't know what to do
I cried when my three dogs died
I am happy and funny

I understand my feelings
I say to stand up for yourself
I dream that one day I will be a vet
I try to listen better than I do now
I hope I will make new friends
I am happy and funny

Jennifer Murphy, Grade 5
Stokesdale Elementary School, NC

Green

Green is grass on a summer day.
Green is seaweed on the beach.
Green is the color of leaves and plants.
Green is the color of my eyes.
Green smells like a freshly mowed lawn.
Green tastes like kiwi in spring.
Green sounds like bugs, making noise at night.
Green looks like a grasshopper in the yard.
Green feels like leaves crunching, crunching.
Green makes me want to go outdoors.
Green is nature.

Lane Hays, Grade 4
Olde Providence Elementary School, NC

Mom

When I am feeling sad,
My mom always makes me glad,
She fills my heart with joy,
Because she gives me lots of toys,
When I'm hurt or sick she always gives me a kick,
We laugh and play,
All through the day,
She is my best friend,
All the way, 'til the end,
Can't you see,
She's been through everything with me,
She always stays calm,
Because she's my mom.

Ashlee Jones, Grade 6
Boiling Springs Intermediate School, SC

The Truth Behind the Door

As people walk by this door thinking about their busy lives,
They never realize inside a man is watching them with sighs.
   He sits in front of the window in a big white chair.
   No one really notices; it's as if no one really cares.
   He sits there and watches everyone go by.
   Sometimes people's thoughts even make him cry.
   He closes his eyes at night and then he starts to dream,
     But everything in his dream is nothing as it seems.
He watches for the wounded and watches for the sick.
He watches for the people in jail; he has no choice, no pick.
   He watches for the laughing and watches for the sad.
   He watches for the kids, even the moms and dads.
He is known as God, and he loves and watches us all day.
   He helps us in the night even when we're feeling gray.
     He lives in everyone's lives and behind that door.
     He helps you resist the evil that forever lures.
   He is there for the plants and everything that breathes.
   He is there for everyone, even in their midst of dreams.
   He is there for the rich, the homeless, the needy, or the poor.
   He is there for everyone behind their made-up doors.

Lyla Mills, Grade 6
Woodward Academy North, GA

Bad School Day

Don't mess with me; I'm having a bad day.
I missed the school bus and ran the wrong way.
I was late for class and I got bit by giant ants!
Worst of all, I forgot my pants!
So forgive me Mr. Burk,
Because of those reasons I lost my homework!

Quinton Smith, Grade 6
Elba Elementary School, AL

Someone Special

Someone special is an inspiration
Who tells me I am a wonderful creation
Trying to find things he left behind
As he leaves

Someone special whispers my name
My heart jumps for joy when I hear his voice
He tells me my eyes are in his reflection
Whose strong hands tuck me into bed
His soft lips plant a kiss upon my head

Someone special sizzles "spinners"
Who admires my imagination
He has confidence in himself
Surely he deserves a standing ovation

The laughter that fills the room is like endless happiness
I fall asleep in his arms
Gentle snores surround my sleeping body
With the powerful hands of Hercules
He lifts me to my bed
I run my fingers across his used-to-be beard; it is rough
It is gray and black
Someone special is slowly aging but still thinks of me.

April Whiting, Grade 6
Williston Middle School, NC

The Color Blue

I love the color blue,
Just like blueberry pop tarts.
The color blue reminds me of the
sky and the ocean.
Blue calms me down when I am frustrated.
Just looking at the color blue makes me
want to eat a blue mix slurpy.
Blue stands for a baby boy.
I listen to the blues every day or so.
Blue is the sound of the water of
the dirty blue ocean.
One day I would love to go to see
the Caribbean clear blue ocean.
I wear a lot of blue jeans to
mean that I am calm and happy
with myself.

Briona Foster, Grade 6
Arlington Middle School, FL

My Mom

My mom is my world!
She means everything to me
Never spiteful
Always full with brightness.

Without her
I'm an angel without a halo
She fills every space in my heart!

She is the reddest rose on a bush
She is the sweetest peach on a tree
She is a gift from God
I couldn't ask for any more.

Sofia Schimpff, Grade 6
Tarpon Springs Middle School, FL

Miley Cyrus

Miley Cyrus is a rockin girl
From the East
All the way to the West
Concert tours all around the world
At singing, she is the best

On the TV screen
She's Miley Stewart
With her friends and family
When she hits the stage
She's Hannah Montana
Singing awesomely

Jake McVay, Grade 6
Arlington Middle School, FL

Softball Fun!

Softball is a blast,
You get to run real fast.
When you hit the ball,
You hope you do not fall.
I take off running to the base,
And hope that I am safe.
Oh this is fun,
As I run home.
When the ball is hit,
You better go get it.
Run, run, run
All the way to home.
Cheer, cheer, cheer,
As you make it home,
Yippee, yippee, yippee.
You made a run.
From this day on,
Softball is in my veins.
I love it…
When we win the game!

Taylor Trogdon, Grade 4
Grays Chapel Elementary School, NC

Welcome to My World

Over this paper,
Past my school,
Beyond the country,
Beside the continent,
Through the atmosphere,
After the world,
Across the galaxy,
Under nothing,
Above air,
Up, up, and up it goes,
Toward unreal,
Away from reality,
Near insanity, but not quite,
Toward fiction,
Within no limits,
Underneath no commands,
With everything known and unknown,
Into my head,
Among my dreams,
In my imagination.

Lauren Ballejos, Grade 6
J E Holmes Middle School, NC

Spring Sunshine

S un all day
U niverse lit up
N eighborly
S treams of light
H ot weather
I ce cream Sundae
N ew flowers
E xcitement

Hans Granger, Grade 5
Queen's Grant Community School, NC

The Christmas Story

On Christmas, the story is told,
And never, ever does it get old.
The King of Kings was born,
But only swaddling clothes were worn.
Christ was there in Bethlehem.
Emanuel was born to them.
Shepherds came to give praise.
They respected the Lord in all their ways.
And still to this day, we celebrate
That He's waiting in heaven at His gate.

Daniela Bolivar, Grade 4
Bridgeway Christian Academy, GA

The Fox in the Bush

Where the red fern grows,
a fox dances in the bush,
in the night he plays.

Connor Howell, Grade 4
PVPV/Rawlings Elementary School, FL

When I'm Bored

Sometimes, when I am bored,
I've done all my homework,
listened to all my music,
and played enough games.
I just lie down,
laying there in the dead silence
on the sofa with my dog
and think, think about life.

Holden Tullier, Grade 6
J Larry Newton School, AL

Poultry

P oultry
O rder
U ses
L ots of
T urkey
R aised every
Y ear

Savannah Taylor, Grade 4
East Jones Elementary School, MS

Valentine's Day

On this Valentine's Day
I want to ask this girl out
I think this girl likes me
But I'm not so sure

The butterflies
They tell me something
Just to get it over
But I just can't help myself
The way she looks at me

So on this Valentine's Day
I will overcome what the butterflies say
I will ask this beautiful girl out
If it's the last thing I do today.

C.J. Williams, Grade 5
Buies Creek Elementary School, NC

Willow Trees

the pretty willow trees
are losing all their leaves
when the windows fog
the great leaves fall

I love willow trees
can't you see,
as I climb in the trees,
my mom rakes the leaves,

that's why I love willow trees

Libby Moses, Grade 4
Pine Tree Hill Elementary School, SC

Javan

Athletic, honest, funny, trustworthy
Son of Lanette and Albert
Who loves family and friends
Who feels funny when talking
Who needs money every day
Who gives love
Who fears snakes, spiders, and cliffs
Who would like to visit Paris, Hawaii, and Las Vegas
Resident of Columbus, GA
Davenport

Javan Davenport, Grade 6
Arnold Magnet Academy, GA

Wild Ride

My stomach did a flip
My insides twisted and turned
As I stepped on the ride of my life

It was scary yet exciting
It was amazing but dreadful
It was full of ups and downs
Twists and turns

It was the rollercoaster of anyone's dreams
It was our friendship

Jenna Rugel, Grade 6
Tarpon Springs Middle School, FL

Spring Blooming

Spring is the trees all blooming and blooming,
Spring is the air so fresh and fragrant.
Spring is the time to spend with your family.
Spring is the best time of the year.

You can spend day and night having fun.
Doing the things you want to be done.
Spring is the best time of the year.
Spring is the thing that makes light velvet flowers.

That all bloom after hours.
Spring is the best time of the year.

Jacob Miller, Grade 6
Chapin Middle School, SC

A Simple Smile

A smile is a simple way to say hello.
It's a sincere way to let your feelings show.
A smile could change the ways of others.
It's as cleansing as rain's showers.

All the people of the world smile.
Short, tall, God made them all.
So pass it on, but don't take too long,
Because the world has a future of smiles.

Margaret McFarland, Grade 4
St Thomas More School, NC

Someplace Special

Someplace special…
Where could it be?
Could it would it have flowers and trees
Butterflies and bees buzzing in my ear

Those butterflies and bees eating
All the honey milk and cookies too

I love this special place
but where could it be?
You just might guess it's my grandma's house
because of the bees, flowers, and trees
the cookies in the oven the milk in the cooler
Can't you just see *my* someplace special.

Evan Wise, Grade 4
Irmo Elementary School, SC

I Am

I am achieving and smart
I wonder if I'll achieve my goals
I hear the sounds of accomplishment
I see my life in the future
I want to live my life right
I am achieving and smart

I pretend that I can't hear the comments
I feel the people staring
I touch the hearts and minds of people
I worry about what they think of me
I cry when I fail
I am achieving and smart

I understand what I'm working for
I say what I think is right
I dream of my future
I try to do my best
I hope I'll have what I've been working for
I am achieving and smart

Shawna Esp, Grade 6
Heron Creek Middle School, FL

Learning Promise

Learning each day,
Each day a new way.
Not wanting to learn,
But my request is adjourned.

I look at the clock
Hoping she'll say
"Everyone line up it's time to play."
The time has come, but it will soon be over,
then we will go home and start all over.

Kaelin Gentry, Grade 6
Philadelphia Elementary School, MS

Pillow

I really love you
I get no sleep without you
You bring me comfort
You are so soft
You are always there for me when I cry
You are so huggable
You make me have sweet dreams
I love you, pillow

Isabella Cody, Grade 4
Pensacola Beach Elementary School, FL

Spring

Warm breeze in the air
Blooming flowers all around
I hear birds chirping

Nathalia Belgrano, Grade 4
Dante B Fascell Elementary School, FL

The Lady with the Brown Bag

There once was a little
Old lady who walked around
With a bag I've always wanted
To know just maybe what was
In that bag was it all her
Life savings or was it just some
Old knickknacks

Jade Gray, Grade 6
St John's Lutheran School, NC

A Friend

A friend is someone,
who believes in you
when you don't believe in yourself.

A friend is
an ocean breeze
that calms you down.

A friend is someone,
who got your back
when there's no one else to turn to.

A friend is someone,
who comforts you
when you're feeling down

A friend is,
Friday night when you're bored
with nothing in the world to do,

A friend is someone,
you can trust,
and talk to about anything.
Don't take a friend for granted.

Callahan Cox, Grade 6
Chapin Middle School, SC

The Legacy of Hope

She was an inspiration to many in just 12 short years,
Everyone cared, her family and peers,
She died at age 12 as you can see,
She loved everyone in her family,
She made everyone happy and put a smile on their face,
Her dad, mom, and sisters loved her much,
Because she left a mark of their heart of a 12 year old girl like you and me,
The mark of a legacy,
The Legacy of Hope.

Olivia Adams, Grade 6
Gold Hill Middle School, SC

Green

Green sprays across grass and paints on leaves,
it is on flower stems and traffic lights.

Some people like green and some people don't.
I like green, how about you?

Green thinks he's awesome because he's on the sea,
he's in the rainbow and he's my dad's favorite color.

Green thinks he's terrible because he's on vegetables some people don't like
he is a color of mold and some people don't want to dye their hair green.

Some people like green and some people don't.
I like green how about you?

Catherine Hoffmann, Grade 4
Youngsville Elementary School, NC

One Grand Grandpa

I call my grandpa Pawpaw Glenn
There is always a huge smile on his face and a big brown beard on his chin
Our family alights after our flight
We arrive at his Victorian house in the middle of the night
I'm as quiet as a mouse when I step through the door
And cats are curled-up sleeping on the floor

His loud, red motorcycle is a train rolling by
While I sit behind him staring up at the sky
The guys watch football on his big TV
While the others laugh and sing karaoke
His big house is filled with antiques of old
The tall Christmas tree sparkles with silver and gold

Every day is a ton of fun
Whether it's sitting in the house or playing in the sun
Piles of presents surround the tree
I tear open my presents just to see
Pawpaw has built a puzzle for me
This all happened when I was three
We pack our bags and step out the door
I hope to return for Christmas once more

Cole Garner, Grade 6
Unity School, FL

Friendship

Friendship is golden,
It smells like a garden full of blooming flowers,
It tastes like an ice cream sundae after a day at the beach,
It sounds like the radio playing old classic songs,
It feels like the sun beating down on you.

Olivia Rosato, Grade 6
Tarpon Springs Middle School, FL

My Home, Georgia

I live in Georgia — a wonderful place,
It is what they they call the "Peach State."
I go to school here, here in Georgia,
And I try not to be late.

It provides good food, really good food,
And clothes and shoes too.
It has really good weather — sometimes,
And all these things are true.

Atlanta is the capital,
In which I live.
So if you plan to come to Georgia,
You might as well come quick.

David Shoneye, Grade 6
Academy of Lithonia Charter School, GA

My Little Puppy

My little puppy is very sweet.
He has white and blonde hair.
He likes to play chase with me.
His favorite things to do are sleep, play ball, and chase me.
My little puppy's name is Pooh Bear.

Lory Miller, Grade 5
West Marion Elementary School, MS

People

I don't understand
   why kids gossip instead of listening
   how a person is amused by being cruel
   why humans are so lazy

But most of all I don't understand
   why people have to *always* look so excellent or cool
   why some girls go shopping for things *all* the time
   how folks can abandon animals to starve and suffer
   why society loves material things

What I understand most is
   why we need our families
   why we have senses
   why we should go to church
   everything happens for a reason.

Morgan Sistrunk, Grade 6
Turkey Creek Middle School, FL

The Haunted House

I live next to a haunted house,
every night I see a floating blouse.

So one day I checked it out,
then I heard a frightened shout.

I ran into the living room,
then I knew I was in doom.

I tried to get out of this haunted thing,
but then the phone rang, "Bring, Bring!"

I finally got out of the house,
now I don't see the flying blouse!

Shelby Robichaud, Grade 4
Chancellor Charter School At Lantana, FL

Gray

Gray, what do you say?
What secret message do you convey?
Are you lifeless folds of baggy skin,
on an elephant shot for his ivory tusks?
Are you mud, having been crawled through,
by soldiers fighting at dusk?
Are you stones thrown at a woman,
who was too quick to sin?
Are you hairs on the head of an aging man,
whose life is soon to give in?
Gray, is that what you say?
Is that the message that you convey?

Elizabeth Kingaby, Grade 5
David Cox Road Elementary School, NC

War (What Does that Spell War)

War is something that makes some people cry.
The reason stays the same, children think their parents will die.
For all you people out there that don't care
Just think how would things be would life be fair?
I don't agree that war is right
But, where would some of us be if we didn't fight
Africans would still be slaves if it was not for the civil war
And just hearing that makes some hearts sore
America would not be
You would not have the life you have now as you can see.
I think all those who have died for my cause
These people are way better than some old Santa Claus
to me war stands for these three words
Warriors are read
That's the deal
I'm proud to be and happy to be where I am today
And these are the finals words I have to say
Then you can stop reading ok
Thank you for all you have done for me and my fellow friends
And sorry to say this is where my poem ends

De'Ericka Payton, Grade 5
St Martin Upper Elementary School, MS

The Scariest Moment Ever
I was walking across the street.
A big truck was coming.
I couldn't move.
Suddenly, I felt a cold shiver
Going down my back.
My heart was pounding.
The truck came closer.
It was beeping its horn.
Then another one came.
I was scared out of my wits!
Then they came closer.
I thought I was gone!
But they stopped!
Donneil Fortenberry, Grade 5
East Marion Elementary School, MS

Spring Has Sprung
Here it comes, here it goes.
Flowers wilt, flowers grow.
Birds are chirping, a lovely sound.
Rain is falling, by the pound.
Feel the warmth, the sun is shining.
Giving the clouds a silver lining.
The pitter-patter of little feet.
I think spring is really neat.
Phoebe Greene, Grade 4
Oak Hill Elementary School, NC

Spring
S unny
P repare for hot weather
R elaxing
I t's swimming time
N ew season
G reen grass
Whittney Cook, Grade 4
Coldwater Elementary School, AL

Courage
Harriet Tubman kind and brave
She was so very bold
She spied on the war every day
At least when she was told.

Harriet Tubman went down to the South
And back about 18 times,
To help 300 slaves escape
And to get to the Freedom Line.

Harriet Tubman was also good
For helping wounded soldiers
She fought for freedom every day,
I want to be more like her.
Maren Hansen, Grade 6
Day Spring Academy, AL

My Little Devil
You are sitting there
Gazing at me with that icy stare
You look like an angel
Looking at me as if I am a fangle
I try and pet you
You bite at my hand
I don't know why
I don't understand
I clean your home every day
I give you food, in some way
Why don't you love me
Why do you attack me
I am not your enemy
I give you water, shelter and food
Your life should be so good
I try to please you every day
I don't know why you push me away
But I love you and that is that
Because either way you are my crazy cat
Ryan Rhodes, Grade 6
Seven Springs Middle School, FL

Wonder
The true blue
Ocean spray
The wind
In my face
The beautiful ocean
In every place
I never knew
I'd feel this way
About something so simple and safe,
But never underestimate
The sea
For it will surely
Put you back
In your place
Bianca Book, Grade 5
Rosarian Academy, FL

Daddy
He's always there.
He's always kind.
He loves me
with a love that's blind.
He holds my hand.
He gives me hugs.
He comes to my room
to squash all the bugs.
He always loves me,
no matter what I do.
He is my daddy.
And I love him too.
Katelin LaRee Isbell, Grade 5
Ranburne Elementary School, AL

Today
The moon cries out to me
Saying that it is nearly dawn.
The wind cries out to me
Saying the day will be cold.
The sky cries out to me
Saying the day will be clear.
The sun cries out to me
Saying the day will be sunny.
It will be a whole new world.
Joshua Chavez, Grade 6
CrossPointe Christian Academy, GA

Capree
C aring
A pple lover
P eas are not my favorite
R eading is fun
E ats a lot
E xcellent jump roper

T all
A aron's sister
Y ours truly
L ions are my favorite animal
O ranges are good
R eading is fun
Capree Taylor, Grade 5
Winona Elementary School, MS

The Beach
Often, I have strolled
along beaches,
feeling the roll
of sand through my toes.
I decide to tiptoe
into the spraying
dark water
as a mouse would.
Grace Turner, Grade 6
J Larry Newton School, AL

Gazing Through the Night Sky
Gazing through the night sky,
While lightning bugs fly so high,
Looking at the stars above,
Dreaming of my one true love,
Soaring high,
Sleeping low,
Shining lights of the moon,
The gazing starlight will end soon,
I rest in peace,
Right where I lay,
Waiting for the unseen day.
Elizabeth Noland, Grade 5
Brooklet Elementary School, GA

Red, White, and Blue
Red, white and blue.
It stands for you.
Red white and blue.
It cooks for you.

Red white and blue.
It's the colors in our flag.
It stands for liberty and justice for all.
Like a peaceful place on Earth.

Flint Dixon, Grade 4
Camden Elementary School of the Creative Arts, SC

My Amazing Home Run
I'm up to bat.
I'm aiming to hit a homer.
I become tense and start to sweat.
The pitcher starts his wind up.
I grind my teeth, anxious to hit.
He finally throws the ball.
I am shocked as I hear a crack of the bat.
The ball rolls all the way to the fence.
I run around base 1, 2, and 3.
I spot home base as the ball reaches the catcher.
I slide into home base.
The umpire shouts "safe" and the crowd cheers.

Austyn May, Grade 5
Grays Chapel Elementary School, NC

Carolina Blue
Carolina Blue, the spirit of your soul.
Carolina Blue drinks water like a dog starving from thirst.
Strong like a tornado.

Carolina Blue is the courage of never giving up.
The person of citizenship.
The one that doesn't let anyone make you believe differently.

Carolina Blue, the color of the sky,
for one's that are in the hospital,
the opinion of lying and
the fairness of letting others play with you.

Carolina Blue is awesome.

Dwayne Macon, Grade 4
Youngsville Elementary School, NC

From Puppy to Dog
Puppy
Fond, playful
Jumping, teething, sleeping
Woof, growth, bark, strength
Sprinting, fetching, smelling
Bright, reliable
Dog

Tyler Plummer, Grade 6
Tequesta Trace Middle School, FL

Blooming Flares
Blazing fire
Flickering flames sweep across land
Scarlet flares dance like graceful lions and tigers
Sprawling and lighting up the dark as if it was almost dawn
Catastrophe

Burnt, scattered ash
Bare, black hole stretches across land
Ash conceals the ground that was once nature's green
New growth eradicates the bare black into a new pool of life
Natural beauty

Madison Kilgore, Grade 5
The Sanibel School, FL

I Wish I Was Still a Tree
Being a piece of paper isn't so great.
Oh, how I wish I was still a tree.
I could still help you and you could help me.
Giving air was one of my best talents.
Now I am just a piece of paper
To be written on and thrown away.
So hear me out and save a lot of trees.
Please, just for me.

Michael Warner, Grade 4
Julian D Parker School of Science, Math & Technology, FL

Love
The love we share the time we spend.
We get together over and over again.
You love me,
I love you.
Why don't we stay together us two.
I want to spend my life with you.
My love is strong and I know yours is too.
This is to you.
Your love is powerful too.

Corey Brandon Smith, Grade 4
Grays Chapel Elementary School, NC

Pizza Pie
I tell you this, I will not lie.
I sure do love my pizza pie.
With pepperoni stacked on high,
and mounds of cheese that touch the sky.

No one knows the reason why,
how much I love my pizza pie.

I wish my pizza pie had an eye,
that way it could see.
How very much my pizza pie,
really means to me.

Joshua Neumaier, Grade 5
Our Lady of Fatima School, MS

Can You Imagine…
Limited Too not at the mall
Or my house not having a hall

No April showers
That bring May flowers

A world without money
And bees not making honey

A clock with no numbers
A house with no lumber

No properties of matter
And cake with no batter

Me in a poetry book
And people come to look?
Ashlyn Howell, Grade 4
William S Talbot Elementary School, FL

Zebra
Long, striped, black, and white
Your tail is so long and thick
Your back is so smooth
Henock Jacques, Grade 4
Park Ridge Elementary School, FL

It Isn't What It Is
As comfortable as a bed with pins on it
As graceful as a monkey driving a car
As clean as a pig in a puddle of mud

As convenient as a dirty room
As reassuring as a dog riding a bike
As exciting as homework

As pleasant as a hot summer day
As welcomed as a pair of muddy shoes
As easy as catching a butterfly with a net
Ashlee Armbrister, Grade 5
Covenant Classical School, NC

My Daddy
My daddy is so fun,
he likes to play and run.
We like to play ball,
even in the fall.
In the summer we like to watch the race,
to see who's gonna save their face.
During the spring we play in the pool,
to see who's gonna rule.
In the winter we hope for snow,
so we can have a row.
Daddy's nickname for me is hun.
Morgan Calhoun, Grade 5
Ranburne Elementary School, AL

Mirror, Mirror in the Sky
Down the sun glistens
as the darkness seems to fall from the starry sky.
When the night is settled in its place, a big, bright mirror glistens,
Almost as bright as the sun in the day.
But no, it's night
With stars in the sky, and the glowing mirror.
It reflects a shimmering light down to the Earth.
The unfamiliar Earth.
But now, all is right.
Why? Because it's night!
You see nothing but the sky,
with its stars and its mirror.
The sky does not need a mirror; it's beautiful and peaceful by itself.
This mirror is to make the Earth beautiful.
All is peaceful in this dark world.
As peaceful as the mirror's light shining down on the still, cold water.
All is calm, there is no sound.
It's all because of the mirror far above the ground.
Haily Collins, Grade 6
Varsity Lakes Middle School, FL

Summer
Sugar and spice, and everything nice is what I'd like to be
With silver bells and cockle shells and nice herbal tea.

Flowers are spreading, birds are bedding, and butterflies fly
Ants die, babies cry, and I ask "Why oh why?"

I like to swim in the summer, but if I don't it's a bummer.
My dad spies seashells in the water. Then he cries "Daughter, daughter!"

When we get out of school our dogs sit down and drool.
It is fun to hang out in the sun and shout "I won, I won!"

Do you like summer? I like it too. Whenever it goes
I don't know what I'll do!
Tamia Brown, Grade 4
St Helena Elementary School, SC

Blind Eyed Television
Me and my friend I had just met
We were watching a show on my tv set.
We watched all day and we watched all night
that both of our eyes were clear out of sight.
I tried to see with all my might
because *Tom and Jerry* had got in a fight.
They fought with fear and fought with might
I wish I could see, but I had no sight.
How I had wished to see that show
I had watched too much tv you already know.
I told my mom about my sight as I bumped and wobbled to and fro.
My mom told me not to fright
for you just need glasses I'm sure I'm right.
Alec Anselmo, Grade 5
Queen's Grant Community School, NC

How Jail Saved Me

Hello, my name is Mr. Jolly Pete.
I was a hobo who lived on the street.
I lost all my money with horrendous fee,
For punching my treacherous enemy Lee.
I was in an extreme need for food,
Without it I got into a bad mood.
My first idea to get food was to beg.
It did not work, and I gained a sore leg.
I only had one idea left,
And it sadly happened to be theft.
I knew I could get food at jail.
I could also stay long, for I had no bail.
I went to K-Mart and started stealing shirts
I was caught by cops and dragged through the dirt.
They put me in their ugly car,
And then they drove me really far.
Later they put me in a smelly cell.
It had bread, bed, water and a bell.
I could finally live with glee,
And that is how jail saved me.

Nikhil R. Gangasani, Grade 6
Woodward Academy North, GA

By Myself

When I'm by myself,
In a room all alone…
Be if far or be it at home,
I close my eyes and think of me,
And all the things I want to be.
I'm a horse — charging through winds,
Even a cat eating catnip,
Chomp — chomp — chomp.
Now I'm interrupted by all types of noises.
Boom, bang, pitter-patter, pitter-patter.
When I'm by myself,
In a room all alone,
I *open* my eyes —
And think of home.

G. Ashley McCord, Grade 4
Irmo Elementary School, SC

Life of African Americans

All African Americans should be honored for their great duty;
Even though most went through hard trials
They were enslaved and worked to death
Which made them want freedom more
Most were picked on because of their race
That doesn't really matter because we are all the same
Right now there is no need to blame
In a very special way we all have fame
No one is not too lame
To just have a bit of fame

Elizabeth Keenum, Grade 6
Saint Pauls Middle School, NC

Animals

A bear is a brown furry mud puddle.
He eats the golden honey from the comb.
It climbs trees to be high and huddle.
Bears try to be as quiet as a gnome.

A dog is a variety of colors like paint.
She eats hard, brown food from a dish.
It crawls into a dog bed to faint.
Some dogs like to eat scaly fish.

A snake is a sheet of mixed color glass.
He munches on field mice and smaller mammals.
It sleeps in a field of high, green grass.
Few kinds of snakes can take down giant camels.

A frog is like slimy gak from a lad.
She eats flies with a sticky hard tongue.
It rests on a wet, floating lily pad.
They jump so high it looks like they got flung.

Charli Kethan, Grade 6
Gold Hill Middle School, SC

The Roller Coaster

My mom says, "Do it if you feel you should."
My brother and my dad say, "Don't be a scaredy cat."
I think that I should do it.
Roller coasters aren't that scary, are they?
It isn't going to kill me, right?

Driss Ziane, Grade 6
Tequesta Trace Middle School, FL

Smoke

I watch the black smoke as it leaves its brick tower.
Moving through the air hour by hour.

Floating carelessly in the breeze,
It chokes my throat and makes me sneeze.

A cat, a dog, no a snake,
Of course I really know all these animals are fake.

The smoke how it billows across the sky,
Enveloping all that I see with my eye!

It is a bit frightening that's for sure,
At least I won't see that smoke anymore.

Josh Morgenlander, Grade 4
St Thomas More School, NC

Ocean

Swish swish ocean waves crashing against the shore.
Clams and seashells slapping and clapping.
Sharks and minnows swimming and splashing.
Whales and seals clapping and plunging into the ocean waves.

Ross Mertson, Grade 6
Gold Hill Middle School, SC

A Ode to Horses
A horse is a friend
They will help till the end.
Do they always receive happiness
From land ahead,
Or do they run free,
Where does the running stop?
Within my mind?
Within our minds?
I do not know,
I do not know, except this:
You cannot build a zoo
Upon a crazy thought.
So, I'm going to believe in my wishes,
Follow them on the run, or
I might lose them all.
Jamie Freeze, Grade 5
Sharon Elementary School, NC

Snow
Snow
So white
Floating down
Many snowflakes
Gone
Max Rutter, Grade 5
Morgan Elementary School, NC

Laurie
I have hair so frizzy.
I have a pet named Lizzy.

I don't like being cold,
But I really love gold.

I like saying "hi,"
But never "bye."

My friends think I'm weird,
But I don't even have a beard.

I like to play fun video games,
But I hate ones that are lame.

My mom says, "I'm a pain,"
But, I wish I had fame.
Laurie Borden, Grade 4
William S Talbot Elementary School, FL

Rain
R ough splashes of water from the sky
A small spring shower
I nside on rainy days
N ice vibrant colors afterward
Olivia Zalecki, Grade 5
Queen's Grant Community School, NC

Practicing Violin
I feel miserable
Like an animal
Locked up in my practice room
And sometimes I feel like a dead broom
My teacher is pushing me
As you can plainly see,
But he has given me permission
To go and audition
When I went to the stage
I was asked my age
Then I played my piece
Until the judge said "PEACE"
Emily Rzepka, Grade 6
Gold Hill Middle School, SC

Dirt Bikes
Dirt bikes are loud and messy.
Dirt bikes can go very fast.
Dirt bikes are very fun to ride,
they go in your garage
when you get done riding.
Morgan Smith, Grade 6
McRae Elementary School, FL

Kitty
Kitty, kitty, kitty
You're so pretty
Kitty, kitty, kitty
You're so sly
but sometimes you're shy
when loud people come by
Kitty, kitty, kitty
You're so beautiful
I'm glad you're not a guy
Kitty, kitty, kitty
Did you just eat?
It made your breath stink!
Salena Swinford, Grade 5
St Martin Upper Elementary School, MS

Running
Horses
Running, running, running
through the fields
blanketed with blue.
As I watch
their hooves
hit the ground
my heart soars.
Running, running, running.
As the moon goes high,
they run away
Running, running, running.
Sarah Boone, Grade 5
North Windy Ridge School, NC

Merry Christmas
Sitting quietly in bed looking
out the window waiting for Santa
and his eight reindeer.
Listening to jingle jingle of
Santa's bells that he hangs on
his reindeer.
Morning is almost here she
said in her head.
Jumping up out of bed gazing
at the presents under the glowing tree.
Megan Carr, Grade 4
Tabernacle Elementary School, NC

Teachers
T rust
E ducation
A pples on the desk
C aring
H onesty
E ncouragement
R espect
S elf-control
Madison Huskey, Grade 6
Tequesta Trace Middle School, FL

The Sea
The sea is like the
Bright blue sky day after day,
Until the sky turns dark,
Just like the black bay
Day after day.
Drew Board, Grade 5
Morgan Elementary School, NC

Angles
You measure them using a degree
They are very hard to see
And they are used in geometry
William Hughes, Grade 6
Gold Hill Middle School, SC

Butterflies
Butterflies flutter
all around in the heavens
flying in the breeze
Elizabeth Bates, Grade 5
Palmetto Christian Academy, SC

Running
"Huh, huh" panting quickly,
thighs cramping, fingers freezing.
Running is not fun you see,
when it's below zero degrees.
Rose Gunn, Grade 4
St Thomas More School, NC

High Merit Poems – Grades 4, 5, and 6

The Darkness

As the darkness closes around me.
I get a quiver in my chin.
The darkness keeps coming.
Until I start to grin.
As I wait to be devoured.
I hear a sound from afar.
The next thing I know.
The darkness starts to break.
As I let out a sigh.
I soon begin to say.
I never thought I would see the light of day.

Tristan Alford, Grade 6
North Myrtle Beach Middle School, SC

Baseball

B atting is the best
A homerun, way to go.
S ummer is the time for baseball
E xtra practice makes perfect.
B ases are square that's how base got in ball.
A triple play, that was awesome.
L anding after a dive for the ball hurts.
L osing is not fun at all

Seth Carpenter, Grade 6
St Francis Xavier Elementary School, MS

Sweet Oreo

Oreo meant so much.
He was the best cat ever.
Every day after school I'd play with him,
we'd play catch the toy mouse,
and get the ping-pong ball.
I fed him
I cared for him
I slept with him
One day after school something went wrong,
something was not right.
Oreo was gone
dead,
By a disease.

Katt Crowdis, Grade 5
Pensacola Beach Elementary School, FL

Fireworks

It was beautiful and a night to remember.
When we shot up the fireworks,
they were gleaming like little meteors
sprouting out of the ground and
falling down like magic dust
sparkling with a tail behind them.
As the screamers shot up into the sky
they screamed and screeched as if to say,
"Look at me, how pretty I am as I dance and scream
as loud as a fire truck's siren in the sparks."

Jerry Marchelletta, Grade 5
Summit Hill Elementary School, GA

Capacity

Oh gallon man, oh gallon man
You are so very large
You're also the biggest
And you are always in charge

Quarts oh quarts
You're the second in line
There are four quarts in a gallon
And they are all mine

After that are the pints
They are bigger than cups
There are 2 pints in each quart
You're the size of my baby pups

And last in line are the cups
There are 4 cups in each quart
Cups are as small as can be
They are not tall but short.

Deja Williams, Grade 4
Egret Lake Community Elementary School, FL

I Am

I am tired
I wonder why I wake up
I hear my alarm clock singing
I see my eye lids closing
I want to fall back asleep
I am tired

I pretend I'm getting ready
I feel like I can't move another step
I touch the hot cup of coco ouch!!
I warn, I won't be able to make it
I cry because I have to go
I am tired

I understand I have to go but I don't wanna
I say good morning and goodbye as she leaves for work
I dream that school will end soon
I try to get ready
I hope to finish
I am tired.

Camille Frederick, Grade 6
Heron Creek Middle School, FL

Fred

There once was a cat named Fred,
Who hit his head on his bed.
Then someone said can you see my face
He hopped up and began running the race
Then at the end Fred said "oh man I'm dead!"

Jessica Kelley, Grade 5
Ranburne Elementary School, AL

Our World

I looked upon the sky, and I wondered why. Has everything changed? Or is it the same? I thought and thought about it as the days passed away. The world is a bigger place. The people around us feel loved and cared for, the place we truly belong in. It is, our world. We love it, we care about it, we respect it. No matter where we come from, Thailand, Italy, or even Africa, we will always be a part of our world. And we will no longer be apart from each other again.

Tacerrah Keokhamdy-Saechao, Grade 5
St Martin Upper Elementary School, MS

Greta's Garden

Greta has a garden that has real red roses, where green grass grows and grapes. It has pretty pink and purple pansies and fantastic fruit. It has beautiful gold bananas and red, green, and yellow apples too. The strawberries are so sweet your tongue will want to sing, and the most gorgeous green grapes you've ever seen.

Macy Myers, Grade 4
Edwards Elementary School, SC

TenBieg Tree

They say three is a magic number, on this I do not agree because there are five in my family!
I have a dad who is tall; he always wins when we play basketball.
Sometimes he lets me help him cook; he has all the recipes in his brain so we never need a cookbook.

I have a mom, who is cool as can be; she is loving and kind and kisses and hugs me all the time.
And then there is me; I am the oldest you see. I am the boss of two little sisters. The first branch of the family tree.

The first sister I have is Kaitlyn. She is 10 going on 11.
We fight and bicker. SHHH! Don't tell her what I really think of her.
She is super and fun to be around; she is a straight out clown!

Then I have a sister who is 4; her name is Brealyn,
In the morning she comes to wake me up; she will stand in front of me screaming,
"I want to see your feet on the floor!" She doesn't leave until I show her the door!

So this is my family in a nut shell and I think they are swell!
A better blessing I will never find than those who love me ALL the time!

Ashlyn TenBieg, Grade 6
Tarpon Springs Middle School, FL

Love

Love is a powerful thing, sometimes we show it with a wedding ring
Love will make anybody smile for a while, but your heart will break into pieces without it.
It will be love all around the world if we just can get along
Instead of fighting, can we just sing a song?
So, if you are out there, you are not alone.
There is somebody next to you that loves you very much
Love is a powerful thing

Talike Brown, Grade 4
Park Ridge Elementary School, FL

Slavery Is…

Slavery is the difference between the way you feel if you would rather to wake up the next day or die trying. Slavery is the hurtful and ugly discipline you have to deal with because you are a different color in race. Slavery is killing you slower and slower until you can feel good about yourself and your escape. Slavery is a hard consequence you feel you do your best but you're still being beat. Slavery is a very low down way to live life as a black person. Slavery is like you being sat on and being treated like a piece of furniture. Slavery is being owned by someone who does not care how you feel — just if you are a good working person. Slavery is when you work in any condition even if your pregnant, sick, or in pain. Slavery is like being chained up like a dog. Slavery is yearning for life to be a free negro. Slavery is what our life shouldn't be.

D'Abra Hinton, Grade 4
Madison Cross Roads Elementary School, AL

Fall
Red, orange, yellow, leaves of every color
Like a rainbow in the trees
Air is cool and crisp
Watch your breath go up in a cloud
Geese are honking in the sky
Swiftly flying away for the winter
It is harvesting season
Down at the farm you can pick out a pumpkin
Shiny red apples ready for picking
Rake up the leaves
Everyone knows fall is here

Mary Bannister, Grade 5
Rosarian Academy, FL

Pen
I am the master of all writing implements,
My writing is very specific,
I sign signatures,
I can be very sharp,
I write for freedom,
For some, I am the best tool,
Like a hammer or a wrench,
I am very useful,
I contain ink,
Sometimes I can run out,
The hands are what hold me,
The pencil is my relative.

William Crockford, Grade 5
Pensacola Beach Elementary School, FL

Anger Is Like a Feather
Anger is like a feather,
It floats and flitters in flocks in you,
And comes out a roaring bear,
Even though it still has that feathery touch.

Anger is like a feather,
It mocks you in the moonlight with its meaningful color,
A flush of red.

Anger is like a feather,
It floats and falls in a fluttery attack,
In a cave just trying to get out.

Anger is like a feather,
It perches on top of the happiness,
Sitting still with its sleek smirk.

Anger is like a feather,
It floats and flitters in flocks in you,
And comes out a roaring bear,
Even though it still has that feathery touch.

Caroline Meisner, Grade 5
Summit Hill Elementary School, GA

Chicken Joe
Chicken Joe…
Depressed, yet still determined,
Has a disadvantage, yet still disturbing,
Discouraged, yet still able to talk about it (crossing the road)
Full of defense, yet still not a discount,
Able to demonstrate his skills (crossing the road),
and not be defeated.
The road crossing champ Chicken Joe.

Lukas Agnew, Grade 5
Summit Hill Elementary School, GA

The Sea
I watch the sunset as I walk on the beach
The waves roll to the surface they reach
The sky is now turned fire red
So I turn around and head home for bed
While in bed I dream of the sea
And finally realize what it means to me

Tori White, Grade 6
Perquimans County Middle School, NC

The Call
I hear the songs, I hear the noise
When you call me, I hear your voice
Sometimes in the room, silence without a sound
When I play basketball
I'm with my friends and they'll call rebound.

I wish you were here again
I miss you and your smile
On text I press the button send and trying my best to smile.
Writing your name in sand all alone
Trying not to miss you because you were long gone.

I try not to have tragedies and sorrow in my diary
I try not to be weary and crying
Those memories are so very fond
I wake up sometimes in the morning of dawn
Still waiting for you to come back.

Jane Farinas, Grade 6
Kernan Middle School, FL

Nature's Year
Leaves plunge every fall,
Each one dancing to it's own little ball.

In the winter they are all gone,
The tree branches sparkling with frosty dew every dawn.

They all start to appear again in the spring,
Announcing it, the birds start to sing.

By summer they are all there,
Each little leaf waving happily in the air.

Hailey Wallace, Grade 6
Gold Hill Middle School, SC

Baseball

I'm the catcher on my team.
I see the ball and its seam.
The batter takes a big swing
Listen to that ball sing.

My uniform is black and red.
The catcher's mask sits on my head.
The field is in front of me…
The dirt at my feet is clay red.

The pitcher's mound is high and round
The batter tries the ball to pound.
White and blue the sky he sees
Turn third base to look at me.

Ball in hand.
My cleats in sand.
I set my feet.
His attempt is in defeat.

Seth Bridgeman, Grade 5
Sharon Elementary School, NC

Land of Hope

A safe place
of hope and dreams.
This vast landscape
its green fold gleams.

These extraordinary valleys
are cosseted in trees.
Protected by nature
as far as the eye sees.

I remember the time
this place was my home.
When I left I was dejected
And now I long to roam.

Carlos Ordonez, Grade 5
Oliver Hoover Elementary School, FL

Martin Luther King

Thank you Martin Luther King,
Thank you for letting freedom ring.
Black people always cry,
Don't ever want to say goodbye.
Thank you, Martin Luther King.

Teeara Carter, Grade 6
Arnold Magnet Academy, GA

Singing Star

Singing star Miley Cyrus
Is as pretty as a springtime Iris
She never pitches fits during her big hits
She also has a wig that fits

Emily Larsen, Grade 4
Pensacola Beach Elementary School, FL

Decisions

One day while out on walk,
I came across a wallet lying on the sidewalk.
It was full of lots of green cash,
For a moment I thought I would take it and dash.
But in my heart I knew it wasn't right,
So I called up the name in the top right.
I gave it to him and he took it in a blink of an eye,
He gave me a money reward and I thanked him then we said goodbye.
That day I felt all good inside,
And I was filled with lots of pride.

Alex Michaeli, Grade 6
Gold Hill Middle School, SC

Life Today

American soldiers searching.
Searching for what you may ask,
Searching for chemical weapons is the answer to that.
An everlasting war of fighting and killing,
But for what,
A safer life?
What and where is this so called safer life?
Because it seems to me that the fighting and killing is everywhere in this life.
Some say this land spoken of is America,
The land of the free and the home of the brave,
But this is not true.
Think for a minute about this sweet land we call home,
Isn't there still fighting and violence?
Yes there is,
There's no doubt about that.
So why, tell me why there is no land of peace.

Michael Canino, Grade 5
Rosarian Academy, FL

A Happy Body

Soft skin protects my happy body.
Fluffy hair covers my happy head.
Eyes help me see the beautiful world.
Ears help me hear when moma's
Calling me to clean my room.
My nose helps me smell delicious cookies baking.
Teeth help me bite the dentist if he hurts me!
My tongue helps me taste a yummy steak at Outback.
Lips help me to smile and talk forever with my best friend.
Arms are for giving and getting hugs from my grandmother.
My elbow is a funny bone!
Hands are for clapping when someone does a good job.
Fingers help to hold a crayon so I can draw a beautiful picture or
Write a lovely poem for my mother.
Nails are for painting with bright, sparkling polish.
My stomach has a cute little belly button!
Legs are for riding my bike, running or walking in the park.
Feet are for tickling. Toes are for wiggling.
Inside this happy body is a great big heart full of love!

Micah Helms, Grade 4
Bostian Elementary School, NC

High Merit Poems – Grades 4, 5, and 6

Music I Sing
Music, music, a glorious sound.
When I hear the music my ears dance around.
Hear my voice sing, the drumbeat sounds,
When I hear the music my ears dance around.

Jared Warner, Grade 4
Barrow Elementary School, GA

An Extinct Species
A gentle creature
Arguing with the grass
Looking for the greenest pasture
Hoping for no disturbance in its royal feast
Its beard tickling at the dirt
Prickly like a porcupine
A species in danger
Which man doesn't notice
There is only one left
And dead it goes

Rene Cuadra, Grade 5
Oliver Hoover Elementary School, FL

Thank You, Amber
I am thankful, Amber is always my friend.
I am thankful, she always listens to me.
I am thankful, she gives me advice.
I am thankful, she does things with me.
I am thankful, I can talk to her about anything.
I am thankful, she is always there for me.
I am thankful, she celebrates my achievements.
I am thankful, that she is my sister and no one else's.
I am thankful, that she lets me hang out with her friends, too.
I am thankful, that she will always and forever be my sister!

Cheyenne Garlock, Grade 4
Sangaree Intermediate School, SC

A Very Special Grandma
My Grandma Judy
Is a very special Grandma
She is deeply dependable
Her heart is as good as gold
She is as sweet as flowers
Her scent is as sweet as sugar
Her smile is a bright sunny day
Her athletic ability is admirable
Her extraordinary elegance exuberant
Her care for me abundant
Her eyes are the bright sun
She is more than I can ever
Ask for in my life
Her unusual abilities I admire
Her niceness is unstoppable
She loves me to death
She will do anything if it makes me happy
Her love for me is endless

Benny Kron, Grade 6
Unity School, FL

Swimming at the Creek
When we went swimming,
It was very fun.
My cousin was swinging on the trees.
Every time we jumped in,
We hurt our knees on the giant, hard rocks.
We were bleeding from head to toe.
My cousin and I were pushing each other, diving,
And being bashful of any other people.
My cousin was bleeding
Because he had busted his head.
We couldn't swim anymore after that happened.

Tarish Mallard, Grade 5
East Marion Elementary School, MS

Side by Side
Two doors side by side
Two doors side by side
I chose the door on the left
I saw my mom leaving in a jet
leaving me behind with another family.
Two doors side by side
Two doors side by side
I chose the door on the right
I saw my mom running and running
she picked me up.
gave me a big huge a kiss on the cheek
Two doors side by side
Two doors side by side
I'm going to choose the door on the right
not the left door.

Chelsey Herrin, Grade 4
Clearview Avenue Elementary School, FL

The Wrestling Ring
The wrestling ring is a fabulous place to be
Great matches are what you'll see

When John Cena comes out he's ready to fight
so hold onto your seat really, really tight,

Unless you want to fly, way up high in the sky

When the songs begin to play, Jillion is ready to say,
where you're from and how much you weigh!

When the divas come out, everybody is ready to shout!!

The Undertaker's eyes flutter and flap
my shoes are ready to tap, tap, tap

Wait is there another match again?
Yes! Wrestling never ends.

Tayler Ramsay, Grade 4
FSU/City of Pembroke Pines Charter Elementary School, FL

My Gifts
I was sent into this world,
blessed with many talents.
And they can very much be
taken away, the same way
they were given.
I could make a wrong decision
and lose my gifts forever.
Or I could do the best I can
and keep them ever after.
My talents will be shared and
loved by the people everywhere.
I will play the guitar with my
fingers so gifted.
And score the winning goal
and with the clapping and screaming
of the crowd I will be lifted.
As I practice every day,
my talents will grow.
With the beauty of my Lord,
my gift of faith will show.
Alex Arthur, Grade 6
Chapin Middle School, SC

Grandma
My grandma is so cool
She picks me up after school
We go to Wendy's for a snack
She talks to me on the way back
My grandma plays games with me
She is even great at the Wii
My grandma has a pool
Gee, my grandma is so cool
Smith Austin, Grade 4
Irmo Elementary School, SC

The Four Elements
Fire burning twigs
Earth is shaking up the ground
Wind blowing the grass
Water gently tugs at me
Nature can be nice or mean
Deanna Taub, Grade 5
The Sanibel School, FL

Skateboarding
Skateboarding is totally cool.
I skateboard in an empty pool.
Skateboarding is wicked fun,
Even in the flaming hot sun.
I like skateboarding a whole bunch,
But not when I hear a horrible crunch.
In skateboarding, you can get a cast
By going dangerously fast.
Antonio Perez, Grade 5
Poinciana Elementary School, FL

My Buddy and I
We will be with each other until the end,
Because Alyssa is my best friend.
Much time together we will spend.
Just me and my buddy,
We are the best of friends!
Mary Woodyard, Grade 4
Immaculate Conception School, MS

Jesus
There is a man
Who died on a cross
Just to save
And help the lost.

He loved us so,
That he died
He loved us so,
He was crucified.

This man is Jesus
So soft and sound
And I am so glad
That I am found.

He saved my soul
And prepared a place
That I am glad to know
I'll go after death.
Tori Williamson, Grade 5
Rock Mills Jr High School, AL

Spicy Feisty
S uper spicy
P eppers hot
I n your mouth
C elsius cold
E ven though burning
S pice
Andrew Medina, Grade 4
Prince Avenue Christian School, GA

The Willow Tree
As awake as the sun
the willow tree whispers
saying hello with a whimper
flowing and blowing all day
her branches are long arms
she is a great, green, graceful tree
everyone loves her
when it is raining cats and dogs
she is quiet as a mouse
when day turns to night
the willow tree howls with fright
Emma Buchanan, Grade 4
Pine Tree Hill Elementary School, SC

Butterflies
Butterflies flying
Flowers blooming in the grass
Sun is shining bright
Ladybugs and dragonflies
Light blue sky glistens above.
Olivia Squires-Propper, Grade 4
St James Episcopal School, FL

The Time Is Summer
The time is summer.
The time is sweet.
I don't know how we bear the heat.
The children will play.
The moms will lay.
I wish that summer could stay.
Summer is great. Summer is grand.
There is no homework or test.
And that's why summer is the best.
Savannah Holman, Grade 5
West Marion Elementary School, MS

My Teacher
My teacher is sweeter than honey
She is also very funny!

She teaches us through the day
Then we get to play!

I love being in her class
Too bad it will not last!

I will miss her next year
Because she is very dear!
Emily Sweatt, Grade 4
Edwards Elementary School, SC

The Lake
The water ripples
Breaking the stillness of dawn,
Animals live here
Fish jumping in the water,
The lake glistens in the sun
Creating a pretty scene.
Marissa Reinker, Grade 4
PVPV/Rawlings Elementary School, FL

A Smilin' Lion
There once was a lion
Who was always smilin'
The zookeeper came in
And made a lion's den
And after that not even
The smilin' lion ever saw him again
Devin Reed, Grade 5
Ranburne Elementary School, AL

Ms. (Mean) Bean

My history teacher is really mean
I am pretty sure her name is Ms. Bean
Although we get homework in her class every day
She lets us eat candy in her class
YEA!!!!!!!!!!

Hailee Zielinski, Grade 6
Arnold Magnet Academy, GA

The Sun and the Moon

I woke up
looking and looking
at the morning sun come out.
I wonder if it is going to come out
but seconds later it was coming up.
I felt so happy looking at it.
It was coming up and up
then the sky got blue.
I went to school and came back from school
hours and hours passed.
It was getting late
the sun was coming down
and there was a sunset.
I looked at something for a minute.
I looked up and saw the moon.
It was dark but the moon was shining.

Lourdes Perez Hernandez, Grade 6
Brogden Middle School, NC

Spring

I see the field of amazing flowers,
I hear the leaves rustle against the hallow trees,
I feel the hot blazing sun beat on me,
I smell the sweet odors in the distance,
I touch the outstanding flowers, trees,
and the beautiful green leaves.

The fields of amazing flowers,
The leaves rustle against the hollow trees,
The hot blazing sun beats on me,
The sweet odors in the distance,
and the outstanding flowers, trees, and
the beautiful green leaves.

Nicholas Hinds, Grade 4
Central Park Elementary School, FL

Mom

My mom is sweet
Like a sugar treat.
At night she glows…
That is when her beauty shows.
She is my mother
And I will love her forever.

Brianna DiJorio, Grade 4
Julian D Parker School of Science, Math & Technology, FL

The Accident

"Waaaaaaaaa!!!!!"
cried my brother.
While my mom was filling up the car with gas,
my little brother had fallen out of the car.
He cried, and cried,
and his arm looked very funny.
My mom took him to the hospital,
only to have a broken arm.
The doctor gave him a splint and a sling.
And a couple days later,
he got a cast which was blue.
So here's some advice:
never fall out of a car
because you're just asking for harm to your arm.

Nicholas Karch, Grade 6
Lake Park Baptist School, FL

The Beach

The beach is cool.
The beach is fun.
I like to play
and I like to run,
along the water in the sun!
I like to swim
and I like to splash,
but if a shark comes
I start to dash.
I wish I could go to the beach each year
and the waves and the ocean I could hear
I would smell the water and the sand
and all day long I would stare at the beautiful land!

Grace Franco, Grade 6
St Francis Xavier Elementary School, MS

Jessica Allbright

This is the story of Jessica Allbright
Who played the computer all day and night.
She sat in her chair
Without a care.
She liked to chat
As she grew pale and fat.
She loved the computer.
She loved it so much.

She grew an unhealthy addiction
With absolutely no restriction.
She denied to reside
Anywhere but the seat where she sat.
They all called her big dingbat.
And she loved the computer.
She loved it so much.

She never left
Until her death.

Melissa Scotti, Grade 6
Challenger K8 School of Science and Mathematics, FL

Why I Like Summertime

Summertime is a time to
laugh and play.
It's beautiful, hot, and sunny.
You can go swimming, go to the beach,
and play with friends.
You will not want summer to leave!
That's why I like summer!

Tori-Nicole Thuy Tien Tondee, Grade 5
St Martin Upper Elementary School, MS

Deer Hunting

Sounds like leaves cracking
Looks like a bunch of trees
Tastes like cedar tree in your mouth
Feels like an old rusty tree stand
Smells like hardwood
It must be spine tingling

Taylor Noles, Grade 5
Ranburne Elementary School, AL

Winter

The wind is howling
It is bitter cold and dark
Snowflakes are falling
From the darkened sky above
To blanket the earth in white

Katherine Strange, Grade 5
The Sanibel School, FL

The Divorce

Arguing, yelling, fighting,
That's all I ever heard.
My dad never came home.

Daddy was at work,
Or either at his shop,
He came home for six hours,
Just to go to sleep.

He never came to see me,
In school functions,
Or even at home,
The divorce finally came.

Still now I suffer,
I want more time with my dad,
I see him and we go places,
But I never think it's enough.

I play sports and have many games,
And all I ask,
Is for him to come to one,
But I guess,
I am asking him for too much.

Breana Hyler, Grade 6
J E Holmes Middle School, NC

Love

I love someone but it seems they don't love me back,
So now an earthquake is going on in my heart and there's plenty of cracks.
My heart is now broken
At the same time my heart is burning and smoking.
So I love her but she don't love me,
My heart is cold and at the same time full of heat.
I love her so that is that
I love someone but it seems they don't love me back.

Tommie Hudson Jr., Grade 6
Philadelphia Elementary School, MS

Sports

Joey
Athlete
Perseverance, loves sports, short, long hair
Lover of hockey, lacrosse, and family
Who believes that Ohio State is the best college
Who wants to make the NHL, play college sports, to get a good education
Who uses the car a lot, sports equipment, TV
Who gives dedication to sports, time to sports, clothes to the needy
Who says sports are the best
Russell

Joey Russell, Grade 6
Broad Creek Middle School, NC

I Am She

A **V** irtuous girl who has an
  O ngoing life. She also
  L oves art
  A nd poetry.
  N ever leaves her
  D evastated friends
  O ut in the open to
  U ndergo something big in their lives.

  G rowing her knowledge every day, she is always trying to be
  R ight. But this can turn out into arguments that go
  O n and on. But they usually end out
  N icely.
" **O** h my god!" is a personal quote of hers.
  W ishing, wondering, and curious is she. Gazing at the billions of
  S tars, she looks for the right one. With my
  K inky hair and my big brown eyes,
  I am she.

Volandou Gronowski, Grade 6
Tarpon Springs Middle School, FL

The Train Is an Iron Snake

The train is an iron snake
Weaving through tunnels as fast as lightning strikes the ground
Twisting and turning around every corner in so much of a hurry
With so much time and people depending on it there is no time to think;
Just time to go faster and faster, with no exact place to go.

Jessica Nolting, Grade 6
R D and Euzelle P Smith Middle School, NC

Sun

My beautiful face watches down on you each day
My warm streams of fire warm you up
And I set in the west with gorgeous colors
I'm a pleasure to every human, plant, and animal

Sara Post, Grade 5
Pensacola Beach Elementary School, FL

Cold December

December is white,
The color of snowflakes falling from the sky.
December feels like the warmth of a chimney fire,
It sounds like smooth classical music.
It smells like pine resin from a Christmas tree,
December tastes like hot chocolate in a mug.
December begins the long new year!

Kevin Noyes, Grade 5
Vienna Elementary School, NC

Martin Luther King

Martin Luther King
Had a dream
He wanted to hear freedom ring
He wanted to see black and white unite
He is a brave man
He took a stand
His voice caused the world to change
He paid the price and lost his life
He fought a great fight
Now people thank him because of his great deeds

Aleyah Julmiste, Grade 6
St Mark's Lutheran School, FL

The Sky

The sky is like a little world of our own.
Like a place to get away and free your mind.
It's an open place to let all your feelings or distractions out.
It's a place where planes fly.
We are like the planes, free and ready to take off.

Summer Hutchens, Grade 6
St John's Lutheran School, NC

Dares

I was once dared to do a dare,
It involved me to shave, shave all of my hair
When it was off, and I saw my head, it was indeed quite a scare
Take my advice, now, never ever take a dare.
The next day at school,
All the kids made fun
I swear I had hands on my head, a ton.
I charged them a buck, a torn, dirty, buck
Then they walked away with pure golden luck.
So take my advice and take it well,
Never do a dare, especially if it involves, your hair
For sure, I'm telling you people will surely stare!

Sean Crosby, Grade 6
Gold Hill Middle School, SC

Multiplication

Multiplication multiplication
You must know your facts
For if you don't
You may just get held back

Six times six is thirty-six
Two times two is four
I think it's time to pick up sticks
Oh I forgot to shut the door

Congrats you just learned
To multiply doubles
If you forget them
You're in serious trouble

Multiplication multiplication
You must know your facts
For if you don't
You may just get held back

Ashabi McDonald, Grade 4
Egret Lake Community Elementary School, FL

Keeping Our World Beautiful

In the beginning our world was clean.
Lovely and charming and all over green,
but something happened that made it go wrong.
Something was happening that did not belong.

The humans made the world old,
the grass turned from a lovely green to a color of gold.
The animals fell down to their knees,
and down, down, down fell the trees.

The cans and gum go flying into the grass,
and alongside the roads rise a harmful gas.
This causes the greenhouse effect,
and it makes our world a wreck.

Morganne Guinther, Grade 5
Queen's Grant Community School, NC

Giving Back

Rivers flow so we can destroy them.
We dig up a single gem,
And chip away.
Trees sway,
So we can cut them down.
We pick cotton so we can just turn it into a gown.
We build on the mountains and just pollute their tops.
Then suddenly our world stops.
We take so much from nature,
And we are nothing but immature,
We don't give back.

Emily Ray, Grade 6
Gold Hill Middle School, SC

Time to Make My Bed
Mom said get out of bed
You sleepy head
Time to make your bed!

Went to get my sheets
And my dirty cleats.

My sheets are polka dot pink
And they really stink.

I throw them in the wash
And boy they are really posh!
Lexie Waterman, Grade 6
St Mary Magdalen Catholic School, FL

The Hawk
Way up above us all,
the hawk flies proud and tall.

Watching us with those sharp eyes,
we all know her turf is the skies.

Protecting her kin she soars,
never afraid of a beast's roar.

She is ever watchful of her flock,
definitely not all talk.

Because all she knows is caring,
the food she gets is solely for sharing.

Come winter come spring,
her flock is under her wing.
Carlton Bone, Grade 6
Bak Middle School of the Arts, FL

If I Was in Charge of the World…*
If I was in charge of the world,
I would cancel school.
Anything I want would be a vegetable.

If I was in charge of the world,
Your mom would stop saying
"stop teasing your brother."
Come to think of it,
you wouldn't even have brothers.

If I was in charge of the world,
We would all have hybrid cars.

That's what I would do
Katherine Call, Grade 4
Irmo Elementary School, SC
*Patterned after "If I Were in Charge
of the World" by Judith Viorst

By Myself*
When I'm by myself
and I close my eyes
I feel like a rocket ship ready
to blast off
I'm a hummingbird ready
to chirp.
I'm a bee ready to buzz.
I'm a book ready to be read
I'm a soccer ball ready
to get hit in the goal
and win the game.
But when I open my eyes
What I care to be is me.
Alexis Mayson, Grade 4
Irmo Elementary School, SC
*Inspired by Eloise Greenfield

Let Freedom Ring!
Freedom shouts "I'm Free!"

He feels like joy
spreading through America

Freedom sounds like
dog tags jingling

He stands like
the Statue of Liberty

Freedom marches like
a soldier going to war

He is an eagle soaring free!
Tyler Brown, Grade 4
Tabernacle Elementary School, NC

Different Ways
Athletic
Fun, sweaty
Rewarding, acting,
Sports, bum
Slow going, easygoing
Slothful, drony
Lazy
Brandon Anselmo, Grade 5
Queen's Grant Community School, NC

Smile
S mile like somebody loves you!
M e and you always smiling!
I love you and you love me!
L augh and laugh that's what we do!
E very day I keep loving you!
Sara Bunker, Grade 5
Summit Hill Elementary School, GA

Clean, Smart, Reason
You walk by a dirty man on the street,
People saying he's dirty
So that is all he knows how to be.
But you think is that true?
Is that all he knows how to do?
He's only seen clean people on the road,
So isn't all he knows,
Clean?
The dumbest person in the world,
People saying that's all she knows,
How to be dumb. But is this true?
She's only ever seen smart people.
So isn't all she's ever known,
Smart?
A dreamer dreaming of a new world,
People saying he's crazy.
No wars no fights.
If he's crazy he's only ever seen reason.
So is he truly crazy?
Reason,
Clean…Smart…Reason.
Ragan Hagey, Grade 6
Gold Hill Middle School, SC

Alphabet Food
A pple, **B** ananas, **C** arrots,
D oughnuts, **E** skimo doughnuts, **F** ruit,
G rapefruit, **H** awaiian punch, **I** talian,
J unk food, **K** it-Kat bar, **L** emons,
M ango, **N** achos, **O** ranges, **P** otatoes,
Q uiche, **R** utabaga, **S** paghetti,
T omatoes, **U** ndersea fillet,
V irgin olive oil, **W** ombat stew,
X treme Doritos, **Y** ogurt,
and **Z** ebra steak.
Mark Gibson, Grade 6
Arnold Magnet Academy, GA

My Past
my past is frightful
and scary all at once
running the night
hoping sobbing
can't wait to be free
almost there
I can see it
just don't get caught
but that has changed now
the north beat the south
KKK's still here and stars and bars
and so am I
living my life and to this day
I am not afraid
Assata Trader, Grade 6
Shorecrest Preparatory School, FL

High Merit Poems – Grades 4, 5, and 6

The Way I Am

Don't change the way you look,
It's written down in His book.

Throwing away all cares,
might upset the big guy upstairs.

But we,
will only know the different between you and me.

So I am happy the way I am
because everything is in His hands

Sydney Derr, Grade 6
Brogden Middle School, NC

Green

Green is on trees
Green is on grass
Green is on lili pond pads.

Green is on a clover
Green is on hats
I love green and I can never change that.

Green is on some papers
Green is on some eyes
Green is on some wacky wigs that I saw at the mall.

Green is on pencils
Green is on erasers
Green is my favorite color and I can't change that.

Nicolas Marquez, Grade 5
Eugenia B Thomas Elementary School, FL

The Road to Love

There's nothing like love,
Love is like a pool of hopes and dreams
Like sapphires, rubies, and golden oak trees
You will never ever beat the road to love
Love is like a helicopter hovering above
And I don't know why, but there's nothing like love
So even if you try your hardest, you won't succeed
Because nobody can beat the road to love, not even me.

Dentonio Utley, Grade 5
Manchester Elementary School, NC

Caterpillar to Butterfly

I watch the caterpillar
With my two eyes
It crawls and wanders.
Wherever eating, crunching and munching.
With all its might but tomorrow
It's a beautiful butterfly.

Nia Anderson, Grade 4
Spruce Creek Elementary School, FL

My Life in Full Colors

White is the fluffy cloud in the sky
Blue is the feeling when you have to say good-bye.

Yellow is as bright as the sun
Green lush grass is where you can run.

Grey is the color of pencil lead
Black skies tell you to go to bed.

Purple grapes are what I like to eat
Red is your face when you turn up the heat.

Brown is the wood I use for a fire
Orange juice is what I mostly desire.

Thomas Delgado, Grade 6
Tequesta Trace Middle School, FL

Friends Till the End

You are the sugar to my Kool-aid,
The ketchup to my fires,
The bun to my hot dog,
The sweetness to my cereal,
The chocolate to my milk,
The laces to my shoes,
You are always there for me through thick and thin,
And that is why you will be my friend until the end.

Kayla Hernandez, Grade 5
Joella Good Elementary School, FL

Addition

One is sometimes lonely
But add another, it's a pair
A pair plus one is three
You won't be lonely there.

Three plus one will equal four
Four is always fun
Four plus one is always five
And now I'm halfway done.

Five plus one is number six
And that's a half a dozen
Six plus one becomes seven
The same age as my cousin.

Seven add one you now have eight
And that is very fine
Because when you add one to eight
You get the number nine.

If you take a one and add to nine
You've finally come to ten
I bet you are all happy it's over
And you can say AMEN!

Rasheed Nembhard, Grade 4
Egret Lake Community Elementary School, FL

The Colors of Autumn

When you see colorful leaves,
You know from the gorgeous trees,
That autumn has finally come,
Summer is now done.
The cool breeze is in the air,
Scarecrows give crows a scare.
Cinnamon is very nice,
Giving the house a smell of spice.
Thanksgiving is a delicious day,
We have dinner in a special way.
Family and friends all come,
Moms, dads, daughters, and sons.
Join for a scrumptious meal,
Share stories that are very dear.
This season in all,
Can't be other than fall.
With pretty leaves, family near,
We know that autumn is here.

Manya S. Goldstein, Grade 5
Brevard Jewish Community School, FL

Classroom

The classroom was new
And colorful too.
Green, Go!
Yellow, Slow Down!
Red, Stop!
Stop at my classroom
December has passed
January is coming
But the classroom is still there.

Heather Hargrave, Grade 4
Lynn Fanning Elementary School, AL

Winter Snowfall

Winter's cool snowfall,
Like little specks of white joy,
Falling from the sky.

Michael Delgado, Grade 6
Gold Hill Middle School, SC

Secret

I have a big secret,
but I just can't seem to keep it.
I always let it out,
in a loud, obnoxious shout.
I've tried tape,
but it flew off like a cape.
I've also tried glue,
but it was unfaithfully true.
I think I've tried the whole book,
but wait, look!
The secret to keeping one,
is only to tell none.

Ellen Johnson, Grade 6
North Myrtle Beach Middle School, SC

Swish

The score is tied. My teammate is dribbling down the court.
He hurls the ball towards me.
With the ball in my hands I bounced the ball on the court floor.
I had two decisions, either to pass or shoot.
With the ball in my hand I propelled myself upward
And released the ball towards the goal.
The ball extended upward and began to go
D
O
W
N.
"Swish" went the ball as it jumped into the net as the buzzer rang
For the final score of 24-22.

Trevor Hinshaw, Grade 4
Grays Chapel Elementary School, NC

I Am Wolf

I dropped down into a low crouch.
The wind whistling through the trees almost made the rabbit bolt.
Winter would be hard for the pack.
I trod softly on the snow through the brush.
The rabbit's ears flickered towards my direction.
The smell of prey clogged my nose, but I waited for the opportune moment. There!
I pounced onto the unsuspecting hare and sank my teeth into its neck.
I spat out the hair from my mouth.
Hunting was a dirty job, but someone had to do it.
It was sad to see the light die out of the creatures eyes.
I suddenly felt sorry for the hare.
Then I remembered the pack.
I dragged the rabbit back to our camp.
I reminded myself once again why I was dragging a rabbit.
I am the crackle of the leaves. I am a warrior.
I am the dead quiet of night. I am a hunter.
I am the rush of the river during the floods. I am a predator.
I am the reason my pack survives. I am wolf.

Christina Potter, Grade 6
Shorecrest Preparatory School, FL

I Used To…

I used to not understand cursive,
But now I am an expert.
I used to suck my thumb,
But now I suck lollipops instead.
I used to crawl,
But now I walk and run and skip.
I used to go to school three times a week,
But now I go five times a week.
I used to ride in the cart at Target,
But now I push the cart myself.
I used to live in California,
But now I live in Georgia.
I used to love Barbies and Polly Pockets,
But now I enjoy e-mail, thrilling books, and of course, the phone.

Kate Dunsmore, Grade 5
Summit Hill Elementary School, GA

God Is Love

God is caring, God is love.
He lives in heaven up above.
He gave His son for you and me.
So we can have life eternally.
When you get baptized you feel like you're born again.
Now that He is in your heart He can be your best friend.
So if you keep believing in Him you will see,
That He loves us. You and me.

Hope Turnage, Grade 5
West Marion Elementary School, MS

I Am a Singer

I am a singer
I wonder if I will become famous
I hear people cheering me on
I want to see people listening to me
I am a singer.

I pretend to be famous when I sing
I feel happy when I sing
I touch other's hearts when I sing
I worry that people will hate me
I cry when people tell me I can't sing
I am a singer.

I understand the song I am singing
I say "I know what songs mean"
I dream that everyone will love me
I try to sing well every time
I am a singer.

Raleigh Prewitt, Grade 6
Boiling Springs Intermediate School, SC

Lizard

My favorite animal does not linger.
Hissing, biting, running away.
Drops his tail in fear and anger.
Has a new one by next week's seventh day.
Cages cannot hold him.
He's colorful, cunning and shy.
Maybe that is why I love him.
Me and Lizards see eye to eye.

Savannah Graves, Grade 5
Abundance Home School, FL

Tyler

My brother is Tyler, sweet and kind.
He is always there for me.
Even thought we fight we love each other.
He is 10th in his class and that is why I look up to him.
His heart is sensitive like a baby's.
I am weak while he is strong.
I love him more than anything.
He understands me in every way.

Bronwyn McDaniel, Grade 6
Gold Hill Middle School, SC

Hope

Moves you on,
The strength you might need.
It's called hope.
you get it from the wonders around you,
They drive you on.
They might depend on you,
They might have faith in your name.
Just know hope will come from what you believe in.
Hope will and can even come from your heart.
It mostly does come from there,
That warm spot in your heart.
No matter where you are,
You have a warm spot in your heart.
Don't ignore it,
Because it's your hope.

Elizabeth M. O'Neill, Grade 4
Olde Providence Elementary School, NC

Rainbow of Our Lives

R ed for the rage of life
O range for the people who open their hearts
Y ellow for the yuckiness of people
G reen for the greatness of living
B lue for the blocks and stones that divide our people
I ndigo for integration in life
V iolet for the violence that weakens our race
    The rainbow of our lives
    Just like life
    Beautiful but harsh

Christie Furtick, Grade 6
Brogden Middle School, NC

Charnita

Kind
Young
Female
Wishes to enjoy life to the fullest
Dreams of going to Disney World
Wants to enjoy her childhood
Who wonders about a lot of things
Who fears danger and bad things
Who is afraid of snakes
Who likes to be surprised
Who believes in God
Who loves the computer
Who loves Disney channel
Who loves God and her family
Who loves to be with her friends
Who plans to finish school
Who plans to be the very best she can be
Who plans to be successful
I can do all things through Christ which strengthens me

Charnita Herrod, Grade 5
Winona Elementary School, MS

Pencil

Under the beanbag chair,
Around the desk,
Beyond the cubbies,
Beside the TV,
Near the blackboard,
On the bookshelf,
Looking around the classroom,
Until I find a pencil,
On the teachers desk.

Ben Waters, Grade 6
McRae Elementary School, FL

Leaves

Something mysterious,
floating in the breeze,
making a lot of noise
under my feet.
comes in red, orange,
yellow, and green
always there,
hanging from a tree.
Won't you say
"It's a great thing!"

Allen Vorn, Grade 6
McRae Elementary School, FL

Death

He knocks on every door,
he comes with surprise.
When you see his face,
it will be your demise.

Coldness will creep up your spine,
your mind will go blank.
You'll find yourself
on a peaceful, quiet ocean bank.

Dizziness will ensue,
you'll be faint and numb.
Soon you'll see a bright light
and hear a distant hum.

Yasmin Ibarra, Grade 6
Turkey Creek Middle School, FL

Dog

I bark at the neighbor's cat
Like a lion's roar
I scratch with my paws on the dirt
Feeling the wind rush past me
I run out into the field
Like a cheetah
I have spotted my prey
An old cat laying down.

Gage Smith, Grade 4
Pensacola Beach Elementary School, FL

Waiting for the Wind

Waiting for the wind,
to pick me up and take me away.
To take me to that place I have been,
that place I've come to love.
Where only good dreams happen,
the place God has told me to go.

Waiting for the wind,
to carry me to that happy place.
Where I'll be in the heavens forever.
Waiting for the place I wonder of,
in God we trust to live in our souls,
and be with us in the afterlife.

Waiting for the wind,
waiting to live in the heavens,
to go to that happy place,
were we walk in life.
Waiting for the wind,
praise to God amen!

Rachel Ring, Grade 6
North Myrtle Beach Middle School, SC

I Try to Remember Her

I try to remember her,
but I can't completely.
I can see her,
but she can't see me.
I want to feel her presence,
but I know she's not beside me.
I try to talk to her,
but she can't hear me.
I love her,
And I know she loves me.
One day I will meet her and say,
I missed you Nanny.

Hayden Clay, Grade 6
Alexandria High School, AL

Peaceful

As I lay so peacefully
and watch the flowers sway
back and forth, back and forth
I sit there in delay.
When I see pretty colors
red, white, and pink,
they make me think of Valentine's
and so I may not blink.
The field of grass waves goodbye
as I am nearly gone
but still I wait
for my very special someone.

Kali Jones, Grade 5
Trinity Lutheran School, FL

What Love Is!

Love looks like
two people holding hands
Love feels like
a heart that's beating
Love smells like
warm chocolate made from the heart
Love tastes like
a sweet piece of wedding cake
Love sounds like
wedding bells ringing.

Allyson Brown, Grade 4
Tabernacle Elementary School, NC

My Girlfriend

Fit,
Smart
Flipping,
Jumping, laughing
Is the best girlfriend
Running, reading
Tumbling,
Attractive,
Lively
BAYLEY

Austin Young, Grade 5
Grays Chapel Elementary School, NC

Katrina

Katrina struck the state
Disaster following its path
The deafening screams before the wait
And the country felt its wrath

Memories talking to the sky
All of them lost
And the sound of a cry
Gave a terrifying cost

In so much pain
But the feeling was gone
A feeling of strain
And the love went on

And then it stops
The destruction paused
And the panic drops
Time to reflect on what has been caused

People brought close
And the feeling is good
In a city of ghosts
The love, grown, like it should

Jacques Lesure, Grade 5
Browns Mill Elementary School, GA

Mother

My Mother sitting next to the counter,
The lights made her lips cherry while she was eating berries.

My Mother heard not a sound of laughter,
Laying on the sand made it look like she owned the land.

My Mother driving the car,
Opening the windows,
Smelling smoke and tar,
While she was riding on the road.

My Mother sitting on the couch,
But not with a grouch,
Because she knows the day is going to end.
But now I have to say good-bye to my old friends!

Michelle Linares, Grade 5
Immaculate Conception School, MS

Nature in the Springtime

See the pretty flowers blowing in the wind
And the bunches and bunches of trees
With colorful leaves on them
And the ants on their anthill
Climbing out and in
The pine straw and the bushes
The pine cones and the leaves
Each a part of nature
A beautiful thing

Kiana Bynum, Grade 5
Southern Pines Elementary School, NC

The Witch

The witch is mean and old
her heart is very cold
her hair is green as mold
and she carries lots of gold.

The witch has a pet
that she never met
and she never calls the vet.

When she uses shampoo
she mix's it with glue.

The witch has a wart
she is very short
and likes to snort
also she's bad at sports.

The witch as a hat
that scares her cat
it even scared her bat.

Caila Bertot, Grade 4
Chancellor Charter School At Lantana, FL

Deep Blue Sea

The deep blue sea so blue and nice
with all the animals that sting and bite
they bite me they sting my knee
I hate the way they be so mean
but I'm so glad they're only in the deep blue sea.

Romesha Smith, Grade 4
Clearview Avenue Elementary School, FL

The Gnat

I saw a bad gnat,
He had a cat.
The cat had a rat.
The rat told the cat he had a house,
The cat said he had a friend named the rat,
So the gnat met the rat.
When the gnat met the rat he said, "Please don't eat me!"
The rat was as hungry as a wolf
And with a chomp! Chomp! Chomp!
The gnat was gone.

Carmen Tamayo, Grade 4
Camden Elementary School of the Creative Arts, SC

Summer

Summer is here let's hit the pool,
now that we are out of school.

Let's have some fun out in the sun,
now that summer has just begun.

We'll wear our new swimsuits to show off our looks,
we'll think about boys and forget about books.

Let's hit beach after beach,
and have fun at each.

We'll have cookouts and eat cool treats,
while dancing to our favorite beats.

We'll have to make summer last,
before we have to go back to class.

Shelby Hill, Grade 6
Boiling Springs Intermediate School, SC

Armando

Armando
Big, strong, athletic, fast,
Brother of Tony,
Cares deeply for baseball,
Who feels accomplishment,
Who needs a travel team,
Who gives support, and help to teammates,
Who fears my bones,
Who would like to make it to the MLB,
Resident of Weston.

Armando Hernandez, Grade 6
Tequesta Trace Middle School, FL

My Friends*

My friends are nice and cool
I see them every day at school
Me and my friends fuss and fight
But all of us are very bright
To know no one will break us apart

Souneke Pratt, Grade 6
Gold Hill Middle School, SC
*In loving memory of Kayla

Man's Best Friend

Are dogs man's best friend?

Dogs are brave,
resourceful, caring, and loyal.
They are a devoted, loving,
playful family member,
and comforting,
when you are sad.
Millions of breeds,
millions of personalities.
From puppy,
to adult.
You could train them,
play games with them.
Eyes bright, tail wagging:
no matter what it is,
dogs always seem to approach everything
with a positive attitude.

Dogs are truly man's best friend,
never a better word spoken,
for it is certainly true.

Serena Mon, Grade 4
Barrow Elementary School, GA

Drought

Drip, drop, pitter, patter, flop.
The sounds I long to hear.
The ground is brown,
All of the lakes are dry;
for the rain is not here.
It all began last summer.
I guess rain went on a vacation.
And decided not to come back.
But I truly do miss it,
And wish it could come back
Our plants are thirsty.
The water's missing.
This is not very pleasing.
Until one day,
I heard a noise,
Drip, drop, pitter, patter, flop
The sound which I longed to hear
Finally came this year.

Emily Eubanks, Grade 6
Brogden Middle School, NC

Graveyard

I stepped into the graveyard and a crazy shiver went up my spine,
The wolves were far in the north starting to cry.
A black velvet blanket was far above my head,
The sun was probably far away tucked inside a bed

The grass was painted with dew,
Graves had slime that started to ooze.
Nasty bugs starting to creep,
Weeds were tingling at my feet.

The graveyard door started to crack,
I run out with cobwebs all over my back.
I sit down and my head starts to spin,
I think to myself, I'm never going in there again.

Chelsea Duke, Grade 5
Sharon Elementary School, NC

I Am Finally Alive

My nana has dark hair
She is excellent to me
She treats me like I am her most honored possession
I am finally alive
My nana is admirable and always gleaming
My nana's heart is gold
Her cooking is like heaven
She is thoughtful with her meals
Corned beef is my favorite
She makes it every time I'm over, she says it's her special meal
I am finally alive
My nana is very active
She is skinny, sweet, and she has a smile that is as bright as a spotlight
My nana used to be a teacher so her mind is filled with knowledge
She has a very good sense of humor, My nana is always elegant
I am finally alive
My nana is sweet like sugar in sweet tea
When my nana comes to visit me my heart fills with adrenaline
It feels like I'm awakened from my sleep of boredom
My life is suddenly cleansed from a fog
I am finally alive

John Linton, Grade 6
Unity School, FL

The Meaning of Life

What is meaning?
I always ask, is it a definition from a dictionary page?
If so then what is the meaning of life?
To me it means many different things.
Sometimes it means sorrow, darkness, war, and hurt,
But it can also mean adventure, happiness, love and fun.
There are tears and tears of joy, two completely different things
And two completely different moods.
I don't know about yours but in my own world,
The meaning of life will always remain unknown and unpredictable.

Jessica Jacob, Grade 6
Freedom Middle School, FL

High Merit Poems – Grades 4, 5, and 6

Kayla
Kayla
Lover, kind, useful, nice
Daughter of Debbie
Lover of beauty, company and learning
Who feels loved, beautiful and lonely
Who needs encouragement, a pet, and a weekend job
Who fears big snakes, frogs, and spiders
Who gives love, kisses, and hugs
Who would like to see New York, Canada and Africa
Resident of Folly Road
Lynard

Kayla Lynard, Grade 4
St Helena Elementary School, SC

My Friends and Their Clothes
Black, green, and a little mean
Better watch out for Madi V.!!!
Black and yellow like a bumblebee,
Allie's crazy can't you see?
The color of money on Mindi's shirt
makes ALL the guys want to flirt!!!
Perfectly PINK in EVERY way,
Savanna adds joy to every day!!!

I love my friends with all my heart and soul,
I would hate it if they moved to the NORTH POLE!!!

P.S. Mindi wants to move to the SOUTH POLE.
She says, "Well, it's warmer down there!!!"
Sooo, who wants to tell her?

Taylor Morrison, Grade 6
Alexandria High School, AL

Diamonds
Diamonds are great
but they are expensive too.
They sparkle in your eye
and go best on a ring.
Diamonds o, what a thing
they make my heart want to sing.
Diamonds are what you want, what you need.
So to have a sparkle in your eye, have a diamond ring.

Abbie Stringer, Grade 5
West Marion Elementary School, MS

Sister
Oh sister oh sister you show me much pain
Whenever I'm around you I go completely insane
Oh sister oh sister you wear funny shoes
She is insane but my parents have no clue
Oh sister oh sister you get me in trouble
And whenever I'm in a trouble you're outside blowing a bubble
Oh sister oh sister just let me tell you the round is not over
I just can't wait 'til you lose your four-leaf clover.

Derek Gordon, Grade 5
Queen's Grant Community School, NC

Looks Matter
This world today is so superficial
Never caring about your feelings
Or your personality
Just how you look
And today it doesn't matter if you're funny
Or kind, fun and sweet
It only matters how you look
Today it matters if you're fat or skinny
Or if your forehead's too big
Or if you have pimples on your face
Today it doesn't matter if you're nice
And that you care
Only how you look.

Montressa Gray, Grade 6
Savannah Middle School, NC

Amazed
Amazed, amazed
With Astro Skate
Amazed, amazed
With the food they make
Churros, popcorn, candy

Amazed, amazed
With the prizes
They have
Light up teeth, hats
And bracelets too.

Amazed, amazed
With the songs they play
Soldier Boy, rock, disco.

Amazed, amazed
With Astro Skate.

Rachel Glenn, Grade 4
Clearview Avenue Elementary School, FL

True Love
Every time when I look outside I see a castle.
I will wear a crown, royal clothes.
But I need to marry.
But is love from first sight true?
Is there really love in the air?
I will search for my true love.
Is he my true love?

The next day of my life.
Just looking at the castle
Will make me feel like royalty
But to enjoy all of this
I need a true love.

Angelix Torres, Grade 5
Trinity Lutheran School, FL

These Memories Will Stay with Me Forever

Memories of the sweet, fresh turkey smell on Thanksgiving Day, and how the delicious scent pulled me into the kitchen.
Memories of Grandma scurrying around in the kitchen, making sure everything was ready for the extravagant feast.
Memories of Grandpa sitting on the living room couch, and talking to us about things that we like.
Memories of eating that delicious, mouthwatering feast, and how we sat together as we ate,
Memories of hearing all the stories about Thanksgiving, and how they interested me.
Memories of how Grandma's eyes filled with pride as she watched her family eat. These memories will stay with me forever.
Memories of going to Dunkin' Donuts with Grandpa, during every cold fall day.
Memories of how Grandpa would steal my food, even though he had his own jelly donut.
Memories of how the chocolate glazed donut melted on my tongue.
I still remember how that sweet donut tasted in my mouth. These memories will stay with me forever.
Memories of Coco and Shane, how they lay their heads on my lap and begged for food.
Memories of strolling around the neighborhood with Coco every day, and how she would get so tired because she's so chubby.
I can still hear her panting in my mind. These memories will stay with me forever.
Memories of going to Plymouth Rock with Grandma and Susan, and how Isabel wouldn't stop talking for the two hour ride.
Memories of going into the little, tiny houses that smelled like fresh bread, and watching them do their "chores."
These memories will stay with me forever.
Memories of all the happy times together, and a few sad times we've shared, too
Memories of all the fun times we've had and memories of the funny things.
All these memories, no matter how long I live, will never fade. These memories will stay with me forever.

Lynny Wheeler, Grade 6
Unity School, FL

An Unforgettable Day

On August 27, a bad storm came to visit the Mississippi Gulf Coast. It made a swoosh, and a bang, and a loud KABOOM. All you could hear was trees falling, houses being destroyed, and the loud whistles of the wind. When you needed help, there was no way to get help. A lot of people were in danger. I was so scared I couldn't even open my eyes. After a while I kind of got used to the loud noises of the storm. Then finally the storm started to slowly fade away.

Torie McCoy, Grade 5
St Martin Upper Elementary School, MS

The Holocaust

H orrid fumes fill the air while gunshots could be heard all around
O thers such as husbands and wives, daughters and sons would be separated from one another breaking families apart
L osing family members, friends, and loved ones was difficult
O ver six million Jewish men, women, and children perished during this tragic time
C rying can be heard from everywhere around the Concentration Camps
A major event in World History that will hopefully never be repeated
U nmerciful people tortured others who were unlike them with inhumane acts
S creams of the people could be heard as they entered gas chambers, knowing they were taking their final breath
T he memory of those who suffered will always be remembered.

Dean Kaire, Grade 6
Highland Oaks Middle School, FL

Beautiful

You can't always see the beautiful things,
like wind blowing through the leaves,
or your dreams lost in your mind that you forgot all about,
and the crystals up in the mountains that you keep searching for but you just can't find.
I keep on hoping that I will achieve to find one of those beautiful things,
and I keep on dreaming and dreaming and dreaming…
Finally I found one of those beautiful things in one of my dreams.
It was probably one of the most beautiful things I had ever seen.
I was sad the next day because I had forgotten the dream I had just dreamed.

Alex Wetmore, Grade 5
Southern Pines Elementary School, NC

I Dream Of…

I dream of a world beyond our own,
A world of the great unknown,
Full of creatures of which we have never seen.
Precious pixies and fluttering fairies,
Gigantic trolls and daring demons.
I dream of characters beyond the ordinary,
Fussy dwarves and elves of speed,
Sneaky rangers and paladins upon their steeds.
I dream of royalty,
Dukes with dreams and duchesses with creams,
Princesses that are prim and princes that are dull.
I dream of kingdoms,
Undersea villages and pretty purple castles,
Evil mountains and dank dark lairs.
I dream of animals,
Fierce tigers and brown bears,
Gliding hawks and kelpies with seaweed for hair.
You see,
I dream of many things,
Because I love to dream,
So will you dream with me?

Dominique McNeil, Grade 6
Milwee Middle School, FL

What Are Colors?

Blue is the color of the pool.
White is the color of a fool.

Brown is the Hershey chocolate bar.
Silver is the color of my mom's car.

Red is the love that she gives.
Yellow is the sunflower that lives.

Purple are the berries falling from the tree.
Green are the apples rolling free.

Orange is when I know summer's here.
Pink tulip petals blowing in my ear.

Jazlee Gomez, Grade 6
Tequesta Trace Middle School, FL

The Ocean

The ocean is so delightful,
The waves go whoosh!
How could we survive without the ocean
One of the wonders of life.

The wondrous glories, and excitement
I wish in my heart,
With a breeze in my hair;
Oh how I wish I was there!

Lauryn Runyans, Grade 4
Providence Classical School, AL

School

Going to school can be quite fun
Working hard until the day is done
Math, Science, Social Studies
Playing at recess with your buddies

Going to school can be a pain
With tests and homework every day
Doing tests that are very long
Going to detention for doing wrong

Even though school can be good and bad
When you graduate you'll be glad!

Lara Lamanilao, Grade 6
St Francis Xavier Elementary School, MS

Live for Today

Live for today,
And you will see a way;
Live for today,
Because every day is special;
Live for today,
You will never regret it;
Live for today,
Because every minute counts;
Live for today,
Great things will happen for you;
Live for today,
You will always see growth,
Live for today,
Your dreams will come true;
Live for today,
You will see a new you;
Live for today,
Because tomorrow is not promised to you,
So live for today,
And make memories that will last for a lifetime.

Tony Jenkins, Grade 6
Brogden Middle School, NC

I Don't Understand…

I don't understand
   Why love lasts
   Why hearts break
   Why love grows

But most of all
   Why people leave and never come back
   Why we cry
   Why we laugh

What I understand most is
   Why we must bear this pain
   Why I am who I am
   Why I love them so much

Makayla Dixon, Grade 6
Turkey Creek Middle School, FL

Rainbow

My colors shine great
I sparkle in the morning
I dance in the sky
I come after a drizzle
I am a little rainbow

Daize Maggio, Grade 4
Pensacola Beach Elementary School, FL

Capers

When I go and see my puppy,
It makes me pity those
Who only have a guppy,
For no fish could ever compare,
To the love my dog and I share,
My dog Capers runs so fast,
He takes off in a blast,
He is always very sweet,
To every animal that we meet,
He always wants to have fun,
Even when the day is done,
And I look into his eyes all I see is joy,
I am proud to say
Capers is my one-and-only
Baby Boy!

Julia Applegate, Grade 6
Gold Hill Middle School, SC

My Mom

My mom is really thoughtful
She is nice to me
She is very helpful
And she is as good as can be.

She can sometimes be serious
And sometimes wonderful
When I ask her for advice
She can because she is helpful.

My mom is cool
She takes me to school,
Is a responsible mom
She has a hard job.

She always nags on me
To play with my sister,
But she bothers me
My sister is mean to me.

My mom is a good mother
She is good at cleaning
She doesn't bother
She is also good at running.

Selena Sanchez, Grade 6
Turkey Creek Middle School, FL

Water's Sad Cycle

Water falls as rain
Plunges from high in the sky
Back down to the Earth
It's as if God is crying
Just to cry and cry again

In its sad cycle
A never ending circle
That goes 'round and 'round
When will it ever be stopped
Or will it always be

James Dowling, Grade 5
The Sanibel School, FL

One Sunny Day

One day it was a
beautiful sunny evening
the clouds were out
all puffy and white.
But all of a sudden
it started to rain.
After the rain
there was a rainbow
red, orange, yellow,
green, blue, purple,
violet, indigo,
even lavender too.

Tonya Cherry, Grade 4
Spruce Creek Elementary School, FL

I Don't Want to Go

You're so kind
I can't get you off my mind
I love you so
I don't want to go
You're so sweet
You make me weak
Please don't make me go
I want to stay
And spend with you, each and every day.
Fine, I'll go
But just remember
I will always love you so.

Savana Earnest, Grade 6
McRae Elementary School, FL

Our Cat

Our cat he loves to eat
He's actually very sweet
But if you make him mad
He'll make you very sad
He'll attack you with his feet

Wyatt T. Massey, Grade 6
Arnold Magnet Academy, GA

Skating

The adrenaline
Standing at the top of the ramp
Vrummm you rush down the ramp
The wind blowing through your hair
No bailing out
It's too late now

Tyler Worbington, Grade 6
Tequesta Trace Middle School, FL

Nature and Its Seasons

Nature is beautiful
It has flowers and animals
And don't forget the nice weather
Sometimes it's cold, warm, and even hot
When it's warm and hot it's pool time
And when it's cold it's hot cocoa time
Those are the best times of year

Kate Paci, Grade 5
The Sanibel School, FL

The Picture

Roses are red
Violets are blue

Pear blossoms
As in the summer sky
With a shade of yellow
On the rising sun of the horizon

The set of blue
Leaving dark in the sky
Sun a canvas of red and yellow
The yellow streaking sun on the horizon
Becoming a sinking drop of red
The darkness where the flower blossoms

The sky bright blue
With the sun bright yellow
At the horizon
Rising to the sky
I see the roses deep red
And violet blossoms

Lauren Aza, Grade 5
Orlando Junior Academy, FL

Snowmen

As the rain and snow fall
Animals surround the snowmen
In the cold night the snowmen
have their shape
But in the morning
they slowly melt, melt, melt away

Samantha Ratliff, Grade 4
Tabernacle Elementary School, NC

High Merit Poems – Grades 4, 5, and 6

Fast
A ball is thrown,
Flying fast through the air.
Spins wildly,
Then goes down, and
I catch it!

Phillip Carter, Grade 4
Indian Harbour Montessori Elementary School, FL

Just Because I'm Mexican
Just because I'm Mexican
   I did not cross the border illegally
   I'm not in a gang
Just because I'm Mexican
   It doesn't mean my favorite food is tacos
   It doesn't mean my favorite candy is Mexican candy.
Just because I'm Mexican
   I don't speak Spanish everywhere I go
   I don't only talk to Mexicans
   I'm not racist to any other race.
Just because I'm Mexican — it doesn't mean I'm different.

Sebastian Ruiz Jr., Grade 6
Turkey Creek Middle School, FL

Heart Attack
I've seen this condition,
many times before.
Seeing her hurt,
My heart it tore.

Lying on the bed,
I rushed into the room.
Yet I was underage,
And in her eyes I saw doom.

Heart monitors and breathing machines,
All I felt was a great sting.

Ever since that awful day a surgeon indeed I will be.
Not regular however, cardio vascular is for me!

Molley Bailey, Grade 6
Philadelphia Elementary School, MS

Seasons
In the summer I'm at the pool.
In the winter I'm at school.
Why do the seasons have to change?
Why do they have to have to rearrange?
Sometimes I wish kids could rule.

In the fall when it's cold,
In the spring when leaves are bold,
Why do good times have to end?
Why do seasons have to bend?
Why do seasons grow old?

John Albaugh, Grade 5
Daufuskie Island Elementary School, SC

I Don't Understand
I don't understand
Why there is vandalism
on the fences,
why kids join gangs at the age of twelve,
why people are so racist,
why people spread lies,
why people spread rumors,
and why kids judge others.
I also don't understand
why kids at school waste their education,
why kids get in trouble just for attention.
What I do understand is why the sky is blue,
why kids run, why people talk,
and why the world is alive.

Savannah Mew, Grade 6
Turkey Creek Middle School, FL

My Grandmother's Birthday
My grandmother's birthday is on March 12th.
She is getting old.
She doesn't want anyone to know.
Even though she's getting old,
We still have fun going to the mall.
I love my grandmother.

Brittney Langley, Grade 5
Ranburne Elementary School, AL

The Witch's Side
This is a different side of Hansel and Gretel.
The side of the witch who almost ate them in a kettle.
The "cute" little children nibbled at my house,
Almost like a pesky little mouse.

Until I alarmed those children at my door,
My house was good but I wanted MORE!
So I thought I might enjoy some little brat stew,
Soon very soon it would brew.

But first I needed to plump them up,
Cause they were so skinny, I needed more than a cup.
But my eyes are not as good as they should be,
So that Hansel boy tricked me!

Gretel and Hansel thought up a plan,
So that's how I'm stuck in this steamy can.
I was almost burnt, very gory,
But I had to tell MY side of this story.
So as you see you shouldn't be mad at me.

I'm the innocent one and they, the real problem,
Lived happily ever after.
But you haven't heard the last of this old witch.

Nikki Van Lanen, Grade 5
Olde Providence Elementary School, NC

Classroom Communication
Pages turning
Pencils scratching on paper
Teacher giving orders
Whispering children
A binder being opened
The hum of the air conditioner
Markers squeaking
Classroom commotion
Alexander Fernandez, Grade 6
Turkey Creek Middle School, FL

Nothing Is Everything
To see what is really here,
You must find what is not!
To find what is possible,
You must discover the impossible!
To know what I'm thinking.
You must understand your thoughts.
There is no such things as nothing.
For everything is something.
Alexandra McWhirter, Grade 6
Scotts Creek Elementary School, NC

Lucky
Lucky is my favorite pet
I remember how we met
I loved his fluffy hair
Then I thought, I want a bear
But I changed my mind
And left the bear behind
Then Lucky died
And I cried and cried
Lucky was my favorite pet
And I'll never forget the way we met.
Tiana Pearson, Grade 4
Pine Tree Hill Elementary School, SC

What Should I Do?
What should I do?
What should I be?
What kind of person
Will life make of me?
Will I go to college?
Will I be smart?
Will I become a surgeon?
And work on someone's heart
How long will it take?
When will I know?
What if I don't make it?
Then where would I go
These questions wander
Through my head every day
That's why I'm taking a hold of life
Because I don't have time to play.
Krystle Turner, Grade 6
Arnold Magnet Academy, GA

My Cousin SFC Jared C. Monti
My cousin Jared is a hero to me.
He gave his life, so we could be free.
Jared and his men were out on patrol.
They were ambushed, and the fight was hard to control.
Jared and his men were now in their own war.
Not once, not twice, but three time he was hit.
He did not let fear hold him one bit.
Derek and Brian were saved.
In came the helicopters, the blades the air shaved.
The helicopter pulled up Brain when it crashed.
Hope for Brain was dashed.
Jared once again left cover.
Over another soldier did he hover.
Patrick was gone before Jared got to him.
Jared was badly injured by an enemy RPG in a limb.
At his funeral, he was awarded a Purple Heart and a Bronze Star.
Jared, Patrick, and Brian are up in heaven with the stars.
This is why my cousin is a hero to me.
He gave his life, so you and I could be free.
Ryan Lindsay, Grade 6
Camperdown Academy, SC

What Do You Think?
Have you ever made something? Something that could move or ring?
Bible times to modern days find inventors try new ways
Get a Bible anywhere; sit somewhere, like in a chair
If you read you'll find in there harps and lyres and scrolls that tear
Later came the printing press, saving writers much distress
Franklin's eighteenth century brought us electricity
Time went on and soon we had telegraphs run by a lad
Steamboats puffing up and down, trains and planes all over town
Now we have TVs and cars, streetlights take the place of stars
Giant factories pollute traffic jams on every route
What do YOU think of it all? Did it grow our country tall?
Did it help to make us fall? What do you think of it all?
Early days to times like now, new inventions may be how
We have busy city life, trouble, problems, angry strife
On the other hand, I know, most inventions help us go
Much more quickly than before; in a way they help us more
But —
Smoky cities full of grime, busy streets full all the time...
Don't you think that in some ways you'd prefer those prairie days?
What do YOU think of it all? Did it grow our country tall?
Did it help to make us fall? What do you think of it all?
Molly Fox, Grade 6
Sturbridge Academy, NC

Back to Class
The sun beams down on the grassy school yard.
Look up. The trees sway, leaves soaring through the air like birds.
Birds sing a love song; the trees are acting like big trolls.
Thump! Pine cones falling from the trees, like incoming bombs.
Ding! Up there goes the bell. Got to get back to class.
Jason Savage, Grade 5
Southern Pines Elementary School, NC

Category 5

Debris floating in the sky moving so swiftly
touching everything in its path.

Outside the wind howls like a freight train
sucking from the drains sounding like vacuums
right at your ears.

Moving so swiftly looking like a gray giant bullet.
Tearing down everything in its path.
Silence for a moment nothing left.
No sign of life visible.

Bobby Y. Clement, Grade 5
Morgan Elementary School, NC

Wondering Years

They just don't spill
"Come on, just tell me the year."
Why is she acting so crazy?
You might ask
Well I'll tell you why
She just doesn't spill how old she is!
NOT my teacher or no one.
Sure they tell me 105
But pish posh!
That can't be right.
Gimme your license!
I say begging and crying
I can't tell you why.
I wonder how old she is
BUT there's no way to trick her
I'm desperate to know.
And oh I wonder more.

Lais Perez, Grade 4
Clearview Avenue Elementary School, FL

I Am

I am confident and forever determined
I wonder if I will be famous or athletic when I grow up
I hear the voices in my head to focus
I want my goal to be straight in front of me
I am confident and forever determined
I pretend I can do whatever I want
I feel the wind of the city blowing in my face
I touch the air and feel the sky
I worry when I am alone and nobody to help me
I cry when I think of my lost ones
I am confident and forever determined
I understand life is a rough place
I say I can do whatever I want
I dream I can control my own life however I want
I hope life will take me somewhere one day
I am confident and forever determined.

Chris Fritz, Grade 6
Heron Creek Middle School, FL

Time

The hour hand is short,
And the minute hand is long.
If you read it backwards,
Then your time will come out wrong!

There are sixty minutes in an hour.
Sixty seconds in a minute.
The time is twelve o'clock,
That's the time limit.

The time always changes.
Tick tock goes the clock.
The time goes by so quickly.
Sometimes that's a shock.

The hour hand is short,
And the minute hand is long.
If you read it backwards,
Then your time will come out wrong!

Rachida Harper, Grade 4
Egret Lake Community Elementary School, FL

Mountains in the Fall

Over in the mountains during the fall,
Is the most beautiful time of all.

Riding on the four wheelers, wind in my face,
The colors flying past as if in a race.

Up and down the mountain, going oh so fast,
Red, orange, yellow are the colors that go past.

Jamie Brown, Grade 6
Gold Hill Middle School, SC

Just One More Time

My friend gave me a red balloon, all rubbery
    and flat.
I took a big breath and blew to try to make
    it fat.

It puffed out just a little, and so again I blew.
And each time that I huffed and I puffed I watched
    as it grew.
I thought I should stop.
But I gave one more puff, and my balloon went
POP!

Kelsey Haizlip, Grade 6
Harold C. Johnson Middle School, SC

Midnight Moon

The midnight moon illuminates the night
The sleeping world at calm
The shadows of the darkened world lying on the ground
The world passes by as the moon fades

Jenelle Acebo, Grade 5
Virginia A Boone Highland Oaks Elementary School, FL

Snow Skiing
Aspen, Colorado was windy and frigid
Snow mass was bright and sunny
the majestic mountains were peaceful
the air was dry and thin
I saw, glistening white powder
baby skiers and old ones
ski lifts, high and numbing
gondolas with a breathtaking view
I did, swift rides through the mountains
on snowmobiles
a leisurely horse drawn sleigh ride
soared up
the mountain in a chair lift
skied the whole way down
I felt, the raw wind hit my face
warmth from the fire
the sweet taste of hot chocolate
amazed at what
God
has created
Elizabeth Hancock, Grade 6
Chapin Middle School, SC

Parker, My Sister
Parker
Brown hair,
Blue eyes
A lot of fun,
Always happy,
Very active
Five years old,
Smart,
Wild,
A sister
In preschool,
Stubborn,
The youngest in my family of four,
Loves sweets and things,
A great friend!
She's my baby sister!
Kate Green, Grade 5
Waccamaw Elementary School, SC

Hide and Go Seek
Eight, Nine, Ten
Here I come
I look here
I look there
Are you there
Are you here
I can't find you
Oh! Here you are.
Summer Nolen, Grade 5
Ranburne Elementary School, AL

What Should I Do?
My mother said to read and write,
my father said to read the bible at night.
My brother said to run and play,
my cousin said to play all day.
My aunt said to sew was fun,
my uncle said go out in the sun.
My grandma said to learn and cook,
my grandpa said just read a book.
But of all the things that I have heard,
the best thing is to read the word.
Kelly Miles, Grade 4
DaySpring Academy, AL

Tornados
Tornados are a deadly thing
From time to time they come
People scream and people run
Trying to get away
I just stay down in the basement
Curled in a ball
Waiting for my call.
Gabrielle D'Amato, Grade 5
Morgan Elementary School, NC

Mama
Carla
Beautiful, great
Strong, happy, joyful
Greatest mom in the world
Mommy
Xaynah Nicholas, Grade 6
Arlington Middle School, FL

Why Oh Why Oh Why
I gave a kid some pie,
And then he started to cry,
Why oh why oh why,
Every time I got near,
His face shot up with fear,
Why oh why oh why,
When he stopped crying,
I asked him "Why?"
He said "I don't like apple pie."
William Bassett, Grade 6
McRae Elementary School, FL

There Once Was a Fish
There once was a fish in a lake
who wished he was a snake.
So he didn't bite any hooks
and he read lots of books,
and he even moved out of the lake.
Reagan Oswald, Grade 5
St Martin Upper Elementary School, MS

Katelyn
K inesthetic
A thletic
T errific
E ntertainer
L ikable
Y oung
N ice
Katelyn Hinton, Grade 4
East Jones Elementary School, MS

Brothers and Sisters
Brothers
Toys, mud
Sweating, dog-walking, stealing
Mess-maker, hunter, glitter, shoes
Styling, flirting, exciting
Good-looking, makeup
Sisters
Tristen Benefield, Grade 5
Ranburne Elementary School, AL

Catching a Rock
It was foggy out.
You could hear the roosters crow.
The boat was clean —
And shiny.
It had white with yellow stripes.
It felt good with the wind on your face.
The sun was hot.
While we waited for a bite,
One of the poles bent down.
It looked like it was going to snap.
Someone grabbed it.
They said it felt like a big one.
It came to the surface
It was a rock!!!
Fire coral to be exact.
We were all sad.
Later on we laughed and joked around.
Instead of a fish we caught a rock.
Jessica Gehring, Grade 6
Lake Park Baptist School, FL

Spring
Blades of grass grow silently,
Reaching for the sky.
Old birds, their feathers preening,
Call to young yearning to fly.
Blossoms humming every hue
Tilt their faces to the sun.
Spring is a promise of renewal
To each and every one.
Michaela Kivett, Grade 4
Pelican Marsh Elementary School, FL

Orange

Orange is as strong as a raging elephant,
he's as smart as Einstein,
and he loves space.

Orange is a spark just waiting to turn into fire,
he's a ferocious tiger just waiting to pounce,
he wraps around fire and sparks,
orange is a juicy fruit.

Orange is a circle that rolls and bounces all around,
he is lava, pouring from a volcano,
he wraps himself around lava,
he splashes orange on the sunrise and sunset.

Graeme Smith, Grade 4
Youngsville Elementary School, NC

Multiplication

Multiplication is the best.
It puts you to the test
It is the opposite of division
In everybody's vision

When you look in an equation
You will find multiplication
It is like art
It is also like a chart

Multiplication, multiplication
All around the nation
I know a great mix
It is two times three equals six

Multiplication is a subject
Which you use many different objects
For the better knowledge of the math we gain
In the end it will stick in your brain.

Korisha Ali, Grade 4
Egret Lake Community Elementary School, FL

Old Schools

Do the bells really chime?
Are they really the color lime?

Did the kids walk home for lunch?
Or did they stay at school for brunch?

Did they really have coal heaters?
Or did they put warm water in bottled liters?

At the end of school, were there herds?
Did many kids follow birds?

Was there really only one room?
Did they spend all day sewing looms?

Stephanie Zhang, Grade 4
William S Talbot Elementary School, FL

In Rain or in Shine

How cute they are with a ball on their nose.
Just let me tell you a strong tale of woe.
One day at Sea World, oh a beautiful day,
I was watching an otter show, which was so very gay.
As I talked to my mom I heard an "or, or, or, or"
And I know at that moment this wouldn't be a bore
The balls went flying like the American flag,
It is just too bad he cannot brag!
And just one moment later I saw in his eyes
The saddest of seals, the saddest of lies.
And I thought to myself "Why isn't he happy?"
For I just hate to see him so unhappy.
Then I understood clear in my mind
That he hates his job in rain or in shine.
So I talked to the owner and he let him go free.
So when I visit the ocean, I see my friend with glee!

Eliza Butts, Grade 6
Brogden Middle School, NC

Storm

Rain hammers the roof
The sky explodes with lightning
The air rings with thunder
The clouds darken
An angry storm begins
It shows no mercy
Striking like a snake at everything
It traps everyone in endless blackness like a black hole
Suddenly the gathering of dark
Dispatches
The rain
The shots of light
The angry noise
All stopped
The sky is peaceful and the blazing hot sun returns
The only evidence of the storm is the puddles
And all is well, except me
I dread every storm that comes this way
Yet I crave every one when it leaves
I crave the darkness and the mystery
Why did it leave?

Cassidy Parker, Grade 6
Gold Hill Middle School, SC

Bengal Tiger

Bengal Tiger
stripes, loud, big, sneaky,
runs fast, sleeps, walks, eats, and hears well,
lives in forests in India, Bangladesh, and Nepal,
amazing hunter
furry large carnivore
Cat

Cori Hupe, Grade 4
Wellington School, FL

The Runaway

The shiny light
is coming from
the warm fire.
the fire is red, and orange, mixed.
It could burn me into dust.
There's peaceful stories about
The Underground Railroad
and how slaves got to freedom.
What is he saying about me?
While I'm by the fire
it makes me feel warm and cozy.
Come sundown
they say we run away.
Come sundown
come sundown
come sundown
run away to freedom.

James Boyd, Grade 4
Pinnacle Elementary School, NC

The Accident

We arrived at Papa's and Granny's,
Put our humongous suitcases down,
And went to catch some z's.
So I chose to wake up
And go take a dip in the pool.
Papa replied, "Don't go too far
Or you will drown."
I answered quickly, "I won't.
I know how to swim."
I put my head under
The wonderful water
To see how long
I could stay.
When I was coming up,
I choked and my face
Was as purple as a rippled plum.

Savanna James, Grade 5
East Marion Elementary School, MS

Agriculture

A nimals
G rains
R aising crops
I ndustrial park
C orn
U sed land
L and
T rees today
U sed combines
R ice
E ggs

Hogan Brewer, Grade 4
East Jones Elementary School, MS

Going Beyond

Departing the pond,
Hopping onto a lily pad,
Alone in my world.

Gazing at the moon,
Sharp and bright in the night sky,
Shining in the dark.

The spry frog yearning,
Yearning to travel beyond,
Beyond the ancient fields.

Down in the forest,
Colors so plain and simple
Brown, green, black, simple?

Finally beyond,
I am in a cherry tree,
Looking at the past.

Rachel Sevcik, Grade 5
Summit Hill Elementary School, GA

Summer

Summer is almost here,
The hottest time of the year
We can go in the pool,
it will be so cool.
Oh, I can't wait till summer!

Shareba Broadnax, Grade 4
Moyock Elementary School, NC

Ode to Mom

She is caring
And loves kids
She checks the kids health
And helps parents
She's talented in music
And creates symphonic sounds
She is very experienced
And always itches for more
She's smart
And assists in others work
She cracks problems for others
She's normally there to help
She's always active
And edges you to also be
She tries to keep you out
But only sometimes succeeds
She's passionate
And uses others' perspective
She creates masterpieces
And makes them taste great.

Patrick O'Leary, Grade 6
CrossRoads Middle School, SC

The Dog

When I was walking by myself,
I heard a sound.
I looked behind me.
There it was;
A dog running right toward me.
I started running.
Then before I could jump
Over the fence,
The dog had grabbed my shoe
And I fell.
The dog went the other way
Meanly.
It jumped on me
And licked my face.

JaNyra Parker, Grade 5
East Marion Elementary School, MS

Faceball

When I was playing baseball
It turned into faceball
It hit me in the chin
And I didn't know where or when

So now I'm more careful
And not quite so dareful
And that's why baseball
Should not turn into faceball

Sam Cromley, Grade 5
Brooklet Elementary School, GA

My Little Brother Willy

My little brother Willy, oh Willy
You are so silly.

When you hop
I want to pop.

Oh Willy, I quite despise
Yet you are only five.

And you best friend Wessy —
Don't get me started on Wessy!
Wessy is so messy!

When we're at the deli
He's always covered in jelly.

You two are just so stupid
You always smell so putrid.

Oh yes I really quite despise
Yet you two are only five.

Nissa Coit, Grade 5
North Windy Ridge School, NC

The Boy That Lost His Toy Truck
There once was a boy,
Who had a big toy,
When he played he was full of joy.

Then his little red truck,
Had got very stuck
In all of the gooey muck.

When he couldn't get it out,
He started to pout,
He go so mad he started to shout!

The boy started to cry,
Then his dad came by,
And when his dad helped him, he made a big sigh,
And said, "Goodbye."
Heather Hochmeister, Grade 5
Jeff Davis Elementary School, MS

The Harsh Cold Wind
As I walked out the house,
I felt the harsh breeze.
I ran to get out of the wind
When I fell and hurt
My knocked knees.
It bled as I got back up to run;
Red blood flowing down my leg.
I can hear my cousin screaming,
"Come on, Fat!"
I knew I could make it through
The cold wind.
I had a pathological fear of the dark
And what I thought was out there.
I will never run in the harsh cold wind again.
TaKizah Alford, Grade 5
East Marion Elementary School, MS

My Precious Beagle
When I was the age of six
A little puppy came to our door.
She had a skin disease our vet had to fix.
She ate like a pig and then wanted more.

Her eyes sparkle
Like diamonds in the light.
She loves all people
but dogs, she loves to fight.

When I pet her she smiles at me
and shakes my hand on the count of three.
If you go to my house you will see
my precious little beagle that we named Mercy.
Marley Melton, Grade 6
Appling County Middle School, GA

Helping
One in a quadrillion people
Or maybe it's a trillion
Whatever it is
You can't hurt if you help
Some need help
We have it
The question is
Will we give it?
Is there any reason not to
Besides pure greed and want?
There are plenty of reasons why we should
Can't you think of one?
All these people need
Is love, care, and devotion
It doesn't take a special potion
We have those three things
Of course we do, we're only human
You have two hands
Use them to help
Elizabeth Panagopoulos, Grade 6
Incarnation Catholic School, FL

A Mother
My mother is the best out of all the rest.
She will love me and hug me forever.
She will hold my hand for a while, but hold my heart forever.
Laurie Xiao, Grade 5
Summit Hill Elementary School, GA

Money Time!
Penny, penny
Easily spent
Chocolate brown
And worth one cent.

Nickel, nickel
Thick and fat
You're worth 5
I know that.

Dime, dime
Thin and small
That's worth 10
"Oh," I spent it all!

Quarter, quarter
Big and bold
You're worth 25
I am told.

Dollar, dollar
Green and long
You're worth 100 cents
"Oh my it's all gone!"
Stephanie Byers, Grade 4
Egret Lake Community Elementary School, FL

Reading a Book

Reading a book,
A whole new chapter,
What will happen next?
Unexpected,
What a surprise,
Every time you turn a page.
Like jumping into a whole new place,
Like looking through another's eyes.
Every book is something new,
You never know what you will find.
Another book read,
Another book started,
A never-ending cycle.
Traveling Pants,
To World War One,
Always something different.
I love to read,
I always will,
Always excited for a new adventure.
Always hungry for another book.

Hannah Lawson, Grade 6
J E Holmes Middle School, NC

The Beach

Every year I go to the beach
It is very fun
I see the waves
And the sand
I go out with my cousins
And have a good time
We play for six hours straight
Until we are tired

At night we have dinner
and watch TV
We see a movie and eat popcorn
It is late
So we have to go to bed
Wake up in the morning
And do it again
I can't wait

Tyson Messer, Grade 5
Buies Creek Elementary School, NC

Tim Tebow

Tim Tebow is great
He is so cute
He is not a brute
Tim Tebow is big and tall
All he does is throw the ball
He won the Heisman award
When he plays we're never bored
Tim Tebow is nice and tan
And everybody is a fan

Taylor Sparks, Grade 4
William S Talbot Elementary School, FL

My Window

I run to my room slam the door and cry
I wish I could run and fly away
To escape this awful dreary day
I don't want to waste another day
I look out my window, do you know what I see?
I see the sea polluted with debris
I see children who are struggling like me
I see the sky gloomy and looms like gray draped across the sky
I hear sirens in the distance
Someone died this instant
I see my reflection and I made a decision that me and only me
Would change the world for the people before and after, just like me

Erika Rivera, Grade 6
Freedom Middle School, FL

The Shining Shark

I went to go fish at sea,
When I saw something shinning with glee.
It had a fin like a rats nose
can it be, can it be, who knows.

It wandered off onto the ocean floor,
I screamed, I screamed like a mad person knocking on the door.
It slowly came up with no harm or fright,
like a cool, soft, sweet dark night.

It was hyper with 5 gills,
like me when I over eat my pills.
It's grey, and white, and big, and strong,
but not as strong as when I play ping, pong.

Now I sit on my thinking bark,
I know what it was, the shining shark.

Luis Gonzalez, Grade 5
Eugenia B Thomas Elementary School, FL

Here Is Where I Lie*

Here is where my journey ends.
My brain cannot think anymore.
My hands cannot feel anymore.
My feet cannot carry me anymore.
Here is where I lie and here is where I wish to die.
I wish to die here in this spot where my body left me,
unable to move, unable to continue my journey, the journey I have started.
I will die here in this spot, unable to move or smile.
I have someone with me, in this spot where I lie.
She is a pretty girl, but she is unable to smile,
for her smile is fading, as is mine.
Here is where I lie, and here in this spot, where my body left me,
is where I am to die.
Good bye.

Jessi Whitacre, Grade 6
Jackson Heights Middle School, FL
*Inspired by a movie about Mt. Everest

High Merit Poems – Grades 4, 5, and 6

Awesome Black

Black is my favorite color.
Black loves math because he likes rounding decimals.
His favorite food is steak and popcorn.
Black loves football and basketball.
Black loves to skateboard.
He likes video games and computer games.
Black plays the electric guitar.
Black is an A++ student on every subject.
Black never makes B's, C's, D's, F's, or E's.
Black's favorite movie of all time is *Over the Hedge*.
He has a dog named Blacky.
He hangs out at the skate park with Red.
He plays basketball with Carolina Blue.
Black kinda likes black popcorn.
Black has a 3-story house.
Black has 26 Webkinz.
Black is a great student in school.
Every time he plays tennis he gets hit.
Black is still a great color.

Britney King, Grade 4
Youngsville Elementary School, NC

The Sunny Beach

Sunny Beach,
You are so crowded.
Sunny Beach,
You are so peaceful.
Sunny Beach
You are so exciting.
Oh, do I like you Sunny Beach!

McKay Harris, Grade 6
St Francis Xavier Elementary School, MS

Can You Imagine…

Life without a video game
Dick Vitale not entering the basketball Hall of Fame

Losing a few loving grandpas
Having too many flaws

Nighttime not dark
Dogs that can't bark

No water in oceans
Scientists not using potions

School with no teachers
The O'Connell Center without bleachers

The Gators not being a sports team
Life with no ice cream

Antarctica with no ice
Dylan Maillart not being nice?

Andrew MacNeil, Grade 4
William S Talbot Elementary School, FL

Life After Death

Life after death,
Would I be a memory?
Or would you carry me on,
When you talk about my life of the good times,
would you laugh and then don't cry,
My life after death would set me free,
no problems or worries,
no longer on Earth,
Where people could hurt me,
Whether I'm glad, sad, or mad,
I knew all my hurt was in the past,
Living life for the world,
but dying for your freedom,
Only hoping you could make it to the Holy Kingdom,
Life after death don't cry,
but rejoice by hearing the sound of my voice,
To all my loved ones,
All I ask of you is to remember me,
Until we meet again.

Desilyn Cobb, Grade 5
Minor Elementary School, AL

I Am Here Grandma

I am here
I came to this country
And behind, I left the delicious food
Of my loving grandma
I am here, missing you
I'm still remembering your beautiful wrinkled hands
That would prepare me meals every day and night
Meals full of love
Good love
I run and jump looking for you but I never find you
Where are you grandma?
I send you a kiss through the wind
So you could feel the love from me
Thank you, thank you Grandma

Martin Villacreses, Grade 6
Varsity Lakes Middle School, FL

I Believe…

I believe
In courage, when all hope is forgotten.

I believe
In freedom, when my heart is trapped in shame.

I believe
In myself, when my dignity is lost.

I believe
In peace, when death engulfs our memories.

Jamie Odzer, Grade 6
Highland Oaks Middle School, FL

My Sister
E mma is
M ischievious every
M oment she is
A wake;

R unning
A round
E verywhere

J umping
O n my
N erves
E very
S econd.

Travis Bodford, Grade 6
Scotts Creek Elementary School, NC

My Life
My life is stressful, my life is hard
Whether I'm playing trombone
Or playing soccer

My life is weird
The clank of first position
The thud of the free kick
The zip of the coat
The gong of the late bell
My life is stressful

My life is stressful
The bam of the nerf gun
The squish of the mud
The pit-pat of the rain
My life is hard

My life is stressful
The tick of the clock
The coo of the bird
The zing of the cash register
The whoosh of the wind
The fizz of the hot cocoa
This is my life and I like it!

David Petmecky, Grade 6
Trickum Middle School, GA

Spring
S mell of flowers
P retty sky
R ipe fruit
I ncredible
N o school
G o outside

Brandon Rew, Grade 4
East Jones Elementary School, MS

Heaven
H eavenly
E verlasting
A bove
V irtuous
E ternal
N oel

Trevor Henry, Grade 5
Ranburne Elementary School, AL

My Mother
M y mother is so nice.
O h, so neat and clean.
T he love I give her.
H as a special ingredient to it.
E very time I see her, I…
R eveal my love to her.

Savanna Bullard, Grade 4
Freeport Elementary School, FL

Spring
S pring break
P lay
R ain
I ce cream
N ice fireworks
G oing on vacation

Micah Heathcock, Grade 4
East Jones Elementary School, MS

Spring
S pectacular
P recious
R ainbow
I mpression
N ature
G reen

Isabella Vallejo, Grade 4
Central Park Elementary School, FL

Summertime
Summertime is here.
The birds are singing.
The clouds are blue.
Ducks are swimming.
Butterflies are flying.
The sun is shining.
Kids are playing.
The pools are cold.
Grass is green.
Parents are watching
And we all say
"Summertime."

Miranda Russell, Grade 5
East Marion Elementary School, MS

Newspapers
N ew news every day of the week
E verything important and interesting
W eather
S ports
P aper cuts and paper to recycle
A ds
P eople and places
E ntertainment
R eporters gathering information
S tories

Hannah Rambo, Grade 5
Bramlett Elementary School, GA

Everyday Life
As life passes you by
Every day is an adventure
Life is too short for people to lie
People die every day
Once you love it can't go back
Every day life consists of food
It is sometimes hard
No one's perfect
Grown ups wish they were kids
Kids wish they were grown
Men do what they want
Boys do what they can
Life is a puzzle
We all put it together
Some don't have a life
But yet they still live
Put it all together
And you get life
Life

Brandon Edwards, Grade 6
Arnold Magnet Academy, GA

Spring
S pring break
P lay in the leaves
R ake
I ce cream
N ature
G ardens

Jade Padgett, Grade 4
East Jones Elementary School, MS

Balls
Balls are fun to bounce,
They only weigh one ounce
Balls are fun
I play with them in the sun
Watch the ball pounce.

Carolyn Wright, Grade 4
Coldwater Elementary School, AL

Friendship

It doesn't matter if you're five, tall, short or if you're nine,
A friend will always be by your side.

No matter what, when, where, or why,
A friend will be there and will not lie.

A friend is like an angel, precious and kind, loving and caring,
and most of all sharing.

Graciela Cordoba, Grade 6
Immaculate Conception School, MS

The Garden

What a wonderful garden
How quiet and still

The blooming roses, healthy and scarlet, every thorn so sharp
With the smell of every flower put together

With the clear, dazzling color of each bush
Green, popping green among the scented flowers
How still, appealing, and sweet
Like a jungle of silence and tenderness
With the feeling of nature and peace

The trees as high as the sky
With the budding sunflower that is as yellow
As the bright new sun even higher than the trees
And the creamy color of the orchid, so purple like a grape
How lovely they look, oh so lovely
In the wonderful garden, they are so different
As each bud grow, they are special in their own way

Nina Alesna, Grade 5
Orlando Junior Academy, FL

Summer

Summer is coming all night and day
All that we would want to do is play
No more pencils, no more books
All we need is a rod and a hook.
We will catch some fish and bass
We can go in the lake and cast.

Rhett Hasty, Grade 6
St Francis Xavier Elementary School, MS

Ocean and Sky

Why can't I fly with the flock of birds?
So I can touch the sky
Well I want to learn how to swim
So I can feel how it is to see a shark swim by
Now you see why
I want to swim in the ocean
And touch the sky

Carlos Taylor, Grade 6
Tarpon Springs Middle School, FL

Heart Means Love

Sometimes it feels so passionate it could make you fly,
Some days it makes you feel so low and others high,
It can be bold or it can be hurt on any given day,
But it will also be there to take my pain away,
My heart will always be there it is my best friend,
And it will remain with me all the way until the very end.

Andrea Marroquin, Grade 5
Joella Good Elementary School, FL

Love

What is this thing we call love?
A wonderful gift from above is love.
It makes us warm inside and out,
The one thing in life that is hard to doubt.
It sends chills up your spine
To hope that person will soon 'be mine.'
It makes your heart beat faster and
Your sweat becomes like plaster.
You fumble your words, you cannot speak.
You think about that person all week.
When you mess up, you are too embarrassed to speak;
But it all turns out well in the end
When that special person becomes more than a friend.

Emily Watts, Grade 6
Life Christian Academy, AL

Good Bye

Daddy how I wish I could see you
just one last time
to tell you that I love you
and how much I miss you
even though I know you miss me too,
every day I think of you
and tears come to my eyes
wishing I could relive the days we fought
or the day you died
Boy I wish I could have known
I wish I could say all the things there are to say
you're my Dad and even though you left painfully
you taught me a lesson that needed to be learned
drugs and alcohol are not the way
they will just end your life with dismay
and now all I have to say is
thank you, I love you, and good bye.

Dani Valdes, Grade 6
Osceola Creek Middle School, FL

Swimming

'Splash' as I leap in the pool
The water feels so cool
As I race to the other side
I'm aching so much I feel like I'm about to die
Yes! I won the big race
The water is dripping from my face

Savannah Fissenden, Grade 4
William S Talbot Elementary School, FL

MoQueshia Ringo

MoQueshia Ringo
Crazy
Nice
Funny
Wishes to be a famous singer
Dreams of being a nurse
Wants to be a lawyer
Who wonders about driving
Who fears spiders and snakes
Who's afraid of alligators
Who likes cats and dogs
Who believes in God
Who loves my grandmothers
Who loves my mother
Who loves my daddy
Who loves my brother
Who plans on having a baby girl
Who plans on having a husband
Who plans on having a baby boy
Plans on having a great life!

MoQueshia Ringo, Grade 5
Winona Elementary School, MS

School

School
Fun, awesome
Playing, learning, laughing
It's The World's Best School
Dover

Alexis Molina, Grade 5
Dover Elementary School, FL

Free from Slavery

quiet
scared, waiting in silence
two blacks climbing
down a ladder
the light is dull
yellow lantern flickers
woman with silver hair
gives a white pillow,
a peace of heaven,
resting,
resting,
resting
until we go to freedom.

Cody Arrowood, Grade 4
Pinnacle Elementary School, NC

End of Day

We've eat'n all our dinner,
Prayed our prayers, wished our wishes.
Now it's time to get to work and
Wash up all these dishes.

Austin Ladner, Grade 6
Holy Trinity Catholic School, MS

My Storybook Sweater

My sweater tells stories, even though it does not talk;
The stories aren't written though, in ink, marker or chalk.

Its stains tell the stories and memories of my past;
I shall tell you these stories from the beginning to the last.

This stain on my right shoulder reminds me of my baby sister
Because she left her spit-up mark when I hugged and kissed her.

I finally conquered a two-wheeler, although the falls left blood on my sleeve;
But now when I look at that stain, "I can accomplish anything," I believe.

The chocolate drop down my front tells of summers at the lake;
When we celebrated my birthday with family, friends and cake.

Once my sweater is washed, all the stains will be gone;
But one thing can't be washed away, my memories will carry on.

Tess Saperstein, Grade 6
Bak Middle School of the Arts, FL

Spring

Spring is a time of awakening.
Spring is a time of joy.
Spring is when wood peckers come out and make quite a shaking.
Baby animals will begin to toy.
Ah yes, spring is a great time to be
Spring is a time for vacation, family, and fun.
Spring is a time of play! What a memory to be.
Spring, when the sun comes out, spring a very fun season of a memory.

Ryan Gorman, Grade 6
Chapin Middle School, SC

I Am

I am full of questions and choices.
I wonder if my fortune of being a lot of things
Is waiting out there in the world for me to find.
I hear voices telling me yes.
I see wonderful dreams that can come true.
I want it all, and it will encourage me to go forward.
I am full of questions and choices.
I pretend to know everything, but I don't.
I feel I'll keep learning and learning and I'll never know everything.
I touch peoples hands to join together.
I worry if it all is a myth.
I cry when I can't understand.
I am full of questions and choices.
I understand that life isn't always easy.
I say keep working and never give up.
I dream that someday all my effort will benefit my life.
I try to gain courage and never lose it.
I hope it turns out the best.
I am full of questions and choices.

Michelle Valkov, Grade 6
Heron Creek Middle School, FL

What Is Love?

Love looks like a brilliant red rose in the wilderness.
Love feels like a soft warm kitten sleeping in the sun
She smells like sweet brown chocolate
Love tastes like sweet red, white, and pink candy hearts
Love whispers sweet words into our ear
She dances and prances in a field of tiger lilies
As she dances and prances she asks,
"Will you be my Valentine?"

Corey Biggs, Grade 4
Tabernacle Elementary School, NC

you left me alone

you were the one i always wanted,
you were the one i could never leave,
you were the one that made me stronger,
you were the one that made me breathe,
you lit up my day,
and darkened my night,
oh how we had a terrible fight,
but you showed me who i am and who i was,
there was a lot of dignity,
there was a lot of trust,
you took my hand,
and you held me close,
you even gave me a rose,
but then for some reason,
my heart had broke,
you had left me all alone.

Breanna Knowles, Grade 6
McRae Elementary School, FL

My Old Friend

My old friend
I recall
You were the best out of all my friends

Our friendship is silver
But the sisterly love we share
Is more valuable than anything in the world

Our emotions are the same
We cry at the same things
And die of laughter

My old friend
We have so many things in common
I love you like a sister
I will never stop

My old friend
You are amazing and different
Just like me
That's why we share this everlasting bond together
My old friend

Anna Collinsgru, Grade 5
St Martin Upper Elementary School, MS

The Unknown World

I have seen the lightning,
but I haven't heard the thunder growl,
part of me is finished,
part of me is still in the ground.
When you start to believe,
and you stop to deceive,
that there is miracles and magic,
you will unlock the doors to the
Unknown world

And when you do,
it's so great,
everything looks well,
your inner feelings…
tell you something changed,
things aren't the same

Is it real or a dream?
Will continue or will end?
Can it last forever?
And lastly,
can your mind be stronger…
Than a simple whatever?

Zue Lopez-Diaz, Grade 5
Eugenia B Thomas Elementary School, FL

My Flowers

In a garden, there's many flowers
big, small, beautiful like a rainbow in the sky.

In a garden there's many flowers
they smell lovely, with many colors
and many forms so the flowers are very beautiful.

I like when I see them open
and I think in my mind that the world
is beautiful because the flowers bloom the plant

Valerie E. Hamer, Grade 5
Eugenia B Thomas Elementary School, FL

Alex

Alex
Smart, loud, funny, happy
Brother of Reginal Williams
Lover of mother, toys, and family
Who feels mad, happy, and shy
Who needs family, games, and love
Who fears anacondas, death, and alligators
Who gives time, toys, and food
Who would like to see Chuck E. Cheese, friends, and parks
Resident of Seaside
Lambert

Alex Lambert, Grade 4
St Helena Elementary School, SC

Why?

Why? That's the question everyone asks? Why do we do the things we do? Why is it so hard to say good-bye? Why is it that people say they have a plan but they really don't? Why do we say we can but we won't? Why does it seem like no one is caring? Why does it feel like nobody is sharing? Why does it feel like no one is listening? Why does the sun come up in the morning? Why does it feel like it never goes down? Why is it that people make fun of others because they're different? Why? That's a question we ask ourselves!

Yonah Austin, Grade 6
Gold Hill Middle School, SC

Rain

The raindrops falling down on the ground. Where are they now, nowhere to be found. I looked down the road with a great bound, but there was nothing to be found.

When it was spring the rain did not come, but one day it came with a thump against the window pane. There are so many things to do in the rain.

Summer then came as usual hot breezy days. The sun did not shine, but the rain came. It came through the fall and into the winter. I hope this following spring will be breezy and hot, but maybe not.

Laney Johnson, Grade 5
Ranburne Elementary School, AL

The Things They Do, the Things They Are

Some are special, some are smart
Each one has their own special thing about them
The one lucky thing that my grandparents have
Is they all have me in common

Most people don't have great grandparents but I have two
They may be older but they act young at heart
But the other three are as scrumptious as eating chocolate cake on your birthday
And all the stories that each one tells have a special laughter and space in my mind
We all play games like apples to apples, dominos, cards, and things like that
We get so competitive with winning and losing, but it all turns out in a friendly game

Everyone is always together for the holidays enjoying the home made recipes
They will always take you places you may not want to go, but because you are together you
have a fantastic time
Some even let you stay up late when your parent's don't know
They all have their own unique smells
Of flowers and stuffy cars
Every birthday you know who will give the best presets year after year
And when the ones I love do something for me, I feel so secure to know they will be there for me
They help me with homework, it's lots of fun
Even knowing some answers are wrong
And those are the memories; so many to count, but there will always be more to come

Shelbey Kreamer, Grade 6
Unity School, FL

New Friends

One minuscule plant is sitting all alone in the wide, bare field. Then slowly a new green sprout shoots up beside it. Day by day, it transforms itself into a graceful and slender rose. It rises until it touches the heavens, and on the twelfth day of its appearance, it gazed down to the poor depressed flower and loudly booms, "You shall not be lonely." Suddenly, petite petals popped out of the ground everywhere. They turned into carnations, tulips, sunflowers, and even petunias. Their beauty crooned to the daisy who's eyes flashed like a mighty lightning bolt with delight. It wouldn't be lonesome anymore, now that it was surrounded by friends. And the wide, bare field was no longer bare, but blooming with gorgeous flowers.

Alexandria Ng, Grade 5
Coral Park Elementary School, FL

The Awesome Astros

"1…2…3…Astros!" said the team,
and it was bottom of the 6th.
The score was 4-2.
Daniel is up and smacks one to the fence,
and he gets a triple.
Now I am up and I get a single and knock Daniel in.
The score is now 5-2, and next up is Chase.
he ends up knocking me in.
We eventually get 4 more runs,
and it's now bottom of the 6th and it's 9-2.
I am at third,
Sam is pitching, and Michael is catching.
Sam pitches to the batter,
he hits it to me,
and I throw him out.
After that Michael throws someone out at third,
and now we have 2 outs.
The next batter gets up,
and Sam strikes him out.
"We did it," I told Sam.

Patrick Shea, Grade 6
Lake Park Baptist School, FL

War!

War, war is wrong but you have to be strong.
Bombs in the air, someone may light a flare.
Hope and pray so many won't lay sleeping, forever.
There will be many names that will say "war is not a game!"
You might load and fire and release a bullet from a gun,
But it's not fun, soon it will be done, and we have won.

Shyan Smallwood, Grade 5
Queen's Grant Community School, NC

Snowball

Snowball
Cute, friendly
Meowing, purring, eating
Terrified of my brother
Rolling, sleeping, leaping
Lazy, happy
Snowball

Dylan Bent, Grade 6
Challenger K8 School of Science and Mathematics, FL

Friends

F unny friends crack jokes all the time
R espect your secrets
I mmediately know when you're sad
E ntertaining laughter
N ever a nervous breakdown
D oubtful of lying
S weet friends are good to have

Leighann Reynolds, Grade 4
Wrights Mill Road Elementary School, AL

When Nobody Is Watching

When nobody is watching are you a back stabber?
Because most of them are destroying other's fame.
How could you live with the shame?
You know who is to blame.
Only a few are friends with them
but you can't trust them
you can barely bust them.
They act all nice
but beneath the blunder
there is a great roaring thunder.
All this time you thought they were your friend
but they waited for a time to twist and bend.
Destroy your lives that's what they do.
Now they're coming after you.

Nick Wells, Grade 6
McRae Elementary School, FL

I Am

I am happy and energetic.
I wonder why there are different belts in tae-kwon-do.
I hear cheering.
I see myself as a tenth degree black belt.
I want to be a helper at tae-kwon-do.
I am happy and energetic.

I pretend I am a black belt.
I feel the rain hitting my face.
I touch a cartoon.
I worry about my dad.
I cry when my family members get hurt.
I am happy and energetic.

I understand my form at tae-kwon-do.
I say I will be a black belt.
I dream of being a black belt.
I try to work hard.
I hope to be a black belt.
I am happy and energetic.

Jaime Mothershead, Grade 5
Stokesdale Elementary School, NC

What I Am

At times I am blue,
Cool and calm like a spring breeze
Forgiving and even-tempered like a true Christian

At time I am green,
Intelligent as a scholar
Yet, new as spring foliage

At times I am red,
fiery and anger-swept
Unable to hold it in, until…
BOOM!

Jonathan Craig, Grade 5
Sharon Elementary School, GA

Light's Enemy

Darkness is the color black,
The shade that's on a tack.
Soon it knocks on my pane,
Later at ten I've gone insane.

Darkness disappears at light,
You can only see it at night.
It moves around from here to there,
After a while it jumps into its lair.

Darkness' enemy is the moon,
When he sees it he knows light is soon.
While you're young it is an enemy,
When I was young it was a friend to me.

Darkness is not so bad,
If it was gone I'd be sad.
Darkness cannot be sold.
This is my story it has been told.

Jenna Tan, Grade 4
St Thomas More School, NC

Summer

S ummer is wonderful
U nder a shady tree on a hot day
M any people on vacation
M any things to do
E veryone has fun in the sun
R eally fun

Christina McCormack, Grade 5
Palmetto Christian Academy, SC

Green

Green is always bright.
He loves to go to school.
Green has scraggly hair,
And wears glasses.

Green loves to eat lime,
And makes people sour.

Green wears rain boots.
He makes the grass green.
It's fun to watch him stomp,
And watering those plants.

Green smells like gumdrops,
And the Christmas wreaths.
His favorite friend is Santa Claus.
He really likes his laugh.

Whenever I think of Green,
I think about the trees
Blowing in the breeze.

Joanna Henry, Grade 4
Youngsville Elementary School, NC

Yellow Lily Pad

Yellow lily pad, you are the one I seek
You are the one I love
You are the one I will always adore
You will be my ember and I will be your soul

Oh yellow lily pad
You will be my sun that I will wake up to every morning
But I will be the moon every night you sleep to
I will always visit you at the pond at noon when you shine the most
Yellow lily pad, you will be mine and I will be yours.

Esteban Calderon, Grade 6
Denn John Middle School, FL

Those Yummy Cookies

On the balcony
Looking over the crystal clear ocean, I hear the waves
I smelled something.
The smell wrapped around me like a silk bow and brought me to the small kitchen
I smelled those yummy cookies

Fresh out of the oven, I counted the cookies 1,2,3, — 24!!!
Grandma said, "Only 2"
I said, "It's a beautiful day outside.
The sun is so bright and the sky is so blue.
Let's bring the yummy cookies to the beach."

When we got to the beach, we sat on the white-tan soft sand
The white seagulls were paparazzi
One by one they wanted those yummy cookies
The seagulls didn't get any.
Grandma and I bite into the crunchy, chocolaty, soft, warm yummy cookies

These cookies were so warm like a hot summer day
I said to grandma, "Where is the milk?" her response was, "Right here."
My grandma is so handy, she brought napkins, plates, cups, and even the milk
The first time I tried those yummy cookies
I went to heaven
I will always remember my grandma, Connie, for those yummy cookies

Carri Glickman, Grade 6
Unity School, FL

Florida

A place where the sun shines
and dolphins roam freely in the waters.
Natural wonders all around,
the Everglades and natural springs abound.
In the center of our state is a magical world to see,
you can take a tour of the world or meet a princess if you please.
Way down south the keys lay
with glorious sunsets to make your day.
St. Augustine, the oldest city filled with history,
drink some water to keep your youth.

Melissa Pierce, Grade 4
FSU/City of Pembroke Pines Charter Elementary School, FL

My Dreams

Miracles happen in my dreams
I think of my life
I laugh and love
I am perfect in my dreams
I am funny
I think of horses galloping in the sky
I think of me riding a dragon
People looking up to me
My real life could not compare
I wake up and my perfect dream world is over

Gabby Lupica, Grade 5
Summit Hill Elementary School, GA

Sounds

Boom! The sound of thunder
Sounds like my grandpa with a broom.
Plop Plop Plop the rain like a keyboard.
Crack! I think I heard my grandpa break his back.

Deantae Gwyn, Grade 6
Challenger Middle School, FL

Life

When I was born, I was the middle child
With big brown eyes and hair that curled wild
Full of tantrums I was never mild
My mother called me her wild child

The years went by as I grew
Too many things I want to do
My mother said she always knew
I'd have to grow and try a few

Now come my teenage years
Full of grown up fears
And full of silent tears
That my friends don't hear

Now some day I will grow old
Never more to be bossed or told
'Til I lay down, my hands to fold
In my grave lying cold

Paige Skinner, Grade 6
Boiling Springs Intermediate School, SC

The Storm

The storm was long, bright, and loud
The thunder shook the house
The lightning was as bright as the sun
As the rain fell harder it sounded like ice falling
The ground muddy and soft
All the cats outside ran for shelter
As I climbed in bed the last roar came — to an end
The lightning stopped and the rain slowed down
The storm was over

Sydney Killebrew, Grade 6
Gold Hill Middle School, SC

Missing Dancer!!!

When I look around all I hear is hissing
When I look around it seems to be like someone is missing.
Oh who is that dancer who has been snaking around
There's that hissing sound.
Have you seen that dancer,
When I call for her she doesn't seem to answer.
If you look around there's no one there.
My heart is filling with despair.
The sound of hope sounds really fair.
There's someone missing who could it be?
This job's too big for you and me.
I finally see her, that silly dancer.
She made me run around looking for this answer.
Indeed we found her now off to bed,
There's a dance competition up ahead!

Natalie Franco, Grade 4
FSU/City of Pembroke Pines Charter Elementary School, FL

An Ode to Jesus

When Jesus' followers pray,
There's light in the day.
They pray with all their hearts,
Their minds, and strength to Jesus Christ.
We praise You Lord for lifting us up,
Up above the heavens,
Does everyone know You?
Only You can answer that
Because You mighty Father see all.
Bless You Lord! We praise You Lord!

Jared Hauck, Grade 5
Sharon Elementary School, NC

Basketball

Basketball is fun.
I like basketball.
After a game, my mom takes me to eat a hamburger in a bun.
It's better than baseball.

I can shoot three pointers.
Basketball is hard.
Every shot I make I get three quarters.
In basketball, three pointers are hard.

My brother played basketball.
It is easy to get a penalty.
My mother did not play basketball.
The people that make penalties are always guilty.

You need to be in shape to play basketball.
I need to get in shape.
I used to play baseball.
I know someone that looks like an ape.

Remington Foxworth, Grade 4
Bayshore Christian School, FL

The Storm

Clouds form,
Fit together like a puzzle,
A gray blanket covers the sky,
With a gloomy mood,

The wind picks up,
Rustling the leaves snug in the ground,
The rain chimes in making a melody,
A rhythmic song.

Thunder rumbles,
Lightning flashes,
Sounds collide, and
Blend together.

Trees sway,
Back and forth,
The rhythmic song continues,
Then fades away.

The clouds clear,
The sun shines through,
The sky opens,
All to reveal a breathtaking rainbow.

Jenna Hill, Grade 6
Chapin Middle School, SC

Cats

Cats are cute
cats are fun
cats love milk
and so do I.
When I go to sleep
they sleep
beside me and
when I wake up
they play with me.
I love cats
and you should too
everyone loves
them except for you.

Courtney Fortenberry, Grade 5
West Marion Elementary School, MS

Angels and Demons

Angels
Good, light
Winged, shining, loved
Holy, perfect, evil, insane
Deluded, twisted, hated
Dark, black
Demons

Tyler Martinez, Grade 6
Oakbrook Middle School, SC

Eric

I like to read
and to feed my dog.
I like to play
and make stuff with clay.
I do work
and wash my shirt.
I like games
and my mom has pretty picture frames.
I wash my clothes
and I like to watch TV shows.
I like to skateboard
and my uncle has a samurai sword.

Eric Varnado, Grade 4
East Jones Elementary School, MS

Déjà Vú

Maybe in a dream,
It seems to me,
A recurring thing,
It's the same experience,
The same feeling,
Except in the past
You can't force it to come,
But when it does
You can see the future,
In a déjà vú.

John Bradford, Grade 6
Brogden Middle School, NC

Missing New York

Born in new York
that's where I was a few years past
then I moved.
So sad and lonely I was.
Missing friends and my relatives.
But now is now
and I am going to make the most of it,
and I am going to enjoy it.
So now that I moved on
with new and good friends
I am happy
but till then I will miss New York

Kevin Legagneur, Grade 6
Varsity Lakes Middle School, FL

The Wind and the Story

The wind tells a story to you and I.
You can't see it nor can I.
But the wind tells a story
so make sure you say hi
Cause the wind comes and goes
Where it ends up nobody knows

Amanda Gray, Grade 5
St Martin Upper Elementary School, MS

Nikki

Shy
Short
Wishes to be a teacher
Dreams of singing
Wants to model
Who wonders about getting married
Who fears snakes
Who is afraid of nothing
Who likes dancing
Who believes in what I see
Who loves Dad
Who loves Mom
Who loves Grandma
Who loves family
Who plans to pass every grade
Who plans to be in college
Who plans to be rich
Loves always

Nikki Austin, Grade 5
Winona Elementary School, MS

Middle School

Middle school
Time of change
Very different
Very strange
Time of renewal
Time of independence
But not time of dependence

Ian Miller, Grade 6
Tequesta Trace Middle School, FL

Sleeping

My sisters are screaming
My mom is cleaning
My dad is sleeping soundly

Everything is crazy
My sisters are lazy
But my dad is still sleeping soundly

My sisters are scheming
My mom is day dreaming
And my dad is STILL sleeping soundly

We walk out the door
And go to the store
And my dad is still sleeping soundly

Then everything is quiet
And nothing is a riot…
And then my dad wakes up

Katie Rozmajzl, Grade 4
Queen of Angels Catholic School, GA

We Love Reba!
Reba was our beloved dog!
She never ate as much as a hog.
Reba even went on my parents' honeymoon.
On weekends, she slept in until noon.
Reba gave birth to seven pups;
I can think of a zillion times they got the hiccups!
Reba was a chocolate lab.
She was a big ball of fun and extra fab!
Reba is not with us now.
We know this, she is better off, some how.

Kajsa Lebo, Grade 4
Spruce Creek Elementary School, FL

Angels Oh Angels
Angels, oh Angels
You're in a better place
I'll have to wait
Until we meet face to face.
Angels, oh Angels
You can fly!
Oh so high with lovely feathered wings
But forced not to cry.
Angels, oh Angels
I know I can't see you
But I've always wanted to free you.
Angels oh Angels
You all do the right thing,
But the thing that proves it is the golden ring
Angels, oh Angels
Take good care of my mom, she is in pain,
But please…don't make it long.
Angels, oh Angels
You have a key,
It will open my soul and
Protect me.

Ciara Elkabbany, Grade 4
Clearview Avenue Elementary School, FL

Men's Best Friend
Bulldogs are men's best friend
Very playful little pups
Their energy may sometimes end
But they will always be men's best friend

Some are nice some are crazy
They will always be there for you
When you're very sad and quite dazy
Your four legged friend will cheer you up

So get a bulldog to be your friend.
Trust me,
Your fun will never end.

Ethan Franks, Grade 5
Buies Creek Elementary School, NC

Summer
Summer is coming and school will be out,
Time for fun and games and ride bikes about.
Playing in the pool is so much fun,
Soaking up all that sun.

Summer is here and it's very hot.
Too hot to play basketball in the parking lot.
Man it's a scorcher, I'm burning up!
Time to go inside and get some water in my cup.

You know you can have fun in the sun.
You can have so much to do
Still take time to pack up a book,
Look it through.

Shawn Williams, Grade 5
Sharon Elementary School, NC

The Tree
A tree growing high
up to the very blue sky
It is beautiful

Josiah Altieri, Grade 4
Camden Elementary School of the Creative Arts, SC

What Winter Is
Winter is snowflakes sparkling in the night
The sound of Church bells make me think winter is coming
The sight of bundled up children makes me feel like winter
Winter is like bare branches in the night sky
Winter looks like horse carriages riding through the night
Winter smells like fresh pine trees
Winter is cold snowballs hitting your side
Winter is icy frozen streams

Kaitlin Beane, Grade 4
Tabernacle Elementary School, NC

My Lazy Dog
My lazy dog's name is Smokey.
He is always kind of dopey.
He never gets in a fight. He doesn't even bite.
You can play with his tail. He won't even wail.
He sleeps all day and runs all night.
He is a baby and he is the handsomest dog in the world.

He never gets in mud
He is always clean.
I don't see how he lies around
and still he's faster than a cod.
He doesn't like guns.
If he hears he always runs.
He never jumps or digs.
If he grows anymore he will turn into a horse.
He is the most lovable dog in the world.
If you see him you will be filled with joy and glee.

Chase Compton, Grade 6
Childersburg Middle School, AL

Tree

A tree is a home
A home for a bee or bird
The bird sings to me
The bee makes honey for me
A tree is a very good home

Chad Harvey, Grade 4
Pensacola Beach Elementary School, FL

Summer

The sunniest days of the year
The schools are out
Hear the kids cheer
The cool breeze blowing
Through your hair
Going outside
To get some fresh air
On a warm day
Playing a lot
Some lemonade
Would hit the spot

Christine Bralich, Grade 5
Rosarian Academy, FL

A Day at the Beach

One day at the beach I,
went to the salty ocean.
The salty ocean was very fun.
I had a great time at the salty ocean.

Ashton Howell, Grade 5
Schley County Elementary School, GA

Pot of Gold

The little leprechaun with a pot of gold
All of his jokes seem to sell.
With a green three leaf clover,
He has luck that gets unstuck.

On St. Patrick's Day, the wee folk
Spread out to find the rainbow.
That leads to the pot of gold.
Don't look — you'll never find it.

The leprechaun hides it so well.
Nobody can disturb the leprechaun
And his pot of gold.

Gabriel Puente, Grade 5
Wynnebrook Elementary School, FL

Inspiration

Everything is changing.
Nothing is staying the same.
What has the world come to?
Maybe we should open our eyes
And make a difference.

Natalie Capshaw, Grade 6
Seven Springs Middle School, FL

Summer Fun

One day we were on the boat
Splishing and a splashing and floating on a float
We were about to take off then…
My aunt Lisa went high in the air like Big Ben.
My sister tried to reach her but it was too late,
Everyone started screeching like a squeaking gate.
My uncle Glen jumped off the boat and paddled out.
Then Winston went to the wheel and started to turn around
We finally found them floating in the lake.
My uncle Glen sure wished this was fake
Because he got in a real lot of trouble.
My aunt Lisa cut him a little grief
Because if she didn't she would have been yelling at him like a thief!

Maddie Finn, Grade 4
Grays Chapel Elementary School, NC

The Beach

I can enjoy the ocean's waves when I am at the beach.
There are some gigantic waves and some are small.
Some of the waves are faraway and some are within my reach.
The waves roar loud like it could take down a wall.

When I was on the sand it was hot as fire.
I raced to the water's edge to get cooled down.
Before I could get there the sand's temperature got higher.
When my foot hit the water, I was happy as a clown.

At the beach, when the wind blows from the east it's mean as a beast.
When it blows from the south the air is warm.
When it blows from the west, it bothers me the least.
When it blows from the north the seagulls swarm.

Jacob Sharpe, Grade 5
Sharon Elementary School, NC

Florida

Florida, so beautiful and so nice
I already live here but I would like to live here twice.
Florida full of history, through the everglades and through St. Augustine;
history is in the air and below our feet.
Florida, it's so fun here, it is so exciting.
Disney World and every other amusement park is in Florida.
Florida, so beautiful and so nice
I already live here but I would like to live here twice.

Michael Manning, Grade 4
FSU/City of Pembroke Pines Charter Elementary School, FL

Life Is Like an Uneven Path

Life is like an uneven path.
It goes up and down and the path ahead is never clear.
You can never take a step without stumbling.
There is never an easy way to do things without missing the true purpose.
There is always something to block your way.

Brandon Meisner, Grade 5
Summit Hill Elementary School, GA

Nothing or Something

Welcome to nothing…
Where something is nothing.
But isn't nothing something?

I don't know…
But nothing is nothing
So it's not something…
Is it?

(Hold on. Let me get this straight…)

If nothing is nothing,
Then it is not something.
But you can't do nothing,
So it's something…
Right?

Jacob Bodtmann, Grade 4
Clearview Avenue Elementary School, FL

Too Late

Look in the air, to the sky
Go higher and what do you see?
Gray, why, more gray, why?
Look!
Do you see it a truck, a long distance truck, gray, more gray.
Look over there, do you see it?
A factory, a big factory, gray, more gray.
Look in the air, black, dark black.
Why is it warmer now?
Look ice, look now, water.
Penguins, more penguins, gone, where did they go?
Look at that wave, a big wave.
Why did it get hotter again, cough, cough, I feel sick.
The wave is coming closer!
I'm too hot too sick to swim or move.
The scientist did warn them, but they didn't listen.
Pollution truck is over there, pollution factory is over there!
Wave coming nearer and nearer…
It's too late to stop it now, we should have stopped it back then
Gulp, gone.

Janay Clytus, Grade 6
CrossRoads Middle School, SC

Ode to My Family

Family, oh family,
You are so nice
I feel so taken care of and loved
I love to hug them and you do too
We sometimes fight, but we get over it
You never leave me if we're at places,
When I have trouble, you always help me,
You're always there when I need to share
My feelings with you
I LOVE YOU SO MUCH!

Natalie Arce, Grade 5
Vienna Elementary School, NC

9-11

"Boom!"
Did you hear that?
Smell that?
It's fire.
I see the smoke, raise higher and higher.
The building is coming down
It makes me sad, and everyone in New York mad.
Why did they do that?
Was that necessary?
Knockin' down the Twin Towers, and makin' airlines scary.
I don't think it's all right, do you?
Well…
I hope we do something new, to protect me and you.
And our landmarks too, because 9-11 is very important.

Eric Waiknis, Grade 6
Seven Springs Middle School, FL

Tonya Jacks

Tonya
Mother
Loving, gentle, caring, enjoys life
Lover of her family, her job at county, her dog
Who believes she can do anything
Who wants a really big house, me to be happy, lot of money
Who uses her intelligence, her heart to care,
her family when she is in a rough situation
Who gives her family love, her mind to think, her heart to give
Who says, "You can do anything you set your mind to"
Jacks

Ashley Jacks, Grade 6
Newport Middle School, NC

Under the Sea

I like the fish under the sea,
they seem to swim a lot like me.
They swish and they swoosh and they zoom like a rocket.
Boy, would I hate to have them in my pocket!

I like the crabs down in their shells.
If I had one I'd name him Mells.
You might think that they sleep all day,
but turns out, they love to crawl and play.

I like the starfish, slow and lazy,
with their eyesight so very hazy.
I think they are very cool things,
but it would be cooler if they only had two wings

Under the sea
is a great place to be.
You won't believe some of the creatures,
but just as amazing is all its features!

Jaymie Danford, Grade 6
North Myrtle Beach Middle School, SC

White Wonderland
White wonderland
Stepping on ice
Potentially threatened
Predator of the Arctic
Life is in jeopardy
Soon to disappear
Paola N. Russe, Grade 5
Oliver Hoover Elementary School, FL

Every Three to Four Years
Moving coast to coast,
Every three to four years.
Florida to California,
Every three to four years.
Losing my friends,
Every three to four years.
Meeting new people,
Every three to four years.
A new beginning,
Every three to four years.
Jorge Rodriguez, Grade 6
Tequesta Trace Middle School, FL

The Ocean
The ocean, the ocean
It's a beautiful motion

You can ride waves
Or explore mysterious caves

The dolphins jump high
In an attempt to wave bye

There's yellow, glistening sand
On this big, beautiful land.
Sarah Netherland, Grade 4
William S Talbot Elementary School, FL

Snow
Snow is white
And very bright
It sparkles in your eye
Like a crystal in the sky
Yellow is yucky
You won't get lucky
When it snows here
You know Christmas is near
As the snow falls
People try to catch it all
I miss playing in the snow
Making snow angels, snowmen
And watching all the snow blow.
Katelyn Ricker, Grade 6
Challenger Middle School, FL

Spring Break
S peck of flowers
P laying games
R inging bells
I n the pool
N eed to take a breath
G oing places

B ring flowers
R olling in grass
E legant flowers
A pple pie
K ittens being born
Madison McLelland, Grade 4
East Jones Elementary School, MS

Dirty Hands
Sappy, itchy
Muddy, crumby
Cold, sore, bumps
Cuts, dirty hands.
Nadine Bausert, Grade 4
Spruce Creek Elementary School, FL

Spring
S wim in pools every day
P erfect days with sun
R emembering that there's no school
I nviting friends over
N o more homework
G oing to get ice cream to eat
Madison Cox, Grade 4
Prince Avenue Christian School, GA

I Am Sea
I feel waves
    Splashing, gliding, crashing,
For I am me
I hear wind
    Howling, soaring, pushing,
Forever free
I see people
    Moving, talking, laughing,
Minds never dark
I smell creatures
    Hunting, swimming, feasting,
A fish, a shark
I touch sand
    Drifting, floating, shifting
A lot like me
I, too, know
    Drifting, floating, shifting
For I am Sea
Nicole Izmaylov, Grade 5
Creek View Elementary School, GA

Kids
Boy
Rough, mean
Falling, hitting, playing
Male, lad/female, gal
Talking, sitting, singing
Girlie, prissy
Girl
Chelsey Davis, Grade 6
Westview Middle School, SC

My Dad
He is wonderful
but not at all dull
He is good
but I dislike his hood
He likes hugs
but does not do drugs
He might be shy
but without him I would die
He loves animals
but doesn't drink Danimals
He minds his manners
and has no banners
He is the master
but never a disaster
He likes to bake
while cooking a steak
He has the magical touch
I love him very much
He never acts bad
and is never really sad
That is my dad.
Taylor Heinz, Grade 6
McRae Elementary School, FL

Hollywood
Stars walk and are in the sky.
Paparazzi's snapping shots.
Sights for you to see.
People are starstruck!
A big white sign is there, too!
Gabriella Manuszak, Grade 4
Pelican Marsh Elementary School, FL

A Joyous Death
Death
Depressed, sadness
Killed, coffin, no more
Extinguished, buried, happy, joyous
Lively, loved, pulse
Distinguished, playing
Life
Sarah Anne Kulakoski, Grade 4
Spruce Creek Elementary School, FL

Don't Eat Bubble Gum!
Some people are just plain dumb
because they like bubble gum.
Ask my teacher, Lum,
she will tell you plums are better than gum.

If you don't believe me.
Go get you a plum tree.
So close your mouth and brush your teeth.
And now they are clean!!!!!!!!!!!
Ashley Yarbrough, Grade 5
Rock Mills Jr High School, AL

Freedom
Freedom is a horse, whose hooves never touch the ground
So delicate, so gentle
Your wildest dream
Soaring through the wind
A poem to their own beat
Muzzles are soft and their mane and tail gleaming in the sun
Trust is on their side
Soaring with the wind, dancing in the moon light
Careful not to hurt the tiniest creatures
Rolling in the sand on a hot summers day
Cooling down in the water with fishes wondering
Horses are sleeping in the sweet, soft grass
Peaceful in the moonlight
Horses are freedom, and freedom is a horse
Amanda Moccia, Grade 6
St Mark's Lutheran School, FL

Hate
Hate should be left alone,
Never to come near my home,
The only place you should see it,
Is in the devil's eye,
That is where it shall stay,
Never to get out just lay,
It lives in all of us,
Sometimes it slips out,
We don't know how to stop it,
It's like a candle that must try not to be lit,
We try to fight it,
Hate is a never ending war.
Carey Kauffman, Grade 6
R D and Euzelle P Smith Middle School, NC

Failure Is…
When you feel you could have done better.
When your goal seems like light years away.
When you get an F on you math test.
When you bake a cake and a burnt aroma fills the room.
Feeling left out when they clap and congratulate someone else.
Massiel Alcantara, Grade 6
Arlington Middle School, FL

Life
L ove everybody no matter what they do to you.
I f you hurt somebody, apologize to them.
F orgive people even if they hurt you.
E ventually you will learn how to forgive everybody.
Marc Genius, Grade 6
Carter Community Charter, NC

Khyra Campbell
Khyra
Young
Pretty
Adorable
Wishes to become a doctor
Dreams of passing school
Wants to do great things
Who wonders why the sky is blue
Who fears snakes
Who likes shoes
Who believes the world is going to change
Who loves Mom
Who loves my step dad
Who loves Dad
Who loves Granddaddy
Who plans to be rich
Who plans to write songs
Khyra Campbell, Grade 5
Winona Elementary School, MS

Cleaning a Bird Cage
Cleaning a cage can be dirty,
If you want a happy birdie,
First you have to take him out,
So he will not pout,
You have to clean out all the poop,
So the cage will not be full of goop,
Then when you have changed the bedding,
You are heading,
Toward perfection.
Christopher Bond, Grade 6
St Mary Magdalen Catholic School, FL

Enemy
Fear is my enemy
A shadow of fear is here
At night a dream — at day a thought
but fear will always be in my heart.

It comes and goes like a roller coaster
I never know when I am finished
fear will always be there in my heart and in my mind.

I never know when to stop or when to start
but my fear is my enemy —
every day and every night.
Amanda Sjoelin, Grade 6
R D and Euzelle P Smith Middle School, NC

April
A pril is springtime
P retty things can happen
R ain like a waterfall
I maginations run wild
L ove is blooming

Matthew Stokes, Grade 4
Pine Tree Hill Elementary School, SC

My School!
My school is awesome
My school is the best
My school rocks
Even some tests!

It is so fun
We learn a lot
I know my math
Right on the dot!

We draw in art
We have PE
We do some music
Even spelling bees!

The principals rock
The teachers are cool
The students are awesome!
Everything rules!

Well, that's it
My school rules
Hopefully, I'm not
Late for school!

Marli King, Grade 5
Brooklet Elementary School, GA

Friends
Friends are friends
they're here till the end

A part of you, they'll always be
the two of us, just you and me

In your heart, they will stay
forever and ever, they won't go away

Without them, you will not live
friendship is what each other gives

The laughs and cries you have shared
will live forever and always be cared

True friends
are here till the end

Megan Bobbitt, Grade 6
Brogden Middle School, NC

Little Boy, Little Boy
Hopping, dancing, leaping around.
The little toddler could not stay on the ground!
Adults couldn't find him when he hid, but he would flee when they did.
So he would run off and be hidden again.
He'd wait impatiently for a minute or three.
Then he would skip off and hide in a tree.
He yelled to give a hint, but that only meant
That he was in a tree, but no one knew which.
It took them a while, but he would only smile because he was about a mile away.
They would drive out a mile and sit for a while
Until one could spot him in that one little tree.

Mattie Earley, Grade 5
Summit Hill Elementary School, GA

Memories of You
I saw a video of you the other day,
and the memories came to my mind and wanted to stay.
I remember when you went away.
My mom sat us down and told us you had gone to a better place.
I remember not crying but sad inside 'cause I would never see your face.
The months went by but I didn't cry.
People started to wonder why, was I heartless? No, that wasn't the case;
I was just too young to really understand about that place.
I miss your hugs, like a blanket they surrounded me in comfort and warmth.
Without you life is getting tough.
You were the family's glue
you kept us together now we're falling apart without a clue.
You made me feel special when nobody did.
I wish I could have said good bye before you left.
It's been three years and I've found comfort at school
with my friends that are like my new crazy family
but you'll always have a place in my heart.
I miss you and love you.

Janel Moreno-Cuevas, Grade 6
City of Pembroke Pines Charter Central Middle School, FL

I Learned That...
I learned that everyone makes mistakes.
I learned that God knows everything.
I learned that you have a choice in life.
I learned that you have to let go.
I learned that you follow your heart.
I learned that friends go with you through the ups and the downs.
I learned that school is the best for you.
I learned that you can't try to be someone you aren't.
I learned that there isn't an easy road in life.
I learned that everyone is good at something.
I learned that everyone comes to the end of life.
I learned that the best thing in life is friends and family.
I learned that if you are alone someone is always there.
I learned that you can't buy friendship.
I learned that you can't get everything you want.

Anna Eades, Grade 5
Northside Elementary School, SC

High Merit Poems – Grades 4, 5, and 6

Lonely

When you're lonely
You sit alone thinking of your life
You think of everything you could have done
To save yourself from loneliness and sadness
But to save yourself you have to try your hardest
You can't think anyone is trying to help you
It's not that you aren't helping yourself
So when you think no one is trying to save you from loneliness
Just think how you can save yourself.

Jody Pike, Grade 6
Tarpon Springs Middle School, FL

Making My Bed

Making my big bed is a lot of hard work,
Especially when your bed gives you a jerk.
I pull and I tug to get the crazy blankets on top,
They will not cooperate; they continue to drop.
Suddenly the monstrous bed starts to try to eat me,
With heavy covers all on top, I struggle to be free.
The mad bed is winning; this is no laughing matter,
Are there others in here? The bed seems to be fatter!
It then spits me out; maybe I don't taste very good,
I landed on my two feet, and there I stood.

Jenna Cocozziello, Grade 6
St Mary Magdalen Catholic School, FL

The Beach

The beach is eternity,
Its horizon stretches on like a timeline.
The endless specks of sand forever flow
Through Cronus's giant hourglass.
The water breathes,
Expanding and contracting like a human chest.
The beach is timeless yet it is always changing.
The beach is a work of art.

Mitchell Madsen, Grade 6
CrossRoads Middle School, SC

My Computer

It's very slow
My computer stinks
When you go on iTunes
It will delete your tunes forever
My mom freaks out when she goes on G-mail
Because it won't give her voice mail

Sawyer Bengtson, Grade 6
Gold Hill Middle School, SC

Dr. Elizabeth Claire Lowery

When I grow up, I want to be a doctor.
My patients will consider me wise and sweet.
I'll run, race, or fly to help those in need.
A better doctor you'll never find.
Introducing, Physician Elizabeth Claire Lowery.

Elizabeth Claire Lowery, Grade 5
Winona Elementary School, MS

I Am

I am a smart and creative person in my own way
I wonder if I will follow my life long dreams
I hear laughter and beautiful sounds
I see only the brightness in the world
I want to be the one who makes peace between people
I am a smart and creative person in my own way
I pretend to be quiet and calm
I feel that people should be treated the same way
I touch and reach out to people in poverty
I worry that the world is not safe
I cry to think that everything isn't good in the world
I am a smart and creative person in my own way
I understand I can't do everything
I say I am smart and creative in my own way
I dream to save peoples lives
I try to be the best I can be
I hope I follow my dreams
I am a smart and creative person in my own way

Patrick Gomes, Grade 6
Heron Creek Middle School, FL

Blue

Blue is shy
Blue doesn't like spinach.
The color blue is very unique
He is fast as lightning zooming through the sky.
Blue loves reading
He is nice.

Blue has curly hair
He is paint that is smooth
He is the tallest person in the whole world.
Blue is the color of my favorite skirt.
The lines of lined paper is blue
Blue is the square shape like a box.
Blue is the most special person in the whole world.
He is helpful in every way.
Blue gazes through the sky
Blue is fun.

Blue's legs and arms are small.
He is tie-dyed the ocean.

Hannah Perry, Grade 4
Youngsville Elementary School, NC

My Dog

My dog is two.
He has a shoe.
He likes to play.
He plays every day.
He likes to run.
My dog has fun.

Carter Kemp, Grade 6
St Francis Xavier Elementary School, MS

I Am

— I am a softball player
I wonder if I will play this sport forever,
I hear people cheering for me
I see birds flying in the sky
I want that championship trophy
— I am a softball player
I pretend I'm in the big leagues
I feel like a superstar
I touch home plate for the run
I worry we might lose the game
I cry when I make an error
— I am a softball player
I understand that I am a winner
I say that I can do it
I dream that I'll play in college
I try my hardest
I hope every game I'll get MVP
— I am a softball player
Brittney Pritchett, Grade 6
Heron Creek Middle School, FL

Winter Snow

Snow
Cold, wet
Blowing, clinging, melting
Makes it cold outside
Crystallizing, brightening, never ending
Cool
Courtney Marie Fletcher, Grade 6
Turkey Creek Middle School, FL

I Am

I am smart and athletic
I wonder how to get college credits
I hear the hitting of a baseball
I see me hitting a home run
I want to graduate college
I am smart and athletic

I pretend I'm the best baseball player
I feel happy when I win a game
I touch a baseball
I worry if I will score a basket
I cry when someone dies
I am smart and athletic

I understand Math
I say I'm good at baseball
I dream about a cool car
I try hard at baseball
I hope for a cool car when I'm 16
I am smart and athletic
Andrew Jent, Grade 5
Stokesdale Elementary School, NC

Hawks

Hawks flying boldly
Streams flowing beautifully
Wind blowing swiftly
Flowers blooming cheerfully
The sun shines brightly above
Ben Higgs, Grade 4
St James Episcopal School, FL

I Love You

I love you
No matter how selfish you are
No matter how ugly or pretty
The love will still be there
I cherish you like a rare gem
To me you are a spectacular person
Never forget
No matter where you are
I Love You!
Christina Wade, Grade 6
Armuchee Middle School, GA

Sports

I am quite short,
I can't play ball on a court.
I can hold my breath,
I swim.

I can't play baseball,
Lord, knows I can't do it all.
I can swim breast,
Trained hard by Jim.

I can't kick a soccer ball,
Can't do it short or tall.
I can't flip on a balance beam,
All I would do is scream!

I love to swim,
It is my talent.
I can do butter, back,
Breast and free.
When I'm in the water,
It's all me!
Caroline Jones, Grade 6
J E Holmes Middle School, NC

Gone Huntin'

It smells like pine trees
It feels like rain
It tastes like leaves
It sounds like a mouse
It looks like woods
James Cartee, Grade 5
Ranburne Elementary School, AL

Love

Love looks like a big heart balloon
Love feels like a velvet smooth flower
in the warmth of the sun.
Love sounds like two blue birds
Chirping in the wind
Love speaks with a hushed tone
Love moves like a nice calm and
gentle breeze.
Brianna Bean, Grade 4
Tabernacle Elementary School, NC

Friendships

You will never be bored,
You will always have friends,
It's like being in heaven.

But when day goes to night
And fun leads to fights
It's boring once again.

But if and when you write a sorry letter
You will be the bigger person
And you will have a very best friend.
Dontavius Newton, Grade 4
Olde Providence Elementary School, NC

Hurricane

As the weather man predicted,
There will be a hurricane.
It will be really rough,
So I called on Jesus' name.
I ran into my bedroom
To prepare and get ready.
When I finished my prayer,
I prayed, "This house will be steady.
We don't want this town to end."
Devon Hawthorne, Grade 6
Mount Zion Christian School, SC

Ice Crystals

I ce falling on the ground
C ement covered with ice crystals
E merging from the sky

C hildren crushing ice crystals
R emaining cold
Y ard work is delayed
S nowing ice crystals
T otally cool
A lways fun
L ots of school delays
S lippery roads
Morgan Duggins, Grade 5
Vienna Elementary School, NC

High Merit Poems – Grades 4, 5, and 6

Nature
I see the birds in the sky
I feel the breeze in my face
I see the leaves fall from the trees
I see the flowers popping out and blooming
I wonder is this the way nature will be in the future
Will there only be buildings and parking lots if there…
If there will be no nature

Braxton Russell, Grade 5
Southern Pines Elementary School, NC

The Clock Chimes Four
School keeps me busy through the day,
So on the couch I do not just lay.
Sitting there, my brain turning to mush
Instead my brain is very lush.

I get to learn and have some fun,
Then go to class, wait, do not run!
Math, Art, Science, Spanish too;
Oh me, oh my, how big my plant in Science grew.

And when that school bell finally rings,
I slowly gather up my things.
I run out the door and down the hall,
Down the steps beside the wall.

I run to catch up with my friends,
And that is how the school day ends.
I shall go home and work some more,
Work I will 'til the clock chimes four.

Madeline Hemmingsen, Grade 6
Gold Hill Middle School, SC

I Am
I'm an artist
I wonder where I go for inspiration
I hear sounds for the part I make
I see my art come to life
I want an art career
I'm an artist
I pretend I'm as good as Leonardo da Vinci
I feel proud of my art
I touch the paint brush and go crazy with it
I worry people might make fun of me
I cry if my art is not good enough
I'm an artist
I understand that becoming an artist takes hard work
I saw I'm a good artist
I dream to be a famous artist
I try to be the best
I hope I become as good as Leonardo da Vinci
I'm an artist

Lawrence Worrie, Grade 6
Heron Creek Middle School, FL

Venezuela Is a Place!!
Venezuela is a place of happiness!!
Venezuela is a place to feel the wind at the beach!
Venezuela is a place to believe in you!!
Venezuela is a place to be you!!

Corina Gornes, Grade 4
FSU/City of Pembroke Pines Charter Elementary School, FL

Death
As you watch a dreadful death,
That person breathes their last breath.
And as you watch them in a daze,
As a mouse in a maze.

Then a question wonders your mind,
"Should I leave that person behind?"
And as the question escapes your thoughts,
They all say it was your fault.

Yes, they say it was you,
But it wasn't you, only some knew.
They knew it was death,
Who took that man's last breath.

As I lay there in fear,
I think, "I'm dying, oh dear!"
So please pass my story on and on,
Because sooner or later I will be gone.

Dalton Jacob, Grade 5
Sharon Elementary School, NC

Super Monkey
There once was a scientist named Norman.
He had a father who worked as a doorman.

Norman spent much time in the basement,
Experimenting with brain replacement.

One day Norman was feeling blue,
He decided to check out a kangaroo

So his dad drove him to the zoo,
In their car which was new

It was there when he first saw a monkey,
He had an idea that was kinda funky

After he found a way to sneak this monkey out,
His plan would work without a doubt

With a brain Norman built from scratch,
He would place it in the monkey's cranium hatch

It would be the world's first known,
"Super Monkey" straight out of Norman's home

Ethan Deal, Grade 5
Brooklet Elementary School, GA

Nature

Waterfalls big and small,
the beauty of them says it all.
Flowers blooming at various heights
such a beautiful, wonderful sight.

The moon, the stars,
that twinkle at night.
So big and bright,
just full of shimmering light.

The feeling of a cool breeze,
the movement and swaying of the trees.
Everything calm and at ease
that's what nature means to me.
Jessica Baumgartner, Grade 6
Seven Springs Middle School, FL

Spring

S unshine
P retty flowers
R eally sweet birds
I mpressive colors
N ice sky
G reen grass
Elisa Nixon, Grade 4
East Jones Elementary School, MS

Musical Amusement*

At the amusement park,
The many sounds make symphonies like
Nauseous people
On their knees.
Some sounds are loud
While zooming by
Like roller coasters in the air
I wonder what it's like up there.

Some sounds are bone-chilling
Like little toddlers
Crying
As they watch their
Balloons go flying.

Laughter,
Giggling,
Ooohs and aaahs
Make us want to take a pause
To breathe in all of the
Wondrous sounds that
Are here and there and
All around.
Jake Tobiczyk, Grade 5
Pinewood Acres School, FL
*Inspired by Arnold Adoff

Crying When I'm Alone

I can't be who I am
Got to keep it all inside
I smile to keep you happy
But alone I sit and cry

I smile to keep you happy
I smile when you're around
Whenever I cry
My life comes crushing down

You talk to me sometimes
Because you think you're cool
The next time you see me remember,
I'm a human being too
And I cry when I'm alone.
Alexis Spikes, Grade 4
Pine Tree Hill Elementary School, SC

The Track

Whoosh, they pass me
I don't care
And I keep running.

They call me slow,
I don't care
And I keep running.

They say I can't do it
I don't care
And I keep running

I get the medal,
I don't care
And I keep running.
Aaron Torop, Grade 6
Pinellas County Jewish Day School, FL

Whatif*

Last night while I lay thinking here
Some "whatifs" crawled inside my ear
And partied all night long
And sang their own "whatif" song
　Whatif houses frown
　Whatif we walked upside down
　Whatif I wore a beautiful coat
　Whatif I fell in an icky boat
　Whatif whales walked
　Whatif fish talked
　Whatif grass made honey
　Whatif I had real money!
Katherine Seamans, Grade 6
Challenger Middle School, FL
*Patterned after Shel Silverstein's
"What If"

This Isn't a Dream…Or Is It?

This isn't a dream…or is it?
I know you're gone now
Please can I feel your touch once more?
You come down to watch over me
Is this a dream?
Who knows?
It feels as if you're physically here
With me…right now
This isn't a dream…or is it?
Carlee Rosenblatt, Grade 6
Seven Springs Middle School, FL

This Morning

This morning I flew in the air,
Just like a bird flying in the sky.
This day I see every tree
Just like a flower.
I see the light just like the skylight.
I see the day every night
and birds flying in the bright sky.
Mackenzie Shore, Grade 4
Cool Spring Elementary School, NC

My Grandfather

My grandfather
my grandfather
oh how he can cook
the fried chicken and the corn
fish, turkey, then cornbread too
but unfortunately he has cancer
cancer cancer
oh how I hate that cancer
but luckily he's out of the hospital
that's only for now
Amonté Blocker, Grade 6
Saint Pauls Middle School, NC

Colors of the World

Brown is the making of a house
Grey is the color of a mouse

Purple is the color of a hair band
Tan is made for your hand

Red is the color of a box
Orange is made for a fox

Blue is the color of the sky
Yellow bee's my oh my

Green is a frog
White is the fog
Karina Gonzalez, Grade 6
Tequesta Trace Middle School, FL

Playing Baseball

Baseball is one of my favorite sports
You run, you hit, you catch, you play
And hitting a home run really makes my day.

Practice, practice, practice is key
The drills from the coach teach us just what we need.

Being part of a team is totally cool
You get to have fun with friends after school.

You learn to never give up and always try your best
And when you believe in yourself you pass the test.

Wesley Foster, Grade 4
Virginia A. Boone Highland Oaks Elementary School, FL

Words of Feeling

A world of beauty,
A song of love,
A time of sorrow,
A cloud up above,
And a place of beauty is filled with love.

A word that you cry,
Is a word that you want or don't want to hear,
A word that makes you smile,
Gives you a feeling of happiness inside,
A word that makes you happy is a great word indeed,
And a word that makes you sad,
It's a word we don't want to hear!

A world of beauty makes you smile,
A song of love makes you cry,
A time of love makes you happy,
A cloud in the clear blue sky,
And a place with words of all different kinds,
Just look and ask for it and you will find!

Tadd Evans, Grade 6
Immaculate Conception School, MS

Dancer's Feet

Dancer's feet are two of a kind
They are unique in their own way.
You cannot get them in short time
They are created like a potter molds his clay.

You have to work and work and work
They do not happen over night.
You have to practice, practice, practice
Until you get them just right.

At times they can be rough and tough
Or soft and painted pink
But most of the time especially after work
They just really, really stink.

Mary Margaret Dyches, Grade 6
Chapin Middle School, SC

The Race to the Veggies

Bouncing and pouncing here they come
jump jump jump run run run
I see a garden so let's get hoppin'
we're gonna get some veggies.
Yikes! Watch out for those hedgies.
Bound bound bound prance prance prance
run run run dance dance dance
we're gonna get those veggies first
so your little legs are now permanently cursed
Now we're winning run run run
Hey all those veggies are already gone
Ha ha ha we got here first
now your little legs are permanently cursed
we used our time to get away
and now we've eaten all the veggies for today.

Michele Lesley, Grade 5
Queen's Grant Community School, NC

Serving the Homeless

The old church, which gave hope,
was in the poorest part of town.
People were selling drugs on the corner street.
The kitchen was dirty, and it smelled moldy,
There were many bugs crawling around.
Shivers go through my body.
Sick crying babies in one dark room with 50 mattresses.
Gloomy church.
Hungry families waiting, watching movies.
Filthy hair salon in the middle of the kitchen.
I was helping to make food.
Asking 4 year old kids to drink expired lemonade.
Please God give these people a home.

Zac Smith, Grade 6
Lake Park Baptist School, FL

Lonely

When you are lonely you feel sad
Sometimes you start crying
Nobody is your friend
No one wants to talk to you
You feel like you are breaking apart
Alone, alone in a dark cruel world all-alone feeling lonely.

I have been lonely once
I know what it feels like
But I know that if you are feeling lonely
Don't be sad
Always know that Jesus is with you
Be kind
Be nice
People would like you
And you will never feel lonely ever again.

Emmanuel Okocha, Grade 6
Brogden Middle School, NC

I Learned
I learned that life is not always what it seems.
I learned that you should always trust your heart.
I learned right from wrong as I learned the rhythm of life.
I learned that friends don't always stay together as a never ending circle.
I learned to take life by the bull's horn no matter what comes at you.
I learned to accept people for who they are, not by their looks on the outside.
I learned that we're all in this together as a family or as a herd of animals.
I learned that dogs are a man's best friend when your world is blue and full of sorrow.
I learned that gold is not always a treasure, but that family is a true treasure.
I learned that a waterfall may not be the end product of many years of water action.
I learned that a baseball game may be fifty dollars, but a homerun is priceless.
I learned that deep down there is such a thing as everlasting love.
I learned that the end is just the beginning.

Marcus Frias, Grade 5
Northside Elementary School, SC

Valentine's Day
Good day, good day, are you happy, let's go to the movies or let's go to Austria or we can celebrate Valentine's Day. We need a lot of supplies and a lot of guests like your mommy, daddy or even your uncles and your aunts. Let's invite them quickly, so the time does not pass. Get the ribbons and get the hearts and let's have a party for our families' hearts. Last night we had a great time I hope you come again to celebrate Valentine's Day.

Harsh Patel, Grade 5
Trinity Lutheran School, FL

A True Friend Forever

I love you so much
We do a lot of things together,
We watch football,
We bet on games,
We play poker,
We go fishing, and we hang out together like were the best of friends.

What I like most is that you love sports…
Just like me.
You're so amazing to me,
Radiant with your smile
Fantastic, and always excited to see me.

Ever since you came from New Jersey
It has been so great to have you with us
I love it when we have our Sunday dinners
We have a great time and you make our whole family laugh.
You are a clown without makeup and the rest of that weird stuff.

I love it when I have a friend over and you, my dad, my friend, and I play poker.
I remember one time when I had my friend Nicky over, you acted like you didn't know how to play.
You said, "So if I have two aces what does that do?" We all folded.
But you really knew how to play, you just tricked Nicky and me
But now I know you really well, I love you so much

Ben Romer, Grade 6
Unity School, FL

High Merit Poems – Grades 4, 5, and 6

Pink
Pink is a small fire on a cold day.
Pink is a shy little girl up on stage.
Pink is a little boy outside on a cold rainy day.
Pink is a small puppy lost on the street.
Pink is a baby outside your door on a cold windy night
hoping that you will open the door for it.
Pink is a storm coming to your house.
Pink is a monster coming out from under your bed.
Pink is the best and saddest color of all.
Pink is your favorite color of all.

Diana Beltran, Grade 4
Youngsville Elementary School, NC

Hope Is…
Hope is a small bird in a giant blizzard
    Coming to you even when it seems impossible

Hope is a helping hand
    Helping you overcome your darkest fears

Hope is a polluted ocean
    Always trying to keep itself clean

Hope is a cheery friend
    Cheering you up when you feel rotten

Hope is an endangered species
    Trying to make a greater population each day

Hope is a cane
    That will never let you fall and never betrays you

Hope is a gift
    That you are happy to get and will use all year

Lillian Rodicio, Grade 4
Dante B Fascell Elementary School, FL

Relay for Life
A day of remembrance
And human endurance
Sharing ideals
Coming together as one
To declare the war on cancer will be won

Those who lost the battle against the disease
And left people behind with their hearts in pieces
Can take comfort watching from heaven
That this war has only just begun

For no disease can overcome
Love and passion from
The determination of humanity

Rahul Chittipeddi, Grade 6
Shorecrest Preparatory School, FL

A Vision for Peace
Peace on Earth is what I see.
What a priority this should be!
The sign is the winged dove.
Peace to me is care and love.

No more fighting, ugly words, or pranks.
No more hijacking or stealing from banks.
If we all strive to make Earth a better place,
We will discover brotherhood in the human race.

Isaac Wilks, Grade 6
Palm Harbor Middle School, FL

Color Feelings
Green is the grass blowing on a summer's day.
Yellow is a flower picked in May.
Red is an apple picked off a tree.
Blue is the fish swimming in the clear sea.
Orange is an orange cut into one slice.
White is me skating on the wonderful bright ice.

Simeon Coby, Grade 5
Coral Park Elementary School, FL

I Don't Understand
I don't understand
why people are racist
why people tell lies about each other
why we tell each others' secrets

But most of all
I don't understand why there are cliques
why people can't get along
why so many teenagers vandalize
why there are gangs

What I understand most is…
why we have friends and family.
why cats meow and dogs bark.
why night turns to day and day turns to night.
why the clouds move.

Nicole Hosmer, Grade 6
Turkey Creek Middle School, FL

Birds
Every day birds are chirping, as they dive and whirl,
Here and there, they dance and sing and swirl.

Everywhere you go, you see the birds they fly,
But if you scare them off, you'll be sure they'll say goodbye.

My mom had a noisy bird, and its name was Sunny,
One day the bird got on her nerves, so she traded it for a bunny.

As you can see we talked about birds, almost the whole day,
So why don't we take a break, what do you say?

Craig Ryu Hyatt, Grade 4
Grays Chapel Elementary School, NC

Ode to Chocolate Cake
Cake, O, Cake
How smooth your icing is.
How chocolaty and brown.
With a white cake center.
I wish I could eat you,
Day and night.
Your chocolaty flavor
Makes my mouth water.
Chocolate cake,
When people eat you
They start to hallucinate.
That is the power of chocolate cake.
Yum!!!
Taylor Coley, Grade 6
Advent Episcopal Day School, AL

In the Movie Theater
    in the movie theater
    there is the popcorn smell
    the rich buttery taste
    in the ginormous bucket
    in the movie theater
    there is the ice cold soda machine
    pouring out thirst-quenching Coke
    in the king size cup
    in the movie theater
    the best part of all
    is when the lights go dark
    and then suddenly the graphics pop up
    and the movie begins
Michelle Palumbo, Grade 6
Challenger Middle School, FL

Love Is…
A magnetic attraction between two.
Nonstop thinking about someone.
Warm kisses upon each other's lips.
Honest between each other.
Passionate love for each other.
Kaiven Humphrey Jr., Grade 6
Arlington Middle School, FL

Christmas
C hrist
H oliday
R unning
I nside
S creaming
T ogether
M any presents
A ll together
S URPRISE!
Dylan Searles, Grade 5
Ranburne Elementary School, AL

I Am in Love
I am in love
With this boy,
He has crystal
blue eyes,
every time I
get around him
I blush.
I like him
But I don't know
If he likes me.
I don't know what to do.
What should I do?
Should I tell him?
Or should I not?
Help me please!
Brittanie Bush, Grade 4
Freeport Elementary School, FL

Basketball
When I play basketball
It makes me feel good
When I bounce the ball
Up and down the court
I feel like I'm flying
That's why I like basketball
Olivia Nichols, Grade 5
Colerain Elementary School, NC

Summer
Summertime is very hot!
But when you get to go swimming
and have no school
it's the best time ever.
    You
      now
        know
          what
            summer
              is.
So have a lot of fun and have a nice
    Summer!
Rebecca Peabody, Grade 4
Spruce Creek Elementary School, FL

Country/City
Country
Quiet, open
Drive, planting, mooing
Building, water, people, food
Working, shopping, talking
Crowded, noisy
City
Catherine Cepeda-Mejia, Grade 6
Seven Springs Middle School, FL

An Ode to My God-Mother
Mother, oh mother
You are so pretty
You make me so happy
When I'm so sad
You're there when I need you
You taught me common sense
You teach me right from wrong
I will love you until I die
You're as good as it gets.
Timothy Jordan, Grade 5
Vienna Elementary School, NC

Friends
Adam
Neat, clean
Working, listening, thinking
Friend, brother, cousin, uncle
Playing, throwing, talking
Messy, dirty
Homero
Homero Bernal, Grade 5
Dover Elementary School, FL

Baseball
B ases to run
A cting crazy in the dugout
S tealing bases
E xciting when you win a game
B lood from sliding
A ll the people cheer for us
L ectures for bad plays
L ots of running
Clark Logan, Grade 4
Elba Elementary School, AL

Please Don't Go
It was one of those blue mornings,
I wake up and you're gone
I don't understand
I don't know what's happening
I feel like I'm swinging on a hammock
into a different world.
My fears are turning into tears.
What did I do?
What did I say?
I feel like something has taken me away
From one place to another,
I'm worried,
I'm afraid,
I don't know who I am anymore,
or who you are.
Please don't go.
Charlotte Koch, Grade 6
Gulf Stream School, FL

High Merit Poems – Grades 4, 5, and 6

My World
The world is built on our nation,
Restless people with determination
We shall never give up because we take risks,
Even as young blacks we endured prejudice.
Segregation is responsible for early life.
We were taken from our sons, loves ones, and even our wives.
It felt like carrying a load —
Our tireless pursuit of a goal.
But now we are all about peace.
Forever let my black butterflies be free!

Demetrius Lewis, Grade 6
M.A.T.S. Middle/High School, FL

Why?
Life is short, why not live it?
Money isn't going to last forever, so why not spend it?
Love is happiness, why not enjoy it?
These are the whys in life, so why not follow them?

Jordan Suber, Grade 6
McIntosh County Middle School, GA

Dishes
Washing dishes takes so long
I hope that I don't wash them wrong

It is always very boring
I sometimes feel like snoring

When it's my turn, there's always a lot
I just certainly cannot

But someone has got to wash those dishes
That I wish I had three wishes

Lloyd Verdeflor, Grade 6
St. Mary Magdalen Catholic School, FL

Penguins
Little and chubby, walking around
Flightless birds I love
Joyfully enjoying the feast they luckily found
All though penguins aren't as pretty as a dove

Flapping their wings
Wiggling their tails
Standing as they gracefully sing
Cautiously avoiding the arctic whales

Deep in my heart penguins have a place
Those little arctic birds are glued in my mind
If they were vanishing I would put one in a case
So there would be no memory of penguins left behind

Those birds are so dear to me
If I could see them I would pay the fee

Katie Ryan, Grade 4
PVPV/Rawlings Elementary School, FL

Blue
Blue sounds like rushing water of a waterfall
Blue is the taste of mouth watering blueberries
Blue is blue jays singing and dancing to their musical note
Blue is the smell of the saltwater sea
Blue is day, Blue is night
Blue is everywhere in sight
Blue is painted all around
Blue is calm, safe, and sound

Alexus Warren, Grade 4
Tabernacle Elementary School, NC

Cheaters
C razy jerks who
H ear or see your answers
E veryone is
A nnoyed by
T heir constant looking over your test
E njoy it while you can, but I won't
R esist from hurting you for long!!
S top looking at my answers!!! RAH!

Jacob Biltoft, Grade 6
Boiling Springs Intermediate School, SC

Brothers
Brothers are the very best
They always help you on your test
You love them like you love your dad,
And they never make you sad.
Sometimes they are really mean,
But at the end of the day you are thankful to
Have your brother around.

Kaitlyn Gonzalez and Madison Turcotte, Grade 5
St Martin Upper Elementary School, MS

Concerned Tree
I am a sad and sorrowful tree.
I look over the environment, oh woe is me.

Things now look trashed,
Beauty is smashed.

What you do leaves the earth destroyed.
Don't you think we trees are annoyed???

Trees are very depressed.
Just clean up and we'll do the rest!

Come help save the forest every day!
Even turning off the lights helps anyway!!!

So get out of the couch, roll up your sleeve,
Throw out the trash, oh please…please…please!!!

William Brown, Grade 4
William S Talbot Elementary School, FL

Sports
Basketball
Inside, court
Bounces, shoots, passes
Ball, gloves, shorts, jerseys
Shirts, cleats, pants
Outside, field
Softball

Football
Brown, oblong
Kicking, passing, scoring
Ball, white, small, round
Throws, hits, home runs
Outside, field
Baseball

Tilandra Staton, Grade 5
North Elementary School, SC

Markeia
M arvelous person
A wesome sister
R espectful child
K ind to people
E nergetic person
I nteresting
A rtistic child

(can do a split
all the way down)

Markeia Anderson, Grade 5
Winona Elementary School, MS

Spring
S pring break
P retty flowers
R epaint
I magine
N ice place
G arden

Zakyia Curry, Grade 4
East Jones Elementary School, MS

My Sister
My sister's name is Mindy.
She goes to North Georgia Tech.

If you try to go in her room
You just might break your neck.

You see her room is messy.
There's clothes all over the floor.

It reminds me of my own room
'Cause I can't even open my own door.

Mallory Cauley, Grade 5
Treutlen Elementary School, GA

Illinois
In my stand I sit, alone and carefree,
Awaiting what may emerge from this endless wooded sea.

While big oaks and friendly folks are common in this land,
A giant deer for which I'm here may be close at hand.

This land I speak of is Illinois, where deer are free to roam,
Though I live in South Georgia, I call it home away from home.

Gage Patton, Grade 6
Appling County Middle School, GA

Gina LaCarrubba
Gina
Tree hugger
Curious, artistic, jovial, Italian
Lover of animals, the environment, and my friends
Who believes that she can do anything she puts her mind to
Who wants global warming to stop, nothing more than a life,
and no more pain in the world
Who uses every minute of every day to live her life to the fullest,
her mind, and her heart
Who gives her brain to fill, her thoughts to the sky,
and her voice to the world
Who says live your life to the fullest no one gets out alive anyway
LaCarrubba

Regina LaCarrubba, Grade 6
Broad Creek Middle School, NC

I'm Talking Colorful!
I'm talking colorful!
I'm talking red!
I'm talking blue, black, brown!
I'm talking yellow, purple, pink, green!
I'm talking vivid, picturesque, bright, gay, rich!
I'm talking brilliant, strong, clear, distinct, splendid, flamboyant!
I'm talking glaring, dazzling, shining, brightness, intense!
I'm talking colorful!

Tyler Luttmann, Grade 4
Wellington School, FL

Talkin' Trash
Taking out the garbage is not the coolest thing to do,
Once a day, or once a week, it's still not that much fun for you.
When taking out that nasty stuff there're some tips I have for you;
Don't touch the garbage cans,
Don't wave to the garbage man,
Don't handle old pots and pans,
But ESPECIALLY don't take that slimy, grimy, no good garbage out!
(Oh yeah, don't wave to the mailman either, he shouts.)

Luke Cory, Grade 6
St Mary Magdalen Catholic School, FL

3 Strikes

Everyone watching me, waiting to see,
If I have what it takes,
To be the best, I know I can raise the stakes,
But first I need to throw 3,
I look at the batter I feel her eyes on me,
I won't let it make me throw so awfully,
I wind up to let it soar,
Then it started to downpour,
It didn't distract me,
The rain drew the batter batty,
So I threw my perfect 3,
And everyone couldn't believe

Savannah Elizabeth Clark, Grade 5
Grays Chapel Elementary School, NC

I Am

I am strong and unique.
I wonder what will cause a beat.
I hear the sound of typing rhythm.
I see the areas that are forbidden.
I want to become a vet someday.
I am strong and unique

I pretend that life is forever.
I feel just as light as a feather.
I touch the wooden desk of life.
I worry that a wrong will be right,
I cry about the problems of Earth.
I am strong and unique.

I understand nobody is perfected.
I say that everyone will be corrected.
I dream of swimming with the dolphins.
I try to succeed in tennis and mini-golfing.
I hope I will achieve my goals.
I am strong and unique.

Jessica Elia, Grade 6
North Myrtle Beach Middle School, SC

Scar

I was playing with my dad around the couch.
Until I felt something 'OUCH'.
I fall to the floor.
I almost hit the door.
My mouth tastes sour.
I sit their for an hour.
It felt like my cut was going to throw out my brain.
It felt like all my blood went down the drain.
My blood looked like squished cherry.
It was really scary.
My dad took me to the car.
What do you know, I still have my scar.

Jaasiel Figueroa, Grade 6
Challenger Middle School, FL

Jake

I have a dog his name is Jake
He is so small he can almost break

He has the most adorable eyes
When he barks it is a big surprise

When he gets bitten I know there is trouble
I check on him on the double

All he likes to do is run
He can never stop having so much fun

My dog is really crazy
I can never think of a time he was lazy

When he is in his cage he starts to whine
He does it every single time

Joseph Hastings, Grade 4
William S Talbot Elementary School, FL

Boredom

Boredom is white like nothing,
And also like seeing blank walls.
It is like just walking through my neighborhood.
It reminds me of the time when I was sitting
And watching the rain.
It makes me feel lonely like I have nothing to do.
It makes me want to find a new friend to play with.

Akash Shah, Grade 4
Indian Harbour Montessori Elementary School, FL

A White Mustang

In the valley below lay a horse
A mustang
Late in summer,
he ran from the valley to find a mate
Not just a mate
An Appaloosa
He searched the mountain peaks
the valleys
the forests
but no luck came
Late in summer
he came back to the valley to join the herd.

Heather Blakeslee, Grade 6
McRae Elementary School, FL

Life Itself

January, February, March.
That is how our life goes.
It is like a clock that goes slow when you want it to go fast
And goes fast when you want it to go slow.
No matter what life goes by fast in the end.
So use your life time wisely.

Amanda Deese, Grade 6
Gold Hill Middle School, SC

Tree Swallows
Their ability to use plant foods
Help them survive harsh weather.
They have great wingspans, like a hawk
Just look at all their feathers.

Open fields and woodland edges
That's where they live.
A beautiful song and ocean blue sight
That's what they give.

They're as graceful as a kite
They're an interesting crew,
They are like a sunset bright
And soar like a balloon.
Corbin Hoffman, Grade 5
Covenant Classical School, NC

Football
My name is Eric.
I like to play football,
I run like Reggie Bush
I run as fast as he to make a touchdown!
Eric Nguyen, Grade 5
St Martin Upper Elementary School, MS

The Ladybug
A ladybug that lived in a car,
Often dreamed of flying very far.
And then one windy day,
She quickly flew away,
Only to land in a giant jar!
Jessica Pettersen, Grade 6
Lake Park Baptist School, FL

Nichole
N ice
I ncredible
C hristian
H oly
O bey people
L ove one another
E njoyable
Nichole McLaurin, Grade 4
East Jones Elementary School, MS

Spring
S pring
P retty flowers
R ed bird
I nclusive
N ice
G round work
Holdin Dutton, Grade 4
East Jones Elementary School, MS

Candy
Candy is yummy
When I eat it I'm happy
Candy has color
Lollipops, mints all that fun
What should I start eating first?
Jillian Richter, Grade 5
The Sanibel School, FL

I Don't Understand
I don't understand
  why my bus driver hates me
  why we can't chew gum in school
  why we have homework

But most of all
  why some boys are jerks
  why some of my teachers are mean
  why we have to go to school
  why we take FCAT

What I do understand
  why softball is fun
  why the Earth rotates
  why we are alive
  why I have friends.
Kelli Tidwell, Grade 6
Turkey Creek Middle School, FL

To See an Angel Cry
My hand lay softly on an angel's wing
A song flows from her gentle lips
My spirit lifts as I listen to her sing

Then I slip back to land
And all Earthly troubles
Darkness, loneliness, demand

A tear slips from her eye
And one falls from mine, too
It tears your heart to see an angel cry
Gabrielle Arnold, Grade 6
Tarpon Springs Middle School, FL

My Friend
There is a little friend I know
  That's very very pretty.
She never ever needs a bath
  She's not the least bit gritty.
She started as a caterpillar
  And formed a great cocoon.
Then opened up and dried her wings
  She'll be flying home soon.
Hannah Levin, Grade 4
Lake Park Baptist School, FL

Color Wonders
White is my mom's wedding dress.
Grey is the dust that makes a mess.

Yellow is the shining sun.
Brown is my hamburger bun.

Black is my dog's wet nose.
Green is the color of my gardening hose.

Pink is a flamingo's wings.
Gold is the color of my sparkling rings.

Blue raindrops fall from the sky.
Tan is the hand that waves good-bye.
Kendra DeStefano, Grade 6
Tequesta Trace Middle School, FL

Converse
Converse
Very cool shoes
All different colors
They are very comfortable
The best
Cara McCurdy, Grade 6
St Mark's Lutheran School, FL

Gentle Dogs
G enerous pup
E nthusiastic pal
N ice and sweet
T o never sell
L oyal to your dog
E normous like a hog

D ependable to you
O bedient since she was two
G entle pup
S oothing pal
Christopher Vanlandingham, Grade 6
Arnold Magnet Academy, GA

Candy
Comes in all shapes and sizes,
Many come with some surprises.
All candy is very unique,
Under the wrapper hides a special treat.
Some is colorful, some is plain,
Some is striped like the candy cane!
All of us have our own flavor —
It is just our behavior.
All of it is quite dandy,
That's why we call it…candy!
Will Waldrop, Grade 4
Olde Providence Elementary School, NC

High Merit Poems – Grades 4, 5, and 6

New York City
The cameras
The action
The big city lights
The best place to be on a mid summer night
Yankees, landmarks, the Broadway plays
There are buildings so high you could look up for days
Central Park, carriage rides, the Plaza, Time Square
When you are in New York City, there's buzz in the air
Shopping 5th Avenue, you could see all the stars
When you turn every corner you hear the honking cars
So make sure that you visit this great shopping town
A weekend in New York City will never let you down

Halee Moore, Grade 6
Shorecrest Preparatory School, FL

Alone
I am a doll
laying on a pillow
in a dark and shadowy basement.
I hear a dull wind
blowing through the opened glass window.
   I wonder
if anyone will find me?
I am scared and frightened.
I hear a little mouse
squeaking in the distance
this basement
is so empty,
   empty
   empty.

Alex Hendren, Grade 4
Pinnacle Elementary School, NC

Kira
A dawn of golden sun
began that Sunday in October.
First comics, then pancakes,
came to the breakfast table.
A classified ad then caught my eye.
A Siberian Husky, with a
lovely coat and eyes.
We called, and arranged for the owner to bring her over.
When there came a knock on the door,
my heart stopped beating.
A lady first came in,
soon followed by Kira.
Kira was a beauty, true,
with a black and white coat
and eyes of blue.
She gave me a giant smile,
and I knew I had to keep her.
So we did, and, I'm happy to say,
we since have loved her,
to this day.

Samuel King, Grade 6
Lake Park Baptist School, FL

Vegetables
Crunchy, crispy, leafy and green
To make us eat them it seems really mean!!
Green beans, cabbage, and a carrot
The whole vegetable idea *isn't so hot*!!
Spinach and broccoli, they make your stomach turn
We'd be better off if only they'd *burn*!!
Snuck into places you'd never even see
Parents don't get it — kids and veggies — it'll *never* be!!
They stick them in your lunch
And they pack a whole bunch.
Drawing in and creeping close
Ah man they sure are gross!!
Fruits aren't so bad…between *just you and me*
But getting rid of veggies, *I'd finally be free*!!!

Morgan Gilmore, Grade 6
Boiling Springs Intermediate School, SC

Georgia on My Mind
Georgia Georgia on my mind
On my mind all the time,
I look out the window and see
The little kids grow-up like you me.

As some grow-up to be teachers and doctors
While some just like to be plain mockers,
I look up in the sky and down in the ground
I wonder if there's any sound.

I see kids and teenagers taking drugs
And I wonder if some of these are in mugs,
Sometimes Georgia can make me mopey and sad
But what I like is when it makes me glad.

So stand up, stand out
Say it loud and proud,
My life is in Georgia State
And I'm glad it's happening now!

Nicole Hill, Grade 6
Academy of Lithonia Charter School, GA

Springtime Beauty
Daffodils
springtime beauty
yellow that's vibrant
luminous, reflecting spring
glowing, resplendent, and brilliant
pleasing and exquisite; tangled and gnarled
twisted, neglected, and dirt covered
nestled in the soil and leaves
implanted and knotted
a tribute of spring
Weeds

Celia Mizelle, Grade 5
St Thomas More School, NC

If I Ruled the World
If I ruled the world,
I'd let everyone have freedom,
Try to keep our world in order,
And find a cure for cancer.

If I ruled the world,
There'd be no war,
No racism,
And plenty of homeless shelters.

If I ruled the world,
You wouldn't have to worry about terrorists,
You wouldn't have to suffer from natural disasters,
You wouldn't have to follow one religion,
Or live a certain way.

If I ruled the world.
Annie Schneider, Grade 6
Shorecrest Preparatory School, FL

Making Crepes with My Dad
Making crepes with my dad,
Makes me very, very glad.
Our crepes taste one hundred times better,
Than crackers with slices of sharp cheddar.
Our crepes have whipped cream and strawberries,
Maybe even sliced up cherries.
Making crepes is very fun,
They taste real good when the job is done.
Quinn McKemey, Grade 6
Gold Hill Middle School, SC

I Am
I am a fish; I never get caught
I am a deer; I walk through the woods
I am a four-wheeler; I ride and explore
I am a boat; I float through the water
I am a fishing pole; I catch the biggest fish
I am a deer stand; I watch for deer
I am a John Deere tractor; I never break down
I am a friend; I'm always there
Adam Woodall, Grade 5
Four Oaks Elementary School, NC

Boarding
I love skateboarding.
I love snowboarding.
I love to fall and get back up.
I love to crash and get bashed.
Sometimes it's a soft fall sometimes it's not.
So all of it's fun to me, even the falling and getting cuts
But I love it all for best or worst.
Caleb Bennett, Grade 6
Gold Hill Middle School, SC

Women
There are mothers, daughters, sisters and aunts
And the best of all has the best laugh

I will give you one hint, just one
She is sweet and kind and she can run

Now can you guess who it is?
If you can't here is one more hint.

You can love her, you can hug her
But you can't out run her.
Amanda Mazzie, Grade 6
Gold Hill Middle School, SC

I Am?
I am a truck, always strong
I am a fish, swimming along.

I am a gun, loud
I am a deer, cautious of my surroundings.

I am a four wheeler, real fast
I am a bulldozer, pushing my way through.

I am a helmet, protecting
I am a tree, tall, reaching for the stars.
Hunter Benson, Grade 5
Four Oaks Elementary School, NC

My New Year's Resolutions 2008
I have a lot of resolutions
There gonna turn into solutions

I would like to make new friends
We're gonna laugh like chicken hens

I want to do my homework good
Checking and checking, better I would

Those A's are gonna jump on my page
And my aunt's bird is in a cage

I would really, really, really like to read
More mystery books
To finally figure it out, see how it looks

I would like to keep my desk clean
Like a fresh swept floor, sparkly and keen

I want my toe touch high
Jumping and jumping, to the sky

My resolutions are really great
I can't wait to accomplish them in 2008
Mikayla Batton, Grade 5
Waccamaw Elementary School, SC

Let's Go
Look at that top!
It says stop.
Should we stop?
Maybe not.
Let's go!
Oh no!
Why not?
We might see a cop.
Let's go back!
We might see a sack.
So?
Let's go.
Where?
To see a bear.
Why?
So we can sigh.
Let's go!
Oh no!
Home?
Let's get gone.

Josh Smith, Grade 4
Camden Elementary School of the Creative Arts, SC

Poems
Poems are fun to write
but hard to describe
Silly willy and don't mean much
But hey!
You never know it could change our minds.

Gabriela Vilar, Grade 5
Eugenia B Thomas Elementary School, FL

Reggie Bush the Football Star
Reggie Bush runs far.
But he is the star.
He jumps and spins,
Just like the wind.
He jumps high,
When is his power going to die?
His name is Reggie Bush and that's who he is.
We all stand to take a glance.
His name is Reggie Bush.

Manuel Plancarte, Grade 6
Saint Pauls Middle School, NC

My Life
I love to play
I can do it all day
That's enough, it's time to pray
We do that five times a day
I love to pray
So I stay in the right way.

Abdullah Leka, Grade 4
Muslim Academy of Greater Orlando, FL

Whatif*
Last night, while I lay thinking here,
Some Whatifs crawled inside my ear,
And pranced and partied all night long,
And sang their same old Whatif song:
Whatif my hair turned green?
Whatif my eyes shot laser beams?
Whatif my arms turned into chicken wings?
Whatif my dog started to sing?
Whatif I got really mad?
Whatif my mom got really sad?
Whatif my brother was mean?
Whatif my face turned green?
Everything seems swell, and then,
The nighttime Whatifs strike again!

James Semiken-Gardner, Grade 6
Challenger Middle School, FL
*Patterned after "Whatif" by Shel Silverstein

Queen Bee and Her Royal Prince
"she" is queen bee — "at least she thinks" —
she has all the clothes, jewelry, and shoes
but most of all she has HIM, the royal prince

the boy that all the girls dress-up to impress
the boy everybody says "they don't" love…
the boy everybody talks about and loves

on the other hand — queen bee that is —
the bee who won't let anyone touch her prince
"we" can't talk to him, "we" can't look at him
what's a girl to do

the queen bee doesn't know
but secretly he's dating someone else
no one has told, cause nobody knows

and finally, it leads down to this — "the day"
the day every girl has been waiting for…
"THE BREAK-UP DAY"

every girls dream has finally been reached
and every girl has figured out we're all…
QUEEN BEES

Brooke A. Forsyth, Grade 5
Ranburne Elementary School, AL

Jomisha
J uicy is my name
O rganized is my game
M y favorite sports are soccer and volleyball
I nteresting as in funny
S mart in school
H elpful for my mom and teachers
A ngel as in cute

Jomisha Dietrich, Grade 6
Arnold Magnet Academy, GA

My Grampster

One of my favorite memories with my Grampster is when I was a youngster and I would go to his house
on sunny spring days and assist him in planting the coral impatiens in the garden.
The garden smelled so fresh and fragrant. Grampster was ready to work with me tirelessly
with a tremendous smile on his face.
Grampster is a busy bee, so very active in his community. He is very artistic and demonstrates it in his photography.
When you look at his pictures, you can almost feel like you are there. His photographs are eye-popping!
His demeanor is pleasant and calm.
Grampster is a very sentimental man he cherishes every memory!
He also likes to try and do new things.
He is certainly a marvelous cook and creates luscious recipes like Picasso created paintings.
Grampster is always up on the latest news gathering information about politics and celebrities.
He delights in all his adorable Labrador Retrievers taking long walks with his faithful companions.
He is a skinny man with short gray hair.
And so cheerful that he always wears a smile
Grampster is one-in-a-million. He has a heartwarming laugh
and all his grandchildren adore him greatly. He always makes everyone feel special.
Whenever I see his glowing face at one of my performances,
I feel like a star on Broadway that he came to see me.
Grampster is like an eager beaver always bustling and working on his projects.
But, he also enjoys his quiet time and hankers for a good book or movie —
Just like me!

Elise Emord, Grade 6
Unity School, FL

You Are Always There

You are always their
You're there when I am weak
You care when I am sick
You lift me up when I am down
You cover me with your love
When I am cold
The love that we share is so special
Your love will follow me through all of my troubles
You protect me when I am in danger
That's why I am so happy
The tears that I cry is always full of joy that's how I know that I could never even ask for any more.

Kimberly Whyte, Grade 6
Varsity Lakes Middle School, FL

But Yet We Are Different

We all live in different places. we come from different races.
We all can hear a bird sing and share the same feelings and pains.
But yet we are different.
The way we talk is not the same. Nor the way we learn or entertain.
We can all enjoy the smell of spring and take a walk out in the rain.
But yet we are different.
We do not worship in the same manner nor do we pledge to the same banner.
We embrace; we hug and show acts of love. We gaze and wonder about the stars above.
But yet we are different.
We live in different countries and far away lands. But yet we are bound together with the shake of a hand.
We care about others and their needs. We show this love through our good deeds.
But yet we are different.
Like links of a chain we are connected and share many things.
But yet we are different.

Bradford Lemmons, Grade 6
Hand Middle School, SC

My Horse
Beautiful, fast, majestic
All of the words I could use
Flowing manes that shine when the sun hit it
Their tails blowing in the wind, full and healthy
Their fur glows and feels like a silk pillow

Their muscles strong and amazing
They run with the wind in their hair
Their hooves beating the ground
Their eyes filled with spirit

Their strong amazing head,
With the eyes of a tiger,
But a gentle soul
Their nostrils flaring with rage
Is my horse.

Kyle Neill, Grade 6
Gold Hill Middle School, SC

Index

Abbott, Samantha 81
Abreu, Boris 157
Abrigo, Luke 144
Acebo, Jenelle 219
Acosta, Kenny 50
Acosta, Vivian 149
Adams, DaraGracen 159
Adams, Isaiah 152
Adams, Olivia 88
Adams, Olivia 190
Adkison, Kris 36
Agnew, Lukas 199
Aguayo, Alejandro 173
Ahrens, Damien 115
Akhtar, Saad 99
Akinin, Arie 117
Albaugh, John 217
Alcantara, Massiel 239
Alesna, Nina 227
Alexander, Kaitlin 66
Alexander, Stephen 182
Alford, TaKizah 223
Alford, Tristan 197
Ali, Korisha 221
Allen, Alex 182
Allen, Julia 62
Alspaugh, Campbell 34
Altieri, Josiah 235
Altnor, Alfredo 169
Alvarado, Dante 128
Alvarenga, Mario 42
Amberson, Jace 120
Amick, Courtney 168
Anders, Dakota 114
Anderson, Bridgett 113
Anderson, Jacob 159
Anderson, Jalon 121
Anderson, Jaron 121
Anderson, Lindsay 88
Anderson, Markeia 250
Anderson, Nia 207
Andreoni, Regina 163
Andres, Rosalinda 63
Andrews, Chloé 28
Andrews, Karli 175
Andrews, Sam 109
Anselmo, Alec 194
Anselmo, Brandon 206
Anthony, Isaiah 184
Applegate, Emma 163
Applegate, Julia 216

Araujo, Ricardo 122
Arce, Natalie 237
Arceneaux, Hailey 102
Archbold, Megan 76
Argimón, Gabrielle 138
Armbrister, Ashlee 194
Armendariz, Christian 129
Arnay, Fernanda 130
Arnold, Gabrielle 252
Arrowood, Cody 228
Arthur, Alex 202
Ascik, Carly 144
Ashby, Robbie 136
Ashman, Mykel 132
Asmar, David 30
Atkins, Emily 39
Atkins, Tori 157
Atkinson, Katherine 14
Atwater, Breonna 152
Austin, Nikki 234
Austin, Sierra 98
Austin, Smith 202
Austin, Yonah 230
Austrie, Kishon 148
Autry, Amber 105
Avritt, Journey 78
Aza, Lauren 216
Badgett, Victoria 108
Baek, Soo .64
Bagley, Demario 111
Bailey, Brandon 166
Bailey, Gavin 50
Bailey, Molley 217
Baker, Kristen 125
Balceiro, Arianna 67
Baldwin, Jacob 158
Ball-Gonzalez, Anais 112
Ballejos, Lauren 188
Ballou, Emilia 69
Balmer, Britney 179
Bang, Victoria 178
Bannister, Mary 199
Banyard, Sara 142
Bar-Haim, Joshua 122
Barahona, Bridget 130
Barnes, Ashlei 178
Barr, Robby 94
Barre, Alyssa 47
Barrick, Andrea L. 99
Barry, Lane 72
Bassett, William 220

Basye, Jordan 116
Bateman, Melody 101
Bates, Elizabeth 196
Batton, Mikayla 254
Baughn, Will 116
Baumgartner, Jessica 244
Bausert, Nadine 238
Baxter, Allyson 80
Beadle Goliber, Skylar 73
Bean, Brianna 242
Beane, Kaitlin 235
Beasley, Amber 152
Beasley, Angela 50
Beattie, Macey Laine 48
Beckham, Griffin 164
Beckley, Asya 145
Beech, Hannah 50
Beecher, Luke 140
Beeco, Drew 84
Belgrano, Nathalia 190
Bell, Travis 80
Belt, Susanna 91
Beltran, Diana 247
Belue, Shelbi 49
Benard, Deionna 65
Bender, Brendan 87
Bendfeldt, Samantha 179
Benedict, Catherine 151
Benefield, Tristen 220
Bengtson, Sawyer 241
Bennett, Caleb 254
Bennett, Jesse 151
Benson, Hunter 254
Benson, Jasmine 139
Bent, Dylan 231
Berg, Amanda 90
Bermingham, Aidan 42
Bermingham, Aidan 126
Bernal, Homero 248
Bernstein, Jason 120
Berry, Kevin 100
Bertot, Caila 211
Bexley, Camille 131
Bhagat, Zainab 170
Bhakta, Shiv 120
Biedenharn, Elaine 141
Biggs, Corey 229
Bilden, Theodore 180
Bilden, Tommy 33
Biltoft, Jacob 249
Bingham, Takara 67

Bitting, Caitlin 183	Brower-Lingsch, Adam 176	Cardwell, Lauryn M. 82
Bivins, Brittany 95	Brown, Allyson 210	Cariello, Lindsey 102
Black, Henry 115	Brown, Gabrielle 52	Carlton, Harry 80
Blackburn, Kirsten 50	Brown, Jamie 219	Carmean, Justin 68
Blackwelder, Katie 132	Brown, Jared 85	Carpenter, Seth 197
Blair, Olivia 179	Brown, Johnny 106	Carr, Megan 196
Blair, Sydney 28	Brown, Morgan 84	Carroll, Lauren 39
Blakeslee, Heather 251	Brown, Olivia 58	Cartee, James 242
Bloch, William 152	Brown, Talike 198	Carter, Kim 176
Blocker, Amonté 244	Brown, Tamia 194	Carter, Maggie Laura 104
Blumberg, Jared 140	Brown, Tyler 206	Carter, Phillip 217
Blyler, Nehemiah 30	Brown, William 39	Carter, Teeara 200
Board, Drew 196	Brown, William 249	Caskey, Adam 25
Bobbitt, Megan 240	Bryant, Caitlin 164	Cassada, Raleigh 154
Bodford, Travis 226	Bryant, Jasmine 150	Castellon, Emely 78
Bodtmann, Jacob 237	Bryson, Chelsea 126	Castille, Caitlyn Alexandra 157
Bogerd, Emma 128	Bryson, Trevin 180	Castillo, Abigail 141
Bolivar, Daniela 188	Buchanan, Emma 202	Castizo, Yesenia 45
Bollock, William 80	Buchanon, Jared 131	Caswell, Jade 162
Bona, Zoe 95	Bueno, Cassandra 144	Catarino, Jose 114
Bond, Christopher 239	Bui, Jasmine 100	Catledge, Katelyn 82
Bone, Carlton 206	Bullard, Kameron 172	Cauley, Mallory 250
Bonham, Becca 132	Bullard, Savanna 226	Cauthen, Chandler 159
Book, Bianca 192	Bullen, Victoria 185	Cavanaugh, Tyler 27
Boone, Sarah 196	Bunker, Sara 206	Cepeda-Mejia, Catherine 248
Booth, Willis 77	Burbank, Anna 79	Cervantez, Noel 80
Borden, Laurie 196	Burchette, Daniel 62	Cesar, Veronika 121
Borders, Nathan 131	Burnette, Emily 180	Ceto, Bradley 24
Boria, Gian 89	Burns, Zachary 141	Chandler, Christian 32
Borsch, Corrine 164	Burt, Edwona 172	Chandler, Sherlee Q. 53
Bosarge, Todd 80	Bush, Brittanie 248	Chang, Joseph 88
Bost, Caylen 46	Butler, Quinisha 81	Chapman, Keara 26
Bowers, Kaelah 151	Butler, Sarah 105	Charre, Carlos 35
Bowman, Summer 34	Butts, Eliza 221	Chase, Alex 106
Boyd, J. 83	Byars, Jonathan 160	Chavez, Joshua 192
Boyd, James 222	Byers, Stephanie 223	Chenet, Nikolai 127
Bozo, Maria 93	Bynum, Kiana 211	Cherney, Shannon 92
Bradburn, Josh 74	Byrd, Chyna 51	Cherry, Frank 61
Bradford, John 234	Byrd, Kennedy 137	Cherry, Tonya 216
Bradley, Aaron 44	Cabe, Aaron 111	Chewning, Reagan 63
Brainard, Kyle 49	Cabrera, Seidy 88	Chittipeddi, Rahul 247
Bralich, Christine 236	Cain, Jonathan 41	Christensen, Shelby 98
Branch, Daniel 143	Calderon, Esteban 232	Christensen, Tyler 178
Brandrick, Dylan 143	Calhoun, Destin 116	Christian, Jessica 60
Brannen, Rachel 180	Calhoun, Morgan 194	Christman, Micah 27
Brennan, Kristina 148	Call, Katherine 206	Chupp, Emily 69
Brewer, Hogan 222	Callais, Connor 92	Churbuck, Amy 168
Bridgeman, Seth 200	Callaway, Nick 123	Churchwell, Fear 62
Bright, Cassie 116	Calvo, Sofia 183	Ciaccia, Andrew 64
Britt, Hannah 154	Campana, Rafael 138	Cisco, Ashely 186
Broadbent, Grace 119	Campbell, Khyra 239	Clark, Haley 165
Broadhurst, Bryan 186	Campos, Esmeralda 137	Clark, Joey 71
Broadnax, Daniel 40	Canino, Michael 200	Clark, Savannah Elizabeth 251
Broadnax, Shareba 222	Cannady, Jashea 145	Clarke, Emma 44
Brockway, Garrison 113	Capshaw, Natalie 236	Clay, Hayden 210
Brooks, Kyle 169	Caradine, Maya 62	Clayton, Ella 170
Brosius, Anna 87	Cardenas, Kristen 32	Clayton, Kaleb 81

Index

Clement, Bobby Y. 219
Cline, Emily 176
Clytus, Janay 237
Cobb, Desilyn 225
Coby, Simeon 247
Cocozziello, Jenna 241
Cody, Isabella 190
Coe, Taylor 150
Coghan, Madison 118
Cohen, Jocelyn 176
Coit, Nissa 222
Cole, A.J. 115
Coleman, Mikayla 98
Coley, Taylor 248
Colley, Damian 25
Collier, Jessica Lynn 80
Collins, Haily 194
Collinsgru, Anna 229
Collison, Kaitlin 73
Combs, Anna 172
Compton, Chase 235
Comrie, Cameron 15
Congress, Joshua 181
Congress, Kelsey 117
Conrad, Christina 109
Conrad, Jonathan 152
Cook, Colton 24
Cook, Whittney 192
Coolican, Shay 114
Coons, Chandler 101
Corbitt, Shelby 28
Corder, Bayley 181
Cordoba, Graciela 227
Cordova, Brandon 170
Corrigan, Jacob 43
Cory, Luke 250
Costner, Sara 116
Cox, Brian 120
Cox, Callahan 190
Cox, Isaiah 59
Cox, Kyle 125
Cox, Madison 238
Craig, Dara 85
Craig, Jonathan 231
Cravey, Clayton 135
Crews, Kaila 71
Cribbs, Seth 29
Crimi, Mallory 129
Crisp, Kelly 79
Crocker, Laura Jane 16
Crockford, William 199
Cromley, Sam 222
Cronin, Megan 34
Crosby, Sean 205
Cross, Tabatha 153
Crow, Hannah 25
Crowdis, Katt 197
Crowe, Cierra 109
Crowley, Hayden 132
Crownover, Jonathan 178
Cuadra, Rene 201
Cue, Denecia 26
Cummings, Casey 55
Cummings, Megan 112
Curis, Cole 80
Curry, Zakyia 250
Curtis, Sarah 24
D'Amato, Gabrielle 220
Dalton, Sydney 38
Daly, Cameron 130
Daly, Heather 176
Daneault, Allison 92
Danford, Jaymie 237
Daniel, Dylan 83
Daniel, Joanna 49
Daniels, Chase 168
Daniels, Chelsey 77
Das, Dillon 36
Das, Shourik 31
Davenport, Javan 189
David, Nicole 128
Davis, Cassidy 162
Davis, Chelsey 238
Davis, Collin 89
Davis, Dalton 47
Davis, Dustin D. 177
Davis, DyneQua 91
Davis, Gina 75
Davis, Leyshaun 107
Davis, Tamrah 60
Davis, Trenton 60
Davis, Tyler 180
Davis, Zac 30
Dawkins, Michaela 124
Dawkins, Talia 44
Dawson, Bayley 184
Dawson, Dakota 55
de la Torre, Joserlys Adriana 65
Deal, Ethan 243
Dean, Tabitha 39
Dear, Allison 30
Deese, Amanda 251
Delgado, Michael 208
Delgado, Thomas 207
Delorme, Darrin 52
Denmeade, Emily 126
Derr, Sydney 207
Derrickson, Rachel 128
DeSilva, Sashinya 160
DeStefano, Kendra 252
Destino, Anna 128
Detlefsen, Rachel 44
DeVita, Adam 178
Deweese, Destiny 140
Dewey, Libby 81
Diaz, Alessandro 62
Diaz, Andrew 105
DiCristo, Alyssa 177
Diepenbrock, Arielle 24
Dietrich, Jomisha 255
Dieudonne, Djwaidah 95
Digney, Matthew 102
DiJorio, Brianna 203
Dills, Matthew 148
Dixon, Dylan 105
Dixon, Flint 193
Dixon, Jacob 82
Dixon, Makayla 215
Dodson, Zana 144
Dolzonek, Shawna 90
Domond, Kezia 133
Dorcely, Madeline 81
Dowling, James 216
Doyle, Clare 98
Doyle, Jacob 132
Doyle, William 183
Drake, Kaelyn 108
Drayton, Tyler 46
Drennan, Matthew 130
Driessen, James 185
Duarte, Juan 80
Duffield, Mallory 149
Duffy, Megan 70
Duggan, Tykirea 133
Duggins, Morgan 242
Duke, Chelsea 212
Dunbar, Andrew 72
Duncan, Stephanie 116
Dunsmore, Kate 208
Dunston, Fredrick 184
Dupper, Ashley 180
Dupuis, Leonie 50
Durley, Justine 167
Dutton, Holdin 252
Dyches, Mary Margaret 245
Eades, Anna 240
Eargle, Koury 103
Earle, Jonathan 48
Earley, Mattie 240
Earnest, Savana 216
East, Tylar 110
Easterling, Armani 46
Eazor, Timmy 88
Echelson, Zachary 27
Edmondson, Kayla 181
Edwards, Brandon 226
Edwards, Danielle 104
Edwards, Tamar 56
Efird, Dakota 105
Egbebike, Jennifer 178
Egly, Erik 79

Elia, Jessica 251	Fornes-Neuharth, Andre 89	Gatewood, Rachel 101
Elias, Caitlin 100	Fornes-Neuharth, Ariana 149	Gatlin, Madison 154
Elkabbany, Ciara 235	Forrest, Jaquavious 126	Ge, Beverly 53
Elliott, Kaleb 151	Forsyth, Brooke A. 255	Gehring, Jessica 220
Ellis, Sara 116	Fortenberry, Courtney 234	Gehris, Brandon 44
Elmore, Logan 82	Fortenberry, Donneil 192	Gell, Emily 138
Ely, Emma 42	Fortenberry, Travis 64	Gelman, Tyla 33
Emery, Maggie 133	Foskey, Haile 153	Genius, Marc 239
Emord, Elise 256	Foster, Anna 42	Gentry, Kaelin 189
English, Alisha 65	Foster, Bridget 41	Gibbs, Caroline 111
Epting, April 61	Foster, Briona 187	Gibson, Mark 206
Ertel, Taylor 24	Foster, Diamond 74	Gilbert, Kennedy 144
Ertzberger, Jacob 81	Foster, James 90	Giles, Bailey 176
Escobar, David 35	Foster, Wesley 245	Gill, Zane 66
Eslick, Liz 130	Fox, Molly 218	Gillespy, Bailey 50
Esp, Shawna 189	Foxworth, Cameron 154	Gillette, Chelsea Grace 107
Espinal, Eber-Andres 59	Foxworth, Remington 233	Gillis, Perry 29
Espinoza, Andrea 144	Franceschina, Brittany 184	Gilmore, Morgan 253
Estermyer, Emily 100	Francis, Mariah 36	Girard, Colton 65
Eubanks, Emily 212	Franco, Grace 203	Glass, Amanda 141
Evangelista, Selene 150	Franco, Natalie 233	Gleason, Ryan 40
Evans, Katlyn 181	Frank, Garet 30	Glenn, Rachel 213
Evans, Tadd 245	Franks, Ethan 235	Glick, Hannah 106
Evans, Travon 37	Frantz, Michael 162	Glickman, Carri 232
Faber, Katie 68	Frederick, Camille 197	Glover, Callie 161
Fairley, Yasmine 69	Freeze, Jamie 196	Glover, Coronda 62
Farese, John 91	French, Jenna 122	Glover, Leila 175
Farinas, Jane 199	Frias, Marcus 246	Godinez, Miriam 43
Farrow, Dustin 56	Friloux, Olivia 142	Goins, Breanna 29
Farson, Alec 172	Fritch, Danney 139	Golden, Ben 113
Fason, Jordan E. 35	Fritz, Chris 219	Goldman, Angel Lynn 183
Felton, Taylor Michelle 158	Fuller, Lucy 143	Goldstein, Manya S. 208
Fenwick, Courtney 172	Fulp, Caleb 42	Goldwyn, David 175
Fernandez, Alexander 218	Furtick, Christie 209	Gomes, Patrick 241
Fernandez, Danny 33	Futrell, Kayla 128	Gomez, Jazlee 215
Fernandez, Veronika 90	Gaines, Tatyana 147	Gomez Cochran, Meranda 68
Field, Patrick 97	Gaither, Clarissa 180	Gonzalez, Chloe 145
Fields, Max 168	Gallagher, Andrew 153	Gonzalez, Kaitlyn 249
Figueroa, Jaasiel 251	Galletti, Wilbert 101	Gonzalez, Karina 244
Finn, Maddie 236	Gamble, Joanna 40	Gonzalez, Luis 224
Firstman, Robbie 29	Gammons, Austin B. 55	Gonzalez, Nicholas 68
Fischer, Zack 110	Gangasani, Nikhil R. 195	Gonzalez, Xavier 48
Fishel, Sarah 84	Gano, Katelyn 153	Goosby, Terriyana 60
Fisher, Brianna 72	Gantt, Jordan 104	Gordon, Aaliyah 128
Fisher, Hayli 28	Garber, Justin 57	Gordon, Derek 213
Fissenden, Savannah 227	Garcia, Agustin 72	Gordon, Khandis 143
Fletcher, Courtney Marie 242	Garcia, Alana 48	Gorman, Ryan 228
Flick, Christian 138	Garcia, Jesus 72	Gornes, Corina 243
Flint, Tyler 92	Garcia, Kirver 167	Gorowitz, Amy 138
Florczak, Spence 27	Garib, Janeen 131	Gouhin, Nicole 30
Flowers, Christian 35	Garlock, Cheyenne 201	Graham, Alyssa 178
Floyd, Dashon 156	Garmager, Tricia 84	Granados, Luis 112
Flynt, Emily Shae 165	Garner, Cole 190	Granger, Hans 188
Foley, Kyle 133	Garren, Hailee 161	Grant, Hannah 96
Folmar, Ada 43	Garrett, Rylee 46	Grant, Mary Beth 49
Fontaine, Natalie 158	Garrison, McKenzie 69	Graves, Savannah 209
Forgy, Meghan 107	Garrison, TreVion 168	Gray, Amanda 234

Index

Gray, Jade 190
Gray, Montressa 213
Green, Caleb Nathaniel 56
Green, Jamie 53
Green, Jessica 74
Green, Kate 220
Green, Tommy 58
Green, Will 55
Greenberg, David 144
Greene, Phoebe 192
Greene, Sarah 159
Greer, Victoria 146
Griffin, Anna 151
Gronowski, Volandou 204
Gross, Jevanté 181
Guiney, Grayson R. 126
Guinther, Morganne 205
Gunn, Rose 196
Gunning, Alexis 126
Guy, Trace 122
Gwyn, Deantae 233
Hagey, Ragan 206
Haines, Pierson 160
Haizlip, Kelsey 219
Hall, Brandon 44
Hall, Darnell 112
Hall, Diane 126
Hall, Kiyhanna 163
Hall, Lindsey 43
Hall, Shacoria 64
Hall, Tanner 123
Hallman, Matthew 91
Hamby, Joshua 155
Hamer, Valerie E. 229
Hancock, Elizabeth 220
Hansen, Emily Dawn 30
Hansen, Maren 192
Hanson, Taylor 55
Hargrave, Heather 208
Harper, Rachida 219
Harrell, Samantha 160
Harriman, Paige 139
Harrington, Kenneth 68
Harris, Jonathan 118
Harris, McKay 225
Harrison, Bridge 63
Harrison, Luke 168
Harrison, Taylor 120
Harter, Michelle 44
Harvey, Chad 236
Haskin, Kayleigh 158
Hastings, Joseph 251
Hasty, Rhett 227
Hatten, Colby 83
Hauck, Jared 233
Hawkins, James 30
Hawthorne, Devon 242

Haynes, Aaliyah 172
Hays, Lane 187
Hayworth, Alicia 34
Hearn, Keith 29
Heath, Candace 70
Heathcock, Micah 226
Hecht, Kaley 139
Heggins, Madison 51
Heinz, Olyvia 25
Heinz, Taylor 238
Helms, Micah 200
Hemmingsen, Madeline 243
Hemmit, Haley 128
Hemphill, Foster 94
Henderson, Jackson 48
Henderson, Jazmin 80
Henderson, Thomas 45
Hendren, Alex 253
Henley, Breana 45
Henley, Elizabeth 124
Henry, Joanna 232
Henry, Kristin 112
Henry, Trevor 226
Hensley, Vanessa 112
Hentz, Samantha 90
Hepner, Kristen 57
Herb, Courtney 31
Herb, Sarah 127
Hernandez, Alan 45
Hernandez, Armando 211
Hernandez, Kayla 207
Hernandez, Lourdes Perez 203
Hernandez, Mirian 82
Hernandez II, Joel 108
Herndon, Tabby 24
Herrin, Chelsey 201
Herrod, Charnita 209
Hettinger, Andrew 157
Hicks, Caleb 158
Higgason, Cameron Brooke 184
Higgins, Avery 76
Higgs, Ben 242
Hill, Jackson 184
Hill, Jenna 234
Hill, Nicole 253
Hill, Shelby 211
Hill, Trenton 155
Hinds, Nicholas 203
Hinkle, Alex 138
Hinshaw, Trevor 208
Hinson, Ashley 41
Hinton, D'Ahra 198
Hinton, Katelyn 220
Hipp, Eric 102
Ho, Lena 90
Hobbs, Matthew 112
Hobbs, Zachary 162

Hochmeister, Heather 223
Hodge, Gavin 62
Hoeun, Richard 94
Hoffman, Corbin 252
Hoffmann, Catherine 190
Hoffner, Grant 66
Holihan, Nora 184
Holland, Taylor 174
Holland, Will 54
Holloway, Lacey 74
Holman, Savannah 202
Holmes, Nathaniel 57
Holshouser, Savannah Rose 92
Honeycutt, Richard 72
Hood, Karrizma 96
Hood, Matthew 24
Hopkins, Jules Pierre 145
Horner, Caitlin 164
Horton, Alyssa 137
Horton, Courtney 161
Horton, Jacob 83
Hosmer, Nicole 247
Hossein, Riisa 84
Houston, James 40
Howard, Santremica 44
Howell, Ashlyn 194
Howell, Ashton 236
Howell, Connor 188
Huayllas, Shoshana 113
Hudson, Blake 129
Hudson Jr., Tommie 204
Hughes, Bradley 123
Hughes, William 196
Huhn, Madeleine 112
Humphrey Jr., Kaiven 248
Humphries, Elizabeth 95
Hunt, Casey 176
Hunt, Sabeth 92
Hunter, Kayla 156
Hupe, Cori 221
Huskey, Madison 196
Huskins, Jesse 152
Hutchens, Summer 205
Hutchins, Ashley 162
Hutchison, Sean 119
Hutson, Collin 67
Hyatt, Craig Ryu 247
Hyler, Breana 204
Hylton, Jessica 167
Ibarra, Gavino 162
Ibarra, Yasmin 210
Imler, Peri 162
Imm, Shane 168
Irwin, Allison 105
Isbell, Katelin LaRee 192
Izmaylov, Nicole 238
Izquierdo, Kelly 171

Jacks, Ashley 237	Keene, Adrianna 184	Lance, Antares 149
Jackson, Denitra 118	Keenum, Elizabeth 195	Lance, Milan 63
Jackson, Lakeland 114	Keith, Alexis 184	Lange, Megan 35
Jackson, Matthew 99	Keith, Andrew 75	Langley, Brittney 217
Jacob, Dalton 243	Kelley, Jessica 197	Langston, Trey 148
Jacob, Jessica 212	Kelly, Ayanna 59	Lanier, Rachel 60
Jacobs, Garrett 174	Kemmerlin, Kasey 149	Larsen, Anna 154
Jacques, Henock 194	Kemp, Carter 241	Larsen, Emily 200
Jaimes, Krystal 89	Kemp, Trey 84	Larsen, Isabella 129
James, Savanna 222	Kemp, Wailes 103	Lawrence, Briona 165
Jamieson, Clare 144	Kendrick, Thomas 140	Lawson, Hannah 224
Jamison, Carrie 24	Keokhamdy-Saechao, Tacerrah . . .198	Layton, Jana 28
Jan, Sahar 169	Kerwin, Riley 110	Le, Michelle 125
Jankie, Cierra 116	Kethan, Charli 195	Leal, Nathlie 111
Jefferson, Alexius 124	Kidd, Stephanie 111	Leaphart, Brett 34
Jenkins, Jordan 144	Kihumba, Leah 116	Leavengood, Alice 59
Jenkins, Madison 135	Kilgore, Madison 193	Lebo, Kajsa 235
Jenkins, Tony 215	Killebrew, Sydney 233	Lee, Brady 64
Jensen, Jason 128	Kim, Jina 100	Lee, Courtney 164
Jent, Andrew 242	Kimmel, Alexa 134	Lee, Jessica 71
Johns, Alexis Nevada 28	Kimple, Kara 61	Lee, Shayla 128
Johnson, Alan 113	King, Ashley 148	Lee, Tavijae 110
Johnson, Blake 94	King, Austin 46	Legagneur, Kevin 234
Johnson, Breanna 158	King, Britney 225	Leka, Abdullah 255
Johnson, Chris 37	King, Julie 95	Lemmons, Bradford 256
Johnson, Dominique 62	King, Marli 240	Lennertz, Parker 105
Johnson, Ellen 208	King, Samuel 253	Lenox, Devin 177
Johnson, Hunter 31	Kingaby, Elizabeth 191	Lesley, Michele 245
Johnson, Jamin 148	Kinter, Marialana 80	Lesure, Jacques 210
Johnson, Laney 230	Kivett, Michaela 220	Levan, Raegan 25
Jolley, Loren 82	Klein, Sarah 76	Levin, Hannah 252
Jones, Aerial 99	Klein, Shaindyl 54	LeVine, Shoshana 117
Jones, Ariana 59	Knight, Ashley 176	Levy, Francesca 95
Jones, Ashlee 187	Knight, Shania 136	Lewis, Demetrius 249
Jones, Caroline 242	Knight, Tierra 186	Lewis, Malik 69
Jones, Kali 210	Knighton, Cyrus 183	Lewis, Quiesha 18
Jones, Kayla 144	Knowles, Breanna 229	Liberty, Robert 109
Jones, Leah 177	Koch, Charlotte 248	Libow, Jamie 26
Jones, Neely 156	Koestler, Carlisle 103	Lilly, Chloe 110
Jones Jr., Jonathan 163	Kokenzie, Nick 109	Lim-Hing, Simone 62
Jordan, Koehna 114	Koppel, Adam 92	Linares, Michelle 211
Jordan, Timothy 248	Kosloske, Destiny 128	Lindsay, Ryan 218
Jozefyk, Brittney 62	Kotlar, Jensen 72	Linhthasack, Nathan 107
Julmiste, Aleyah 205	Kramer, Brooke 106	Linton, John 212
Jumapao, Oni 52	Kreamer, Shelbey 230	Llorens, Autumn 174
Jurgrau, Taylor 92	Kron, Benny 201	Lockhart, Prima 58
Kaire, Dean 214	Kulakoski, Sarah Anne 238	Lofton, Emily 131
Kalio, Nemi 125	LaCarrubba, Regina 250	Logan, Clark 248
Kaloplastos, Alexandria 66	LaChance, Elizabeth 65	Longstreet, Lizbeth 37
Kant, Adrian 161	LaCoe, Russell 156	Lopez, Bryan 33
Karch, Nicholas 203	Ladner, Austin 228	Lopez, Cecilia 162
Karwatsky, Jay 28	Ladnier, Keelee 62	Lopez, Emil 51
Katz, Morgan 26	Lalla, Caroline 110	Lopez, Gabriel 166
Kauffman, Carey 239	Lamanilao, Lara 215	Lopez, Patrick 67
Kay, Angela 169	Lamb, Josh 113	Lopez-Diaz, Zue 229
Keating, Shelby 17	Lambert, Alex 229	Louden, Elizabeth 60
Keator, Maya 32	LaMon, Triston 157	Love, Bryson 104

Lowder, Jennifer 108	Mathis, Maleah 19	Messer, Tyson 224
Lowe, Raphael 148	Matthews, Samantha 78	Messinger, Christianna 94
Lowery, Elizabeth Claire 241	Mauldin, Meredith 147	Mew, Savannah 217
Lowinski, Ben 122	Mauro, Christian 174	Meyerowitz, Eliana 42
Lowinski, Jane 68	May, Austyn 193	Micallef, Taylor 38
Luckie, Bridget 132	May, Lindsey 155	Michael, Jacob 177
Luna, Stephanie 91	Mayer, Zachary 141	Michaeli, Alex 200
Luper, Brandon 56	Mayo, Colton 167	Mikszta, Luke 132
Lupica, Gabby 233	Mayson, Alexis 206	Miles, Kelly 220
Lusco, Tony 28	Mazzie, Amanda 254	Miller, Ashley 24
Luther, Philip 75	McAllister, Jennifer Marie 96	Miller, Ian 234
Luttmann, Tyler 250	McCain, GeeKeyvia 96	Miller, Jacob 189
Lutts, Matthew T. 163	McCall, Jenah 65	Miller, Jennifer 127
Lynard, Kayla 213	McCartha, Grace 26	Miller, Lory 191
Mabe, Kristian 48	McCarthy, Abby 65	Miller, Olivia 83
MacFarland, Zoah 90	McClellan, Cyrique 93	Mills, Lyla 187
MacGeorge, Kendra 72	McClellan, Lee 106	Mingo-Watts, Trevin 80
MacNeil, Andrew 225	McClure, Matthew 28	Mininni, Stephen 178
Macon, Dwayne 193	McCord, G. Ashley 195	Miramontes, Wendy 62
Madsen, Mitchell 241	McCormack, Christina 232	Mitchell, Ayauna 114
Maggio, Daize 216	McCoy, Torie 214	Mitchell, Zack 165
Mahoney, Lauren 55	McCraw, Monica 74	Mitra, Vidush 77
Maillart, Dylan 88	McCurdy, Cara 252	Mizelle, Celia 253
Maldonado, Mathew 121	McDade, Andrew 90	Mobley, Keanu 46
Malinowski, Krystyna 76	McDaniel, Bronwyn 209	Moccia, Amanda 239
Mallard, Tarish 201	McDonald, Ashabi 205	Modla, Dorothy Jane 147
Mallet, Holly 134	McFadden, Jacob 56	Moffett, Raven 73
Mann, David 50	McFarland, Margaret 189	Mohr, Maddie 97
Manning, Michael 236	McGee, Davin 120	Molina, Alexis 228
Manuszak, Gabriella 238	McGee, Mallory 164	Mon, Serena 212
Marchelletta, Jerry 197	McGill, Jasmine 122	Montgomery, Justin 161
Marinace, Angeli 95	McGovern, Wesley 53	Monticello, Micah 129
Marinak, Stevie 155	McGuire, Fiona 58	Mooney, Jordan 39
Marine, Kahlyn 43	McKemey, Quinn 254	Moore, Brittany 140
Marino, Julie 36	McKenzie, Bethany 114	Moore, Halee 253
Marquez, Nicolas 207	McLamb, Kayla 124	Moore, Matthew 162
Marro, Fred 132	McLamb, Michael 140	Moore, Tori 146
Marroquin, Andrea 227	McLaurin, Nichole 252	Moose, Carissa 144
Marsden, Andrew 67	McLelland, Madison 238	Moose, Nathan 96
Marsh, Dustin 80	McNamara, Katy 92	Moreno-Cuevas, Janel 240
Marsh, Kendall 136	McNamara, Lexi 124	Moretz, Santana 71
Marshall, Brandon 77	McNeil, Dominique 215	Morgado, Dereck 72
Marshall, Courtney 41	McNeill, Cameron 115	Morgan, Kiana 143
Marshall, Erica 127	McQuaig, Jessica 107	Morgan, Melody 41
Martensen, Jake 30	McVay, Jake 188	Morgenlander, Josh 195
Martin, Aurora 58	McWhirter, Alexandra 218	Morin, Thomas 177
Martin, Connor 77	Meadows, Elizabeth 158	Morris, Hunter 97
Martin, Gabbie 59	Medina, Andrew 202	Morris, Lee 128
Martinez, Alexis 130	Medlin, Krystal 96	Morrison, Aleah 148
Martinez, Leobardo 144	Medoff, Samantha 116	Morrison, Hayley 123
Martinez, Skyler 158	Meisner, Brandon 236	Morrison, Taylor 213
Martinez, Tyler 234	Meisner, Caroline 199	Moseley, Chase 32
Martoccia, Adam 146	Melton, Marley 223	Moses, Libby 188
Masse, Anna 132	Mercado, Brenna 57	Mosser, Valerie 118
Massey, Wyatt T. 216	Merrill, Megan 43	Mothershead, Jaime 231
Mateer, Maddie 147	Mertson, Ross 195	Moulton, Angela 106
Mathews, Maya 131	Meschke, Sabina 158	Mouna, Sarah 141

Mullins, Jacob 82	Odzer, Jamie 225	Pfeiffer, Robert 152
Murphy, Connor 64	Oeth, Alexis 34	Pham, Paul 93
Murphy, Jennifer 186	Ojeda, Abby 166	Phillips, Wyatt 100
Murray, Alexandra 66	Okocha, Emmanuel 245	Philpott, Liana 154
Murray, Martin 49	Oldfather, David 85	Picado, Kimberly 165
Musgrove, Cooper 145	Olson, James 31	Pickerign, Samuel 176
Myers, Macy 198	Olson, Julie 93	Pierce, Anna 36
Myrick, Allyson 119	Ordonez, Carlos 200	Pierce, Jimmy 179
Nadler, Kyle 76	Ortega, Juan 145	Pierce, Melissa 232
Nance, Jonna Leigh 106	Osorio, Maria 146	Pierre-Louis, Steve 103
Nance, Mason Joel 169	Oswald, Reagan 220	Piesco, Greyson 59
Naylor, Jessica 87	Otowchits, Riley 153	Pignataro, Nicole 181
Nazario, Ashley 148	Otranto, Nicholas 135	Pike, Jody 241
Neal, James 167	Outlaw, Ashante 48	Pilcher, Brianna 170
Neal, Suzanna 112	Overman, Gloria 79	Pilipiak, Milagros 47
Neill, Alyssa 85	Owens, Lucas 182	Pinkel, Rebekah 27
Neill, Kyle 257	Pacheco, Adrien 175	Pippins, Shavaunte 174
Nelson, Andy 61	Paci, Kate 216	Pires, Shawn 71
Nelson-Gauthier, Mia 61	Padgett, Jade 226	Pittman, Chelsea 157
Nembhard, Rasheed 207	Palumbo, Michelle 248	Pittman, Kylee 50
Nereau, Christian 185	Panagopoulos, Elizabeth 223	Pizzuto, Barak 131
Nesmith, Regan 33	Paredes, Natalia 25	Plancarte, Manuel 255
Netherland, Sarah 238	Parker, August 64	Plondke, Marissa 34
Neumaier, Joshua 193	Parker, Brittany 93	Plondke, Savannah 76
Newman, Sydnie 173	Parker, Cassidy 221	Plott, Sarah 112
Newsom, Hollie 81	Parker, Dalton 82	Plummer, Tyler 193
Newton, Dontavius 242	Parker, JaNyra 222	Poe, Amy 124
Ng, Alexandria 230	Parsons, Jackie 170	Ponce, Kimberly 20
Nguyen, Brian 51	Parsons, Tyler 44	Pope, Samantha 74
Nguyen, Eric 252	Pasnon, Ava 122	Porter, Kayla 120
Nicholas, Xaynah 220	Passamonte, Alexandria 114	Porter, Ross 25
Nichols, Janay 76	Patel, Alisha 94	Post, Sara 205
Nichols, Olivia 248	Patel, Harsh 246	Poteet, Arianna 146
Nicoletti, Emily 150	Patterson, Riley 160	Potter, Christina 208
Nivard, Kimberlie 127	Patton, Gage 250	Poulson, Rena 121
Nixon, Elisa 244	Patton, Tatiana 88	Powell, Clarke 174
Nixon, Jayme 73	Pavarini, Maribel 60	Powell, Gracie 140
Noble, Matthew 176	Pavlica, Taylor 53	Pratt, Souneke 212
Noland, Elizabeth 192	Payton, De'Ericka 191	Presley, Alie 35
Nolen, Summer 220	Peabody, Rebecca 248	Prewitt, Raleigh 209
Noles, Taylor 204	Pearson, Lauren 140	Pribil, Gina 71
Nolting, Jessica 204	Pearson, Megan 78	Price, Brianna 48
Norman, Ajare' Y. 143	Pearson, Tiana 218	Price, Christopher 74
Nowall, Neil 156	Peeling, Sarah 72	Price, Max 52
Noyes, Kevin 205	Peeples, BuNorris 45	Pritchett, Brittney 242
Nugent, Jonathon 88	Peeples, Logan 100	Proctor, Amelia 146
Nussbaum, Chad 33	Pena, Marco 71	Prospere, Stervensky 105
Nutovits, Ilana 182	Pennington, Sarah 87	Puente, Gabriel 236
O'Brien, Ian 110	Perdue, Amber 172	Pulliam, Lyndsey 137
O'Brien, Michelle 77	Perez, Antonio 202	Pura, Gabrielle 47
O'Donnell, Patrick 132	Perez, Lais 219	Purner, Sean 166
O'Hare, Daniel 64	Perry, Hannah 241	Putnam, Ben 78
O'Leary, Blake 108	Perry, Ja'Quan 81	Quesenberry, Sedona 111
O'Leary, Patrick 222	Perry, Jenna-Lee 73	Quinones, Kayel 85
O'Neill, Elizabeth M. 209	Perry-Smith, Carissa 173	Quinton, Melody 51
Oates, Gray 46	Petmecky, David 226	Raba, David 36
Odom, Clayton 98	Pettersen, Jessica 252	Radicchi, Gina 35

Index

Radwan, Jemini ... 60
Ragazzo, Phillip ... 49
Rahn, Marissa ... 119
Rambo, Hannah ... 226
Ramirez, Jasmin ... 134
Ramirez, Jesse ... 149
Ramirez, Nana ... 98
Ramos, Zenaida ... 36
Ramsay, Tayler ... 201
Ramsland, Danny ... 106
Ratliff, Samantha ... 216
Ravaschieri, Mia ... 146
Rawls, Katie ... 34
Ray, Emily ... 205
Reddy, Rohit ... 32
Reddy, Theron ... 104
Reed, Devin ... 202
Reed, Kaitlyn ... 96
Reese, Cheyanne ... 147
Regan, Terrence ... 88
Register, Dakota ... 56
Reid, Clare ... 186
Reid, Tiffany ... 122
Reider, Caleb ... 183
Reinker, Marissa ... 202
Remson, Jordan ... 58
Rew, Brandon ... 226
Reyes, Juliana ... 38
Reynolds, Leighann ... 231
Rheinheimer, Andrew ... 136
Rhoden, Lindsay ... 184
Rhodes, Ryan ... 192
Richards, Myranda ... 129
Richter, Jillian ... 252
Ricker, Katelyn ... 238
Ricketts, Peyton ... 28
Ring, Rachel ... 210
Ringo, MoQueshia ... 228
Riopelle, Haleigh ... 34
Riopelle, Holly ... 53
Ritter, Samantha ... 52
Rivera, Christian ... 43
Rivera, Erika ... 224
Rivera, Kenneth ... 133
Rivera, Madelyn ... 72
Rivera, Mariella ... 40
Rivera-Velazquez, Andrea E. ... 124
Robb, Madeline ... 140
Robbins, Danielle ... 82
Roberts, Nicole ... 120
Roberts, Summer ... 34
Roberts, Taylor ... 51
Robertson, Shelby ... 56
Robichaud, Shelby ... 191
Robinson, Aaron ... 48
Robinson, Crystasia ... 58
Robinson, Shekeydrah ... 133

Rocco, Kendall ... 88
Roche, Spencer ... 72
Rodicio, Lillian ... 247
Rodriguez, Antonio ... 40
Rodriguez, Gabriel ... 48
Rodriguez, Hunter ... 154
Rodriguez, Jorge ... 238
Roger, Grant ... 29
Rogers, Bevan ... 57
Rogers, Jordan ... 128
Rogers, Megan Michele ... 171
Romer, Ben ... 246
Romer, Caroline ... 21
Romero, Tori ... 96
Rone, Garrett ... 66
Rosato, Olivia ... 191
Rosenblatt, Carlee ... 244
Ross, Cecilia ... 153
Ross, Sunny ... 152
Rossell, Rose ... 68
Rossi, Taylor ... 67
Rowe, Charlotte ... 131
Rowe, Jessi ... 142
Roxas, Robert ... 46
Royer, Brai ... 113
Rozecki, Braeden ... 26
Rozmajzl, Katie ... 234
Rubin, Kyle ... 132
Rudolph, Jenn ... 34
Ruelle, Kate ... 135
Rugel, Jenna ... 189
Ruiz, Analisa ... 28
Ruiz Jr., Sebastian ... 217
Runyans, Lauryn ... 215
Rupert, Dylan ... 168
Rush, Gabby ... 24
Rushing, Reed S. ... 158
Russe, Paola N. ... 238
Russell, Braxton ... 243
Russell, Joey ... 204
Russell, Miranda ... 226
Rutter, Max ... 196
Ryan, Katie ... 249
Rzepka, Emily ... 196
Sachdeva, Sarika ... 78
Sadler, Nick ... 84
Saffer, Ethan ... 100
Safrit, Allyson ... 86
Sage, Ali ... 111
Saliba, Amy ... 69
Salmeron, Noe ... 154
Sanchez, Ashley ... 37
Sanchez, Jordyn ... 122
Sanchez, Kaitlyn ... 57
Sanchez, Kimberly ... 75
Sanchez, Kirsten ... 140
Sanchez, Selena ... 216

Sanders, Tucker ... 115
Santiago, Christa ... 139
Santiago, Melissa ... 123
Santos, Amanda ... 89
Santostefano, Marianna ... 113
Saperstein, Tess ... 228
Sarko, Peyton ... 133
Savage, Jason ... 218
Savoie, Evy ... 37
Sawyer, Jamie ... 44
Scarberry, Jacob ... 36
Schafer, Geena ... 27
Schafer, Lauren ... 89
Schauer, Katherine ... 76
Schimpff, Sofia ... 188
Schmehl, Blake ... 74
Schmidt, Kiersten ... 108
Schmidt, Samantha ... 178
Schnegelberger, Shenelle ... 138
Schneider, Annie ... 254
Schotter, Colin ... 42
Schultheiss, Stephanie ... 47
Schultz, Grant ... 171
Schumacher, Paul ... 137
Schwarzenberg, Sofia ... 154
Schweiger, Jessica ... 116
Schwenk, Emily ... 66
Scott, Devon ... 142
Scott, Jonathan ... 103
Scott, Serina ... 160
Scotti, Melissa ... 203
Seamans, Katherine ... 244
Searles, Dylan ... 248
Sefo, Anna ... 40
Selby, Katie ... 137
Sellers, Garrett ... 106
Semiken-Gardner, James ... 255
Senter, Sammy ... 171
Sepulveda, Nico ... 92
Serra, Sean ... 54
Serrano, Michelle ... 63
Setzer, Anna ... 58
Sevcik, Rachel ... 222
Sevin, Robert ... 41
Shackelford, Devin ... 177
Shah, Akash ... 251
Sharpe, Jacob ... 236
Shea, Patrick ... 231
Sheffield, Wesley ... 63
Sheir, Samantha ... 116
Sheldon, Drew ... 111
Sheldon, Jacob ... 60
Shelton, Sara ... 167
Shirey, Christen ... 185
Shockley, Cody ... 162
Shoffner, Amanda ... 59
Shomar, Joseph ... 151

Shoneye, David 191	St. Jean, Sarah 31	Taylor, Savannah 188
Shore, Mackenzie 244	Staley, Hannah 121	Taylor, Taliah 94
Shuler, Maya 92	Stallings, Haley 135	Taylor, Zoë 34
Sides, Caleb 85	Staton, Mel 117	Tejeda-Manzano, Aidee 125
Siegman, Reuben 103	Staton, Tilandra 250	Telfort, Fabrice 56
Silver, Blake 106	Stegall, Paul 30	Teller, Barrett 155
Simmons, Chance 169	Stennett, Ashton 55	Temmerman, Timothy 172
Simon, Sheree 112	Stephens, Tuh'nesia 175	TenBieg, Ashlyn 198
Simpson, Najja 160	Stetzer, Erica 83	Tenorio, Sam 174
Sinatra, Tia 100	Stevenson, Willie 64	Thakur, Sona 116
Singam, Deepti 89	Stewart, Brendan 40	Thaxton, Charles 41
Singh, Tanay 173	Stewart, Corey 168	Theodore, Kailey 148
Singley, Allie 176	Still, Samuel 78	Therathanakorn, Andy 168
Singley, Hannah 159	Stilphen, Samantha 86	Thigpen, Garrett 110
Sistrunk, Diamond 34	Stiwinter, Chanda 165	Thigpen, Kellé 99
Sistrunk, Morgan 191	Stokes, Matthew 240	Thomas, Betty 50
Sjoelin, Amanda 239	Storms, Bailey 176	Thomas, Breyanna 87
Skeen, Kyle 145	Straka, Nicole 173	Thomas, Chloe 140
Skelton, Caroline 76	Strandberg, Ryan 56	Thomas, Izayah 115
Skinner, Paige 233	Strange, Katherine 204	Thompson, Charlotte 75
Skolnick, Rebecca 75	Streitman, Ashley 171	Thompson, Jarrett 110
Sloan, Seth 116	Strickland, Kayla 52	Thorburn, Mackenzie 53
Small, Zahrea 98	Stringer, Abbie 213	Thorton, Bailey 162
Smallwood, Shyan 231	Stromberg, Kiley 160	Threatte, Nicholas 100
Smith, Adam 80	Strong, Alaysia 104	Thrift, Donnie 83
Smith, Alison D. 110	Stubbs, Shannon 136	Thurow, Austin 179
Smith, Brianna 135	Suarez, Michael 33	Tidwell, Kelli 252
Smith, Caitlin 60	Suarez, Renee 76	Tillman, Travis 82
Smith, Cheyenne 164	Suber, Jordan 249	Timpanaro, Jake 126
Smith, Corey Brandon 193	Subido, Paulo-Emmanuel D. 103	Tischler, Kalei 32
Smith, Cullen 100	Suglia, Julia 148	Tiwari, Shom 56
Smith, DeTrea 29	Sulen, Shandy 125	Tobiczyk, Jake 244
Smith, Donneisha 91	Sullivant, Hannah 159	Tolbert, Kaley 93
Smith, Gage 210	Sullivent, Kaitlyn 170	Toles, Drico 183
Smith, Graeme 221	Sumaljag, Alyssa 47	Tondee, Tori-Nicole Thuy Tien 204
Smith, Jon Paul 129	Summers, Katelyn 45	Torop, Aaron 244
Smith, Josh 255	Summerset, Wayne 185	Torres, Angelix 213
Smith, Lindsay 110	Sutterfield, Alex 29	Torres, Edward 33
Smith, Morgan 196	Swayze, Sara 96	Torres, Henry 173
Smith, Quinton 187	Sweatman, Clint 172	Torres, Karla 156
Smith, Quitman 97	Sweatt, Emily 202	Torricelli, Zachary 108
Smith, Romesha 211	Swinford, Salena 196	Trader, Assata 206
Smith, Sadie 50	T., Jacob 94	Trexler, Colton 63
Smith, Samoriah 56	Tagaras, Krista 110	Trogdon, Taylor 188
Smith, Wesley G. 186	Talledo, Emmanuel 103	Tronzo, Victoria 86
Smith, Zac 245	Tamayo, Carmen 211	Trotter, Cameron 48
Snook, Tyler 168	Tan, Jenna 232	True, Mariah 40
Sommers, Zachary 141	Tarver, Selenia 82	Truesdale, Kiaundria 119
Soule, Suzette 162	Tate, Lexi 32	Truong, Jenny 74
Southerland, Cameron Roosevelt ..179	Tatum, Arlena 60	Tullier, Holden 188
Sovern, Sydney 104	Tatum, Jonathan 44	Turcotte, Madison 249
Spain, Jessica 139	Taub, Deanna 202	Turley, John Haymond 92
Sparks, Taylor 224	Taylor, Annie M. 80	Turnage, Hope 209
Spikes, Alexis 244	Taylor, Capree 192	Turner, Grace 192
Spisak, John 180	Taylor, Carlos 227	Turner, Hannah 139
Spivey, Ahija 172	Taylor, Margaret 127	Turner, Krystle 218
Squires-Propper, Olivia 202	Taylor, Peyton 157	Turner, Lynzee 112

Index

Tuttle, Kristen 154
Tuttle, Victoria 170
Ulyatt, Connor 79
Umstead, Alex 176
Underwood, Monica 146
Utley, Dentonio 207
Valdes, Dani 227
Valkov, Michelle 228
Valle, Jose .52
Vallejo, Isabella 226
Van Allen, Maria 81
Van Lanen, Nikki 217
Vance, Blaise 22
Vangiller, Alexis 79
Vanlandingham, Christopher 252
Vargas, Elizabeth 161
Varma, Ashima 97
Varnado, Eric 234
Varner, Jessi 109
Varnum, Jessi Rae 82
Vasandani, Nimisha 124
Vaye, Stephen 184
Velasco, Matilde 132
Velez, Alexis 175
Velez, Lauren 161
Veliz, J. B. 61
Vencil, Christen 97
Verdeflor, Lloyd 249
Vessell, Kori 39
Vestal, Eli 156
Viana, Humberto 50
Vidal, Theysi 54
Vilar, Gabriela 255
Villacreses, Martin 225
Villamonte, Flavia 61
Villamor, Maria 136
Voit, Jasmine 66
Vorn, Allen 210
Votaw, Caroline 136
Wade, Christina 242
Waiknis, Eric 237
Waldman, Alison 23
Waldron, Ashley 40
Waldrop, Will 252
Walker, Alex 110
Walker, Amber 51
Walker, Arabia 88
Walker, Kristian 167
Walker, Naquira 51
Walker, Nykia 181
Wall, Julianna 93
Wallace, Antonio 183
Wallace, Hailey 199
Waller, Prescott 185
Walters, James 50
Walton, Jeffery 185
Ward, Ashley 126
Ward, Caroline 182
Ward, Stephen K. 90
Warner, Emily 32
Warner, Jared 201
Warner, Michael 193
Warren, Alexus 249
Warrington, Summer 46
Wash, Alena 147
Washington, Demeric 65
Waterman, Lexie 206
Waters, Ben 210
Waters, Caroline 96
Watjen, Rachel 97
Watson, Jazmine 66
Watson, Suzi 26
Watts, Emily 227
Webb, Jorge 53
Weigel, Madi 168
Welch, Avery 97
Weldon, Coleman 149
Wells, Hannah 37
Wells, Nick 231
Wenz, Adrianna 62
Wenz, James 142
West, Jay 161
West, Jessica 109
Westby, Maya 130
Wetmore, Alex 214
Wheeler, Hallie 123
Wheeler, Lynny 214
Whiddon, Tyson 117
Whitacre, Jessi 224
Whitaker, Amber 88
White, Chantal 126
White, Dalen 172
White, Fletcher Allen 87
White, Garry 48
White, Logan 89
White, Mackenzie 66
White, Rachel 106
White, Tori 199
Whitehead, Hannah 144
Whitfield, Tiara 107
Whiting, April 187
Whyte, Kimberly 256
Wibowo, Wally 133
Wichterich, Jonah 155
Widere, Jeannine 163
Wiggins, Brian 79
Wigginton, Randy 37
Wiggles, Rae-Shawn 101
Wilbon, Jonnay 142
Wilkerson, Leah 122
Wilks, Isaac 247
Williams, Andesha 178
Williams, Ashley 47
Williams, C.J. 188
Williams, Clara 45
Williams, Deja 197
Williams, Hailey 107
Williams, Jessica 28
Williams, Khayla 89
Williams, Krishauna 73
Williams, Shawn 235
Williams, Trent 31
Williamson, Sierra 50
Williamson, Tori 202
Willis, Kayla 31
Willis, Savannah 96
Wilson, Allie 93
Wilson, Anna 44
Wilson, Calista 142
Wilson, Cameron 126
Wilson, Christian 143
Wilson, Daryen 155
Wilson, Hali 99
Wilson, Matt 75
Wilson, Tiffani 66
Windsor, Treavor 122
Wing, Amanda 57
Winters, Madison 77
Wirtes, Joey 30
Wise, Evan 189
Witner, Jack 31
Witt, Trace 171
Wittmann, Bailey 70
Wolf, Taylor 125
Wolfanger, Courtney 35
Wood, Eryn 169
Woodall, Adam 254
Woody, Jasmin 50
Woodyard, Henry 60
Woodyard, Mary 202
Worbington, Tyler 216
Worrie, Lawrence 243
Wright, Antwon 155
Wright, Carolyn 226
Wright, Ka'Travia 145
Wylie, Scott 27
Xiao, Laurie 223
Yang, Lydia 163
Yarbrough, Ashley 239
Young, Adrianna Rose 128
Young, Austin 210
Young, Kaishanna 121
Young, Rebecca 122
Zaeh, Katie 129
Zalecki, Olivia 196
Zapata, Vanessa 52
Zavala, Alberto 40
Zeledon, Natalie 24
Zhang, Stephanie 221
Ziane, Driss 195
Zidek, Andrew 117

Zielinski, Hailee 203
Zimmermann, Daniel 101
Zindel, Carolina 119
Zindel, Rudy 116
Zombek, Chandler 186
Zwolski, Devin 150

Author Autograph Page

Katherine Atkinson
(page 14) Be Creative!

Author Autograph Page

Author Autograph Page

Author Autograph Page

Author Autograph Page

Author Autograph Page

Author Autograph Page

Author Autograph Page

Author Autograph Page

Author Autograph Page

Author Autograph Page

Author Autograph Page